# RE-WRITING AMERICA

# Re-Writing AMERiCA

*Vietnam Authors in Their Generation*

PHILIP D. BEIDLER

THE UNIVERSITY OF GEORGIA PRESS   ATHENS & LONDON

© 1991 by the University of Georgia Press
Athens, Georgia 30602
All rights reserved
Designed by Richard Hendel
Set in Janson and Gill by Tseng Information Systems
Printed and bound by Thomson-Shore
The paper in this book meets the guidelines for permanence
and durability of the Committee on Production Guidelines for
Book Longevity of the Council on Library Resources.

Printed in the United States of America
95 94 93 92 91   5 4 3 2 1

Library of Congress Cataloging in Publication Data
Beidler, Philip D.
   Re-writing America : Vietnam authors in their generation /
Philip D. Beidler.
       p.   cm.
   Includes bibliographical references and index.
   ISBN 0-8203-1264-9 (alk. paper)
   1. American literature—20th century—History and
criticism.   2. Vietnamese Conflict, 1961–1975—Literature and
the conflict.   3. War in literature.   I. Title.
   PS228.V5B6   1991
   810.9′358—dc20   90-37804
                    CIP

British Library Cataloging in Publication Data available

*For Ellen Eddins Beidler*

The things they carried were largely determined by necessity.

They were called legs or grunts.

To carry something was to "hump" it, as when Lieutenant Jimmy Cross humped his love for Martha up the hills and through the swamps. In its intransitive form, "to hump" meant "to walk," or "to march," but it implied burdens far beyond the intransitive.

For the most part, they carried themselves with poise, a kind of dignity.

—Tim O'Brien, *The Things They Carried*


I think a lot of us vets came to the wrong conference; we should have been at a conference entitled "America Reconsidered."

—Leland Labinski, from the floor, "Vietnam Reconsidered" Conference, February 6–9, 1983, University of Southern California

# CONTENTS

PREFACE
  *Re-Writing America* : xi

ACKNOWLEDGMENTS : xv

INTRODUCTION
  *Vietnam Authors in Their Generation* : 1

THE LIFE OF FICTION
  *Tim O'Brien, Philip Caputo, Robert Olen Butler,*
  *James Webb, Winston Groom, Larry Heinemann* : 9

AMERICAN DRAMATIST
  *David Rabe* : 104

POETS AFTER OUR WAR
  *John Balaban, W. D. Ehrhart, David Huddle,*
  *Yusef Komunyakaa, Walter McDonald, Bruce Weigl* : 145

THE LITERATURE OF WITNESS
  *Gloria Emerson, Frances Fitzgerald,*
  *Robert Stone, Michael Herr* : 206

CODA
  *The Colors of the Spirit* : 288

NOTES : 301

BIBLIOGRAPHY : 315

INDEX : 327

# PREFACE

## Re-Writing America

The war is not even over before it is transformed into a hundred thousand printed pages and set before the tired palates of the history-hungry as the latest delicacy. It seems that the instrument is almost incapable of producing a strong and full note, no matter how vigorously it is played: its tones at once die away and in a moment have faded into a tender historical echo. Expressed morally: you are no longer capable of holding on to the sublime, your deeds are shortlived explosions, not rolling thunder. Though the greatest and most miraculous event should occur—it must nonetheless descend, silent and unsung into Hades. For art flees away if you immediately conceal your deeds under the awning of history. He who wants to understand, grasp, and assess in a moment that before which he ought to stand long in awe of as before an incomprehensible sublimity may be called reasonable, but only in the sense in which Schiller speaks of the rationality of the reasonable man: there are things he does not see which even a child sees, there are things he does not hear which even a child hears, and these things are precisely the most important things: because he does not understand these things, his understanding is more childish than the child and more simple than simplicity—and this in spite of the many cunning folds of his parchment scroll and the virtuosity of his fingers in unravelling the entangled.
—Friedrich Nietzsche, "On the uses and disadvantages of history for life"

"I deal with people; you deal with facts. Facts," said the Mississippian without explaining whether he was talking in metaphysical terms, "bear no relation to truth."
—William Faulkner, "Interview with Betty Beale"

"We can truly be transformed, and even possibly redeemed, by electing to write at times of what happened—but also of what might have happened, what could have happened, what should have happened, and also what can be kept from happening or what can be made to happen. . . . Words are all we have." These words happen to be my own. This is to say at least that I spoke them once on a formal occasion and that they have

subsequently been printed and ascribed to me. They may be found, specifically, in the proceedings of a symposium, "The Vietnam Experience in
American Literature," held at the Asia Society in New York in May 1985
(Lomperis, 87). They have their origin, however, in words to similar effect
spoken at the same conference by the fine novelist Tim O'Brien, who in
turn had also made an earlier version of them the words, in his *Going After
Cacciato*, of the fictional protagonist Paul Berlin. These may be found in an
initial section, where Berlin ponders the troublesome business of Cacciato
and the latter's decision one day in Vietnam to leave the war and strike
out for himself on the Road to Paris. "What, in fact," he asks himself,
"had become of Cacciato? More precisely—as Doc Peret would insist that
it be phrased—more precisely, what part was fact and what part was the
extension of fact? And how were facts separated from possibilities? What
had really happened and what merely might have happened? How did it
end?" (28).

The myth, as it might be called, of putative origin, inscription, and
reinscription posed here, I wish to suggest, is itself an encapsulated version
of the point of this book. In these words, fashioned out of experience into
imaginative art which in turn inscribes itself into the larger discourse of
culture, we find a call, a challenge, and even, given the richly generative
concept of language they propose, a medium of enactment for a new art
that would be a kind of ultimate cultural revision. It is an art that, even as
it acknowledges the painful memory of Vietnam, would make possible the
imaginative projection of that memory into new dimensions of consciousness, private and public, individual and collective, often providing equally
new insights into knowledge, meaning, and value. Such words are a call,
then, on the part of Vietnam authors in their generation, to do nothing
less than re-write ourselves, and apace, to re-write America.

It is that particular generation of authors who occupy my concern
here, and the degree to which they have in an impressive number of instances made their going back to Vietnam in various forms of literary
expression a going ahead as well into a diverse and complex body of literary mythmaking that has become part and fabric of our national existence
as a culture. And to this degree, what Paul Fussell has written of the great
project of literary-cultural reinscription accomplished by the British war
generation of 1914–18 may thus now be said with great justice, I believe,
about this American generation of Vietnam as well. "At the same time

the war was relying on old myth," Fussell writes, "it was generating new myth, and that myth is part of the fiber of our lives" (ix). For indeed, if there now appears to have been a single distinguishing feature of the most significant American writing about the experience of Vietnam from the earliest days of the present, it has been the attempt to forge myriad forms of new and creative alliance between literature and the work of cultural revision. Across a whole vast spectrum of literary enterprise and a near-infinite range of subject, genre, and mode, Vietnam authors have attempted to carry their re-writing of themselves and their America into crucially enlarged designs of common insight and understanding. To use the acute phrase Thomas Myers has applied to the major narrative literature of the war, their enterprise has been to write new "compensatory history" (*Walking Point*, 9) in the deepest sense, at once mythic explanation of history and creation of history as reconstituted and newly possible redemptory myth. For their recognition has been that particular one which nations, after their wars, have always found it too easy to forget: that to see ourselves clearly in any historical moment, before, during, and after our wars, is to see ourselves always both as ourselves and as our own mythic creations. Or, as that quintessential Vietnam-era writer Kurt Vonnegut, Jr., has phrased it in broader terms, yet with characteristic simplicity and exactitude, "we are what we pretend to be, so we must be careful about what we pretend to be" (*Mother Night*, v). And so, in the last decades of the century that mythographers of culture will surely know as the American one—and the one thus in which America finally came to confront in agonizing self-critique its most cherished visions of what it had always pretended to be—Vietnam authors in their generation have carried their crucial enactment of that mythic self-critique into the very center of our national literature and consciousness at large.

# ACKNOWLEDGMENTS

Initial work on this book was made possible through a leave granted by the University of Alabama's Office of Academic Affairs. Continuing thanks go also to Claudia Johnson, English Department chair, who devises schedules that make life happy in the classroom and at the word processor. I am particularly grateful to Michael Fellman of Simon Fraser University, whose invitation to write a paper became the genesis of this project. Invaluable assistance on various sources and points of reading has been offered by John Balaban at Penn State University and William Jewett at Yale, by Alabama colleagues including Robin Behn, Richard Rand, Marcel Smith, Bill Ulmer, and Mathew Winston, and by a graduate research assistant, Dan Peightel, whose contributions have likewise been collegial in the finest sense.

I would like to make special mention of the guidance and support, during the last two years, of Bill Lerner and Harriet Myers. I similarly appreciate the encouragement and advice of Malcolm Call and Madelaine Cooke of the University of Georgia Press.

Two final expressions of indebtedness remain. The first is to Dwight Eddins, faithful friend and constant companion on the long march. The second is to the extraordinary person named on the dedication page, Ellen Eddins Beidler, whose husband I am privileged to be.

Parts of this text have appeared in *Genre*, 31, No. 4 (Winter 1988), © 1989 by the University of Oklahoma; and in *America Rediscovered*, edited by Owen Gilman and Lorrie Smith. New York: Garland Publishing, 1990. Reprinted with permission.

Grateful acknowledgment is also made to those who hold copyright for poems quoted in this volume:

W. D. Ehrhart for "A Relative Thing."

Harper & Row, Publishers, Inc., for excerpt from "Wichita Vortex Sutra" from *Collected Poems*, 1947–1980 by Allen Ginsberg, © 1966 by Allen Ginsberg. Reprinted by permission of Harper & Row, Publishers.

Michael Pettit for "American Light."

# INTRODUCTION

*Vietnam Authors in Their Generation*

We cannot live in associations with the past alone. . . . if we would be worthy of the past, we must find new fields for action or thought and make for ourselves new careers. But, nevertheless, the generation that carried on the war has been set apart by its experience. . . . in our youth our hearts were touched with fire.
—Capt. Oliver Wendell Holmes, 1885, quoted in John Wheeler, *Touched with Fire*.

I have traveled to a place where the dead lie above the ground in rows and bunches. Time has gone somewhere without me. This is not my country, not my time. My skin is drawn tight around my eyes. My clothes smell of blood. I bleed inside. I am water. I am stone. I am swift-running water, made from snow. I am stone, chipped from giant granite boulders, small shards, jagged and sharp-edged, sliding down the rockface past the timberline. Chips and flakes break away from me, and sparks sometimes. I have not come home, Ma, I have gone ahead, gone back. There is glass between us, we cannot speak. I hear voices, I have seen a wraith, Ma. He wore black boots and britches and strange livery. He talked to me, he whispered, he laughed. He touched my stomach with the back of his hand, like people will put an arm on your shoulder when they speak, and it burns.
—Larry Heinemann, *Close Quarters*

Among the most visible aftereffects of the Vietnam war is one that, at the time perhaps, might have seemed among the least expected: it turned a significant number of American participants in the experience of that war to the life of writing. Of this resolutely anguished and sense-resistant passage in American life, history, and culture, there came, on the part of many who had undergone it at first hand, an impassioned effort at literary sense-making. And of that effort came a number of texts now recognized as some of the major achievements of the past two decades: novels such as Tim O'Brien's *Going After Cacciato*, Robert Stone's *Dog Soldiers*, Larry Heinemann's *Paco's Story*, and Stephen Wright's *Meditations in Green*; collections of poetry such as John Balaban's *After Our War* and Bruce Weigl's

*Song of Napalm;* memoirs such as Tim O'Brien's *If I Die in a Combat Zone,* Philip Caputo's *A Rumor of War,* and Ron Kovic's *Born on the Fourth of July;* works of social documentary and observer report such as Gloria Emerson's *Winners and Losers,* Frances Fitzgerald's *Fire in the Lake,* C. D. B. Bryan's *Friendly Fire,* and Michael Herr's *Dispatches;* oral histories such as Al Santoli's *Everything We Had* and Mark Baker's *Nam,* Wallace Terry's *Bloods* and Kathryn Marshall's *In the Combat Zone.*

The purpose of this book is to study the ongoing work of Vietnam writers in their generation and to talk about the ways in which that work continues to place many of them at the forefront of current American literary endeavor. For indeed an impressive number of them have now come to establish themselves as major interpreters of contemporary American life and culture. Often, they have applied many of the hard-won lessons of literary sense-making learned in initial works attempting to come explicitly to terms with Vietnam. Accordingly, as predicted in such early texts, they have continued to move across a nearly infinite range of subject, genre, and mode. And as a result once again their achievement often continues to be measured by a uniquely impassioned intensity of literary engagement. Their sense of profound experiential authority in the same moment allows them to make their largest meanings through the bold embrace of new strategies of imaginative invention; and thus, precisely, in the inscription out of memory into art, they become in the fullest sense the creators of cultural myth for new times and other. Moreover, in making this claim, I should say that one now finds it hard to overstate the degree to which such a body of writing has also suggested a major direction for the national literature toward an access of renewed creative energy. It proposes, for example, and in many ways has already demonstrated, a possible way beyond what became known in the 1960s and early 1970s in the metafictionist argot as "the literature of exhaustion," a literature of immense creative inventiveness, yet condemned, through its increasing sense of experiential insubstantiality, to obsessively contemplating mainly the forms and processes of its own inscription. (If anything, in fact, I will suggest that the work of Vietnam writers continues to bespeak a major fulfillment of the true "alternative" spirit of the youth culture of the era, the belief in acts of imagination, often conceived in some new, unmediated relationship with experience itself, that could do nothing less than change the world.) And now later, the new American writing of Vietnam authors in their generation also suggests at least one direction of major possibility beyond the succeeding poststructuralist impasse of texts as endless critiques of language, representation, and authority equally condemned to remain, as Gerald Graff has put it, "allegories of their own unreadability" (241). What is proposed here in contrast, I would assert in a vast number of cases, is a literature that would quite literally *create* precisely as it arises out of various critical deconstitutions — social, historical, political, cultural, and thus in the largest sense, mythic — of traditional views of language, representation, and authority, and of various totalizing structures of consciousness with which these views have traditionally sanctioned their claims to truth, value, and meaning. To borrow a term from my title, it is possible to suggest often here a way in which the very idea of authorship itself, in the wake of much poststructuralist conversation regarding its demise, proposes now to reconstitute itself on the ground of cultural mythmaking precisely as the new *cultural product* of its own radical self-critique.

Finally, with regard both to a sense of epochal historic positioning and to a resultant sense of common, even desperate literary enterprise amidst the competing claims of history and myth, I would propose that a serious comparison of these writers of Vietnam, on the basis now of both their initial works and their subsequent careers, to the American and Anglo-European generations of the Great War, is not in the least ill taken. Indeed, as our vision of the experience of Vietnam comes increasingly into historical and literary relief, the mythic-cultural analogies meanwhile grow increasingly breathtaking. Like their forebears of 1914–18, the American generation of Vietnam fought a war not of their own making but of the making of politicians and experts, a war of ancient animosities that cost nearly everything for those involved and settled virtually nothing. They also brought to it at least at the outset their incorrigible native idealism and convictions of geopolitical omnipotence, and in their case, with such visions coupled often as well, at least initially, to a peculiar sense of high generational hope, the legacy in spirit of a fallen young president they had so brightly claimed as their own. They fought it for the most part under conditions of bitter stalemate, with frustration and disillusionment often measuring themselves out into savagery with proportional exactitude. They also fought in the increasing realization of an equally bitter and brutal war within their own ranks born of the most deeply engendered conflicts of power, race, economic production and distribution, and educational and class relationship. At the end, sometimes as little as an overnight trip from a horror, lay a world that once passed for normality; but if that world (and that is actually what they called it: "The World") did still seem in many ways as familiar as yesterday, it also now greeted them as spooky, undesirable aliens, Melvillean isolates sentenced to solitary confinement with the memory of what they had undergone or witnessed on the grounds that even if they could find forms of sense-making appropriate to it, there would be virtually no one interested in what they had to say. And afterward, they remained expatriates within the land, primary legatees of an old history at once meliorist and rigorously amnesiac now come to final crisis of historical self-critique. To use Malcolm Cowley's classic figure of characterization for his own great literary generation of war, "exile" had again become the order of the day. "Return" continues to be less than complete.

"Look down and swear by the slain of the war that you'll never forget." Precisely because Siegfried Sassoon wrote this first in his version of "Aftermath," Philip Caputo no doubt saw it specifically as more than fit to appropriate as the concluding epigraph to the memoir in which he announced to his own age the Vietnam author's new commitment to a major literary calling (338). Present at the end of empire and at the beginning of postmodern America, Vietnam authors wrote, albeit at first with their writing consigned to an admonitory silence. Still, they wrote. And of their writing has now come and continues to come nothing less than a major reconstitution of the very myth of national culture itself, an attempt to reinscribe themselves and their America into new dimensions of creative possibility.

The magnitude of their achievement in this regard has been prodigious. Novelists such as Tim O'Brien, Philip Caputo, James Webb, Robert Olen Butler, Winston Groom, and Larry Heinemann have now produced among themselves a body of more than twenty-five works of major importance. Poets such as John Balaban, W. D. Ehrhart, David Huddle, Yusef Komunyakaa, Walter McDonald, and Bruce Weigl have become major voices not only in poetry but in fiction, autobiography, and criticism as well. The playwright David Rabe, in an achievement equaled perhaps only by Sam Shepard and David Mamet, stands among the dominant figures of his generation of dramatists. Several other highly celebrated interpreters of the American experience of Vietnam—"veterans" in the long-honored tradition of writers whose art has arisen out of the literature of experiential witness — Gloria Emerson, Frances Fitzgerald, Robert Stone, and Michael Herr — now stand, in their continuing work across a vast range of genre and mode, among our most important chroniclers of American life in the last quarter of the twentieth century. Historical observers turned novelists such as Ward Just and novelists turned futurist historians such as Stephen Wright write the "story," to use Peter McInerny's suggestive phrasing, that "history" itself cannot write (187), detail the necessary historical and mythic self-deconstitutions of American vision after Vietnam upon which only can be built truly creative projects of necessary historical and mythic self-reconstitution.

Estimations of the work of these Vietnam writers in their generation have now regularly evoked comparisons of them with figures ranging from Joseph Conrad and Stephen Crane to Jorge Luis Borges and Bertold Brecht, from Ernest Hemingway and Robert Graves to Graham Greene and Joseph Heller, from Walt Whitman and Wilfred Owen to Ezra Pound and T. S. Eliot. The list of their awards is virtually — and often, in multiple number — a roll call of American literary honors: the Pulitzer Prize, the National Book Award, the American Book Award, the Maxwell Perkins Prize, the Yale Poetry Prize, the Tony Award, and the New York Drama Critics Award.[1] Significant critical-academic discussions likewise now proliferate in major books, essay collections, and articles and reviews in prominent national and international journals.[2]

But most important, of course, has been their achievement upon the ground of the text itself. And to look at that work of achievement is to see a single recurrent focus: the desire, born of their immediate sense of the impact of the American experience of Vietnam upon American cultural mythology at large, to reconstitute that mythology as a medium both of historical self-reconsideration and, in the same moment, of historical self-renewal and even self-reinvention.

The breadth of the enterprise alone continues to re-write our definitions of literary possibility. In genre, it has ranged across letter, diary, journal, memoir, autobiography, short story, novel, poem, play, oral history, documentary, and journalistic report. Beyond, it has also frequently embraced and enlarged the forms and strategies of postmodernist new writing that now place themselves at the forefront of contemporary literary endeavor: the neo-journalistic experimentation — as evidenced in the

American works of Truman Capote, Joan Didion, Norman Mailer, Tom Wolfe, Hunter S. Thompson, and Michael Herr—of what John Hellman has aptly termed "fables of fact"; and on the other, imaginative hand, the "magical realism" of such postmodern masters as Borges, Grass, Marquez, Calvino, Kundera. It has embraced strategies drawn from television in every dimension from social documentary to sitcom. It has explored film from grim, visceral, minimalist vignette to surreal apocalypse. It has appropriated popular print from the critical essay to the western, the hardboiled detective story, and the comic book. It has forged new and creative alliances with further possibilities of visual art presented by photography, photo-journalistic documentary, painting, and even the newly rediscovered creative enterprise of book art itself.

In subject, the work of Vietnam writers in their generation has likewise come to comprise nothing less than a whole vast American heterotopia. A few representative examples must suffice. The novels of Tim O'Brien, following upon his magnificent memoir, *If I Die in a Combat Zone*, comprise importantly, as a host of major commentators have observed, one of our most sustained and serious contemporary meditations on the "courage" of cultural sense making. They extend from *Northern Lights*, a rather traditional work of acceptance and return, to *Going After Cacciato*, a highly acclaimed achievement in the attempt to address the experience of the war itself in the terms of postmodern experimentalism, and then beyond to the futuristic neo-realism of *The Nuclear Age*, a work beginning in collective memories of fifties bomb scares and sixties student radicalism and moving eventually on to American premonitions and anxieties as yet undreamed. And most recently now, in a return to the experience of Vietnam coupled with latest excursions into imaginative inquiry, they continue in *The Things They Carried* to extend relationships of factual and fictive meaning into new dimensions of creative reciprocity. The novels of Philip Caputo, likewise arising out of a watershed work in American personal narrative, *A Rumor of War*, embrace, in *Horn of Africa*, the latest version, post-Vietnam and now in mercenary dress, of the American myth of the frontier hero run amok; in *Del Corso's Gallery*, equally inspired by the experience of Vietnam, of the myth of the celebrity adventurer-journalist; and in *Indian Country*, of the traumatized veteran's attempts to return to some common sense of origin in a suspenseful drama of friendship and family set against the mythic forest landscape of the northern midwest.

Aftermath novels by Robert Olen Butler such as *The Alleys of Eden* and *On Distant Ground* explore the particular problems of veterans both in postwar America and in postwar Vietnam with the Vietnamese whose lives and their own have become inextricably of a piece; others by the same writer such as *Countrymen of Bones* and *Wabash* explore further mythic dimensions of American history as diverse as the World War II atomic bomb project and depression-era labor upheavals in the urban Midwest; a most recent one, *The Deuce*, with its titular hero a young Vietnamese-American set adrift in nightmare Manhattan, carries the vision of aftermath forward through the new generation of literal children of the war. In drama, David Rabe has interwoven his achievements as a Vietnam playwright in such works as *The Basic Training of Pavlo Hummel, Sticks and Bones*, and *Streamers* with corresponding extensions of mythic inquiry into major works such as *In the Boom Boom Room*, a harrowed tour of our domestic mythography of violence particularly as it pertains to American women, and most recently, *Hurlyburly*, the old tragedies of men and women now transported to the vapid, menacing air of a dream and drama factory called southern California. In poetry, John Balaban continues postmodern extensions of his view of the poet as cultural artificer out of an already expansive range of vision into new affiliations with both American and Vietnamese language and myth. Similarly, the poet Yusef Komunyakaa has now created an impressive body of work speaking eloquently his role as a post-Vietnam poetic mythmaker out of the vivid context of black American life and culture. In the literature of experiential witness, Gloria Emerson has gone on from the monumental *Winners and Losers* to find the domestic supplement of many of its central preoccupations in *Some American Men*. Frances Fitzgerald, after her controversial masterpiece of Vietnam-era comparative cultural anthropology, *Fire in the Lake*, has subsequently produced, in *America Revised*, an important study of the politics of public school versions of American history, and in a more recent volume, *Cities on a Hill*, a bold and brilliantly eccentric survey of contemporary communities continuing the American search for a sociopolitical utopia. Robert Stone has followed the award-winning *Dog Soldiers* with the uncannily prescient *A Flag for Sunrise*, a tale of intrigue and revolution set in contemporary Central America, and also, recently, with perhaps the most chilling Hollywood novel in the long tradition of that dread-inspiring genre, *Children of Light*. Michael Herr, by many accounts the most celebrated chronicler of Vietnam in the literature of experiential witness, has in a vein similar to that of his celebrated *Dispatches* gone on to major writing in film for the legendary *Apocalypse Now* and the more recent and acclaimed *Full Metal Jacket*. Further, in the aptly titled *The Big Room*, he has gone on with the painter Guy Peellaert to an unnerving mixed-media study of Las Vegas, final gold mine and ash heap of the dream, pleasure dome and charnel house of American virtue. And most recently in *Walter Winchell*, a work described in prepublication notices alternatively as a "novel-cum-docudrama" and "fiction as screenplay," he now pursues further perhaps *the* great, dread, cultural news story of our time, the media myth of American celebrity.

Works continue now to be produced by Vietnam authors in their generation for which we literally have to invent categories. In *Brothers in Arms*, for instance, William Broyles details a veteran's and writer's odyssey of return to Vietnam and his meetings twenty years after their war with the men and women whom he once tried to kill and who once tried to kill him. In *These Good Men*, tracing out the lives of his fellow survivors of a catastrophic ambush on a now-forgotten morning of the war, Michael Norman similarly pursues a journey of memory and reunion into a brave, composite history of a generation. Arthur Egendorf's *Healing from the War* becomes a watershed work of psychological inquiry in post-Vietnam America by enlarging the concept of healing to embrace a nation as well. John Clark Pratt's *Vietnam Voices*, a work of criticism and cultural documentary, styles itself "collage"; but in its wildly eclectic appropriations from high art and low, novel, poem, and play mixing with document and journalistic report, memoir and diary, popular song, soldier anecdote, latrine-wall graffito, it probably comes off best as something like mass-media assault, the combined hubbub and blare of the experience in a single book. Neil Sheehan's *A Bright Shining Lie*, a conflation of documentary, history, biography, moral anatomy, spiritual exemplum, makes the parable of an American life served in Vietnam, that of Lt. Col. John Paul Vann, into nothing less than national allegory. Thus Vietnam authors in their generation continue to write that particular kind of "true war story," as Tim O'Brien has put it, which is in a very distinct sense "never about war" really, but rather "about love and memory," "about sorrow," "about sisters who never write back and people who never listen" (*The Things They Carried*, 91), the kind of true war story that is truest by being about us all.

# THE LIFE OF FICTION

*Tim O'Brien, Philip Caputo, Robert Olen Butler,*

*James Webb, Winston Groom, Larry Heinemann*

True, he was afraid. Doc was right about that. Even now, with the night calm and unmoving, the fear was there like a kind of background sound that was heard only if listened for. True, but even so, Doc was wrong when he called it dreaming. Biles or no biles, it wasn't dreaming—it wasn't even pretending, not in the strict sense. It was an idea. It was a working out of the possibilities. It wasn't dreaming and it wasn't pretending. It wasn't crazy. Blisters on their feet, streams to be forded and swamps to be circled, dead ends to be opened into passages west. No, it wasn't dreaming. It was a way of asking questions. What became of Cacciato? Where did he go, and why? What were his motives, or did he have motives, and did motives matter? What tricks had he used to keep going? How had he eluded them? How did he slip away into the deep jungle, and how, through jungle, had they continued the chase? What happened, and what might have happened?
—Tim O'Brien, *Going After Cacciato*

Paco stares hard at the bus, broadside (seeing the whites of the old woman's tiny eyes), until it slides down the ramp and is gone—thinking, This sure ain't the first fucking time I've been left behind; thinking what any grunt would think to himself, Whatever happens after, Jack, whatever comes next (and I just about give a sweet fuck, you understand), let's just get a fucking move on and get to it.
—Larry Heinemann, *Paco's Story*

The Vietnam war has produced and continues to produce a remarkable body of important fiction. Three Vietnam novels, Robert Stone's *Dog Soldiers*, Tim O'Brien's *Going After Cacciato*, and Larry Heinemann's *Paco's Story*, have won the National Book Award. Others, such as David Halberstam's *One Very Hot Day*, Josiah Bunting's *The Lionheads*, John Clark

Pratt's *The Laotian Fragments*, James Webb's *Fields of Fire*, John Del Vecchio's *The 13th Valley*, Gustav Hasford's *The Short-Timers*, Ward Just's *The American Blues*, and Stephen Wright's *Meditations in Green*, have won for their authors both critical acclaim and national celebrity.[1] Still other, less well known novels such as William Pelfrey's *The Big V*, Charles Durden's *No Bugles, No Drums*, and Larry Heinemann's *Close Quarters* endure as works of extreme power and accomplishment. Even now, more than fifteen years after the last American helicopter lifted out of Saigon, the production continues with such notable works as Jack Fuller's *Fragments*, Ronald J. Glasser's *Another War, Another Peace*, Donald Tate's *Bravo Burning*, Joseph Ferrandino's *Firefight*, Richard Currey's *Fatal Light*, and Tim Mahoney's *Holloran's World War* and *We're Not Here*.[2]

I propose here to discuss the post-Vietnam careers of six figures in particular: Tim O'Brien, Philip Caputo, James Webb, Robert Olen Butler, Winston Groom, and Larry Heinemann.[3] Each is a "Vietnam" novelist who has clearly become a major American novelist as well; and each thereby, in an era of crucial postwar reflection, now continues to inscribe the fictional memory of Vietnam into a sustained and major encounter with the very forms and processes of cultural mythmaking at large.

On one hand, then, as already suggested, their work has often appeared in a tradition uniquely historicist in direct lines of acknowledgment and provenance. As Thomas Myers has shown, for instance, the war novel itself (or, in some cases, the "literary" memoir) in which most of their careers originate is inherently a "historical" form, one in a single moment setting itself forth as "self-conscious aesthetic expression" and as "genuine historical hermeneutic" (*Walking Point*, 9). Not surprisingly, a number of subsequent works by these and other major Vietnam writers described above thus follow such an overtly "historical" direction. They range from Robert Olen Butler's *Wabash* and *Countrymen of Bones*, Winston Groom's *As Summers Die*, and James Webb's *A Country Such as This* to Philip Caputo's and Robert Stone's large novels of adventure and political revolution such as *Horn of Africa* and *A Flag for Sunrise;* and they also include more immediate chronicles of American politics and manners ranging from the establishment fables of Ward Just such as *Nicholson at Large, The American Blues*, or *Jack Gance* — not to mention extraordinary story collections such as *The Congressman Who Loved Flaubert* or *Honor*,

*Power, Riches, Fame and the Love of Women* — to the redneck comedy of Winston Groom's *Forrest Gump* or the fifties and sixties nostalgia-satire of Tim O'Brien's *The Nuclear Age.*

Meanwhile, however, at the other extreme, the historical novelist has also found his vision joined (and at times, as in the two works just mentioned, simultaneously) with that of the experimentalist-fantasist in works such as Tim O'Brien's *Going After Cacciato*, Larry Heinemann's *Paco's Story*, and Stephen Wright's *Meditations in Green* and even further, in Wright's more recent *M31: A Family Romance*, for example, and the nonveteran David Winn's remarkable *Gangland*, the futurist and science fictionist. Indeed, across an array of major works, the very ideas of categories such as history and imaginative art themselves would often seem mainly to continue, as has often been the case with Vietnam writing, to become occasions of radical inquiry into their own categorical status. To seek the point, for instance, where literary memoir and self-conscious artifice become indistinguishable would seem to be among the chief issues of Ronald J. Glasser's *365 Days* or William E. Merritt's *Where the Rivers Ran Backward*. In their very different ways, Ron Kovic's *Around the World in Eight Days* and, as will presently be noted, Tim O'Brien's *The Things They Carried* seem on the other hand designed to create fantasy insofar as possible as absolute matter of fact.

A Vietnam novelist in his generation whose work has inscribed itself across virtually all of the directions of genre and mode described above, Tim O'Brien began his writing career auspiciously with a classic of American memoir, *If I Die in a Combat Zone*. This he followed with *Northern Lights*, an austere and moving novel of homecoming and self-recuperation and a work concealing beneath its essentially realistic surface the stirrings of a stylistic experimentalism of uncommon power and originality. That experimentalism would shortly find its flowering in *Going After Cacciato*, acclaimed as one of the most powerful novels of the Vietnam war and in the same moment instantly recognized as a postmodernist classic of magical realism.[4] Next, O'Brien continued on to *The Nuclear Age*, a work at once, as mentioned above, both brilliantly futuristic and deeply evocative, in the veins of both satire and nostalgia, of the experiential mood of the American 1950s and '60s. And most recently, in *The Things They Carried*, he now continues to work masterfully at the intersection of old dreams of remembrance with new imaginings of meaning and moral possibility. At once, this latest text returns us historically to Vietnam *as experience* only to take us back as well to the future, so to speak, in an ongoing quest toward sense making itself as the ultimate form of literary production. As has been his direction from the outset, O'Brien continues to seek a fiction in which cultural memory and imaginative invention would find a new domain of mythic alliance, a ground of original creation on which each might most fully partake of the shaping and transforming power of the other. It is a fiction in which the vision of the merely plausible continues to trace out other and better visions of the newly possible.

O'Brien's themes from the outset have been the old ones, the fundamental ones, the great ones: discipline, honesty, integrity; understanding, acceptance, endurance. Milton J. Bates, for instance, in a study of *If I Die in a Combat Zone* and of the succeeding novels, notes O'Brien's preoccupation with a "myth of courage" in its largest sense that places him "in the tradition of our great war novelists—Crane, Hemingway, Jones, Mailer, Heller, and Vonnegut" (263). Marie Nelson similarly sees his works as all turning on a question of "conscience" conceived of as a conflict between, in Erich Fromm's terms, the "authoritarian" and the "humanistic" (267). And as with most of his fellow Vietnam writers, his vision of those themes is shaped by a particularly radical form of twofold recognition: of the degree, first, to which moral individuality, as chronicled brilliantly, for instance, by Paul Fussell in his study of the English literary generation of 1914–18, is always a function of preexistent literary mythologies of culture; and of the corresponding degree, second, to which a literary art envisioning an individuality sufficient unto other times and better can only be one that, even as it honors the body of myth whence it derives, must in the same moment undertake its wholesale imaginative reshaping.[5]

This dual recognition is instantly apparent in *If I Die in a Combat Zone*. It is in fact apparent, we eventually see, even as early as the title. This masterwork of the American tradition of the contemplative, an odyssey of consciousness in the lineage of Shepard, Edwards, Woolman, Thoreau, and Henry Adams, introduces itself in a blare of martial false bravado, the first line of a boot-camp marching song out of a long provenance of many designed over the years to persuade American boys on their way to war that they are in fact men.

I know a girl, her name is Jill,
She won't do it, but her sister will.
Honey, oh, Baby-Doll.

I know a girl, dressed in black,
Makes her living on her back.
Honey, oh, Baby-Doll.

I know a girl, dressed in red,
Makes her living in a bed.
Honey, oh, Baby-Doll.

I don't know, but I been told,
Eskimo pussy is mighty cold.
Am I goin' strong?
Am I right or wrong?
Sound Off!

If I die in a combat zone,
Box me up and ship me home.
An' if I die on the Russian front,
Bury me with a Russian cunt.

Sound Off!

Sound Off! The soldier-memoirist anchors his new, post-Vietnam vision of national consciousness in a titular phrase summoning up a long tradition of cadence calls for this century's American wars. Thus, from the title page onward, he reveals to us that he has somehow known the nature of his project from the outset. To be in generational particular the child of his parents, he realizes, is from the outset also to be ineluctably the child of a whole mythic America:

I grew out of one war and into another. My father came from leaden ships of sea, from the Pacific theater; my mother was a WAVE. I was the offspring of the great campaign against the tyrants of the 1940's, one explosion in the Baby Boom, one of millions come to replace those who had just died. My bawling came with the first throaty note of a new army in spawning. I was bred with the haste and dispatch and careless muscle-flexing of a nation giving bridle to its own good fortune and success. I was fed by the spoils of 1945 victory. (20)

It is all there. Teachers: "brittle old ladies, classroom football coaches, flushed veterans of the war" (20). Sports: experience with "the Rural Electric Association Little League Team" and memories of his father's love-affair with the 1950s Brooklyn Dodgers (21). American rituals: "Sparklers and the forbidden cherry bomb were for the Fourth of July: a baseball game, a picnic, a day in the city park, listening to the high school band play 'Anchors Aweigh,' a speech, watching a parade of American Legion-aires" (21). From the outset, O'Brien recognizes in mythic foreshadowing the figure he will soon be in enactment as well, the young centurion, latest comely heir of the empire. Yet in the same moment, the self-conscious sense of such a mythic foregrounding also provokes a most profound sense of difference. Precisely because he is expected to be at one with his fellow draftees, the narrator-memoirist thereby recognizes most crucially that he is not like them and, by implication, he realizes in the same moment, the America assumed to have commonly produced them. Early on in boot camp, his recourse becomes to dream other lives and better. He thinks literature. He makes a friend of common disposition. He indulges in a futile charade of attempted desertion. He passes into war.

Now, in Vietnam, the quest for self-knowledge deepens into larger contemplations and larger understandings, often at once experiential *and* mythic—about courage, about virtue, about wisdom, about wise acceptance. At times they are couched in the classic documents of wisdom and bravery, Plato's *Laches*, Wilfred Owen's *"Dulce et Decorum Est,"* Ezra Pound's "Hugh Selwyn Mauberley." Yet now also, as if his particular experience cannot dictate otherwise, the mythic exempla the young narrator comes increasingly to confront most deeply and pervasively are those prior ones imaging his Americanness. Arising, in fact, directly out of his experience in the fullness of its old American contextualizations, the spectacle increasingly comes to surround him, a whole grand American panoply. For courage, there are "John Kennedy, Audie Murphy, Sergeant York," with the curious addition, at the literary urging of his friend Erik, of the English maverick-hero T. E. Lawrence. There are also his favorite American "make-believe men": "Alan Ladd of *Shane*, Captain Vere, Bogart as the proprietor of Café d'Americain, Frederick Henry" (142). For the attempt to assess the "rightness" of a war there are Ernest Hemingway and Ernie Pyle (96–97). For the fear and the ceaseless thought of ever-threatening violence, there is the narrator's boyish misreading, as at once naively and dreadfully American as such a thing can be, of "guileless, gentle Ichabod Crane" (92). Apace, cultural archetype mixes itself with popular caricature. In the paddy, one wishes to be Tarzan, "able to swing with the vines" (126). After a rest on the march, one arises "like a wooden man, like a toy soldier out of Victor Herbert's *Babes in Toyland*" (126). When an exceptionally aggressive and unpopular battalion commander is reported dead as the result of an attack by enemy sappers, the response of the American boys is pure Hollywood. "A lieutenant led us in song, a catchy, happy, celebrating song," O'Brien recalls: " 'Ding-dong the wicked witch is dead' " (114).

Yet precisely in the wholesale embrace of this vast, giddy heterotopia of collective myth comes in the same moment the opportunity for new individual self-recognition and self-reconstitution. The possibility of this, albeit modest, O'Brien has signaled early on. "Do dreams offer lessons?" he has asked. "Do nightmares have themes, do we awaken and analyze them and live our lives and advise others as a result? Can the foot soldier teach anything important about war, merely for having been there? I think not. He can tell war stories" (31–32). (And here again, from the outset, O'Brien strikes a major tone of his creative career. One of his best-known recent works, published first as a short fiction and then included as a central text in his later collection, *The Things They Carried*, is in fact entitled "How to Tell a True War Story.")

Appropriately, in keeping with the austere, contemplative mood that prevails throughout, *If I Die in a Combat Zone* does conclude with its own prize of experiential-mythic wisdom, a moment of transformation in which the embrace of an oddly old sense of an ending may yet become a place of movement toward new beginnings. "You add things up," O'Brien tells us.

> You lost a friend to the war, and you gained a friend. You compromised one principle and fulfilled another. You learned, as old men tell it in front of the courthouse, that war is not all bad; it may not make a man of you, but it teaches you that manhood is not something to scoff; some stories of valor are true; dead bodies are heavy, and it's better not to touch them; fear is paralysis, but it is better to be afraid than to move out to die, all limbs functioning and heart thumping

and charging and having your chest torn open for all the work; you have to pick the times not to be afraid, but when you are afraid you must hide it to save respect and reputation. You learned that the old men had lives of their own and that they valued them enough to try not to lose them; anyone can die in a war if he tries. (294)

In this intensely written book, the conclusion returns both history and myth to their deepest ground of linguistic origin, which is of course not the language of writing but the language of speech. The newest attempt at sense making becomes new only as it acknowledges its patrimony in the oldest. (In a neat postmodern twist on these figures of language, it should also be noted, a passage incorporating virtually the same words will appear again in *Going After Cacciato;* and, not surprisingly, there the experimental novelist will in fact make the memoirist's "ending" — now rendered as the protagonist Paul Berlin's crucial recognition of the abyss still to be traversed in sense making between "fact" and "imagination" — the literal source of a new "beginning" [288–89].) Across the spectrum of language one tells stories. If stories out of new historical memory honor certain old myths, there must be no particular surprise. If they lead to morals, just as well. If they lead just to simple lessons, as is most often the likelier case, better than nothing. Even if they lead exactly back to the ironic amendment or deflection of what was supposed to be their purpose, just as well also. There in fact may lie the new secret of revisionary relation between history and myth that has been waiting all along. Words are all we have.

Nowhere is this point more fully reinforced than in the book's concluding paragraph, where the quest after mythic signification finds its truest moment of ritual closure precisely in the punctuating irony of the actual. O'Brien is at last coming home. The plane begins its final descent. In one last grand operatic gesture the narrator removes himself to one of the rear rest rooms and exchanges his uniform for some blue jeans and a sweater. Here, after all, will be an end to it, the defeat of the green machine. Here indeed, will even be a further demonstration of control, not only the end of something, but also the beginning of something else. "You smile at yourself in the mirror," he recalls. "You grin, beginning to know you're happy." But then, of course, also comes the attendant revelation. "Much as you hate it, you don't have civilian shoes." Even as the after-image of what you have been begins to enfold into the new reflection of what you may or might wish yourself again to be, you wear the baggage of what you are and have been. Grunts have to walk in the shoes they are issued. As O'Brien tells us in the work's last sentence, it is impossible to go home barefoot (205).

"All it takes is guts—right, O'Brien?" These have been the parting words of the drunken, demented Major Callicles to the narrator-memoirist near the end of *If I Die in a Combat Zone* (201). As with most of the myths of American manhood O'Brien has run into in his experience of Vietnam, this one too has ultimately come to carry some measure of its own ironic truth. For as noted by a host of interpreters, including those already cited such as Bates and Nelson, as well as others such as Thomas Myers and Daniel L. Zins, something like "guts" crudely personified—experiential self-exploration coupled with the new courage of an ongoing quest after larger patterns of sense making—remains effectively O'Brien's great theme; and his early novel, *Northern Lights*, in 1975, proves a first overtly fictive attempt to confront that thematic imperative full face. For the novel is indeed, explicitly, beyond all else, a profound and insistent meditation on the very idea of courage, its origin, its definition, its promise, its possibility.

Set in the dark, northern forestlands of upper Minnesota, *Northern Lights* nonetheless does concern itself almost immediately once again with the experience of Vietnam, in this case the predicament of the returned, half-blinded veteran Harvey Perry; but it also quickly comes to locate Vietnam so considered as the "case" of Harvey's brother, Paul Milton Perry, as well and as a condition of the larger domestic landscape both now inhabit. The latter is a county agricultural agent in a dying office in a dying upper Minnesota lumber town where the two brothers have lived out their youth under the crabbed, eccentric theology of their self-styled minister-father and its omnipresent tyranny over their own shared search for vision and belief. The former now comes home from Vietnam to rejoin that search, introducing into it the new emotional legacy of the war; and events in turn then become further complicated through the impact of Harvey's return upon a set of complex relationships including that of Paul with his wife, the great-hearted, nurturing Grace, as well as those of both brothers with the wild, elusive Addie, her suggestion of Indian blood locating her somewhere between the backwoods honky-tonk and the dark, northern landscape of forest and lake.

The deepest meanings of this novel of homecoming and readjustment come ultimately to reside somewhere beyond the domestic, however, in the domain of the pure elemental, the precinct of nothing less than American wilderness myth itself. And from the outset, one senses this direction in undercurrents of theme: the air of sexual conflict pervading the brothers' relationship and their understanding of their relationships with the two women; the concomitant tension arising out of the attempts of both to cut free of the spectral dominion of the dead father; the sense of the omnipresence of nature and of its possibility as a means of returning to a sense of whole relation to the world. Likewise, this same sense of the elemental is suggested from the outset as a function of overall design as well: the book in fact has no chapters; rather (in anticipation of a similar recent work, Philip Caputo's *Indian Country*), it is structured according to various figurations of American Indian legend.

Finally, one also feels from the outset the omnipresence of myth in the dimension of the overtly symbolic. Harvey returns from his war with a dead eye, now in Hemingwayesque parody, the blinded-bullock poet of his lost destiny. The brother, Paul, in his confused relation to both brother and father, is as often Perry, the individuating Christian name persistently confused with the patronymic. In a recurrent primal scene out of memory, while the old man dies upstairs banging away at his spit cup, the loyal Harvey digs away at a last pet project of spirit-mad paternal dementia, a bomb shelter (and now in anticipation of O'Brien's own *The Nuclear Age*), while the recalcitrant Paul/Perry shirks, Hamlet-like, with his doubts and gripes. The iconography of heroism turns numbingly self-parodic, as Harvey finds his pain and sacrifice trivialized at a high school football game in a fuddled, snow-blown halftime show of patriotism, and later in a dismal memorial parade in which Harvey seems ultimately less hero than some grotesque exhibit. Correspondingly, for Paul, a beery evening's expedition with Grace, his brother, and Addie, to the local parking spot, the village dump, becomes a Skunk Hour measure of small-town despairs imaged conclusively in his abortive swatting away at a defiant rat.

It is only at the last, however, that the novel finds its true mythographic culmination, in a festival weekend of ski races at the Grand Marais and the return of the brothers alone, through a cross-country odyssey of courage, illness, abandonment, and ultimate communion. And in the same moment, precisely as the work makes its critical turn toward some new sense making about America in the wake of the newest of its wars, it also acknowledges its indebtedness to older American mythmaking as well. The literary forebear invoked specifically is Hemingway. In theme, *Northern Lights* may indeed be said to summon up the tales of survivorship and self-reconstitution such as "Soldier's Home," "In Another Country," or "A Way You'll Never Be." In setting, it also speaks on virtually every page, again, as will Philip Caputo's *Indian Country*, of the great Nick Adams tales of communion in the dark forests of the great northern midwest. Similarly as well, the tone throughout is dark, muted, austere, controlled and precise, and cadenced by the careful rhythms of speech and the repetition of key terms and phrases.

As becomes increasingly clear as the novel progresses, however, the Hemingway most explicitly invoked in *Northern Lights* is the Hemingway of *The Sun Also Rises*. (Indeed, as Milton J. Bates points out [264], at least one contemporary reviewer, Roger Sales of *The New York Review of Books*, found the inscriptions of this text so oppressively dense as to require his entitling of his essay "Fathers & Fathers & Sons.") The climactic ski races at Grand Marais and the frenzied partying with which they are accompanied clearly image the festival scenes at Pamplona, even down to Addie's playing Brett Ashley to her Pedro Romero of a young Olympian. The ski adventure undertaken by the brothers on the return home, until it is turned deadly by a sudden blizzard, likewise recalls the subsequent fishing expedition of Jake Barnes and his spiritual kinsman Bill Gorton to the stream at Burguete. And this too has its precise signature even in the degree to which the bond of language — for example, the common use of the word "bloody" early on, or a later embrace of the word "stellar" — becomes a signature of male comradeship. Dialogue throughout suggests literary homage issuing a challenge of near parody. "Came home from . . . feeling like a bum," Harvey mutters through his hangover at Grand Marais. "War and all. Wasn't so good, you know. I told you something about it last night, didn't I?" Paul replies: "Just a little. You were drunk. I forget" (144).

In sum, this first novel by the memoirist of *If I Die in a Combat Zone* becomes the announcement of a distinctly "literary" writer in the best sense of the term, one testing out his vision, his voice, and his new mythic enterprise against the explicit acknowledgment of a highly honored one that, in analogous circumstances, has gone before. Indeed, in this first novel, O'Brien already is the writer to be described much later by his friend and fellow Vietnam author Philip Caputo as "solidly within the tradition of midwestern soldier-poets, which includes Hemingway, Dos Passos, Jones, and O'Brien's fellow Minnesotan, Fitzgerald." From the outset, O'Brien acknowledges the mythic provenance of his art, even as he tests out its new imaginative dimensions.

The explicitly "literary" quality of O'Brien's fiction, and particularly his explicit concern with the exploration of experiential or historical memory through the newly creating and transforming power of imaginative myth, would shortly find its full flowering in the highly acclaimed *Going After Cacciato*. In a return to many of the concerns of the earlier memoir, *If I Die in a Combat Zone*, it is ostensibly O'Brien's "war" novel arising out of the experience of Vietnam. Yet, as Richard Freedman in *The New York Times Book Review* put it acutely, at the same time "to call" *Going After Cacciato* "a novel about war is like calling *Moby-Dick* a novel about whales" (1). And the precise analogy is not in the least ill taken. For the enterprise, albeit in the new vein of postmodern "magical" realism, is very much Melville's own, and on the same scale: to devise a grammatology, a linguistic rendering of felt experience that might project it imaginatively into new dimensions of knowlege, meaning, and value. Indeed, in *Going After Cacciato*, we are confronted with the prospect of a new imaginative fiction of the American experience of Vietnam that would propose ultimately to reify itself *precisely through imagination* into nothing less than redemptory cultural fact.

The work makes this creative task clear from the outset: "Paul Berlin, whose only goal was to live long enough to establish goals worth living for still longer, stood high in the tower by the sea, the night soft all around him, and wondered, not for the first time, about the immense powers of his own imagination. A truly awesome notion. Not a dream, an idea. An idea to develop, to tinker with and build and sustain, to draw out as an artist draws out his visions" (27–28).

Thus begins a novel that, as one quickly sees, is actually two, or possibly three, novels, each of which, moreover, can be read only in terms of its other or others. In a guard tower by the South China Sea, Specialist Fourth Class Paul Berlin stands lonely vigil and thinks out at once a fact-book and a fantasy-book, a book of memory and a book of imagination. Connected by frequent interchapters in what perhaps might be considered a third book—entitled, appropriately, "The Observation Post,"—the other two flow in and out of each other at will until all boundaries of vision and consciousness seem dissolved. And within this structure, as Thomas Myers writes, "experience and imagination" thus "face each other, but they also compose a continuum, a different kind of frame tale of which the architecture, like the eye-fooling geometry of an Escher print, seems to defy natural laws of space and proportion. Reality tests the limits of imagination in *Cacciato* as imagination enters and informs the nature and quality of memory. By extending rather than abandoning the reality of the Vietnam War, O'Brien simultaneously speaks more fully of it as he enfolds that experience with larger issues" (173). Or, as G. Thomas Couser has put it, the novel's "major narrative line is" thus "a story that never gets told about an adventure that never happened. But in spite of the muteness of the central character and his impotence to realize his dreams, the novel does not condemn his desperate use of this imagination. Rather, it portrays it as necessary, worthwhile, and even redemptive" (10).[6] And what results from all this, then, is a whole far greater than the sum of its parts, a ground of original creation on which Berlin ultimately re-writes himself and his America into new dimensions of individual and collective insight.

The domain of fact or memory is a nightmare-continuum of particular horrors. Frenchie Tucker gets shot through the nose. Bernie Lynn dies of a tunnel wound, shot from his chest straight down into his vitals. Billy Boy Watkins dies of fright on the field of battle, screaming his dreadful scream, trying to lace back on the boot that holds what used to be his foot. Buff winds up ass-high in the air, "like a praying Arab in Mecca" (283), his upturned helmet holding all that remains of his disposable humanity in the muck of his shot-away face.

Then, suddenly, in the midst of everything, exit Cacciato. Cacciato. "Dumb as a bullet," says one GI. "Dumb as a month-old oyster fart," says another (2). Dumb perhaps, but apparently not crazy. Or maybe just dumb and crazy enough to think he can pull it off. "Split, departed," says Doc Peret, and somehow, incredibly, miraculously, "Gone to Paris" (2–3). So, in *Going After Cacciato*, the real quickly begins to meld into the imaginative, the factually just plausible into the fictively just possible. Cacciato goes. Berlin and the others follow. Apace, Berlin ponders: "What part was fact and what part was the extension of fact? And how were facts separated from possibilities? What really happened and what merely might have happened? How did it end?" (28).

The fictive road to Paris does somehow magically end there, and in the negotiations that ultimately terminate American participation in the war. At the same time, the novel remains firmly anchored in the experience of the battlefield and centered on the movement of Berlin's particular experiential consciousness toward the recognition of new possibilities of acceptance and understanding. Within this twofold movement, the complex play of style re-engenders that whole vast collocation of memory, myth, metaphor, slogan, political shibboleth, and popular cliche that was in fact America in Vietnam.

It will be remembered, for example, that "The Road to Paris" was the literal expression used by bureaucratic and journalistic phrasemakers to describe the tortuous and often nearly absurd labors—including some prolonged squabbling over the shape and dimensions of a conference table—of getting the peace talks set in motion. It will also be remembered that "The Road to" any number of places once supplied the title to any number of innocently ridiculous American movies that made comedy, in some of the bleakest times of war, out of danger and dire predicament. Here Berlin finds his Dorothy Lamour—it is hard in fact to think of the new model as being clothed in anything but a sarong—in Sarkin Aung Wan, his Vietnamese companion and spiritual guide. He persistently finds himself playing pensive Crosby to wisecracking Hope in the nimble Doc Peret. Peril mixes with pratfall all the way. They and the rest of Cacciato's pursuers barely escape death at the hands of the Shah's dreaded Savak. They miraculously avoid detection as they slip ashore in Greece. They traverse the breadth of Europe looking over their shoulders for pursuers.

In Asia itself, they have already fallen, Alice-in-Wonderland–like, through "A Hole in the Road to Paris" (82) and have wound up seeing "the Light" at the end of General Westmoreland's "Tunnel" (111). The "Light" turns out to be a periscope manned by an aged Vietnamese who is himself a deserter condemned there now for ten years. Berlin, looking through the eyepiece and seeing in imagination, he realizes, Bernie Lynn and Frenchie Tucker in precisely the same moment of his experiential memory of their descent and death, understands for a split second that here the Americans have the chance to see the war from the other side. It is too late. Berlin's platoon leader, a sick, aging relic of American wars, destroys the periscope with six rounds from his M-16 (84). Shortly, they all fall back out of the

Hole on the Road to Paris and, the lesson of perspective lost, continue on their weary, imperiled way.

Through such fantasy wordplay in *Going After Cacciato*, the vision of this latest of myth-haunted American wars is also grounded further in mythic memories of other times and other wars and empires as well. One of the roads on the Road to Paris turns out to be the Road to Mandalay (111). What is sought by those who have gone after Cacciato, the most recent in a long line of historical belligerents, is the "Peace of Paris" (290). Shortly after they arrive, Berlin finds a *New York Herald-Tribune* carrying news of the death of Eisenhower. On the front page are two pictures, one of Eisenhower as a cadet at West Point, the other of "him riding into Paris, the famous grin, the jeep swamped by happy Frenchmen" (304).

Berlin reads on. So at the end, even as at the beginning, he sees, it remains all of a piece, the world, himself, his America:

> The world went on. Old facts warmed over. Nixon was President. In Chicago, a federal grand jury had handed down indictments against eight demonstrators at the Democratic convention the previous summer. He'd missed that—the whole thing had happened while he was in basic training. Tear gas and cops, something like that. No matter: Dagwood still battled Mr. Dithers. What changed? The war went on. "In an effort to bring the Peace Talks to a higher level of dialogue, the Secretary of Defense has ordered the number of B-52 missions over the North to be dropped from 1,800 to 1,500 a month"; meanwhile, in the South, it was a quiet week, with sporadic and light action confined to the Central Highlands and Delta. Only 204 more dead men. And Ike. Ike was dead and an era had ended. (304)

So it goes in "The Observation Post." Still, if nothing has really changed, by Berlin's keeping faith to the end with a new vision of creative possibility born equally of the claims of both experiential memory *and* imaginative invention, a very great deal may yet have been learned and gained. The mythic cycle may persist, but one may also still elect not to succumb to its grim dominion. Like Yossarian, Berlin elects to persevere. "Insight, vision. What you remember is what you see, and what you see depends on what you remember. A cycle, Doc Peret had said. A cycle that has to be broken. And this requires a fierce concentration on the process itself: focus on the order of things, sort out the flow of events so as to understand how one thing led to another, search for that point at which what happened had been extended into a vision of what might have happened" (207). Persevere. Seek the possibility in the face of all of it still to be able to say the two words with which the novel ends: "Maybe so" (338).[7]

Tim O'Brien's third novel, published in 1985, is *The Nuclear Age*. Although a putative chronicle of 1995, its mode nonetheless, unlike that of *Going After Cacciato*, is essentially realistic, a domestic narrative in retrospect of the coming of age of the protagonist, William Cowling, in the America of the Cold War 1950s and the turbulent, angry, counter-culture '60s and '70s and of his subsequent attempts now to live down new, midlife versions of old familiar desperations—both of his own and of his culture at large—in the amnesiac post-Vietnam America of the '80s and '90s. Yet beneath the work's deceptively realistic surface, O'Brien also continues to enlarge on many of the preoccupations, formal and thematic, that have characterized his earlier career: the relationship between reality and imagination, language and consciousness, form and possibility. Like its predecessor, *The Nuclear Age* is a book about what happened but also in the same moment a book about what might have happened, what could have happened, what should have happened, what may be kept from happening, or what may be yet made to happen.

The novel is narrated in the first person by the protagonist, William Cowling, a kind of domestic Paul Berlin—thoughtful, cautious, endlessly self-contemplative—cast in counterculture obverse. And structurally, the novel is also highly reminiscent, albeit in a less radical degree of overt experimentalism, of *Going After Cacciato*. If the dominant mode of the work is a putative realism, one must remember, for instance, that it is set in 1995; and as we proceed through the essentially matter-of-fact recitation of the memories and loves and despairs of a seemingly middling American life, we also ultimately find ourselves making our way across an imaginatively created and reconstituted terrain of consciousness that is nothing less than the world of the radical sixties and seventies returned to us often in mad, garish, even surreal relief. Indeed, in its combination of quiet experiential authenticity and whacked-out panoply of comic invention, *The Nuclear Age* is basically the story of a post-Vietnam, post-sixties, postmodern everyman—a leftover Weatherman Moses Herzog, perhaps (Cowling's first words to us are, "Am I crazy?"), or, in the fullness of a rocket fear

now gone irretrievably intercontinental and ballistic, a Tyrone Slothrop—
now transported to the eve of the twenty-first century.

As the work begins, Cowling is forty-nine years old, living in rural
Montana and building a bomb shelter. His wife and preadolescent daughter
have written him off as "nutto," "buggo." Cowling knows himself better
as simply veteran of the second half of his century, out of date and with
nothing to show: "Times change—take a good hard look. Where's Mama
Cass? What happened to Brezhnev and Lester Maddox? Where's that old
gang of mine, Sarah and Ned and Tina and Ollie? Where's the passion?
Where's Richard Daley? Where's Gene McCarthy in this hour of final
trial? No heroes, no heavies. And who cares? That's the stunner: Who
among us really cares? A nation of microchips. At dinner parties we eat
mushroom salad and blow snow and talk computer lingo" (8). It is time to
dig and mind one's business. "The year is 1995," Cowling writes. "We're
late in the century, and the streets are full of tumbleweed, and it's every
man for himself" (8).

Cowling's credentials as veteran of his era are impeccable. The present
construction, we soon discover for instance, is the final flowering of a long
dream of annihilation that has led Cowling as a boy, in the small-town,
bomb-haunted boyhood of the late fifties, to labor endlessly at convert-
ing his basement ping-pong table to a shelter. Later, in the early sixties, at his backwater midwest state college, he has taken it upon himself
to become a solitary voice of antinuclear protest. In short order, along
with an ad hoc band of ragtag comrades—cheerful, demolition-mad Ollie
Winkler; fat, unhappy Tina Roebuck, "two hundred pounds of stolid medi-
ocrity" (81), with her Mars bars and her resolutions; Ned Rafferty the
jock, patient, easygoing, infinitely generous; Sarah Strouch, cheerleader-
goddess of Cowling's adolescent dreams now, suddenly, improbably, his
lover and on her way toward a lifetime as terrorist passionaria—the unlikely hero finds himself fully enlisted in the radical counterculture. By
1968 he is a draft evader, and, with the complicity of his parents and the
help of his friends who have now gone on to high-grade radicalism, he
is completely underground. There follows a trip to Castro's Cuba where,
ever the unlikely hero, he proves a washout at terrorist boot camp and
spends the rest of his counterculture interlude as a courier and general
factotum of the revolution. Then, finally, toward the end of the seventies,
his guerrilla phase concludes. Searching out and marrying finally the enig-

matic, elusive stewardess-poet Bobbi, whom he has met during his initial journey and has subsequently chased, years later, halfway around the world and along a trail of discarded husbands and lovers, he returns home to Montana where they have a child, and Cowling, in ironic consummation of both his bomb madness *and* his childhood fascination with rocks, makes a fortune as a uranium prospector. There, Sarah, Ned, Ollie, and Tina, co-investors in the uranium scheme, shortly show up, along with their old guerrilla boot-camp instructors Nethro and Ebeneezer Keneezer, bearing the ultimate prize of their long terrorist endeavors, a captured nuclear warhead. Suddenly, Sarah becomes ill from a herpes simplex infection, the familiar blister of passion that through long years of the sixties and seventies has come for Cowling to seem a kind of bright badge of revolution. Inexplicably, the infection moves, a "viral migration," Cowling tells us, "along the pathways between lip and brain" (294), and she dies agonizingly of encephalitis. The others leave. They all die shortly thereafter during the summer, we are told, in a TV-spectacular shoot-out and fire. In the autumn Cowling suffers "a minor breakdown" (295). Bobbi asks for a trial separation. It is the end of 1993. Now, in 1995, stretched at last to the limit of holding on, Cowling digs.

Apropos of what might be called Cowling's progress, by now along the way the work at large has become a kind of mythic travelogue through American consciousness during the last half of its century of empire. Thanks to Cowling, we receive recurrent thumbnail summaries of major passages in the era, complete with lists of big events, pop icons, media shibboleths, major- and minor-league heroes and villains. 1958: CONELRAD; Strontium 90. 1962: the Cuban Missile Crisis. 1964: the Chinese A-Bomb; Khruschev "on the skids"; Marines in Da Nang; Jane Fonda "a starlet" and Abbie Hoffman "a nobody" (66). 1966: Westmoreland in Saigon and Rolling Thunder over Hanoi; Dean Rusk, Richard Nixon, Robert Kennedy, Richard Daly, Eugene McCarthy, Robert McNamara. 1967: Abbie Hoffman a "somebody"; Jane Fonda "making choices"; Sirhan Sirhan "taking target practice"; LBJ "on the ropes"; Richard Nixon "counting noses"; Robert McNamara "having second thoughts"; Dean Rusk "having bad dreams" (112). 1969: Vietnamization; Judge Julius Hoffman in the courtroom; Weathermen in the streets; the Mets in the Series; monsoons in Quang Ngai; Ronald Reagan governing California; the Stones singing "Let It Bleed"; the moratorium (222–23). 1970: Cambodia and

Kent State (226). 1971: Calley on trial; peace talks in Paris; Cambodia on fire (239).

The years and the events crowd, shove, compress, Doppler-like. 1974: Nixon says good-bye and gets a pardon. 1975: Saigon is finished. 1976: Gerald Ford fumbles, tall ships sail the harbors, and America goes forgiving and forgetful (261). 1977: Pres. Jimmy Carter shoots ten thousand draft dodgers "full of Novocain" (262). 1980: the uranium strike comes in, Cowling and his friends get rich, and a long decade issues forward, in Sarah's acute phrasing, of "memories moribundus" (280).

As for Cowling's America, so for himself, it is all there: the bomb; toilet training; Vietnam; the counter-culture; Watergate; seventies aftershocks; the age of post-war retrenchment and retreat; eighties amnesia. And so onward for William Cowling it has continued from the outset now into the last years of the century: a trail of crazed mythologies, beginning with his father's annual death in the role of General Custer in the town pageant and ending in a last American conflagration of self-consuming idealism where everything burns. Everything. It is the American way in the last years of the century. On national television, his friends and their safe house and their stolen warhead burn. And so everything, he sees, in the Nuclear Age, is "combustible." "Faith burns. . . . there is only nothing" (303). In General Custer's America, it is the end of the nuclear age, and now only the hole beckons. Having lived his life and the mythic life of his times, Cowling asks at the end the question he already knows must now always be without an answer. "Where on earth," he says, "is the happy ending?" Meanwhile, he realizes, "Kansas is burning. All things are finite." Yet still he dares to provide an answer. "Love," he says, "feebly."

"The hole," he goes on, "finds" such a proposition "amusing": "*I am all there is*, it says. *Keyhole. . . . your Ace in the Hole*" (298).

His wife and child sedated and ensconced in the darkness beneath, for Cowling it is time to climb in and blow. Still, there remains that matter of the happy ending. "If you can imagine it," Cowling keeps telling himself one more time, "it can happen" (301). Mockingly, insistently, the hole contends otherwise. In the end, it says, there is only *Nothing*. (304). And Cowling sees the attraction of the argument: "I want to know that the hole knows. The hole is where faith should be. The hole is what we have when imagination fails" (306). Yet just as he is down to last questions, the child, Melinda, wakes. Frightened, angry, they quarrel. At last he holds her as she cries. "I touch her skin," he says. "It's only love, I know, but it's a kind of miracle" (311). In the hole, at the end of history and faith and imagination, a communion of souls may yet bring a new revelation to pass, a dream of what has been now inscribing itself into a consciousness of what yet may be. And so the novel concludes. The child is in the shower. Bobbi drinks coffee with Cowling at the kitchen table. Cowling blows the hole empty. Nothing really has changed. Yet again, through the shaping and transforming power of the imagination, a very great deal may have been earned and gained. "One day my daughter will die," Cowling admits. "One day, I know, my wife will leave me. It will be autumn, perhaps, and trees will be in color, and she will kiss me in my sleep and tuck a poem in my pocket, and the world will surely end." It is one thing to "know this," he concludes, however. It is quite another to "believe," as he does, "other-wise." In the Nuclear Age, at the end of the breakdown of history *and* sustaining myth into bad dreams and old terrors, Cowling still believes in the possibility of a strength of imaginative conviction that may yet outrun science and geopolitical madness: "Happily," he says in the end, "I will . . . will somehow not quite balance" (312).

"A thing may happen and be a total lie; another thing may not hap-pen and be truer than the truth" (89). So a newest Tim O'Brien narrator continues to speculate, William Cowling–like, Paul Berlin–like, and now, once again, most suggestively as well, Tim O'Brien–like. He does so, not surprisingly, in the midst of a story about story telling entitled "How to Tell a True War Story"; and this text, in turn, is planted well along in O'Brien's latest book-length work, a collection of Vietnam and Vietnam-related fictions entitled—after an opening section which is, in contrast, a story about bare itemization of fact—*The Things They Carried*.[8] Indeed, with the appearance of this latest remarkable text, it would be possible to measure the ongoing achievement of Tim O'Brien with a certain truth of utter simplicity just by saying that he is still telling Vietnam stories after all these years. And this itself would be appropriate. For as this book tells us again and again, and as the others have before, such must be one of the crucial tasks of the storyteller in a country whose resolute belief in its historical exceptionalism, even after its involvement in a geopolitical tragedy like Vietnam, continues to be predicated on its easy capacity for historical amnesia. But now too, of course, the stories continue to seek out, and often precisely through the medium of their elemental simplicities, their connections with that spirit of fictions Melville called "the great Art of Telling the Truth" ("Hawthorne," 1160). They are relentlessly, at the deepest levels of consciousness, about stories and their making, about how the truth of anything ever gets told in ways by which we might be still transformed and even possibly redeemed. The real war story here, then, is a single story, a story told as many times and in as many ways possible and beyond, about the processes of experiential *and* literary "truth-telling" encountered at their primary nodes of human conjunction.

The selection noted is a case in point. "How to Tell a True War Story" is, for instance, a meditation on story telling anchored on a rather specific story. The latter, moreover, is a fairly straightforward story, and one also, if we are to believe the narrator, essentially "true." Yet exactly there, as we eventually learn, will also come the astounding fictive crux. For indeed as it unfolds, its "truth" comes to encompass a terrible power of unbidden disclosure that art itself would seem taxed to imagine. It is about two buddies, Rat Kiley and Curt Lemon. They play a game of toss with smoke grenades, a kind of burning-fuse variant of chicken where they pull the pin, as they would, presumably, with a "real" grenade, and toss the cannister back and forth, each figuring to leave the other holding it at the point of explosion. The one who throws too early is yellow. The one who throws too late is a fool and make-believe dead. One day, during a trail break, they are playing the game. Their buddies watch. Suddenly, Curt Lemon steps on a booby-trapped artillery round which disintegrates him before everyone's eyes. As the narrator and another GI named Dave Jensen pick what is left of him from the trees (or at least as it now comes back to the narrator twenty years later) Jensen is singing the popular Peter, Paul, and Mary song "Lemon Tree." Meanwhile, as we have been learning all this, however, there have also turned out to be other stories involved as well. As we learn first — and it is in fact the very first thing we learn — Kiley has written a letter to Lemon's sister full of the most arrant fables of bravado and buddy lore about her dead brother. (And they include at least one, validated in a whole other Curt Lemon story just following entitled "The Dentist," in which we learn that he truly *has* stripped himself near-naked one October night in the war, painted himself up, put on a skull mask, and gone Halloweening.) Then, shortly, we are also told, Kiley, still raging at Lemon's death, viciously kills, literally by shooting it apart piece by piece by piece, a baby water buffalo before his comrades' eyes. (And here, even as they stand mute at the atrocity perpetrated upon creation itself, the soldiers themselves know they are present at a story as yet to be written. "We had witnessed something essential," the narrator tells us, "something brand-new and profound, a piece of the world so startling there was not yet a name for it" [86].)

Meanwhile, still other stories have arisen and become likewise intertwined. Mitchell Sanders has told one, part of which he has had later to recant as embroidery, about a patrol in the fog-shrouded Highlands calling in air strikes on a mythic, monstrous Viet Cong cocktail party and music reception they have been forced to listen to in silence for six long days. And, Mitchell Sanders–like (it is his appointed role throughout the book), he even supplies this one with a "moral." "You got to *listen* to your enemy" (83), he says first; and then later, even when he admits he has perhaps exaggerated about the glee club and opera part, he still holds at least to the listening idea. "That quiet," he says, " – just listen. There's your moral" (84).

And while all *this* is going on, the search for the "true" war story, the narrator himself has come upon his own "morals" in a "true" way that the "truth" alone would never have allowed itself to provide. One accepts the fact that "in a true war story nothing is ever absolutely true" (89), or that perhaps often "there is not even a point, or else the point doesn't hit you until twenty years later, in your sleep, and you wake up and shake your wife and start telling the story to her, except when you get to the end you've forgotten the point again" (88). But even as one reaches for after-the-fact epiphany, one also recalls how it has been to stand stock-still in the midst of some war stories even before they have become war stories and to have already known a truth beyond art. So Mitchell Sanders hits it right on the head, for instance, on the day of the baby buffalo massacre. "Well, that's Nam," he offers, pulling out his faithful yo-yo, "Garden of Evil. Over here, man, every sin's real fresh and original" (86). And such also is the truth, the narrator himself tells us, "after a firefight," when "there is always the immense pleasure of aliveness." He goes on:

> The trees are alive. The grass, the soil—everything. All around you things are purely living, and you among them, and the aliveness makes you tremble. You feel an intense, out-of-the-skin awareness of your living self—your truest self, the human being you want to be and then become by the force of wanting it. In the midst of evil you want to

be a good man. You want decency. You want justice and courtesy and human concord, things you never knew you wanted. There is a kind of largeness to it, a kind of godliness. Though it's odd, you're never more alive than when you're almost dead. You recognize what's valuable. Freshly, as if for the first time, you love what's best in yourself and in the world, all that might be lost. At the hour of dusk you sit at your foxhole and look out on a wide river turning pinkish red and at the mountains beyond, and although in the morning you must cross the river and go into the mountains and do terrible things and maybe die, even so, you find yourself studying the fine colors on the river, you feel wonder and awe at the setting of the sun, and you are filled with a hard, aching love for how the world could be and always should be, but now is not. (87–88)

And meanwhile even now, in the same war story and maybe in another, this one absolutely made up, you have plunged on in still another way to the very axis of the real. There is the one, for instance, the narrator proposes, the one we've all heard, about four guys on a trail, a grenade, and one guy that "jumps on it and takes the blast and saves his three buddies." On the other hand, he now says, there might also be the opposing one, just "for example": "Four guys go down a trail. A grenade sails out. One guy jumps on it and takes the blast, but it's a killer grenade and everybody dies anyway. Before they die, though, one of the dead guys says, 'The fuck you do *that* for?' and the jumper says, 'Story of my life, man,' and the other guy starts to smile but he's dead" (89–90). Now "that's a true story" he concludes, "that never happened" (90).

What is true and what is false in such cases, he asks? It is an important question, and further, he asserts, "the answer matters" (89). Indeed, the truth, he proposes, will be measured exactly in the quality of the questions we ask for the very sake of the answers we might get. And that is why, he tells us near the end, we have to keep going back and going back to the old stories, to the openings of the big questions, back there in that one particular war story of that one particular day in the war where all the other stories seem to be lodged. "Twenty years later," he says,

> I can still see the sunlight on Lemon's face. I can see him turning, looking back at Rat Kiley, then he laughed and took that curious half

step from shade into sunlight, his face suddenly brown and shining, and when his foot touched down, in that instant, he must've thought it was the sunlight that was killing him. It was not the sunlight. It was a rigged 105 round. But if I could ever get the story right, how the sun seemed to gather around him and pick him up and lift him high into a tree, if I could somehow recreate the fatal whiteness of that light, the quick glare, the obvious cause and effect, then you would believe the last thing Curt Lemon believed, which for him must've been the final truth. (90)

To be sure, as the narrator tells us in conclusion, the story will sometimes get lost in the circumstances of the telling; and he will just have to say, for instance, of a well-intentioned lady after a reading, like Rat Kiley does of Lemon's sister when she doesn't even write back, "*dumb cooze*" (90). ("Send guys to a war," he has warned us, "they come home talking dirty" [77].) Still, it is the attempt that counts:

All you can do is tell it one more time, patiently, adding and subtracting, making up a few things to get at the real truth. No Mitchell Sanders, you tell her. No Lemon, no Rat Kiley. No trail junction. No baby buffalo. No vines or moss or white blossoms. Beginning to end, you tell her, it's all made up. Every goddamn detail—the mountains and the river and especially that poor dumb baby buffalo. None of it happened. *None* of it. And even if it did happen, it didn't happen in the mountains, it happened in this little village on the Batangan Peninsula, and it was raining like crazy, and one night a guy named Stink Harris woke up screaming with a leech on his tongue. You can tell a true war story if you just keep on telling it. (90–91)

So, in the work at large, this intense structural dialectic of texts and intertexts—facts and fictions, memories and imaginings, morals and meanings—recapitulates itself at the level of textual construction at large. And so, accordingly, across a surface where all categories seem seamlessly conjoined, it becomes at once both a medium of structure and a dialectical critique of structure as well. This is to say that the "moral," such as it is, of "How to Tell a True War Story" also becomes at once in theme *and* form the "moral" of *The Things They Carried* as composite text. It is at once a summation of Tim O'Brien's re-writing of the old dialectic of facts and fictions and a literally exponential prediction of new contexts of vision and insight, of new worlds to remember, imagine, believe.

A single story, without a trace of metafictive grandstanding, moves from the realm of the quotidian into the full domain of the fantastic. In "On the Rainy River," for instance, the draftee-narrator of *If I Die in a Combat Zone* literally recreates himself in a story "never told before" (43) of a preinduction attempt to flee across the border to Canada, only to have past and future history of both himself and his America arise before his eyes in full phantasmagoric imaging of the inevitability of his aborted moral choice. ("I survived," he tells us at the end, now at once in advance and in conclusion, "but it's not a happy ending. I was a coward. I went to the war" [63].) So, similarly, in "The Sweetheart of the Song Tra Bong," a GI choppers in on resupply his back-in-the-world girlfriend, only to lose her literally to the war. Inexorably, she moves deeper and deeper into the action, first leaving her medic-lover for the Green Berets, then too crazy even for them, and now probably somewhere with the Montagnards: just out there now, beyond, Mary Anne from Cleveland Heights "wearing her culottes, her pink sweater, and a necklace of human tongues" (125).

Various other tales, themselves of strange fictive complexity, similarly seek closure only to find their deepest meanings somehow at once recapitulated and newly completed in further ones to follow. "Enemies" is succeeded by "Friends," "Stockings" by "Church," "The Man I Killed" by "Ambush," each story in fact needing the other for its own completion. And so likewise, in increasingly complex multiplications across the text, a relationship of two extends into a configuration of three, three into four, and four into others in rich proliferation of narrative authority seemingly engendered of its own autonomous creation. In "Speaking of Courage," for instance, Norman Bowker attempts amidst the loneliness of return from the war to explain impossibly, to somebody or something— a dead friend, an old girlfriend, his father, an intercom box at the Mama Burger drive-in—the incident of war in the shitfield where he let Kiowa drown and thus missed out on winning the Silver Star. Then, in "Notes," we are given the presumably "actual" story of the narrator's correspondence with Norman Bowker (three years later a suicide by hanging "in the locker room of a YMCA in his hometown in central Iowa" [178]); of an initial version of "Speaking of Courage," excluding the shitfield part, once planned for *Going After Cacciato* but eventually extracted; and of the present re-writing where, he at last tells us, "in the interests of truth" he must now also add "that Norman Bowker was in no way responsible for what happened to Kiowa. Norman did not experience a failure of nerve on that night," he concludes. "He did not freeze up or lose the silver star for valor. That part of the story is my own" (182).[9] Then, further, in "In the Field," he in effect post-writes both story lines by telling what really happened in fullness of dramatized fictional detail. (It has in fact been another soldier—almost certainly himself, we are later led to infer—who has failed during the mortar attack to keep Kiowa from drowning in the slime.) And then with equal suddenness, in "Good Form" he announces any and all versions of stories here and throughout the book to be at once on and off. "I'm forty-three years old, true," he confesses up front, "and I'm a writer now and a long time ago I walked through Quang Ngai Province as a foot soldier." Yet "almost everything else in this book," he continues, "is invented." Still, "it's not a game," he says. Rather, he goes on, "it's a form," and a form, moreover, staking its own imaginative existence precisely on its capacity for experiential explanation. "I want you to feel what I felt," he says. "I want you to know why a story-truth is sometimes truer than a happening-truth" (203). For "what stories can do," he speculates, "is make things present. I can look at things I never looked at," he says. "I can attach faces to grief and love and pity and God. I can be brave. I can make myself feel again" (204). Most importantly, he can talk to his daughter:

"Daddy, tell the truth," Kathleen can say, "did you ever kill anybody?" And I can say, honestly, "Of course not."

Or I can say, honestly, "Yes" (204).

So, now, afoot doubly in fact and fiction, the book text relentlessly imaged in its composite title begins to make its final forays between old nightmare and new dream of meaning. In "Field Trip," the narrator returns with Kathleen to Vietnam and the old shitfield, somehow the same and completely different, deep shit once and now "too ordinary" on "a quiet sunny day" (210). With Kiowa's old war hatchet, so prominent once among the things they carried, he now plunges under again, swims deep, finds the place, lets the burden go. "I tried to think of something decent to say," he tells us, "something meaningful and right, but nothing came to me." But just then suddenly do come the words, exactly the ones, themselves at once old and new: " 'Well,' I finally murmured, 'there it is' " (212).

An old Vietnamese farmer has been watching. As father and daughter prepare to leave, Kathleen glances back across the scene.

"That old man," she said, "is he mad at you or something?"

"I hope not."

"He *looks* mad."

"No," I said. "All that's finished" (213).

Yet now, even as memory is put behind, so it returns most fully in imaginative presence. In "The Ghost Soldiers," a GI named Tim, shot twice and now out of battle, tries to take revenge on the medic who has failed to treat him for shock on the battlefield and almost killed him by trying literally, through a nightmarish hoax, to scare the latter to death. And then, directly, in "Night Life," Rat Kiley really does go crazy from imaginary things, gabbling finally just before he shoots himself out of the war about "Curt Lemon and Kiowa and Ted Lavender, and how crazy it was that people who were so incredibly alive could get so incredibly dead" (251).

Then, now, and beyond, this book tells us, and as the title of its final chapter makes explicit, that will be the way of it. Vietnam must remain just there, out somewhere between memory and imagining, the place of "The Lives of the Dead." But a bad scene for memory, it continues to insist to the last, may yet be a good scene for imagining. Memory may be true, the two foregoing stories tell us, as old nightmare endlessly recapitulated. "But this too," the concluding text now begins, "is true: stories can save us." For "in a story, which is" itself "a kind of dreaming, the dead sometimes smile and sit up and return to the world" (255). In this case the roll of dead is long. One is an old man killed by artillery fire and lying near a pigpen and the first man, in fact, the narrator has seen killed in the war. Another is Ted Lavender, from the first story, "The Things They Carried," dead of tranquilizers and gunshot on another mellow morning in the war. And still another, he now sees, as he has also somehow seen back then on his own first day of the war, is the truly first dead person he has ever seen: Linda, a childhood movie date, a first love, she with a brain tumor lost like all the others to random death. He is tempted now, as a writer, he confesses, to save Linda's life. But now he also realizes he has already done that once back when Tim was Timmy. He has already dreamed her alive. And she, in the dream, has likewise *really* said "Timmy, stop crying. It doesn't *matter*."

And so, along the way, he now recalls, he once came to learn of other ways "of making the dead seem not so dead," some good and some not so good. One bad way was of shaking hands with corpses; another, barely better, was of talking it down with GI bravado. A better one by far was of keeping "the dead alive with stories" (267). And so now, even as he writes, that same better way continues to open. Stories of Ted Lavender and Curt Lemon now mix once more with stories of Linda and of Kiowa, and stories of Linda and of Kiowa with stories of Ted Lavender and of Curt Lemon. Now, exactly, upon the textual space of "The Lives of the Dead," the dead again do literally have lives and have so forever in a realm where death is at once quite real and simply not possible: "And yet right here, in the spell of memory and imagination, I can still see her as if through ice," the narrator writes of Linda, "as if I'm gazing into some other world, a place where there are no brain tumors and no funeral homes, where there are no bodies at all." And so now likewise, he continues, "I can see Kiowa, too, and Ted Lavender and Curt Lemon, and sometimes I can even see Timmy skating with Linda under the yellow floodlights. I'm young and happy. I'll never die. I'm skimming across the surface of my own history, moving fast, riding the melt between the blades, doing loops and spins, and when I take a high leap into the dark and come down thirty years later, I realize it is as Tim trying to save Timmy's life with a story" (273).

Here, then, at the latest stage in the career of Tim O'Brien, is the work of literature as personal sense making and cultural revision in the largest sense. But it is finally much less a summation than a prediction and, as I have suggested, a promise. It would be possible to call *The Things They Carried* a novel. It has characters who act in character; some grow, some stay, and a lot die. It has a kind of plot and, for extended passages, a complex narrative evolution and even an occasional moral. It is also a spiritual autobiography, a new masterpiece of the private confessional coupled in the broadest terms of collective culture with the anatomy of a war, the whole basic load. It is an ancient romance of consciousness and a postmodern epic of something that looks like—here a quaint term, but one that seems to apply—heroism. And in the same moment, it is also a complex treatise on the possibilities of language and representation, a metafictive critique of the forms and processes of fictions both in and of their making.

Structured, as with much postmodern writing, so as to make us reinvent our very categories of factual and fictive structure, *The Things They*

*Carried* yet also remains then, in the same moment, but the newest version of art's old impossible project, "to make the stomach believe" (84). With just such an intention and such a claim wrote the middle-aged sergeant from the Midwest whom O'Brien cites in his epigraph: one John L. Ransom, still trying those nearly two decades after Andersonville somehow to make it mean something. "This book," he averred, "is essentially different from any other that has been published concerning the 'late war' or any of its incidents. Those who have had any such experience as the author will see its truthfulness at once, and to all other readers it is commended as a statement of actual things by one who experienced them to the fullest" (7). And so, in *The Things They Carried*, "a work of fiction by Tim O'Brien," as it is billed on *its* title page, a middle-aged sergeant from the Midwest, two decades after his nightmare of war, continues to honor the same project: Tim O'Brien, a Vietnam writer in his generation, still discovering how to tell a true war story after all these years. "I feel guilty sometimes," he confesses.

> Forty-three years old and I'm still writing war stories. My daughter Kathleen tells me it's an obsession, that I should write about a little girl who finds a million dollars and spends it all on a Shetland pony. (As opposed, one surmises, to one named Linda who dies inexplicably and dreadfully before the wondering eyes of her classmates, of a brain tumor.) In a way, I guess she's right: I should forget it. But the thing about remembering is that you don't forget. You take your material where you find it, which is in your life, at the intersection of past and present. The memory-traffic feeds into a rotary up in your head, where it goes in circles for a while, then pretty soon imagination flows in and the traffic merges and shoots off down a thousand different streets. As a writer, all you can do is pick a street and go for the ride, putting things down as they come at you. That's the real obsession. All those stories. (38)

Although in radically more traditional form, similar to O'Brien's in its range of ambition and achievement has been the career of his contemporary Philip Caputo. It begins, moreover, much like O'Brien's own, in another classic of memoir, *A Rumor of War*, a work once again distinguished, like *If I Die in a Combat Zone* and Ron Kovic's remarkable *Born on the Fourth of July*, both for its eloquent authority of personal witness and for its self-conscious capacity to merge experiential vision and literary-cultural myth in new and important forms of creative statement. Indeed, introducing his recent important discussion of the Caputo text, Thomas Myers notes its particular relation to *If I Die in a Combat Zone* in a way which aptly summarizes their shared quality of historical-mythic genius:

> Intensely personal and allusive, broodingly and brutally honest, both works conduct tests of preexisting myths as forms of confession, means to offer individual guilt and expiation as small models for collective peripeteia and catharsis. Neither work claims to be more than one person's story; both achieve a synchrony of individual and national tragic knowledge rare in either the novel or the personal narrative of the war. Like O'Brien, Caputo creates a carefully modulated narrative voice that describes implicitly its own development as American symbolic action of the most significant kind. (*Walking Point*, 89)

And so now the career thus begun, like O'Brien's, has subsequently continued in a similar vein with the publication of a series of popular and well-received novels including, in the present case, *Horn of Africa, Del Corso's Gallery*, and, most recently, the haunting and powerful *Indian Country*. And if seemingly divergent from O'Brien's neorealist experimentation in its emphasis on a literature of action and adventure, Caputo's fiction nonetheless reveals in equally profound ways a fundamental and complex pattern of literary-mythic reinscription, a re-writing of major archetypal forms of American consciousness into new dimensions of imaginative possibility.

Not surprisingly, given what might be called the "neotraditionalist" character of Caputo's work as well as the experience out of which it was derived—infantry officer, combat correspondent, award-winning international journalist, novelist of action and adventure—the chief American literary progenitor presiding over much of his writing is Ernest Hemingway. (Indeed, in contemplating the idea of literature as cultural revision in Caputo's work, one finds among the most compelling features of his career his seeming cultivation of a consciously Hemingwayan myth of literary personality as well. His post-Vietnam credentials as a combat journalist include subsequent dangerous passages with guerrilla forces in the Ethiopian desert regions of Eritrea, in war-torn Beruit where he was machine-gunned in the legs, and once again in Saigon during the last days in 1975 before the city's fall. His current home is Key West.) Other major American presences include Fenimore Cooper and Stephen Crane. As might be predicted as well, his writings often owe much to related moderns such as Robert Graves, Siegfried Sassoon, Joseph Conrad, and Graham Greene. And as with all the great survivor-moderns, American and international, Caputo takes his fundamental function as the post-Vietnam American novelist to be the work of literature as both personal odyssey of knowledge and quest for mythic self-reconstitution: the characters in his spare, disciplined realism are always, unknowingly or otherwise, both intensely themselves and in the same moment the full-blown embodiment of cultural archetype. Indeed, as the evolution of Caputo's writing has now revealed, the nature of his particular project of literary-cultural revision could not seem more clear: like his Vietnam contemporary Robert Stone, whose work his own frequently resembles, Caputo seizes exactly upon the explicit embrace of literary tradition—in this case the direct political lineage of Cooper-Crane-Conrad-Hemingway-Greene—to make complex mythic reinscription a major achievement of art.

In *A Rumor of War*, the basic terms of this achievement find themselves assembled in a prefiguration that now seems astonishingly complete. As a war memoir, it speaks with an experiential authority unparalleled save in comparable works about Vietnam by O'Brien, Kovic, and perhaps a few others and an authority that also places it, in the larger myth-literature of war *as experience*, in the distinguished modern memoir tradition of Robert Graves, Farley Mowat, and William Manchester as well. At the same time, as critics such as Cornelius A. Cronin and Peter McInerney have noted in their studies of the work's complex structure as "literary" narrative and narrative of "literary" invocation,[10] it also clearly stands in that distinguished tradition as a major study itself *of* war memoir and the reporting of war as it relates to the forms and processes of cultural mythmaking at large. Old veterans such as Shakespeare (*Henry V, Julius Caesar*), Vegetius, and Jomini mingle with Kipling on empire ("the splendid little war" [66], one of Caputo's officer comrades has called it during the first days of adventure) and, as might be expected, with the great Anglo-American voices of the generation of 1918—Sassoon, Owen, Hemingway—in all the power of their grim anthems to *pro patria* and lost youth. There is Thomas Hobbes on life, now quite altogether "solitary, poor, nasty, brutish, and short"

(225). And likewise, albeit now quite unsatisfactorily for a young lieutenant with a belly and head full of jungle combat, there is Dylan Thomas.
"I didn't know much about Dylan Thomas' life," the narrator remembers
thinking at the time, "but I guessed he had never been in a war. No one
who had seen war could ever doubt that death had dominion" (245).

Most crucially in immediate reference, the work likewise positions
itself fully in American myth, literary and popular. A child of the American suburbs, of a world of "post-war affluence" and "VA loans" (4), and of
Saturday afternoon showings of *Sands of Iwo Jima* (6), *Guadalcanal Diary*,
*Retreat Hell* (14), the boy-marine is also equally a soldier of "the King
of Camelot" with Vietnam "our crusade" (69–70). A refugee village becomes "Dogpatch" (107); the jungle beyond the wire is "Indian Country"
(108); the suspense of waiting for combat becomes the worst line in every
western: "It's too quiet," the narrator remembers telling himself and adds,
"Well, it *was* too quiet" (84).

In echo of all the movies and all the books, the boot lieutenant is likewise the Crane-Hemingway-Mailer initiate, complete with the requisite
hard-bitten, foul-mouthed NCO and a ragtag, unruly, melting-pot platoon. His forebears include the uncle who has been on Iwo Jima, the older
cousin who has served with Patton in France. His command constitutes
nothing less than the general leavings of "the ragged fringes of the American dream" (27). He himself, he realizes, comes to war in the charming
literary ignorance of having read "all the serious books to come out of the
World Wars, and Wilfred Owen's poetry of the Western Front" (81).

"Before you leave here, sir," Caputo later remembers one of his ser-
geants telling him, "you're going to learn that one of the most brutal
things in the world is your average nineteen-year-old American boy" (137).
And apropos of this dire warning, he has watched the evolution of more
than one Norman Rockwell kid into an ear collector. By now, however,
he too has walked ever deeper into war. In some goofy parody of a bad
movie, he himself in fact has jumped up in the middle of an ambush
screaming "HO CHI MINH SUCKS. FUCK COMMUNISM. HIT ME
CHARLIE." He has *become* "John Wayne in *Sands of Iwo Jima*" and "Aldo
Ray in *Battle Cry*," even as he has really remained in the same moment, he
realizes, just "a young, somewhat immature officer flying on an overdose
of adrenalin because I had just won a close-quarters fight without suffering a single casualty" (269). But by now sustaining self-awareness of any

sort has become at best a fragile illusion. As a graves-registration officer
he has already dreamed of the men he has lost, limbless, gutshot, rank on
rank, marching in death. Shortly afterward he allows discipline in his platoon to dissolve into a riot of destruction culminating in the burning of
an entire village. Finally, he assents to an assassination-snatch scheme that
results by mistaken identity in the murder of a local informant. It has all
become a black-and-white melodrama gone hideously wrong. At the specific moment of crisis, he recalls, the onset of "unreasoning fear," he has
come quickly once more to feel that same "sensation I had often had in
action: of watching myself in a movie" (314). Accordingly, now, white has
become black, and black has become white. Caputo and other members of
his platoon implicated in the scheme, trained killers on their government's
service, are tried for murder. At the last, as a consequence of command
pressures and a plea bargain, they are all acquitted. With a letter of repri-
mand in his file, Caputo is sent home. Shortly afterward he is discharged.
His war is over.

As may be inferred from this summary, *A Rumor of War* thus becomes at once the account of a young American's initiation into battle
and a larger, consciously composite book of American initiation myth at
large. To be sure, the memoirist has begun by asserting that his book is
"not a work of the imagination" (xix). Yet throughout, he has also been
very like the young lieutenant in the prisoner's dock at the end who now
realizes how fully he has "learned about the wide gulf that divides the
facts from the truth" (329). And thus as if in testimony to the need finally
to locate experiential witness within some larger contextualizing vision of
history, likewise, in a historical epilogue detailing the narrator's return to
witness the final fall of Saigon to the North, the text re-writes at the last
its own structure in the largest sense to become in conclusion *and* closure not one Vietnam book but two. In the first, and by infinite measure
the longer, there has been the private odyssey of consciousness within the
larger structure of myth: From "the splendid little war," Caputo has moved
to become "the officer in charge of the dead," until ultimately he too even
in life dwells unendingly "in death's grey land," indeed to the degree that
a murder is required to secure his release. In the second book, by infinite
measure (as the narrator now as journalist goes back to cover the war's end)
the shorter, it is the structure of myth itself that is the subject. Hence it
becomes to the first as signature and coda, the means by which the former

is returned to full terms of new mythic apprehension. The "second" book growing out of the "first" book is in sum the mythic abstract or epitome of what happened there. "Old" Indochina hands (340) race for helicopters on abandoned mission compound tennis courts, prepare to lift off from one last hot LZ (344). " 'You go home now?' " the narrator hears an ARVN militiaman call out to him. " 'Americans di-di?' " " 'Yes,' " he remembers replying, "feeling like a deserter, 'Americans di-di' " (343). Later, safely lifted out, he sits by an embassy diplomat who keeps muttering to himself. " 'It's over,' " he says. " 'It's the end. It's the end of an era. It was a lousy way to have it end, but I guess it had to end some way.' Exhausted and sweating, he just shook his head. 'The end of an era' " (346). "Americans di-di." "The end of an era." The brown-bar lieutenant who marched off with a head full of slogans for boyish American bravado ("AMBUSHES ARE MURDER AND MURDER IS FUN" [36]) now returns to hear it end for the record, all the voices of history and myth now commingled in the latest polyglot echo of their eternal complicity.

The literary project of historical-mythic inscription so considered becomes the dominant, even the obsessive center of both of Caputo's first two novels, *Horn of Africa* and *Del Corso's Gallery*. And in both instances, that project is undertaken through a conscious attempt to reinscribe — again much in the fictional vein of another major Vietnam contemporary, Robert Stone — the modern political novel in particular, in each case with specific attention to an important modern predecessor. In the first, a dark, sprawling tale of intrigue and guerrilla combat set in the wastes of desert Eritrea, the literary mythic father is clearly Joseph Conrad, albeit with ample acknowledgment of Graham Greene and, in peculiarly American echo, Fenimore Cooper.[11] In the second, although the world-ranging precincts haunted by its titular hero, a celebrated combat photojournalist — Cyprus, Belfast, Biafra, 1975 Saigon, 1976 Beruit — will once again invoke the memory of those regions of historical-political darkness familiar to readers of Conrad and Greene, the chief modernist forebear invoked will be clearly Ernest Hemingway; and the re-writing will thus also be of the particular American myth of the American adventurer-journalist — Crane-Hemingway-Caputo-Herr — as at once traditional man of courage and newest hero of postheroic consciousness as well.

Of the first voice of literary-cultural myth encountered here, there can be no mistaking. From the initial page onward of *Horn of Africa*, the chastened, somber witness bearing of Charlie Gage reinvokes Conrad's Marlow in eerily precise and arresting reecho. Likewise, as to Marlow, Kurtz, so to Gage, Jeremy Nordstrand: the latter from his first entry into the narrative line becomes the new American representative of empire literarily inscribed into in his much older literary-mythic role as well. And presiding over all, the ghost-tone is eerily exact, its echolalic strangeness precisely familiar. Of Nordstrand and the whole business of "Operation Atropos," Gage hastily avers, "I am not trying to place all the blame on him," adding, "this story may be an exorcism of sorts; but it is not an apology for the things we did and the things we allowed him to do out there" (4). If anything, he goes on, it is the account of his own culpability as well. Of what became Nordstrand's unspeakable savageries, his hurling himself ultimately into "the moral abyss where a man becomes capable of anything," Gage writes, "I had done nothing to curb him from satisfying his violent lusts before it was too late. My own ethical antennae were blunted, blunted even before we went out there." Of all of them, he writes, himself, Gage, Nordstrand, Harris, Colfax, Moody, and all the rest, quintessential Conrad-Greene adventurer outriders and spiritual isolatos, their source of common weakness and culpability in this dark region of the earth and of the soul has lain in a gross failure "to inoculate ourselves against the diseases of the spirit men are prey to in such places" (6).

Indeed, as the novel makes its meanings from the outset in deliberate echo and reecho of its literary and political provenance, it is the very deliberateness of all this that is also from the outset in many ways itself the chief literary *and* political issue. Here is history Conrad-Greene *and* history American, post-Vietnam burnout — as it will be also in Del Corso's Saigon and Beruit, or later, in Robert Stone's *A Flag for Sunrise*, Frank Holliwell's Tecan and Compostela — rendered in strange literary after-echo and thus most deliberately attended to as great and complex mythic reinscription.

Accordingly, the tale itself is a vast, sprawling spectacle of violence, intrigue, and adventure, involving a plot, arising out of a dark nexus of geopolitical vectors, to supply modern technological armaments to rebel tribes of the desert and eventuating ultimately in Nordstrand's savage installation, amidst the savage swirl of ideology and fanatical warfare, of himself as white-barbarian king in the forbidden land of Bejaya. And Kurtz-like throughout he is shown to have fixed his gaze fastly on seeing through to some greatness of horror he knows to be lodged in himself to the end.

Indeed, midway in the text, Gage finds a diary, volume the eighth in the life record of this dark soul and volume the eighth over a trail, he also finds, examining previous ones, beginning in "a place called Walton, Minnesota" and extending across "Cairo, Beruit, Tel Aviv, Saigon" (195). And now, appropriately, for the current date Gage finds the ominous inscription, prefaced in previous entries by random musings on Nietzsche, "ON THE THRESHOLD" (194). (Not surprisingly, a companion volume is soon revealed to be a rucksack copy of *Beyond Good and Evil* [199].) "I see, I see," are the repeatedly reinvoked (456, 457, 459–60, 466, 471) last words Nordstrand has been heard to utter, as present as history itself to Charlie Gage who surmises that in that moment what he saw was in fact "his soul" (472) and who has already known for the sake of his own that in that soul Nordstrand has been simply "what he was: neither madman nor monster, but the embodiment of all that was wrong with me, all that is wrong with our crippled natures" (398).

Yet the ultimate political significance of this postmodern reinscription of Conrad lies with the fact that it has now become a distinctly American reinscription as well. Conrad, in sum, and the tradition of the modern political novel have now become a rich and suggestive palimpsest, as it were, for a new inscription of the post-Vietnam American soul. For it is, in fact—and we have not been surprised from the outset when we have learned it—Vietnam that has effectively brought Nordstrand to Africa. It is there, Gage tells us, that Nordstrand has effectively apprenticed to a horror. ("Jesus," he has said early on of this place where, it turns out, both have learned the dark flower of violence in their souls, "the things you could learn about yourself over there. You must have. Things you never imagined" [122].) But beyond ultimately lies a deeper American knowledge as well, so Gage reveals to us through his eyes, a knowledge he sees and we come also to see profoundly as one rooted in the deepest springs of the national character. It comes to him, in fact, in what really becomes the novel's primal scene, his witness of Nordstrand's blood-soaked baptism-initiation into the tribe of his savage kingship in his desert imperium. There, in the moment of ritual consummation, Gage tells us, he sees it all, as "Nordstrand executed a slow turn to display the proof of his manhood to his chanting, clapping, writhing brothers, Natty Bumppo in Africa. The man who lived apart in the woods. And I saw in Nordstrand's movement another kind of turning, a turning of his back on all civilization and on all society except for the savage brotherhood that had embraced him. He had meant what he said; there would be no going back" (397). Thus now we see Nordstrand-Leatherstocking but now no longer, in Cooper's classic formulation, "the man without a cross," but rather the man no longer without a cross, the post-Vietnam outrider, the man without a cross who in howling, delirious blood rite has now crossed all the way over.

So, in post-Vietnam writing by the American generation of Vietnam, we once again witness that other going back that is the profoundest source of a going ahead, that past reinscribing itself as mythic present, that re-writing of post-Vietnam American consciousness out of myth and archetype lodged at the deepest springs of the national memory. Thus we see Nordstrand, Vietnam renegade spook now in his moment of "apotheosis." He is all of the old ones. He is Kurtz; he is Leatherstocking. He is "Gordon of Khartoum." He is "Custer at the Little Big Horn, ready to go out in a blaze of self-destructive madness" (449). He is them all and necessary last term in a most recent American retelling. And if Charlie Gage, survivor, will have to assent at the end to a sanitized telling of the whole business for politics' sake (albeit at the decisive refusal to accept payment for doing so—a "last gesture of loyalty," perhaps, both to Nordstrand and to his own self-respect [486]), with the tape recorder off he can still speak and at least know the secret of it, for both of them, the missing place in Nordstrand's American soul that is equally the post-Vietnam sign and index of his own: "He lacked restraint," concludes Gage, old Nordstrand and America-hand, "and he couldn't love" (485).

The novelistic precincts of *Del Corso's Gallery* return us to a similarly postmodern domain, in this case extended across the titular protagonist's career as a combat photo-journalist to embrace a roster of dark places of the earth as real as yesterday's newscasts: Cyprus, Biafra, Belfast, Xuan Loc and Saigon just before the end, mad, savage (and the particular dark place that will ultimately claim him as well) Beruit—the full complement of "those parts of the world," as the narrator puts it, "where the Geneva Convention has about as much application as the mandatory eight count does in a street fight" (45). Yet as mentioned earlier, what is also staked out here in the depiction of protagonist Nicholas Del Corso is the particular mythic provenance of the Hemingwayan adventurer-artist as culture hero and cultural mythmaker, and once again, it is a provenance so decisively and calculatedly summoned up as to call attention to such an invoking as a deliberate act of mythic reinscription. Del Corso's art, we learn from the outset, is that of "recording things as they are" (3), an art of the "fact" that in the same moment would not "destroy the essential mystery underlying the fact" (5). Always, above all, "he wanted the photograph to do what the actual event had done to him" (5). It is an art of an unstinting concreteness, one in which the good photograph "would be complete and not need any manipulation afterward" (83). It is, in sum, an art of discipline and integral will, one which requires "more than vision and manual dexterity; he had to be thinking clearly, his feelings had to be in harmony with those of the moment, his intimacy with his camera had to be such that his use of it at the decisive instant was reflex action, an immediate union of the tangible and intangible, of hand and eye, mind and heart" (83).

To his adventurer colleagues he is also an artist with a "personal mission," a mission "to take the war photograph," as one of them phrases it, "to end all wars" (42). In this assessment, however, they are only partly correct. Most crucially, what they cannot know is that the particular art of Nicholas Del Corso, the American in the last quarter of the twentieth century, is an art of expiation as well; moreover, as if inevitably, the thing to be expiated is again Vietnam, and here specifically a massacre that he has at once watched and photographed, his witnessing art the emblem of his own moral complicity. "I went to cover the war, and the war covered me" (20), Michael Herr wrote in one of the most famous passages in his master text of journalistic witness to Vietnam, *Dispatches*. Now here, in the fictional literature of the war, Del Corso bears a comparable legacy of witness, the vision of the "monster" (223), as he calls it, this thing that drives him ever afterward. It is his particular visitation of the Kurtzian "horror," Vietnam version. Look at it, the old photos seem to say, locked away in a forbidden file drawer, "Del Corso's Gallery" (222), "*this is inevitable*" (224). Yet of it comes as well his greater function as artist, his true source of integrity and purpose. For now he chooses, must choose, simply to be present at history and in his photographs to speak its vision, to expiate that old, evil thing at Rach Giang and to bear witness, to say somehow, once and for all, "*this is what we are doing to each other*" (62).

He is in sum a post-Vietnam re-writing of the Hemingwayan artist as cultural mythmaker, now come to his mission from the latest of misbegotten American wars to bear witness in our time. And it is precisely in this driven sense of vocation that Vietnam in particular now calls him back to

what will become something like, in the photographer's attempted trans-
mutation of experience into some larger, possibly redemptory vision of art,
the work's great existential moment, the apotheosis of his passion and the
prophecy of his own end. Indeed, even as Del Corso finally does resolve,
for the sake of his wife and children, to put behind him his dangerous calling for a safe, lucrative commercial career, he finds that he cannot, in fact,
not return, not return to Vietnam at the end (and to new bitter rivalry,
it turns out as well, in extension of the art fable, with an old mentor—
clearly modeled on the photographer David Douglas Duncan—whom he
now sees as a glamorizer of old American wars), Vietnam the place where
once he spilled his blood and his anger and his youth. And there he sees
it, Saigon on the eve of apocalypse, rotten to the last at its ripe decadent
heart, aswarm with news vultures, "the old whore," as his friend Bolton
puts it, turning "one last trick," "the Paris of the Orient" about to "become Moscow with palm trees" (197–98). So also Long Binh, he wonders,
must now perhaps look not unlike "the Roman camps in Gaul and Britain"
in the years just after "the legions called it quits" (94). And similarly at the
withdrawal itself, would that have been the photograph? Romans in Britain, "Napoleon" at "Moscow," "the British at Kabul?" (194). He becomes
present witness to the fate of empire in precise garish detail. "Captain
Midnight in drag," one of his friends calls the rakish Vietnamese helicopter pilot who will fly them into doomed Xuan Loc: "He looks like he
ought to be hustling tricks on Sunset Boulevard." "That's probably what
he'll be doing when the war is over" (95), another replies. It is the fate of
empire, indeed, in truth of detail that is always the truth of its own larger
mythic inscription as well.

Accordingly, Vietnam this time brings him what he believes to be his
masterpiece, the work of a career, the photograph of an ARVN soldier in
the moment of his dying that says, far beyond the work of fellow "por-
nographers of violence" (126), simply, "this is what it's like to be mortally
wounded, this is what it's like to feel your own death and there is nothing
dignified about it, nothing to redeem it, nothing to mitigate it" (124). The
art-product is truly, as even the old mentor-rival can see, the flower of
his "genius," "all the agony, the sadness and hopelessness of this defeated
country . . . compressed into that one image" (137).

Yet the quest for such an achievement of historical-mythic return is
also one for which Del Corso will pay ultimately with his life. For although

he once again survives Vietnam, safe at home with his beautiful, brittle, upper-class wife, his bright, remarkable children, his townhouse in Brooklyn Heights, his work loft in Soho, the "monster" will not sleep. Shortly he is back with Bolton, the old rival Dunlop, and all the rest of the "action junkies" (219), this time in Beruit, with its full complement of "Looney Tunes," factions, parties, militias, splinter fanatics, "the Hatfields and the McCoys raised to the thousandth power" (234), as Bolton puts it, all trying to murder each other "for a Holiday Inn" (232). And there, this time, he finds the death he has so long owed, but not before taking also the other picture, he somehow knows before the last, that has somehow paid the "final installment," given him some final release of "grace," one last murder-atrocity shot presided over by the vision of a pair of killer's eyes (the eyes of the man, it turns out, who will shortly kill him as well) in which he has truly seen once and for all "the face of the beast" (333). And so in a sense, it can hardly be otherwise than that death, when it comes for Del Corso himself, will be mainly stupid, random, a bad run-in with one last nut carrying an AK, or that his final word, out of which friends for the sake of his wife will have to fashion, Marlow-like, some better, civilized lie, will have been, simply, "Shit." Someplace else, a price had been paid in full. Even in the shit-passion of his dying, "Del Corso had not lost all his luck, his gods had not entirely withdrawn their benediction. They got him out" (348).

"Though he was done with the war, it was not done with him. The war had started again on September 21, 1981" (107). So in direct Hemingwayan invocation, Caputo in his third novel, *Indian Country*, addresses yet another case of the tragic purchase of Vietnam upon American souls, this time in a tale of love, harrowed memory, guilt, and self-regenerative expiation, set in the dark forest wilderness regions of Northern Michigan. As may be noticed, the invocation is conscious indeed even down to both title and locale. In another country. Indian country, up in Michigan. It is Hemingway country in the fullest sense of the term (by way of signature origin, the protagonist Christian Starkmann's birthplace is noted as Oak Park), after our war, in our time. As this large and complex novel evolves, the list of reinscriptions almost endlessly extends: "In Another Country," "Soldier's Home," "A Way You'll Never Be," "Up in Michigan," "Indian Camp," and, of special importance in crucial concluding scenes, "Big Two-Hearted River." But it is also now Vietnam country as well, as we are carefully reminded even in an introductory gloss: Indian Country—"1. term used by American soldiers during Vietnam conflict (1961–75) to designate territory under enemy control or any terrain considered hostile and dangerous 2. [*fig.*] a place, condition or circumstance that is alien and dangerous." And specifically, in complex Vietnam reinscription, it is that alien and dangerous country permanently inhabited by American survivor victims suffering that newest form of combat exhaustion for our age, the disorder of delayed posttraumatic stress.[12] In sum, the domain of *Indian Country* is both literary-mythic country of the highest order and the literal-historical country of experience and memory called Vietnam from which many of its actual survivors still struggle to return. To this degree, as Thomas Myers observes, *Indian Country* might thus be considered a kind of creative obverse and supplemental reinscription of *A Rumor of War*, with the early work in the status of "classical autobiography as painful confession" and the most recent one in that of "the novel as healing ritual, a work in which Caputo becomes shaman for personal and historical afflictions" (225).

In this particular case of posttraumatic stress so conceived, case study as it really actually turns out to be, Christian Starkmann suffers from an accident of war, specifically the death in Vietnam combat by "friendly fire" (he has called in the wrong coordinates for a napalm strike) of his boyhood friend and blood comrade, an Ojibwa Indian youth named Boniface St. Germain. In opening scenes we are also shown, moreover, that this same Bonny George has once, on a north woods fishing trip, saved Starkmann from drowning and that Starkmann, partly in debt of his rescue and partly in rebellion against his own stern fundamentalist-pacifist minister father, has in effect, or so he thinks, unwittingly engineered Bonny George's deadly passage to Vietnam by enlisting himself and electing to accompany him. (Only at the end is it revealed to us that it has been not Starkmann but Old Louis, Bonny George's Ojibwa sachem grandfather, who has been responsible for the boy's choice not to evade the draft.) In Vietnam, Bonny George has been killed by Starkmann's mistake. Now, fourteen years later, in the place of their boyhood, Starkmann still tries to live with it all, increasingly in the form of a never-ending nightmare buried deep in his consciousness, a nightmare so self-torturing and hideous that he has never been able to speak the story of it to anyone.

The story of *Indian Country* becomes in effect the story of that nightmare story, an odyssey of recuperation and ritual atonement for an old memory of horror endlessly revisited. It is at once an intensely American *and* intensely particularized and immediate post-Vietnam tale of the means by which one veteran, a forest cruiser for a timber company, and his wife, an ex-waitress, ex-divorcee with a dismal job as a welfare counselor and a boundless love for her husband's troubled soul, attempt to attend to his version of the story that is the whole nightmare memory of the war. In close view, the rhythm becomes the now too-predictable one: the recurring nightmares and blackouts; the isolations, hostilities, violent outbursts, drinking, brawling, spouse abuse, job paranoia, dismissal; the gradual dissolution of marriage and love. Soon come visitations from old combat friends long dead, ghost meetings, conversations. There are security preparations, the gate at the driveway, the perimeter fence, the bunker redoubt in the swamp. Meanwhile, the wife, June, and eventually Eckhardt, the VA psychologist, newest master exegete of unpenetrated mysteries of spirit, race to avert the disaster. As things turn out, however, just at the moment the dreadful story has come to the top, the "monster" brought into the present living light, so comes also the final explosion. June, returning home, finds madness fully regnant: Starkmann commits anal rape upon her, the suspected unfaithful wife, now also the Vietnam whore. Shortly afterward, when she has managed to escape, he assembles the weapons, the explosives, wires the place for final destruction. He readies himself for the one last firefight, the one imaged in the Billy Joel Vietnam song that has been going around in his head where "*we would all go down together*" (364). Yet June and, embodied in her, love itself persevere. The moment of dreadful consummation has in every respect arrived. "Let's get this done," he mutters to himself, and waits for the final assault. Instead, June returns, and with her, somehow he must know as he suddenly races to prevent her tripping the electricity in the house with which the explosives are wired, the love that in her has persevered and in him now will begin the process of healing and return.

The voyage back is undertaken initially in a VA ward full of detritus from all our American wars, where it is possible, Starkmann finds, even in new friendship with a gay ex-medic weeping for the Vietnam soldier-lover who has died in his arms, for the darkness to be shared; and it is completed with a final return in both a physical and a spiritual sense to the "Indian Country" of first memory and love for his own old friend

and lover Bonny George as well, to the wilderness camp of old Indian
shaman, Wawiekumig, called by white men Old Louis the fishing guide,
and grandfather of the Indian boy called by him "my grandson and my
son both" (405). So Starkmann returns also on the same journey at last to
that stream from so long ago where a debt had been created and where
the same debt now can be paid. And it is at this point as well that the
novel as complex narrative unfolding also comes to final union and reconciliation with its own other dimension that we now see we have been
concurrently reading throughout, the story of the true "other" story of
"Indian Country," as well: the set of inter-chapters describing Wawiekumig's own passage toward healing from what he has called "a death out
of season," "a sign of trouble in the world" (264). Indeed it is that whole
other pattern of story, present throughout the novel as strangely evocative
supplement and analogue, which we now see has been present precisely to
complete the novel's most crucial meanings and to complete them moreover in a language, Indian, elemental, before Vietnam and after our wars
to come as well, language at last and once again born of a sense of some
new possibility of whole relation to the world. It is language specifically,
as Louis tells Starkmann, at the old man's "Ghost Supper" (265) at which
he has come to partake, where there is no word for forgiveness because it
is an alien concept implying debt, responsibility, causality, all the burdens
of a petty egotism which the survivor of a death out of season, if he is to
survive in that Indian Country of memory which is the guilt-ridden soul,
must once and for all cast off and be done with. "What you want to know,"
the great secret, Louis tells him, "is how to live with yourself" (410). And
so Starkmann realizes, this is the secret of Indian Country, the acceptance
of his place now in *this* place where he has so long dwelt, the world of water
and fire, fire and water, as hideous and time bound as a terrible accident of
war, as grand and timeless as the elements themselves. ("*Water . . . Saved
me . . . Fire, killed with fire,*" he has spoken over and over to us in the text
through that old, ever-returning dream, "*he saved me from the water but I
killed him with the fire* [201, 342].) The secret of Indian Country, at once the
burden of Starkmann's historicity and the possible promise of his mythic
liberation from history, will be the newest vision of an old Indian wisdom,
the acceptance of a world, like that imaged in the text itself, that will always
be at once a place and an exile, here and other. "He saw himself as a kind
of halfbreed: his hair and skin were pale, but the war had made him an

outsider in the land of his people. The war had reddened his heart." And from there he now returns with the old red wisdom, the Indian way, the old red wisdom known *only* to the sufferer and the survivor: "Life was a song, a gift, a prayer." And so finally at the old stream come predictably a ritual immersion, less a white baptism, however, than a simple red cleansing of the dream of murder, and a new ritual preparation, the medium of newly empowered passage for this man, Christian Starkmann, the latest of the survivor returnees in the extending genealogy of Philip Caputo's post-Vietnam mythic fictions, toward the place newly pointed toward in all of them, the place indeed pointed toward here even down to this novel's very final word: "Home" (419).

The outsider at once at home and abroad, the alien adrift in the country that remains the war, burdened with the ceaselessly recurring scenes of survivor memory: these are some of the the central, repeated imagings of the project of literature as cultural revision in the post-Vietnam fiction of Robert Olen Butler. Moreover, in three of the six major novels he has now contributed, *The Alleys of Eden, Sun Dogs,* and *On Distant Ground,* Butler may claim the linkage of such a major theme also with a distinctive major innovation of technique among Vietnam writers of his generation engaged in postwar mythmaking. For in them he has developed the figure of the recurring memory of Vietnam as national dream-nightmare into the basis of what might be called a Vietnam cycle of fiction, with major recurring characters, incidents, scenes, and master symbologies from one often appearing and reappearing suggestively in each of the others. And in two other works, *Countrymen of Bones* and *Wabash,* he may make an additional claim to uniqueness among his Vietnam contemporaries in having embraced also in conscious mythic reinscription the traditions of popular historical fiction, in the first centering on events related to the 1945 New Mexico atomic bomb experiments and in the second dealing with depression-era labor unrest in the steel mills of the industrial Midwest. Finally, in a most recent work, *The Deuce,* narrated by a seventeen-year-old Amerasian runaway in the canyons of New York, he may also make the distinctive claim, along with Bobbie Ann Mason, of producing a new, literal second-generation literature of Vietnam as well.

A major distinguishing feature of Butler's Vietnam trilogy involves, in each novel, the placement of a protagonist bearing a deeply particularized nightmare memory of Vietnam—all three have served together there, it turns out, as part of an American intelligence-interrogation unit stationed at "Homestead," as it is called by them, near Saigon—in the literary domain of what might be called the existential thriller, the world, to borrow a characterization from Robert Stone's *A Flag for Sunrise*, of "a ride on the edge" (338). It is a world of physical extremity and often of metaphysical as well. Clifford Wilkes, in *The Alleys of Eden*, an American deserter, and Lanh, his Vietnamese lover, must escape from Saigon during the last days before the fall and then make their way through that equally perilous, labyrinthine, and unknown foreign world that is the America of their return. In *Sun Dogs*, Wilson Hand, Wilkes's fellow enlisted man, carries the unfinished war in his soul into a desperate investigative mission (one that will ultimately claim his life) and drama of industrial espionage played out in the vast, frozen, frontier wastes of the other true last American frontier of Asia, the North Slope oil fields of Alaska. Capt. David Fleming, in *On Distant Ground*, returning to America to face court-martial for his bizarre, reckless rescue and release of a high-ranking Viet Cong officer from the tiger cages of Con Son, finds himself, in suggestive obverse of Wilkes, also ultimately returning to Vietnam to claim a lost Vietnamese son and the memory of a love brutally sacrificed in the confusion of war.

Similarly, and most importantly to Butler's achievement, out of this recurrent characterization and interweaving of major incident and theme rises a master vision of Vietnam memory fashioned out of something like a set of archetypal scenes. For Wilkes the one in question is that of a Viet Cong prisoner naked and collapsed on a stream bank (Fleming is present as participant-witness as well), a soaked handkerchief eerily masking his harrowed face, dead of a freak heart attack in the midst of a brutal torture-interrogation. For Hand, the scene is that of his kidnapping by the Viet Cong (in compounded irony, it has occurred during a visit by him to an American-supported orphanage for children of the war) and solitary captivity, culminating in a bloody rescue (by Fleming, his commander) in which all of his captors are slaughtered. For Fleming it is that of a crucial encounter, by yet another stream, on Con Son Island, with the prisoner Tuyen, his brave, ironic enemy, this other, who, on the basis of a scrawled prison-wall graffito—"Hygiene is Beautiful" (15)—has become his obsession; and now, in that existential moment, the American, in total abandonment of cause or ideology, stands crazily about to liberate his foe while the two of them, as if in some queer recognition of mutual plight (one that will be repeated at the end when Tuyen, a member of the new provisional government, repays the absurd act by enabling Fleming to leave the country with his son) share in the manic laughter that is the war. In each case, these haunted dreams of memory, recurring as they do in and among the texts, begin to return to us with a sensation of force so strange and immense as to suggest that they are perhaps our own.

And that of course is precisely Butler's aim. The drama of flight, of return, and ultimately of parting and new departure, for instance, as David Wilkes must ultimately separate again from Lanh in a post-Vietnam America—a place, as Thomas Myers has acutely put it, "where they are both spiritually and culturally displaced, strangers in a transformed historical landscape" (222)—is precisely calculated to have us see ultimately that we all in significant ways continue to live on a landscape where America and Vietnam remain a single country of displaced spirits. Which alleys do we wander? the book seems to ask. In what Eden? Where does the new labyrinth of post-Vietnam history tend either in the old country, to borrow Michael Herr's phrasing, that was the war (*Dispatches*, 3), or in the new Land of the Free and Home of the Brave? And so we ask the same questions with Fleming, who, father of an American son in the land where he has become a stranger, must return to that other country (and truly now, the other country by old literary fiat where the wench is dead, by Marlowe through Hemingway to Butler), must travel to the distant ground of memory to reclaim that other son equally his own and the figure of history to which he must be reconciled. We ask some of the same questions even with Wilson Hand, in perhaps the least overt of the three novels in symbolic reinscription. For the Alaska of this novel is clearly much in the vein of Norman Mailer's *Why Are We in Vietnam?*, which in many large ways Butler's significantly resembles. Like Mailer's Alaska-Vietnam, it is the primal last American frontier, true west and magnetic north, end point of our hoarded technologies and rapacities. And Hand himself, with his own memories and his "mission," is still (even down to an almost giddy final irony that the "industrial espionage" he has been investigating has been in fact a newspaper fabrication hatched by rival factions of the national media) in the country that is the war still seeking the death that will be memory's last and only certain surcease. "Eat, it's finished," he tells the gathering ravens at the end as he sits lost and alone, the white serenity of arctic death enveloping him. *Consummatum est:* all the flashbacks, the dreams, the composite nightmares can now be ended. All the way from the orphanage in Hanoi and the grinning VC in the cell and mad Beth, his suicide wife, herself dead of the war in New York, he can now come here to the frozen edge of America in the last quarter of the twentieth century and in this place find "only a humming at the far horizon" (218).

Of coequal significance in postwar writing to Butler's depiction of the power of memory in his Vietnam-haunted American protagonists, and of the degree to which the experience of the war has inscribed itself upon their spirits, is his depiction, particularly in *The Alleys of Eden* and *On Distant Ground* (and most recently again in *The Deuce*) of Vietnamese figures often conceived and fashioned in profound rhythm of counterinscription and design. Indeed, a great measure of his achievement lies precisely in his rendering of the memories of the war and their burdens for Americans and Vietnamese alike through specific issues of consciousness *and* language. For he is often thus able to speak, as an American writer (like the poet John Balaban, Butler is himself a student of Vietnamese), from precisely within the horrendously tangled dialectic of cultures themselves that became, as Frances Fitzgerald and others have shown us, the source of some of the truest tragedy of the war. More often than not, for instance, when Americans and Vietnamese speak in these works, they speak Vietnamese. As a consequence, the dialogue often creates a literary effect suggesting almost complete transliteration, an achievement of style as subtle and precise as the newly imagined circuits of vision it has awakened and traced out. We hear in the language the figure and pattern of the previously unheard and unknown, and it creates in us the sense of a whole world of nuance and gesture, of custom, tradition, and observance, a world of the other which precisely to that degree becomes at least for a moment our own. And the effect thus becomes, significantly, for us, something of our own version of the interior dialogue that finally makes David Fleming understand, for instance, what he has seen inscribed in that graffito he believes to be Tuyen's in Bien Hoa: "David had seen himself on that cell wall; he'd seen the pattern of his own mind, in its aloofness, its irony. Tuyen was not a face, he was a mind, and David had seen himself there as clearly as he'd seen himself when his son was lifted by the nurse" (211). One reads history equally in the mind of a brave enigmatic Vietnamese enemy and in the fact of a newborn American child. And this in turn becomes the circuit of consciousness that must constitute nothing less than a new vision of history.

A similar rhythm of consciousness embracing the self and the other is likewise engendered in the historical fictions of Robert Olen Butler. In each, there is a painstaking recreation of language, incident, setting, theme, action, event. And in each, as in the Vietnam fictions, the special burden of consciousness recreated and reinscribed is the burden of American history. In *Countrymen of Bones*, the vision of history is focused in the conflict between Darrell Reeves, the archaeologist, racing to preserve in his precious burial-ground excavation a suspended moment in the continent's savage past, and Lloyd Coulter, science-mad disciple of Oppenheimer, plotting the means of ritual death for a new, savage, post-atomic future; and by domestic extension, it further plays itself out in their shared obsession with the woman, Anna Brown, for one the embodiment of the saving power of love and for the other the object-image of the cold rapacity of his doomed, violent American soul. In *Wabash*, the vision of history is more simply focused in the struggle of one plain, decent man, Jeremy Cole, with the forces of economic and political exploitation on one hand and the new forces of violent revolution on the other, necessity and change, bosses and owners, agitators and workers. Yet interwoven here is the old, domestic history-plot of love as well in the co-inscribed struggle of Cole's wife, Deborah, to navigate the domestic conflict–world of family and marriage as correlative of his own, equally troubled and shadowed with misguided zeals and hates. And here too the doubled lines of force also finally converge, in a desperate final scene where she prevents him from carrying out a political assassination and, for a moment at least, redeems historical madness through new possibility of love.

As perhaps these summaries make clear, Butler's mode once again here, as in the Vietnam fictions, is essentially that of neorealism, closely symbolic, often with an almost Hawthornean exactitude of design, economy, and psychological penetration, all with the effect often of something like a postmodern morality play. In *Countrymen of Bones*, for example, Reeves, in his exhumation of the ritual site of an ancient death cult (and soon to be the bomb site of the newest one), reads the bones themselves: an Indian king lies amidst his doomed consorts; on the periphery of the magic circle of death, and even in his own death violating it, lies in eternal threat the murdered rapacious prisoner-Spaniard. Reeves thus witnesses and participates in nothing less than a playing out of the old imperial drama of the New World precisely at ground zero of the newest revisitation of history. And his lesson of it all (and ours as well) is nothing less than that imaged precisely and without mistake in the gorget he has exhumed, his only relic, "of grief at what men do" (217). So likewise Jeremy Cole, in his simple grief-haunted impotence, the memory of a lost daughter, the ever-extending vision of friends and fellow laborers, one by one jobless, dispossessed, consigned with their suffering families to poverty and violence, struggles toward the discovery of conscience and personal resolve, in the face of dark threat and even attempted murder, not to let evil prevail in the world of striving men and women of good will; and so concurrently, in the other great rhythm of the book, Deborah confronts the troubled work of her world, the world of women and the family, the grandmother, the crazy aunts, the impotent husband silent in the passion of his suffering. The old world and holy war of faith and the new world and holy war of labor become co-equal and co-valent, facing worlds of history, connected at their interfluence by the whole human drama of hatreds, violences, pains, lonely exclusions. And thus at the end, *Wabash* does become nothing less than, in single moment, world historical class struggle complete with slogans, July Fourth parades, and riots *and* one woman's attempt through love to save a husband who would only be if he somehow could, she knows, in the words she has heard of a priest who has known the husband's struggle as well, simply "a man trying not to inflict pain" (176).

Thus, in the self-conscious embrace in his fiction of distinctively American forms of literary-cultural myth, Butler continues in a major way the project of the main body of American writing of Vietnam, a literature that often achieves its finest insights through the calculated fusion of qualities of experiential truth telling with complex and ambitious new strategies of imaginative invention. Throughout his work, for instance, there is the subtle manipulation of point of view in a way often coextensive with all the various activities of consciousness, inner and outer, reflective and active, experientially constitutive and imaginatively recreative, there depicted; and the result of such experimentation is thus not so much any particular "truth" or "meaning" as a complex intertextualization of "truths" and "meanings" born of their suggestive commingling. To this end, his fiction is frequently a reminder, then, of R. D. Laing's dictum, appropriate for one of the most explicitly, in the contemporary sense of that term, "political" novelists of his Vietnam generation, that "perception, imagination, fantasy, reverie, dreams, memory, are simply different *modalities of experience*, none more 'inner' or 'outer'"—and therefore, by novelistic implication here, true or false, actual or imaginary, real or unreal, factual or fictive—"than any other" (20). Indeed, with Butler, as with Tim O'Brien and (as will be seen directly) Larry Heinemann in particular, the only "true" fiction would be some overt intertextualization of such modalities that can thus add up to some new, whole, complex and "open" rendering of lived experience in its fullest dimension.

A related achievement of Butler's experimentalism—again connecting him with O'Brien and Heinemann as well as with Philip Caputo and Winston Groom—is the complex and creative ordering of time. Time past becomes time present and future, just as time future frequently becomes reinscription of present and past, of experience, history, place, event. The drama of experience rendered in and across time becomes symbolic correlative of the dialectical complexities of consciousness at large, an ever-enlarging play of creative opposings and juxtaposings, imagings, counter-imagings, interimagings. The result is a fiction of brilliant doublings and traces, imagery conceived of not as frozen dialectic but rather as metaphysical supplement, shadow and image of the eternally present other. We read in every moment in *The Alleys of Eden* and *On Distant Ground* across the dual precincts of vision that are America *and* Vietnam; the combat zone of Vietnam recapitulated in *Sun Dogs is* the perilous, threatening last frontier of American space, the Asia-wilderness empire country of the north; the savage ground of *Countrymen of Bones* is at once that of death cults ancient and contemporary; the two domains of ritual struggle in *Wabash* reinscribe the new holy war of labor in the terms of the old one of love and faith. Indeed, across the range of Butler's art, the renderings of the local and immediate ceaselessly search out their larger mythic textualizations. To choose one composite example, we discover, for instance, depending on the order in which we have read Butler's texts, that the great ancient Indian mound of *Wabash*, a place near the begrimed city and its Hooverville suburbs where Jeremy and Deborah Cole take a picnic and for a moment find peace from the twin struggles of history and faith, is the same place recalled by the archaeologist-anthropologist Darrell Reeves in *Countrymen of Bones* as that which he knows to be sign and image of origin for the great pre-American civilization that once flourished in the New World. Here, across the work of literature as mythic-cultural revision, we encounter the project of the archaeology of culture at large, writing on the shared ground, the bone palimpsest of American myth itself.

In Butler's most recent novel, *The Deuce*, the doubled discourse of world-historical myth and particular human experience that speaks is again that specifically of American consciousness in the era after Vietnam; and it does so now for the first time uniquely, albeit somehow inevitably, given the course of the fictional imagination at work, through the single voice in which for the first time those discourses comprise an authority that is also a quite literal genealogy: the voice, now itself at generational fruition, of an Amerasian child. And if by that voice, as the novelist Scott Spencer has astutely observed, Butler returns "to what might be his great obsession, the American misadventure in Vietnam, with the sexual collision between G.I.'s and prostitutes serving as a symbol of that war," he now also uses that voice as the central means whereby he "immerses us in the cultural dislocation of our time" (10).

"I wish it was simple just to say who I am," the narrator begins, "just to say my name is so-and-so and that makes you think of a certain kind of person and that would be me" (7). "But me," he goes on, "I've got three names. And so I've got to go through all this bullshit just to start talking. I'm Anthony James Hatcher, Tony. I'm Vo Dinh Thanh. And I'm The Deuce. Don't ask me which one I use. It's too early for that. I've got to tell you some things first" (7).

At once Huck- and Holden-like, with nods to other nighttown travelers of this century ranging from Joyce's Stephen Daedalus to James Leo Herlihy's Joe Buck, this latest adolescent American isolato inscribes the particular merging of history and experience his book will be about, the experience of being at once American *and* Vietnamese in the generation after our war. And exactly in the naming, the convergence of the authority and the genealogy, lies the tale. Anthony James Hatcher is the son of Kenneth Hatcher, an American GI who fell in love with a bar girl and fathered a child by her; who, in the last days of the war returned to Saigon, found the child and the mother, now wasted and strung out on her drug habit, and has literally bought his son's way to America; who in the decade ensuing has attempted, while pursuing a career as an aspiring young DA in a place called Point Pleasant on the New Jersey shore, to give his son something like a happy suburban childhood. Vo Dinh Thanh, on the other hand, is the son of Vo Xuan Nghi, a bar girl from the Texas Girls saloon who used to pray to her ancestors' spirits in a room amidst the Saigon alleys she has shared with a succession of GIs; who, inevitably lost somewhere between her drugs and her sorrow, traded her son for money from the child's American father to get him to America; who eventually vanished in the war to live now only in a GI photograph stashed in the duffel bag of her runaway son in the nightmare ruins of New York. The Deuce, finally, is the hero of the novel at hand, the New York friend of Joey Cipriani, the vagrant ex-Vietnam GI who has named him for the Hell's Kitchen combat zone of Forty-second Street near the Port Authority Terminal where they make their perilous existence together; who shares with a half-breed runaway from his old war food, a deserted building, and what is left of an addled veteran's vain, alcoholic nostalgia for a place and a youth called Vietnam; who dies for the whore he loved and the war buddies and valor he has imagined in a final, feckless attempt to save his adopted son from the rapacious creatures of the urban jungle.

With both the book and its protagonist bearing this newest in-country name, the war has come home with a vengeance. The Deuce is street smart in the way that only recent American history can be, street smart from the alleys of Saigon to the sinister labyrinthine hell of midtown New York. And his odyssey continues to chart out the newest pathways into this century's teeming American corruptions. The moral morass of Vietnam has now become a domestic urban nightmare. "They call Forty-second Street out there the Deuce," Joey tells the boy on their first meeting, shortly after the latter has been mugged, robbed of the money and the bus ticket that were to take him to join the Vietnamese community of Montreal, and cast into his first nights amidst the human refuse of the streets, "and you're gonna have to watch out for that street. You haven't been in the city long, have you" (22). It is full combat orientation. "You watch out for the motherfuckers out there," he goes on, "who want to eat you alive. But that street is still the Mekong, the river that runs right through all of us around here. And something else, and you're going to get pissed off at me again. You can't bullshit me. You're two things. You're Vietnamese and you're American. A deuce" (22). He is the deuce. It is the Deuce. Again, it is the old theme in Butler's post-Vietnam cartographies of the American soul. Here is there; there is here.

Tony-Thanh-the Deuce, attempting to work a past through a nightmare present into a usable future, reconnoiters the memory of Vietnam on maps in the New York Public Library (129, 231). What he must now face in reality, however, is the latest version of it in the corrupt, stinking streets, where anything and everything is for sale, and the more corrupt and hideous so much the better—peep shows, needles, nickel bags, hookers, pederasts, street vermin of virtually any description imaginable. As the worlds converge, so do the patternings of more immediate experience old and new. Running from one messed-up American vet with money and a job to a messed-up American vet without money and a job, the Deuce trades one father for another (167) only to find out that they are quite disappointingly alike. For all his lurid stories, Joey has been just one of the nameless clerks and jerks looking for a lost war. Or, as Kenneth has put it from his side with a redeeming honesty of the prosaic, "We've got all this stuff. . . . We've got a quiet street and neighbors who talk about the weather and about the Yankees and we've got food and money and clothes and daily work that absorbs us, but because we've been to Vietnam, all of this just doesn't measure up. It's not important enough" (282). Like Kenneth, Joey has fallen in love with a bar girl too, whose picture he keeps, a soldier snapshot very like that Tony keeps of his own bar-girl mother. His fathers have been whore lovers. Tony becomes a whore lover (202), the lover now of Norma, at first just another kid, a sad runaway working on a habit, pretty soon a hooker. There follows a brief adolescent idyll, for the Deuce a sweet initiation. But soon the apprentice hooker has become hard-core. Like "sweet Nghi," "fastest pussy east of the Pecos" (19), Norma has now become Nicole, because, as she tells him, "Hey, everybody who's in love is French, Right?" (225).

As events take their course, virtually everything else as well begins to get doubled, deuced, for Tony-Thanh adrift in American nighttown. A bum gets torched like the homeless veteran once in the circle off Le Loi (220–21). He watches a woman, clearly a whore in the last throes of desperation, sell her child to Treen, the homicidal pederast whose death he himself will later exact in vengeance for the latter's knife-murder of Joey Cipriani (215–16). Shortly, he finds himself, now on a runaway poster, once again for sale for a ten-thousand-dollar reward (238). Yet increasingly now, he sees, for all the old congruencies, the old maps will no longer do any good. "The only thing about Vietnam," he decides on a return visit to the library, "is that it's not Forty-second Street or the East Village, and I know already that if I start roaming the alleys of Saigon with my fingertip, I'll only end up running out into the streets of New York because it's not Vietnam" (231).

But even if the map is different, many of the hard-won values now seem newly to apply, and with new enlargement of vision and possibility. Nighttown truly has become but the latest version of the combat zone. Stephen finds Bloom and the buddy system. The Deuce watches out for Joey. Joey watches out for the Deuce. Joe Buck and Ratzo Rizzo plan their DEROS. Predictably, it is too late. Joey doesn't even make the bus, instead takes on the murderous Treen, winds up knifed for his troubles and stashed under a stairway. But now a new story takes up as well. The Deuce, after all, is Vietnamese. He can still speak to Joey in The Kingdom of the Dead (259). And the code still obtains—never leave a buddy behind. "And I realize I'm talking to an empty room. But what I'm saying is still right. Even if you die in Vietnam, there's some other guy as fucked up as you who gives a shit about it, and they keep on shooting the guys who killed you" (262).

Unsuccessfully, he tries the police. For his pains, he gets sent back to Kenneth and Point Pleasant. There he realizes that it is time to accomplish the mission by other means. Accordingly, he returns once more to become the true urban guerrilla, and in the end, it is mission accomplished. Treen is bigger, stronger, well-armed, but in his greed, his lust, his absolute certainty of being beyond the law, he makes the crucial mistake of being led onto Thanh's turf. For now it is night in the streets, not eternal daylight in the Port Authority Terminal. And night in the streets finally belongs not to Treen but to Thanh. The chase ensues, breathless, cat-and-mouse, New York end game. Then, finally, Treen is dead, impaled in the tiger pit of an abandoned cross-town expressway—full of steel rod and concrete spike pissed and shit on by a whole night underculture of bums and whores— the Lord of Fairyland dead of his own lust and corruption.

At the end, Tony/Thanh is back with Kenneth in Point Pleasant, trying to make a new go of it (302). "Even now it's not easy feeling anything strong about my father. But sometimes it's right to follow your feeling and other times you have to be smart and figure out what's right, and then you tell your feelings to get fucked and you do the right thing. In America kids don't hang around their parents for the rest of their lives anyway.

But Kenneth deserves something and so do I" (302). He is the legacy, and he will have to make it part of him. And the terms, he knows, will be the lesson of history and genealogy that he and his America will have to come to know and understand as profoundly their own. It is a new story that will take some working out. But it is also, he realizes, in good Tony/Thanh fashion, something of an old story as well, something like perhaps the Vietnamese one about the cicada and the great ritual cycles of things that, given a new chance, still just might find its new home as well. "And I remembered how the crack grew along my own spine," he tells us, "as I lay there and I yearned to climb out and sing in my own voice. And now I know what voice I have and who it is I am. A guy on a beach in Vung Tau tells me I'm Vietnamese. A civics teacher in Point Pleasant tells me I'm American. Kenneth James Hatcher tells me I'm his son, and I'm the son of a woman named Vo Xuan Nghi who's lost somewhere half a world away. I'm a lot of things but I'm one thing, and I have no doubt about that. I'm The Deuce" (303).

At the end, as in the beginning of *The Deuce*, here is there, and there remains here. The doubled discourse of history and the voice that speaks in latest versions of street smart is the voice that was America in Vietnam.

This, then, is the major project of Butler's fiction, the post-Vietnam exploration and reexploration of American time and American space. In the war cycle, including the trilogy and, most recently, *The Deuce*, the locus of such exploration is specifically that space of history shared by Americans and Vietnamese; in the history texts, it is history present as at once history future and history past. In the New World, we all continue to navigate the alleys of Eden, make our way on distant ground that is our America, with our countrymen of bones, the scene of an "ancient act of rage" (180). The vision of this writing is nothing less than the old dream of origin that is our own.

In radical contrast to the fiction of his Vietnam-generation contemporaries, the work of literature as cultural revision in James Webb's career as a novelist has thus far been revisionist in quite the literal sense of that literary-political term. In three novels to date, *Fields of Fire*, *A Sense of Honor*, and *A Country Such as This*, while acknowledging the full confusion and outright horror of Vietnam and the price of moral and emotional bankruptcy ultimately exacted by it upon the American soul, Webb at the same time affirms the old soldierly virtues of dignity, honesty, and integrity. His great subject, in a word, is honor. In each of his works, Vietnam as the latest of American wars becomes, even in the acknowledgment of national failure, a possible new ground of chastened and wise reaffirmation and thereby of return to a renewed sense of national purpose.

In *Fields of Fire*, the essentially conservative and revisionary nature of Webb's mythic project as to theme *and* form is announced from the outset. An acknowledgments page, with a familiar assertion of "fictional" liberty even as faith is kept to "actual experience," enlists the work in the traditional novelistic service of representation. The bargain is then sealed with the announcement—a feature likewise of no small "conservative" suggestiveness, given the function of many works of Vietnam literature as explicit critiques of issues of language and representation—of a glossary. (On a succeeding leaf is a map, as well.) Then, announcing the further enlistment of representation in the traditional novelistic service of social analysis, a table of contents projects a three-stage development: "The Best We Have"; "The End of the Pipeline"; and "Vestiges: Virtues Rewarded and Other Crimes."

The opening scenes of the work insert the action firmly into the landscape of the traditional fiction of war. The men depicted are combatants, in the midst of the campaign, vigilant, taking food and a little rest, mud smeared, weary, defiant, cynical, comradely. The place of combat happens to be Vietnam. In many ways it could as easily be Vicksburg or Verdun.

The text then drops back to the assembling of dramatis personae; and it does so, as Edward F. Palm has pointed out, with the index of an essentially conservative marriage of vision and technique here again inscribed as the adoption, in Vietnam updating, of perhaps the most tried and utilitarian of all the strategems of modern war fiction conceivable: the melting-pot platoon (105). (Further, I should add, in anticipation of my own argument, Palm is entirely correct, I believe, about the thematic consequences of such a marriage. "The theme of the novel," he writes, "is the ethic of selfless, mutual concern which existed on the small-unit level in Vietnam and which Webb obviously feels was the war's one saving grace as well as the factor generally responsible for its excesses" [106–7].) Thus we first meet Snake, corporal by battlefield promotion, badass urban drifter, delinquent with a poet's soul; then Hodges, Robert E. Lee, lieutenant, rawboned Scots-Irish son of warriors, last of his line, his real genealogy that of the history of American wars; Goodrich, the Harvard drop-out, platoon intellectual and general misfit; then Dan, the VC conscript with a murdered family as the price of his desertion, now serving the other side as a U.S. Marine interpreter-scout. Then also eventually come the rest of the grunts, American boys, as an epigraph has noted, out at the end of the line—Ogre, Baby Cakes, Phony, Cat Man, Doc Rabbit, Vitelli, Homicide—their various combat epithets the new poetry of naming for America's draft-eligible castoffs (and themselves, with such names and in their new mythic "platoon" status here and in Vietnam novels of various political positionings, as C. D. B. Bryan has rightly noted, now something like a cliche of a cliche ["Screams" 67–69]). "And who are the young men we are asking to go into action against such solid odds?" an "anonymous general" has asked a fictive "correspondent." "You've met them. You know. They are the best we have. But they are not McNamara's sons, or Bundy's. I doubt they're yours. And they know they're at the end of the pipeline. That no one cares. They know" (1). And now, as Hodges sees upon his first meeting with them as a new platoon commander, they have all come further to that common condition where simply "they've all been beat and one more *fuck you* to some mindless order isn't going to sink them any deeper, and they know it" (64).

So also, with the assembling of the traditional cast, comes the generating of the traditional dramatic action that will provide the novel's moral and political center: the movement of a group of men, mainly young, undereducated, and in various ways socially marginal, through pain and bewilderment, fear and loneliness, anger and progressive brutalization, to what becomes a primal scene in Vietnam narrative, some ultimate confrontation with atrocity—in this case the killing of two Vietnam civilians in retribution for the capture and murder-mutilation of two marines—that becomes the index of individual and national horror. And it is horror, one must emphasize, that remains the operative term throughout the text. In fact, *Fields of Fire* captures unrelentingly, as few other Vietnam novels have managed, the virtual ecstasy of horror that was often for many American combatants the primary experience of the war. For while the novel throughout, and particularly at its conclusion, strikes a clear position against the liberal antiwar intelligentsia and their privileged activist children and thus in the process powerfully enlists our sympathies in behalf of the lost Americans we sent to fight there, the war itself remains continuously and, from nearly any perspective imaginable, simply a mess.

"It is such a game" (145), reflects Dan, the Chieu Hoi, upon the complex of forces destroying his land and people from within and without. For the Americans, at the tactical level, it is always but "the Battle of Latest Trailbend" (216). It is a matter, Snake tells Hodges upon their first meeting, of finding a home in "Mother Green, the Killing Machine" (69). Or, as Baby Cakes tells Goodrich, "That's the game out here. That's what we're here for. To kill gooks." Goodrich has replied, "Funny. I thought there was more to it." And so he is right. "There is, Senator," Baby Cakes goes on. "There is. But it all goes together. Kill gooks and make it home alive. Once they're dead, they leave you the hell alone" (223–24). Gilliland, the platoon sergeant, speaks from his perspective the same lesson of pain and pointless murder-sacrifice. "We been abandoned, Lieutenant," he tells Hodges. "We been kicked off the edge of the goddamn cliff. They don't know how to fight it, and they don't know how to stop fighting it. And back home it's too complicated, so they forget about it and do their rooting at football games. Well fuck 'em. They ain't worth dying for" (175). And even Hodges himself, latest in a line of American warriors, and with a faith in the fraternity of battle he keeps through grievous wounding and finally even unto death, knows at the deepest level that he is not unlike "a wounded cock being re-razored and tossed back into the dust arena. His only option was to win another fight, for the glory of the owner, or to die" (246).[13] Accordingly, responsibility breaks down not to politics, positions, even "medals." "Relevance was Snake and Cat Man and Cannonball. Importance was keeping them alive through another week" (283). Or, as Goodrich puts it most succinctly, "the only meaning was the thing itself" (167). It was all, simply, "like existentialism, climbing the hill. Suffering without meaning, except in the suffering itself" (209).

"But no one would understand that if I told them" (209), Goodrich goes on. In his capacity for moral and intellectual articulation of issues, he is essentially "right" about the war. But the novel at the same time makes it clear that he is not its true moral and intellectual conscience. He is rather, in the terms he thinks to himself as he prepares to report the slayings by fellow squad members of the two Vietnamese after the murders of Ogre and Baby Cakes, a "moral purist" (277). He is also—and this is absolutely crucial to our understanding of Webb's revisionist mythology of the Vietnam warrior—in a world where one survives if at all only through martial discipline and abiding loyalty, a poor soldier.

In an early experience of night combat, he fails to act resolutely in seeking help for a comrade who by morning bleeds to death. He persistently
sulks, obfuscates, complains. In action he is indecisive, abstracted, unreli-
able. After a crime in which summary justice has been executed upon the
two Vietnamese who very likely have been implicated in the killings of
the two captured fellow marines, he takes it upon himself to report the
murders. It is his error in combat at the end, albeit a humanely motivated one—he keeps a comrade from firing at a little girl only to have
him killed by a Viet Cong sniper concealed in the bushes behind her—
that precipitates the action in which Snake and Hodges are killed, with the
former in the process of saving Goodrich's life, and in which he himself
loses a leg and is also seriously wounded in the shoulder. Indeed, his true
achievement of moral status comes only at home, when, back at Harvard,
he is asked to speak at an antiwar rally and when instead of playing to the
festive self-righteousness of the crowd, with their chants and Viet Cong
flag, he honors the dead, the corpses, the ghosts, the fallen brotherhood.
"ISN'T THAT WHY YOU CAME HERE? TO TRY AND END IT?"
he shouts out to them. "THEN WHY ARE YOU PLAYING THESE
GODDAMN *GAMES*? LOOK AT YOURSELVES. AND THE FLAG.
JESUS CHRIST. HO CHI MINH IS GONNA WIN. HOW MANY
OF YOU ARE GOING TO GET HURT IN VIETNAM; I DIDN'T
SEE ANY OF YOU IN VIETNAM. I SAW DUDES, MAN. DUDES.
AND TRUCK DRIVERS AND COAL MINERS AND FARMERS.
I DIDN'T SEE YOU. WHERE WERE YOU? FLUNKING YOUR
DRAFT PHYSICALS? WHAT DO YOU CARE IF IT ENDS? YOU
WON'T GET HURT" (338).

Here is the real revisionist myth of *Fields of Fire*, the myth of the
forgotten cast-off legions of the empire, of the Americans sent to fight in
nightmare brotherhood of battle a lousy misbegotten war and then forced
in national memory to become the pariah-scapegoat embodiments of the
shame of its pain and loss. And the core here is not revisionist political
polemic of a particular party coloration—although Webb subsequently,
as an assistant secretary of defense for reserve affairs and later as secretary of the navy, would as a matter of public record advance the familiar
thesis of an "unwinnable war," a war that was lost not by the soldiers but
by the government that waged it. Rather, it seeks access to some older
sense of national regeneration through at least an honoring, on the part

of the memory of those who carried the battle, of the old values of sacrifice and loyalty and the continuity of national tradition of service and responsibility gained through the bond of combat. "I hate it. Goddamn it, I *hate* it," Hodges intones, as he looks at himself in the mirror in Okinawa after his wounding. "But I miss it" (246). (Why did he come back? Bagger asks him upon his return. "Christ, I don't know," he has replied. "Style, I guess" [264].) "Some days you count the meat," he has also remembered Bagger saying, "and some days the meat counts you" (286). At the same time, this thing he must come back to is older and bigger than any current war or present individuality or fear, old as "a jungle clearing on Saipan" or "in the sweet spring grass at Shiloh" (291). It is all there, he sees, in "the bald, red hills with their sandbag bunkers, the banter and frolic of dirt-covered grunts, the fearful intensity of contact. It was too deep inside him, and he had not yet done enough to be free of it" (258). And so the same poetry of comradeship and action penetrates to the soul of the mean, amoral, streetwise Snake, ultimate castoff-survivor reborn of combat into the brotherhood, the legion. "He sensed that it was all here, everything, and there was none of it there. All of life's compelling throbs, condensed and honed each time a bullet flew: the pain, the brother-love, the sacrifice. Nobility discovered by those who'd never even contemplated sacrifice, never felt an emotion worth their own blood on someone else's altar" (276). To be sure, it is nobility hard bought, even at the price of murder. "Baby Cakes was a good dude, you know?" Snake's litany concludes. "He'da died for me. And I killed 'em back for him" (276). This *is* murder pure and simple. What the novel demands is that it at least be assessed against the price of war exacted upon the souls of those who, in becoming its agents, came likewise to bear the primary burden of it for us all. "Look, man," Goodrich exclaims at the end to the protest leaders attempting to enlist him. "I fought with myself about this for *months*. I even turned a guy in for murder. I thought it was my duty. But I just *don't know anymore*. What you guys are missing is the confrontation. It loses its simplicity when you have to deal with it" (336).

Thus, it must be insisted, the revisionary myth of *Fields of Fire* is itself a claim, particularly on the part of those who actually underwent the experience of Vietnam, mainly to confrontation with experiential complexities. It neither excuses murder or atrocity nor endorses the traditional warrior virtues of the American citizen-soldier simply in latest democratic incarnation; rather, it proposes the critique, albeit from a conservative posture, of a larger American tendency to simplistic, callow ideologies in general and in particular to those of recent political fashion whereby certain older ones have been summarily dismissed and dishonored. The simple American conviction of ideological virtue, the work seems to tell us, whether enthroned at the right hand of power or at the left, expresses itself in American wars and in their aftermath always to the dishonor of those who have carried the battle. And to this degree, *Fields of Fire* (in distinct contrast, one should add, to Webb's subsequent fiction) is not simply a revisionist or neoconservative minority report on liberal interpretations of what happened to us in Vietnam but rather a more general call to moral self-contemplation on that account, and one allowing for the complexities of issues as imaged especially in the experience of those who actually fought there. Indeed, it is one despite the ostensible expression, in the coming of age of "Senator" Will Goodrich, of something like a repentant liberalism that carries to the end the deep anguish of our own larger spirit of national irresolution. It will take more than valedictory speeches, the novel seems to say, to get us over Vietnam. In fact, if the work "ends" anywhere in this respect, it does so not in Goodrich's concluding confrontation with the antiwar crowd but really rather with the last two items in the appended glossary. For there the image is not so nearly of closure but rather of something more like ongoing unresolved juxtaposition. "The WORLD": reads the first of the two. "The United States, where, supposedly, sanity reigned" (344). Here in the guise of a gloss is clearly political opinion. "ZULU": reads the second and last: "A casualty report." Imaging more closely the text at hand, it is in contrast the language of the war pure and simple, pain and waste rendered only as ongoing accounting of fact.

It is precisely this image of a military-political tradition at war with itself that becomes the dominating figure of Webb's second novel, *A Sense of Honor*. And again—as with *Fields of Fire* and as will continue to be even more pronouncedly the case with a third work, *A Country Such as This*—the basically conservative and revisionary nature of Webb's project of re-writing post-Vietnam American cultural myth is signaled from the outset in his deeply conservative, indeed almost perversely anachronistic choice of fictional mode. Here that medium is the chronicle of the military academy—part of a literary-cinematic tradition embracing examples from

*Brother Rat* and *The Long Gray Line* to modern updatings of the form such as Pat Conroy's *The Lords of Discipline* or Lucian Truscott IV's *Dress Gray;* and here again the issue is the idea of national honor measured against the complex challenges of the codes of the soldier and now specifically the codes of education and personal discipline of the professional soldier traditionally called upon to fight American wars and preserve American peace while training new generations to do so as well.

The place is the U.S. Naval Academy in early 1968. And although the book opens with a brief scene from June Week exercises of that year, the major action takes place in February roughly during the crucial Tet Offensive. The story centers on the intertwined destinies of a small collection of figures: marine captain Ted Lenahan, tactical officer for a battalion of midshipmen, a badly wounded Vietnam veteran with a chest full of decorations, a head for poetry, a bad attitude toward petty discipline and the small minds of martinets, a divorced wife and beloved son, and an ongoing guilty affair with the wife of his former academy roommate and best friend; Wild Bill Fogarty, a senior midshipman much in Lenahan's cut, tough, irreverent, focused, taking the chickenshit and the discipline for what it is and giving it back in puzzled love, a marine all the way, now with a mission to honor the memory of a best friend killed in Vietnam; John Dean, a plebe, unformed, intellectual, a "sea lawyer" (19, 50) and "shit magnet" (49), as he is known, who thinks too much and hesitates too often, now become Fogarty's special project. "Either go home or square away," the latter puts it to him. "You can't have it both ways, Dean, because I won't let you. Now what'll it be?" (70).

What it will be turns out to be the shaping up of John Dean and his coming to understand, almost as if in some fifties movie voice-over, the mystery of the code, "Men of Annapolis," as he puzzles over it early on, "immaculately groomed, fiercely disciplined even though they resisted every element of the discipline, a paradox, proud of the very things they hated" (52). By the end, the shaping up is in fact accomplished. Dean, through the endless "come-arounds," the inspections, the constant physical and spiritual harassment, finds his place in the order of things. But the achievement comes at considerable cost. Through the intervention of a liberal-hearted chemistry professor, a civilian who has managed to extract from Dean, his prize student, after the latter has failed an exam, that he has been unable to study because of hazing, Fogarty is ultimately convicted under recently instituted rules of protection and expelled from the academy. Lenahan, who has increasingly come to look the other way both with the specific issues in question and with questions of petty discipline at large, takes Forgarty's part even to the point of a special appeal to the academy commandant and for his pains is removed from duty and transferred. Moreover, and this is quite important to note, the fates of both Fogarty and Lenahan come through the workings of an "honor" system that operates exactly as it should. Indeed, the point of the text would seem that while the system remains intact, and to the point of claiming the loyalties of good, natural, albeit rough-edged men such as Fogarty and Lenahan even to the extent of their own undoing, it has now fallen into the hands of sentimental civilians such as Thad, the professor (portrayed as relentlessly soft, ingratiating, effeminate, and, in one scene, possibly homosexual), and brigade tactical officer Pratt, the mad martinet (and likewise portrayed, especially in one important scene with his wife, as being of dubious sexuality). By the end, Dean will remain at Annapolis where he has begun to find, he senses somehow, his personal portion of self-discipline and pride. Fogarty is likely to go on to Marine OCS and then inevitably to the war. Lenahan is on his way back as well. It is where he belongs, as he tells the nurse who along the way has become his adoring lover. (The work, it should be mentioned, involves a number of sex-romance subplots presumably designed to elaborate further the complex specificities of the warrior code of the military professional; but it does so, as will *A Country Such as This*, by subjecting women to various reductive categorizations — the patient and sexually nurturing Penelope, the predatory slut, the castrating mother-bitch — familiar to readers of male romance.) "I'm coming back, Goodbody," Lenahan tosses off, with the ease characteristic of his frequent invokings of lines from Pound, Coleridge, Shakespeare, Dylan Thomas. "I'm just not worth a damn when it comes to dying" (304).

It is perhaps almost too easy to identify the points at which this novel gives in to popular stereotype and cliche. As a form, it is a vehicle finally not so much of mythic revision as reversion, mythic reinscription almost to the edge of the caricatured and unintentionally parodic recapturing of some lost vision of other times and better. The relationships between men and women and the corresponding relationships between the "good" military man and the "bad" military man or his civilian alter ego (it is an index of the true conservatism of this novel that the sexual dynamics of the two orders or categories of relationship are much alike) fill us with the memories of an entire genre of military fiction arising out of World War II and remaining popular precisely until Vietnam made it all look absurd. That Webb takes it so seriously and makes it, for the most part, work—and the book as a depiction of the life of the military academy does great justice to the complexities of love, anger, pride, and self-discipline involved, often in ways quite provocative and moving—becomes a testimony to the power of the conservative and revisionist myth he attempts to reinstitute. The good men are off to Vietnam to serve and perhaps die for a code of honor that they have elected to accept as the central fact of their admission into the professional brotherhood of arms. The civilians and intellectuals and military bureaucrats at home will continue to work their will and presumably prosper and ultimately prevail. The former, in this text, have their small moments of dramatic vindication, Lenahan in his laughing cavalier farewell to Goodbody, Fogarty in a brief showdown, before a classroom of students, with the craven Professor Thad (where he backs off, finally, so as not to endanger his chances for OCS). But it is clear that the latter now own the system all the way up the chain of command. The good men have only self-respect and pride of profession and possibly death.

In *A Sense of Honor*, while Vietnam is almost exclusively offstage, it is clearly the model of the national psychodrama that has become Webb's primal scene: the betrayal of men who often find their sense of worth and dignity in the old military virtues of duty, honor, courage, self-discipline, and personal sacrifice, by an American majority who find it easier and more attractive to take the alternative way of compromise, self-indulgence, and personal aggrandizement and gratification. In Webb's third novel, a whole large canvas of American war, peace, and generations entitled *A Country Such as This*, that mythos of Vietnam is carried all the way back into its immediate post–World War II context and then brought back up to a post-Vietnam present in the full spectacle of a tragic American fall from historical purpose and collective commitment. And here, even more explicitly than before, such a legend of the fall foregrounds itself in a quite specific, and by now quite familiar, political argument: that the true tragedy of Vietnam lay in a massive failure of national purpose and specifically, from the perspective of those who underwent the experience of the war, in the sacrifice of a generation of young American soldiers to a war effort structured from start to finish by the attitudes of American civilians and their political representatives so as to be impossible to win. (And so Webb himself said as much at an Asia Society conference on the literature of the war, noting his basic agreement with "the validity" of the American mission in Vietnam, along with his corresponding belief "that it was our flawed government policy that made the war unwinnable, and therein pierced us through our national soul" [Lomperis, 17].) Such an argument inscribes itself repeatedly throughout the text and almost always, as might be expected (except for one rare case of a senator, sitting in an early briefing in Saigon and recognizing the idiocy of "experts" and "planners" for what it is from the outset [278–79]), through the sober analyses of military professionals bearing the burden. "We're in this one, and I think the only way out is to fight like hell," an embattled advisor tells navy commander Red Lesczynski, one of the book's trio of male protagonists, on an early fact-finding mission. "They've beat us bad where it counts, and it'll take years to straighten that out. If we've got the guts to hang on that long" (289). Shortly, it is Lesczynski himself speaking, now aboard an aircraft carrier and flying severely restricted missions over the North, who articulates the position. "The North Vietnamese are clearly trying to take over the South by military force," he says. "It's the North Vietnamese who have almost their entire army in the South right now. We have stated to the world that the South should not be subjugated against its will. If that's worth fighting over, then it should be worth a serious, total effort. How long is it going to take Johnson to understand that the North Vietnamese believe they're winning, and that this sort of bombing reinforces that belief?" It is the military man who reads best the callow administrators and the idiot politicians. "I'll tell you the truth," he concludes. "I don't think McNamara has the guts, and I don't think LBJ has the clarity of thought, to fight this war. It's that simple" (337). In homespun version, Judd Smith, Lesczynski's Annapolis classmate and marine hero of Korea, now a "fighting preacher" from the mountains of his native Virginia about to become a fighting congressman, makes the same basic point. As he tells a reporter, "If you love somebody, you don't up and quit on them when they start having problems, and it's the same thing with a country. Now, I believe we had a reason to go into Vietnam, and if President Johnson's messed it up, the thing to do is try and get it right, not tell your sons to turn their backs on their country." It is an old American problem, he says, and it has a traditional solution. "Every war we've ever fought has had major problems in its implementation," he concludes. "The thing to do is correct the mistakes, not quit. If our leaders plant the flag, you follow it" (372).

Not surprisingly, as meditated in the forms of his first two works, Webb's radically revisionist political mythology now moves even further in his third novel, an extremely conventional assemblage of virtually all the available gestures and reflexes of popular, mass-appeal, best-seller fiction, toward some ultimate conservative direction of formal correlative, revision becoming increasingly something more like entrenched reaction. The key to the controversial achievement of *Fields of Fire* — its strengths as a graphic and moving depiction of the brotherhood of men in battle, albeit coupled with its insistent undertone of conservative political apologetics — lies in its powerful reshaping to the terms of Vietnam of the dynamics of the traditional novel of combat in the vein of James Jones and Norman Mailer. Likewise the appeal of *A Sense of Honor*, whatever one's opinion of the work as political argument, may be said to rest in the strong reappropriation of the conventions of the "service" or "academy" novel to the complex terms of contemporary military-civilian relationships in a democratic society. In *A Country Such as This*, Webb's choice of form, as if bespeaking his increasing political intransigence (and echoed in a vein of literary pronouncement, one should add, in public laments at the same Asia Society conference mentioned above concerning a liberal "antiwar" strain in the publication of Vietnam writing that had stifled voices of conservative interpretation [Lomperis, 15–19]) is almost defiantly reactionary. Indeed, in choosing here the popular historical epic as practiced by such forebears as Irwin Shaw, Anton Myrer, and Herman Wouk, Webb would seem committed at once to working literarily against the tendencies of Vietnam fiction as a rapidly evolving post-modern genre and to seeking ideologically as well the larger audience — something, in fact, like the old "silent majority" — who might yet form his true political base. The literary politician, in short, attempts to take his case to the people. Accordingly, plot here becomes grandly stylized and almost operatic, character verges incessantly on domestic and sociopolitical caricature, and theme becomes pure political argument. The fiction of conservative revision becomes popular entertainment as reactionist propaganda.

A novel of generations extending from the years just after World War II to the post-Watergate era, *A Country Such as This* centers on the intertwined narratives of three 1951 graduates of the Naval Academy: Judd

Smith, as already noted, first to become a decorated marine officer in Korea, next an FBI agent, then a country preacher in his native mountains of western Virginia, and finally a U.S. congressman; Red Lesczynski, the big Polack from the grim Pennsylvania company town, naval aviator, member of the Blue Angels, North Vietnam POW, lifelong devotee of Asia and student of America's destiny there; and Joe Dingenfelder, Jewish intellectual, MIT aerospace prodigy, air force captain with missile command who sells out for the affluence and comforts of industry, self-consigned at the last to petty viceregal splendors in old outposts of the far American Pacific. The book opens with the three swearing a blood pact of reunion in an Annapolis tavern. It follows their lives, marriages, families, achievements, sufferings, tragedies, triumphs. Smith, the war hero, "fighting preacher" elected to Congress, loses his wife, the old Virginia senator's beautiful daughter, and then regains her (steals her back, in fact, from another husband, a scion of Richmond tobacco money who stands in his way as his chief political rival), commits himself to the fight for a politics of honor, traditional value, and common sense. Red and his beloved Sophie marry, persevere together across myriad duty stations and farewells and reunions, raise a family, undergo the wait of Korea and later his interminable years of torture in North Vietnamese prisons, only to have him die from old buried World War II ordnance as he explores, on a reunion with Smith, Dingenfelder, and his old Japanese friend Kosaka, a battlefield cave site on Saipan. Dingenfelder too marries, the liberal-activist-feminist Dorothy Edelson, daughter of Viennese immigrant Jews, soon to see his aerospace career eclipsed, first in the military and eventually with civilian contractors, by her overweening ambition which carries her into the antinuclear, civil rights, feminist, and antiwar movements, and ultimately, just ahead of Smith, into the halls of Congress.

As these summaries may suggest, *A Country Such as This* thus becomes a grandly ambitious attempt to capture the whole complex panorama of the crucial American decades of the 1950s, sixties, and seventies, the "years," as the jacket copy would have it, "when America would reach out and touch the heavens, only to be defeated and torn apart by internal conflict, and a war in Southeast Asia." And in great measure, it does achieve these ends, particularly once again as a precise and reasoned inquiry into the code of the military professional called upon to bear the burden of American policy in the latest and most ill of all American times of war.

Simultaneously, however, it also embraces its more explicit polemical purpose as a medium of broader political dialogue, and always to essentially conservative and revisionist ends, over a complex of issues articulated basically from two extreme positions: that of the liberal, intellectual (and by constant implication, sexually hysterical), contentious (and again, by constant implication, Jewish), polemical, invariably strident, and relentlessly self-righteous Dorothy Dingenfelder; and that of the traditional, unapologetic, inflammatory but somehow frustratingly reasoned, conservative, common-sensical, earthy Judd Smith. Throughout, they become the designated representatives of the two political discourses contending for what Red Lesczynski has given thanks for, on his return from POW captivity, as "a country such as this" (494). On occasion the confrontations are head to head. Early on they debate civil rights, the policies of "social engineering," and what Judd calls "reverse discrimination" (288–89). Later, in a set piece in Congress, they manage also, in two relatively brief contending passages of counter soliloquy, to cover Asian genocide, Watergate, and ERA (476–79). In solo, Judd speaks most often from the accredited forums of the pulpit, the newspaper interview, or the campaign platform. Dorothy is consigned basically to hectoring confrontation with anyone who is available to be quarreled with: Joe, her husband; Sophie or Red; Judd on virtually any occasion on which he happens to be present.

Between these poles of polemical argument, in the trappings of historical panorama, *A Country Such as This* becomes a museum of major fifties, sixties, and seventies issues: nuclear disarmament, civil rights, women's liberation, the counter-culture, the New Left, the antiwar movement, Watergate, defense spending, abortion. Throughout, one must acknowledge, Webb truly does make something like a genuine attempt to render the complexity of the matters at stake, but the formal alignments of the text at large relentlessly give way to a basically conservative and even reactionary sympathy. Special attention is reserved, as might be expected, given the dialectic of character into which the novel eventually takes shape, for the antiwar and women's movements. (There is an artful dodging of civil rights, the third major piece of the dominant trinity of American political counter theologies established here. Predictably, it is one of the first of the truly consuming political passions of Dorothy Dingenfelder; but the issues are persistently defused through Smith's positioning of himself as a southern "realist"—and in his own person a mountain Celt carrying in his own veins the dark blood of Indians—in the face of pie-eyed northern liberal self-righteousness.) The antiwar students in particular are shown as indulged, narcissistic publicity seekers, abetted by a liberal press and the fact that they are present before the cameras while their less-privileged peers are doing America's everyday jobs or fighting its current war, off on a political joyride fueled by tuition checks and their parents' liberal sympathies (448–49). Antiwar revolutionaries become defined by their analogy to the craven and misguided anti-Lincoln party of defeat during the Civil War (452). Likewise, the emancipated female, Dorothy, as she progresses in the novel, becomes more of a power precisely to the degree that she becomes explicitly less a woman (220). Seated in the halls of government, she becomes fat assed (474). Reliably contentious *and* defensive as in every male traditionalist's bad dream, even down to her posture at a doorbell, she holds her small paws in front of her kangaroolike (273). Decked out in western sporting regalia, presumably the badge of her countercultural affiliations, she looks like something ready "for a costume ball, a thirty-four-year-old Austrian-born, New York–raised, Jewish law student dressed up like a cowgirl" (273).

Indeed, as the novel progresses, and almost as if against the author's own will, Dorothy Dingenfelder herself, as embodiment of all the liberal issues, increasingly, in one walking, talking, nagging, moralizing persona, quite literally gathers unto herself the book's entire energy of focus. She becomes, in short, the incarnation of "what is wrong" with America. She is a mouthpiece of abrasively righteous liberal pieties, finding her "fulfillment" (359) in whatever cause presents an occasion for blind, self-gratifying activism. She is always "there." She has been a "final editor" of the "I have a dream" speech of Martin Luther King, Jr., and is also allowed, in a subtle novelistic deflation of that particularly electric moment of American political drama, to deliver the historic conclusion informally to Sophie Lesczynski well before the event itself takes place (294). She revels in what she sees as her own heroic part in the March on the Pentagon (357–59). The salutation "Congresswoman Dingenfelder?" rings in her ears as if someone has said *"Princess?"* (389). She is a bad mother and a callous wife who rationalizes her neglect (359). So likewise, in dress and adornment, she comes to hate, we are told explicitly, "the implements of femininity" (359). By the revisionist political agenda of this text, from theories of governance and social action to those of gender and familial responsibility, she is in a word a traitor. Across a relentlessly self-aggrandizing career of what we are clearly to regard as destructive, loose-cannon activism, her life has all come to culminate, as she sees it in her own righteous eyes, at least, in nothing less than a necessary and ever ongoing "battle of provocation"; and "the enemy," moreover, "was the United States government" (360). Indeed, the particular moment of antiwar apotheosis in which this recognition is gained becomes something like the novel's moral climax, its roster of villainy filled out by the titles of the divisions in the activist army at which she marches in her function as "a general" (360): "the Women's Strike for Peace, the New York Peace Council, the Chicago Parade Committee, the Southern Christian Leadership Conference, the Ohio Area Peace Action Council, the Students for a Democratic Society, H. Rap Brown's SNCC, various pacifist, socialist, Maoist, communist, and Trotskyite fringe groups" (361). The focus of political rancor is indeed so concentrated here that the remainder of the novel—even including the turbulent events of the last days of the war and the dying Nixon presidency, not to mention the truly horrific scenes of Red Lesczynski's imprisonment as a Communist POW, his homecoming, and his eventual death in the cave explosion on Saipan—assumes the status of something like background contrivance, almost as if it were part of a different text. In sum, Dorothy Dingenfelder literally steals the novel, presumably much in the fashion whereby she and her kind have stolen America.

In this respect, again by intention or otherwise, the work's conclusion in particular turns out to be emblematic, even architectonic. For the story ends where it has begun, literally in the same place. But now two of the men are missing. Red, as noted earlier, having survived Korea and Vietnam, has now been killed in the bizarre cave accident on Saipan while trying to restrain his Japanese friend and alter ego Kosaka from rooting through the detritus of battle in some final expiation of his old Pacific war of pain and loss. Dingenfelder, who has survived the explosion, remains tucked away in happy exile on Guam. In their place, eventually, meeting Judd, who has come to open an old safety deposit box and drink a ceremonial survivors' bottle of twenty-five-year-old whiskey, is of course Dorothy (who has been asked by her absent husband, we are told, to come as his representative). The two argue, joust, flirt, throw out sexual overtures in rank challenge, come close to a restaging of the old blood pact once enacted by the three midshipmen (she backs out at the last moment), and finally draw apart into their ancient, uncompromising, and unresolved enmity, the voices of their America. Later, he passes her standing by the waterfront, gazing moody and perplexed into the darkness of the bay, tells her not to jump into what he is sure must be the maw of her old liberal suffering. She has no intention of doing so, she returns, as long as people like him might have a chance of running the country (534).

The novel's conclusion is a fair epitome of the dialectic of history and political myth inscribed and enacted throughout. And it is in this valedictory context that we must attend to the true symbolic politics of gender, conflict, and ideology that emerge. As is characteristic throughout, Smith comes away with the prize of sympathetic and attractive depiction. Dorothy has the last word. The drunken nostalgist from the last man's celebration of the warrior's old belief and mission passes by the tense, wary, defiant harpy-virago at the seawall, his personal representative of the contemporary political and cultural fates. In Webb's neoconservative rendering, it is an iconography of the national impasse, an image summoned up from the deepest recesses of nostalgia, perplexity, betrayal, and loss — in the most profound sense, a lovers' argument, a quarrel with America bitterly unresolved.

Winston Groom began his career as a novelist with an extremely traditional "big" novel of war, much in the vein of Webb, entitled *Better Times Than These*. This he followed in 1980 with *As Summers Die*, a novel of love, violence, intrigue, and suspense set in his native Gulf Coast region of Alabama. Along the way, he also coauthored, with Duncan Spencer, the Vietnam chronicle of prisoner-of-war Robert Garwood entitled *Conversations with the Enemy* and published as well a young people's book, *Only*. A subsequent return to the subject of Vietnam in the contexts of American myth, past, present, and, in imaginative inscription, future, came in an acclaimed tale of the heroic American half-wit, the good old boy triumphant, *Forrest Gump*. His most recent work, a combination of themes and preoccupations from earlier texts — Vietnam and national memory, the historical South, American politics and their relation to mass-media popular culture — is the novel *Gone the Sun*.

Especially among major novels of Vietnam to appear over the last decade, *Better Times Than These* strikes the contemporary reader (as will perhaps only a few other works such as James Webb's *Fields of Fire* or John Del Vecchio's *The Thirteenth Valley*) as rather anomalous, if not downright anachronistic. Eschewing, for instance, the complex experimentalism of Tim O'Brien or Stephen Wright, the black humor of John Sack or Charles Durden, or the existential cinema verite of Gustav Hasford or Larry Heinemann, Groom embraces instead the older tradition of war fiction handed down by James Jones, Norman Mailer, Irwin Shaw, and others. (Indeed, as noted by recent Jones biographers such as Frank McShane [286] and Willie Morris [217–18], during Groom's writing of *Better Times Than These*, James Jones himself, in his last years, befriended the younger writer and personally served as his literary mentor.) Accordingly, Groom's work stands as one that, precisely as it succeeds according to many of the prior canons of the American novel of war, again also betrays often the particular difficulties of the earlier form in coming to terms with the new and complex realties peculiar to the experience of Vietnam. It is conceived at a high level of ambition and is executed from start to finish with a sustained energy. What one remembers most, however, is not some overall accomplishment of design but rather a collection of individual vignettes and episodes in which the novel is often quite literally captured by the random plenitude of the horror it has attempted to depict.

Above all, *Better Times Than These* is a "big" novel in terms of being vastly peopled. Its dual protagonists, lieutenants Frank Holden, an eastern blueblood from Princeton serving as general's aide, and Billy Kahn, a savvy southern Jew suddenly thrust into command of a rifle company, occupy much of the novel's focus of point of view. But, as revealed by the prefatory "Table of Organization and Roster" the novelist provides for his mythical "Fourth Battalion, Seventh Cavalry (Airmobile)," they are but the principal actors in a much larger cast. There is the whole hierarchy of officers: Lt. Col. Jason Patch, the battalion commander and horse cavalryman out of date; Dunn, the over-the-hill communications officer, on his third war and carrying the secret of his terminal foul-up in Germany; McCrary, the cheerful, ice-cream–swilling graves-registration lieutenant; Sharkey and Donovan, rugged commanders of Kahn's first and second platoons; Brill, the OCS misfit and borderline psychopath, with the troubled third. There is also the full complement of enlisted men: Trunk, the stalwart first sergeant; Crump, the slow-talking southerner; his friend, DiGeorgio, the street-smart yankee; Carruthers, the illiterate black; Spudhead Miter, the U.S. representative's son. At home, Holden's girlfriend becomes an antiwar activist and falls into an affair with one of her college professors who is a leader and major celebrity in the movement. Spudhead Miter's congressman father writes him consoling letters about patriotism and sacrifice.

Eventually, as might have been expected, the initial roster turns out to be a roll call of casualties as well, with only the lucky ones spared. Of the two protagonists, Holden, increasingly disillusioned by the vast spectacle of upper echelon idiocy he is forced to witness, volunteers for the field, where, near the end of the novel, he is killed serving as one of Kahn's platoon leaders. Kahn, on the other hand, survives the endless and brutal fighting, only to be sent home in dishonor for an incident that has happened in his absence, when Brill's renegade platoon has gang raped two female Viet Cong prisoners who have been subseqently executed by Brill himself. Kahn's crime, it turns out, through a series of complications and petty compromises, has been his failure to make a proper report. Courtmartialed and separated from the service, Kahn returns home where, in a last scene, he attends Holden's funeral.

As this synopsis must surely reveal, *Better Times Than These* is thus an extremely traditional novel of war in the old, epic vein. Yet even as it works the ground of familiar convention and, perhaps too often, even cliche, it also does come ultimately to encapsulate, in any number of telling moments of vision, the fullness of the peculiar horror that was America in Vietnam. It is relentless in its depiction of the noise, panic, and confusion of combat, of the particular savagery and shock of a jungle warfare that ultimately comes to seem mainly, as Groom tells us of the Ia Drang, just "killing for killing's sake" (221) and for the price it ultimately exacts on the combatant. The world Groom depicts is, in sum, the unceasingly pitiless one of Vietnam, a world, as he tells us, in which on any given day, "Sorry about that" will pass the unsmiling lips of hard young American boys "at least six thousand times between Reveille and Taps" (261).

It comes as no surprise, therefore, that *Better Times Than These* finds its real formal and thematic climax—in distinct unison with a number of other major texts including Philip Caputo's *A Rumor of War*, Ron Kovic's *Born on the Fourth of July*, James Webb's *Fields of Fire*, and Larry Heinemann's *Paco's Story*, as well as Groom's own subsequent *Gone the Sun*—in an atrocity. In fact, such a climax seems to have been waiting there all along. At one point, indeed, the faithful Trunk warns Kahn explicitly of what we have come to sense from early on: that this particular cast of

American boys in a war novel has somehow gone far west of mythic or military convention. "The thing is, Lieutenant," he says, "some of these shitheads are getting a little crazy" (270). And so, even as the novel moves on to whatever conventional conclusion, it is this vision of the particular madness engendered by Vietnam in the American soul—the horror of it all rendered if possible even more horrific by immensely confused issues of complicity and responsibility—that, along with "the former commander of Bravo Company" (411), this work most fully and finally brings home.

Groom's somewhat curious second novel, *As Summers Die*, marks the extension of the career of this particular Vietnam writer in his generation into a mythic mode—partaking of at least two long-accredited American permutations of the novel genre—perhaps most accurately characterized as hard-boiled southern gothic. Set in 1959 in the steamy port city of "Bienville" (one may read Mobile), it centers on a small-time jailhouse lawyer, Willie Croft, and his attempts to prevent the rich and prominent Holt family from seizing newly identified oil lands secretly deeded years earlier by their father, Jonathan Holt, to a black woman, Elvira Backus, by whom he has fathered two illegitimate children, the one, Priscilla, Croft's maid and the other, Daniel, a Shakespeare-quoting assistant principal in a black county school. This matter is in turn further complicated by Croft's impassioned and carnal love affair with the voluptuous Holt cousin, Whitsey Loftin, and also his attempts to prevent the rapacious Holt siblings, the vicious Percy, the craven Brevard, and the dissolute Marci, from acquiring yet other lands held by Whitsey's addled and eccentric aunt, sister to the dead Jonathan, Hannah Holt Loftin. Finally, there is in addition Croft's eventual engagement with a cartel of black investors, among them the black Holt son, in the Obsidian Oil Company, a venture that threatens and ultimately succeeds in breaking for the first time the old local hegemony of power and wealth.

Along the way, the novel surges with tumult and dark emotion. Percy and Brevard Holt, along with their old-money attorney, Augustus X. Tompkins, hire two henchmen, The Roller and Snake Crenshaw, renegade Holt stevedores from the Bienville docks, to retrieve a conclusive deed reputed to be in Elvira Backus's possession. In the process, she is supposedly killed when her cabin is burned to the ground, but the murder has been a case of mistaken identity. (That it has been another woman, an old, mad, local vagrant, we learn shortly as Croft attends the purported funeral. It remains for the Holts to find this out when Croft eventually produces the living Elvira as a surprise courtroom witness.) Then, toward the last, Croft himself is also nearly murdered by the two assassins. In a climactic struggle, he kills one and captures the other, but only after they have shot to death Guidre, his old friend and fishing guide. By the novel's end, however, justice, insofar as it may prevail in the precincts of Bienville and the newly oil-rich Creoletown, has triumphed. Obsidian Oil flourishes, and the brothers Holt, along with the family attorney, are in jail awaiting trial for double murder. Croft's affair with the passionate Whitsey, on the other hand, has foundered, as has his flirtation with old-family Bienville society. If nothing else, he has had at least the satisfaction of having taken their measure, for all their pretense to position and power, at the old game of money that is their ancient secret corruption. "*Me!*" he says to himself, "and not quietly," in the old downtown park that has always symbolized at once his attachment to and his exclusion from the old Bienville elite. "I *did* it!" he cries out. "By God, I *did* it! I really *did* it!" (277).

In summary, then, *As Summers Die* is clearly a work of ambition. At the same time, however, it is relentlessly melodramatic and insistently overelaborated. Indeed, as James Jones had been Groom's mentor with *Better Times Than These*, one wonders if Jones's *Some Came Running* (by no coincidence, Whitsey mentions the work at one point as a new paperback title having recently arrived at her bookshop) may not have been something of a model here as well. For if both possess the merits of expansiveness, complex design, and a passionate grasp of experience, they both suffer similar defects as well. Although Willie Croft is interesting, for instance, in many of the same ways as is Jones's Dave Hirsh (and as is in her own way the passionate and enigmatic Whitsey Loftin), most of the remaining characters, in particular the scheming Holts and the villainous old-money attorney, incline toward the cardboard. Dialogue and description are often awkward as well, and plot turns too repeatedly on surprise, random social encounter, and outright novelistic coincidence. *As Summers Die*, in sum, remains the work essentially of a journeyman novelist, still in search of an appropriate mode and voice, a novel that may finally be said at best to make general merit of its various and incidental defects. As a hard-boiled tale of action, mystery, and romance, it is complex and interesting, with — as before, in the large and elaborately conceived *Better Times Than These* — an enormous energy of execution. With regard to its depiction of class relations and the politics of race during the last days before mass integration, it may also make claim to considerable achievement as social documentary. Finally, with its dark strains of violence, greed, and passion, it also stamps itself as unmistakably southern in the tradition extending backward from Faulkner to Mark Twain and forward to such contemporaries of Groom's as Bobbie Ann Mason and Barry Hannah. It is by no coincidence at all, indeed, that the main character introduced in the first chapter of *As Summers Die* is the land itself. In his second novel, Groom clearly takes his regional stand and announces, as will shortly be realized in the third novel to come, his most creative fictional domain.

It is in Groom's third novel, the hilarious and tragic *Forrest Gump*, that he most clearly finds his southern vision *and* his southern voice as well. Indeed, in that text of complete conjunction, *Forrest Gump*, he finds it all, his voice, his metier, his donee: the domain, in this case Alabama, as his southern contemporary Barry Hannah has said in the work's jacket copy, of the great American galoot—a character that the New South has now presented to us as nothing less than a "national treasure," at once ourselves and just "simply realer and profounder than the rest of us shadow-idiots."

The work itself amply fulfills that claim of large provenance. As in the Benjy section of *The Sound and the Fury*, for instance, *Forrest Gump* is throughout quite literally a tale told by an idiot. Yet this is no tortured recluse languishing before the kitchen fire in the ancestral mansion. Although "bein an idiot," as Gump puts it early on, may on a multitude of occasions prove to be "no box of chocolates" (1), he ultimately makes more of it and of life itself than virtually any common mortal one might imagine. At six-feet-six and 242 pounds, he becomes a star high school running back on the basis of his not-so-idiotic conclusion—closely linked to the native sweetness of heart that has made him an abject failure on defense—that when someone is chasing you on a football field with the intent of striking you and throwing you violently to the ground, you probably ought to try to outrun him. His high school exploits in turn carry him briefly to the university, where he stars for a single glorious semester for Bear Bryant and the Southeastern Conference while earning an A in an esoteric graduate physics course and flunking remedial English and phys ed. ("Idiot Savant," the doctor up in Tuscaloosa calls him while putting him on display to parade another of his hidden talents—playing the harmonica. And so "idiot savant" he will remain indeed in passing definitive return judgment on all those who so judge him throughout: "Shit on them people" [33].) Drafted into the army, he is sent to Vietnam, where he wins the Medal of Honor and is sent home for a special presentation at the White House by President Johnson, where he in turn answers Johnson's display of his famous gall bladder scar and the president's query about his own scars from his wounding by dropping his pants and quite literally showing his ass. (His most memorable form of public statement, it turns out, he has already perfected years earlier at the state all-star football banquet following high school. Invited to the podium to receive his prize, the victim of a jammed zipper, all he can think to say into the microphone is "I got to pee" [13]. Involuntarily, it continues to pop up on any number of occasions of high seriousness throughout his life, a recurrent echo of his wondrous capacity for misadventure.) Later, there follow a trip to Red China as a member of the U.S. Ping-Pong team (where, to the consternation of his State Department companions, he saves Mao Tse Tung from drowning during the chairman's legendary Red River swim); a flight to outer space as an astronaut; a four-year survival, after the space vehicle's crash, among New Guinea cannibals (where he survives by keeping at bay in game after game a Yale-educated cannibal chess master); a last-minute escape shortly thereafter from pygmy headhunters; a stint at professional wrestling; a brief albeit abortive foray on the silver screen with Raquel Welch; a return home to a successful entrepreneurship in the big-time Gulf-Coast shrimp business; and a gloriously misbegotten run at the office of U.S. Senator. ("Look," he has told his campaign advisor, "I am just an idiot. I don't know nothin' about politics." No matter, the advisor has replied, "Then you will fit in perfectly" [214–15].)

In the midst of all this, he also manages to conduct a passionate, if ultimately ill-starred, love affair with his darling Jenny Curran carrying him all the way from the Alabama Redneck Riviera to the hallowed precincts of Harvard Yard and back at the end toward the South where it is revealed to him that he has fathered her son. And so along the way, as we discover, he has also managed to cover virtually every significant event or occasion of the American 1960s and seventies. Moreover, idiot savant that he may be, he has also nonetheless managed to provide the era with many of its most appropriate linguistic moments of truth. As his high school coach has told him after that first memorable "I got to pee," "Gump, you sure have a way with words" (14). And so it proves particularly for Forrest with the most significant event of the Gump era, the Vietnam war. "It is," he says, "a bunch of shit" (75).

Thus in *Forrest Gump*, even more fully than in *As Summers Die*, Groom embraces the distinctive tradition of southern literature, and in particular, in the newest work, the long and distinguished tradition of southern humor. Yet it is now southern humor in a new key. It is the humor perhaps of a Mark Twain, a William Faulkner, a Eudora Welty, or a Flannery O'Connor, but it is also the humor of the rambunctious and bustling New South, the humor of a Roy Blount, Jr., a Dan Jenkins, or a Lewis Grizzard. At the same time, it also suggests its affinities with the more complex literary humor—the bizarrerie, for instance, and the black-comedy grandstanding—of a Beth Henley or a Barry Hannah.

The most distinctive achievement of *Forrest Gump*, however, both as a novel in its own right and as a significant stage in the literary evolution of its author as a major southern and American author, lies in its sustained, affirmative, ebullient sense of voice. Forrest Gump is a representative not only of endurance and acceptance but also of possibility, an atom cast about in this dark, violent, wicked world who will always believe that it has a better side, a lover-not-a-fighter who proves through a life of fighting a near-infinite capacity for love. He is also, particularly in his imaging of the experience of Vietnam, exemplary of the new and imaginatively inventive sense making, often resulting in new levels of insight and acceptance, achieved in second and third novels by writers of that war. Most of all, he is among the most recent and brilliant in what has proved a long line of rumbustious, ill-mannered, and great-hearted southern galoots, ones who "still got dreams like anyone else." After all, he concludes, "well, so what? I may be an idiot, but most of the time, I tried to do the right thing— an dreams is just dreams, ain't they? So whatever else has happened, I am figgerin this: I can always look back an say, at least I ain't led no hum-drum life" (228).

So to the end he continues to sustain us with the heroism—at once a wise idiocy and often a prize of idiot wisdom—of his attempts to project that life into an ongoing enterprise of sense making. "You know what I mean?" (228), he offers at the last, speaking for himself, his generation of Vietnam, his New South, and his America, and giving us a conclusion that is an ongoing invitation as well.

Groom's fifth and most recent novel, *Gone the Sun*, combines many of

the preoccupations and interests evidenced in his career to date. Apropos
of the echo of military tradition in its title, it returns explicitly, like both
*Better Times Than These* and *Forrest Gump*, to the experience of Vietnam
and its enduring effects upon the lives of those Americans who underwent
it. Like *Forrest Gump* and *As Summers Die*, however, it also commits the
focus of its emphasis on the function of the novelist as cultural mythmaker to the particular vision of southern history. In addition, however,
somehow appropriate to the extended work of this Vietnam author in his
career, it conflates these two major preoccupations within a work that is
also at its formal *and* its thematic center an extended inquiry into the life
of writing itself. The work's protagonist, Beau Gunn, is a Vietnam veteran
and ex-reporter and columnist for the Washington *Times-Examiner* (his
claim to comic celebrity there is that he has utterly blown Watergate), who
has now returned at the behest of an old military school friend to edit the
Bienville *Courier-Democrat*. There, in the city of his birth, he launches—
eventually at the cost of his own life—an investigation into a local murder and, as a consequence, a massive oil-export and price-fixing scandal
involving the district congressman and a large collection of prominent
citizenry. At the same time, however, the protagonist is also Beau Gunn,
rising young American playwright, celebrated author of a first play, *Such
a Pretty Girl*, of a second one later a Broadway hit, and then of a couple
of flops, but now currently working on the *opus magnum*, as the novel's
narrator describes it, which he feels will redeem a flagging career. Not
surprisingly, it is about Vietnam. ("The subject," we are told, "was one he
now felt enough distance from to write about sanely, more or less" [6].)
And more specifically, it is also about an incident in which he has been
crucially involved, one in which, he learns, through a reunion with his old
radioman, he himself in the middle of a torture-interrogation session has
suddenly, inexplicably, drawn his pistol and murdered a Viet Cong prisoner. Not surprisingly as well, in the almost completed play, it is now the
interrogation scene itself that will not allow the work to be completed.
There will be the murder of the prisoner. How will it be accomplished?
As the play stands, the murderer must be the sergeant. He will shoot the
prisoner. When the lieutenant enters, he will then explain the shooting
by saying that he has put his pistol on the table as a threat and that the
prisoner has grabbed it and shot himself before he can be stopped. The
problem on the part of the prisoner, the playwright sees, is one of "moti-

vation." Yet it must be worked out. "A play, after all," he tells himself, "was just a play. Characters could be made to do what the playwright wanted them to do—and *had* to, if the play was to be a success. But this play was different. It was such a part of Beau he sometimes didn't know where the play began and reality left off—or vice versa" (71).

Nor, accordingly, will the interrogation scene and the questions thus leave him in his workaday life, where, along with the memory of a doomed, disastrous attack on a hill called the "Fake" (and to compound the connections of this tale of a Vietnam writer with Groom's own career, both the interrogation scene and the attack have their exact prefigurations in *Better Times Than These*), it has for years returned and now continues to return. Indeed it is itself now, of course, the genesis of the play, insistently, naggingly, as a single, mad, ever-evolving dream of past ineluctably present and equally shadowed by the same questions of agency, purpose, motivation, design. In short, as for Philip Caputo's Christian Starkmann or Robert Olen Butler's Clifford Wilkes, Wilson Hand, and David Fleming, for Groom's Beau Gunn, Vietnam remains whether he is asleep or waking the single haunted dream of memory to which ongoing life and here art as well must consistently attend.

The rendering of all this comes in the form of a posthumous narration by an old Bienville friend, "Pappy Turner," the one in fact who as owner of the Bienville newspaper has brought Gunn home in the first place. As such, it is something of a document issued after a death certificate, he tells us, "a Life Certificate, if you will—which could contain some brief statement for historical purposes that could explain how a person lived and what they accomplished and where they failed and why" (3). And much of it, as things turn out, is devoted to a complicated romance intrigue plot—indeed, one again so insistently abounding in melodramatic congruencies as to seem almost surreal—involving a network of figures from Gunn's life: old Bienville boyhood friends, including the narrator, "Pappy" Turner; Tommy Brodie, the accused murderer whose suicide opens up the larger investigation; Eric Pacer, the schoolmate who has also served as his Vietnam radioman (and who has revealed his agency in the killing of the prisoner); Dan Whittle, an old prep-school adversary now a congressman deeply involved in the payoff scandal and soon to become Gunn's excecutioner; sundry lovers, including Katherine Whittle, Gunn's college fiancée now the congressman's wife, and an ambitious current flame, Sheilah Price, herself an investigative journalist who in turn has been sexually involved with the legislator as well; and various political officials and members of the city's law, banking, and business community including Gunn's own father. Nonetheless, the formal and thematic center of this "Life Certificate" remains the dream of memory that is Vietnam, the dream that will not work itself out in art, the dream that equally haunts the life, the dream that, it turns out, can be ended for Gunn only as it ultimately issues itself into new historical reality as the means of his own death. For, by the novel's end, the murder mystery has been resolved and the oil scandal unraveled, and a special exposé edition of the paper Gunn has labored so mightily to resuscitate as a medium of truth is in the very process of going to press. Now, however, Gunn also faces Whittle, once the prep-school persecutor and now the congressman deeply implicated in the cover-up threatening him with murder with a .45-caliber pistol. And there, as events near their culmination, Gunn does truly see it all, memory and dream strangely commingled in a final vision of truth. He does not face down an old boyhood enemy, a corrupt official wildly waving a gun. Rather, it is again "the night of the attack on the Fake. He had cocked the pistol and aimed it at the Vietnamese's head. And the boy had stared at it, at the black hole of Beau's .45" (299). Except now too there is the old dream as well, and a scene, he somehow now remembers at the last, where it has also been the sergeant with the gun, and Beau exhorting him to stop. And now also, finally, it is Beau facing the black hole of the .45 and seeing that it is in fact his own death that he has been facing all those years in the dream: "It was *him! Him!* He was the one who died" (300). And so now greedily revisited in the latest postwar corruptions and violences, the dream reifies itself into final fact. The Vietnam drama script of memory completes itself in the moment of the dying that it has all these years prefigured.

There only remains, then, an epilogue. Beau Gunn lingers on in a coma. Meanwhile, the world mostly goes on. The scandal revealed, its major participants are dealt with but are mainly in short order back on the street. Those who loved Gunn try to honor him in their own lives as he has them in his life and death. Finally, almost as something like an afterthought, we are told that just before Gunn's death (he has lingered on a year and a half), the Vietnam play has finally been staged, first in repertory and later in Off-Off-Broadway, where it has received mainly good reviews. In fact, the narrator observes, "All the notices were pretty good except that nobody liked the shooting scene. The critics were pretty much in agreement that it just didn't work" (302). The scene of memory that could not get itself rewritten in the dream or the play has of necessity found its ultimate true revision only in life, and with (as the major chapters of narrative development in the novel are headed) American "vicissitude" writing the script. Or, as the narrator has put it early on, "Beau was a good man; decent, but regrettably unfinished. Regarding what happened in the end, I think he'd been honest with everyone but himself" (7). The consequence has been, as with the memory of the war itself, an ongoing tragedy of faulty revision and testament, the long haunted exemplum, Vietnam. It is the old flawed script, a memory drama without a climax, the one where we still struggle to tell ourselves the truth about the country that was the war and what happened to us there.

It is altogether fitting that this chapter on Vietnam novelists should conclude with the latest of them to come to important national recognition. That figure is of course Larry Heinemann, author of the widely acclaimed novel of combat *Close Quarters* and now also of that second major work of post-Vietnam memory and winner of the National Book Award, *Paco's Story*. Indeed, in these two works he may stand as a virtual paradigm to date of the Vietnam author in his generation and of his continued rewriting of the literary memory of the war into an ongoing revisionary encounter with the sundry mythologies of the national culture at large. In the first, a private education in horror becomes an archetypal odyssey through the darkest secret recesses of national vision and belief; and in the second, the Vietnam figure now finds himself afoot on the new mythic landscape of American aftermath as well, the nation and people that now comprise, in Thomas Myers's apt and moving characterization, "imaginative ghost country for the returned veteran" (*Walking Point*, 223).

A standard characterization of *Close Quarters* has been as an extraordinarily powerful rendition of the experience of combat. (Indeed, a quite enlightening study of the novel, Cornelius A. Cronin's "Historical Backgrounds to Larry Heinemann's *Close Quarters*," "reads" the depiction of combat there in the context of U.S. Army training methods of the era, which in their emphasis on the responsibility of the individual soldier to "put out fire" made it easy for the individual combatant to translate the idea of mission into killing, pure and simple [119–30].) What has been slighted in this emphasis on its evocation of the special savagery of Viet-

nam and the almost unspeakable brutalization of the souls of the young
men sent to serve there is a highly developed imaginative structure as well,
an attempt also to trace out time-honored myths of national character and
collective purpose at a level of monstrosity commensurate to the price of
horror exacted upon the American soul at large. Indeed, this is just the
grimly creative function of the "actual" here, to become in itself a reality
so overwhelmingly hallucinatory as to render indistinct and almost im-
perceivable its frequent crossings over into the domain of the imaginative
other. Accordingly, our most deeply imagined horror here is often exactly
the function of our sense of its origins in the actually experienced. A year
in the life of a combat infantryman also becomes a fantasy tour through
the great American mansion of death, one last grand hallucination of geopolitical virtue reared upon Asia as final mythic stage of national destiny
and faith.

As a novel of initiation in combat, the experiential narrative begins
predictably. Fresh from the armor school at Fort Knox, Philip Dosier
is quickly introduced to mechanized warfare Vietnam style. Under the
tutelage of a canny, irreverent, constantly stoned, and incessantly profane
buddy named Cross, he learns of Mogas, machine guns, constant cuts and
blisters from adjusting track tensions, tightening road-wheel nuts, washing
down weapons in sweat and gasoline. He eats dust in the driver's hatch,
drinks warm beer, smokes Cambodian dope, smells bad, stays spooky and
constantly on edge, fighting the fear and the endless waiting for the horror that inevitably comes. He shoots it up in a first ambush (his bumbling
patrol leader has led them by mistake into a nearby unit of ARVN militia)
and gets initiated into the scungy delights of Claymore Face, the platoon
whore. Already, since he is from Chicago, he is worth an epithet, not
Dosier any longer now but "Deadeye." Soon comes the first bad one, the
death of a close friend, and also his own introduction to the very actual
horror of killing of an enemy soldier by strangulation with his bare hands.
Thenceforth, it is deeper and deeper into war. Cross is replaced by an
equally canny, irreverent, stoned, and profane buddy named Quinn. The
GIs fight the enemy, kill and wound, get killed and get wounded, stay
stoned, live from day to day, beer to beer, ambush to ambush. When they
are not fighting the enemy they fight each other, whites against blacks,
draftees against lifers, field soldiers against REMFS and housecats.

Dosier gets letters from his girl, finds out his brother, an in-country marine, has been badly wounded, learns of the death elsewhere in the war of a cherished friend from basic. Quinn gets a newspaper photo from home showing five soldiers, including himself, in a pose from his own basic training. Quinn has a duplicate in his wallet. Three are already dead. And the fourth, "that dufus Teleck," he ominously avers, "ain't all that bright" (143). Stoned and drunk on stand-down, Quinn gets into his private war as well — first with Surtees, the black lifer platoon sergeant, and shortly with the black tunnel rat Lavery, who winds up in the Long Binh jail for pulling his M-16 in answer to Quinn's crazy provocation. (To a man, the white soldiers lie on the latter's behalf and about the fact that he has been armed with a knife.) Eventually Dosier gets R&R and the Tokyo delights of Suzie and the Perfect Room Hotel. Back to war the day after Christmas, he intentionally kills a prisoner he has been set to guard, alleging he has tried to escape. (Again, all the witnesses lie.) Shortly, on New Year's, comes the monster battle of Suoi Cut, a whole endless night of it, and The Great Truce Day Body Count (247–50). By now Dosier and Quinn are getting old on war. "And tell the folks back home," shouts Quinn, John Wayning it up with Dosier and the rest for a *Newsweek* reporter, "that we're all gonna re-up and stay on till the last dog is dead" (250). One more firefight on one more hot day blends into the next and the last. After one of them, Quinn loses it all in a delirious rage, methodically, metronomically swinging his rifle butt down like an axe, reducing an enemy corpse to bloody mush. Dosier, eventually, having survived long enough, gets his orders. There is a party, and he goes home. Back with Jenny and long days of silent solitude, it begins to fall away. Then he gets the letter telling him Quinn is dead, in a truck accident of all things, and what is there to say?

> I mean, Quinn was this short, light-haired guy, quick and clever as anything and smart as hell. Asleep and dreaming nightmares he was arm and leg better than any three dudes I ever rode with. Stoned or sober or ass-whipped tired, he knew the tracks and the killing and the staying alive. I mean, he and I stood back to back many a night. So how come? You cover me and I'll cover you and we'll all go home, and I read Dewey's letter again. And I cried like a kid, the tears coming like an old man's birthdays; like old women keening over a coffin — that special feeling laid out among candles. (329)

Shortly, Dosier and Jenny get married. One morning, Dosier gets up and realizes that he must honor the dead. He finds Quinn's parents in Terre Haute. They all stay close, Dosier and Jenny, Rollie and Jason Quinn. Finally, he has to go see it. At Quinn's grave, on a chill day of a lowering sun, the novel ends. "Quinn the laugher," Dosier thinks to himself. "Quinn so mean and evil. Quinn dead a year and a half but the grave looking fresh, as though the dirt was still loose and the flowers were colder than his body. . . . 'Goddamn you, Quinn,'" he says (336).

Thus we have the essentially conventional narrative development of *Close Quarters*. But it is a narrative of experience that by now also has generated, in complex terms of imagination, its own larger poetic of design. The text overall, for instance, episodic and first-person and rendered in the flow of immediate consciousness, is at the same time given seven distinct and essentially poetic formal divisions. Each is given a highly evocative heading. The beginning, breathing in: "Ugly Deadly Music." The baptism into a first friend's death and one's own capacity for murder: "Moon of Atevo." Revving up and charging in, the whole nine yards: "Torque." The warrior's interlude: "The Perfect Room." Back to knee-deep in death: "By the Rule." Survival and farewell and departure: "Coming Home High." Back in the World and alone with it: "Climbing Down." The sections are not so much chapters as stanzas, long and short, pointed and complex, replete and resonant with association of theme and motif. As dictated by stylistic design in the largest sense, a unrelentingly realistic narrative of fact plays itself out *as* a highly complex poetic structure of imagination.

Most important, however, in this relation is how the fact book here is always—in a structure akin to the highly meditated ones of distinctly related works of fact and fantasy commingled such as Tim O'Brien's *Going After Cacciato* and *The Things They Carried* or Stephen Wright's *Meditations in Green*—at any single moment* a fantasy book as well. Indeed, the difficulty and the genius of this text often lie precisely in the ease with which one mode of consciousness slides into the other, fantasy arising in stoned efflorescence of what a second before was the most quotidian fact, fact bringing extended fantasy back to earth with all the grim reality of a shudder. The workings of this dynamic operate at any number of especially significant points in the text. In the first ambush, frenzied digging in the dirt becomes in memory one's self among other children making angels in the winter's first snow (52). On R&R the name alone of the Perfect Room Hotel is enough to summon up paragraph upon paragraph of a sybarite's wet dream of an oriental pleasure dome. Dosier kills the prisoner and realizes that "the day after Christmas I stood over a weak wounded kid and saw his grave and my grave, and the grave of those around me—a deep smooth-sided shaft and you will never fill it" (220).

The clearest and most complex working out of this creative dialectic of fact and imagination takes place, however, in the scene that comes to stand increasingly as the book's archetypal moment, at once its experiential *and* its imaginative center. It is the visit of Dosier and Quinn, on stand-down, drunk and stoned as usual, carrying a hot case of beer and two pilfered steaks, to the firebase chapel, a couple of scared boys looking for a little peace and quiet in the house of God and unaware that they have instead entered the mansion of death. Things begin simply enough. Dosier has gotten a letter telling of the death of his friend Willie O'Neal from basic training. Quinn has gotten the ominous news photo. Nursing their drunken, stoned spookiness, they find the unoccupied silence of the chapel. There, they honor memory, telling stories, the way foot soldiers have always done (147–50). Apace, Dosier begins to see in ways unexplained and unpredicted how truly far both of them have come to this place. Looking out at Nui Ba Dinh, Black Virgin Mountain as it is called by them, he meditates, "It's a goddamned fucking shame the world is not flat. Then I could sit up or stand up, shade my eyes from the yellowed tinted light, Indian fashion, and see home. I could gaze out under the eaves, and there it would be, morning. Smoky and greenish in the light of a long-shadowed, wet, and chilly sunrise" (151). The two of them meditate on old habits of churchgoing, sloppy crucifix workmanship, Quinn's spooky picture. Shortly, they are interrupted by Surtees, the black lifer platoon sergeant, who has staged a move-out in their absence and now threatens them with charges. But their stoned drunken distance is even too much for him to travel. As Quinn launches into a version of "The Little Boy Who Cried Wolf," doing all the parts himself, the sergeant departs. They are too far into the mansion of death, Quinn with his photo-premonition already of a bad end, Dosier with all the "horny-headed whispers" he has started to hear, has been hearing for a good while, he realizes, hears now only and incessantly (160). "Die, die, die" they chant, "I'm gonna pound

you down to pulp and bad dreams, pound you down to whispers" (160).
The whispers speak, and the vision enlarges:

> I stand in some mansion foyer amidst the thirty-two polished points
> of the compass rose parquet, head craned at the oval spirals of ma-
> hogany railing rungs, and stomping little feet and corduroy trouser
> legs thrown over the banisters. Round and round I turn, following
> the race, round and round. Die, die, the little brats chant, la-la, la-la,
> upsy-daisy, and then they begin tumbling the bodies out and over.
> The legs and arms flail, the green jungle shirts with slanted breast
> pockets, billowing and flapping. The high-pitched, death-rattle, wide-
> eyed screams echo down the floors. (161)

The housecats watch TV, switch channels, mutter " 'Tsk-tsk' and
'Can't *someone* get those children to be still?' " (161). Meanwhile, "the gen-
erals and chicken fucken colonels and rah-rah senators lean over the upper-
most railing, grinning and smiling perfect ear-to-ear smiles, and pound
each other on the back jolly-good-show fashion and pass around glad-
hand handshakes." Amidst "martinis" and "rotgut bar scotch" and cocktail
plates of "liver pâté" and "beef tartare" in cocktail helpings, "General
Westhisface keeps saying over and over, 'They're damn fine killers, eh?
*Damn* fine' " (161). Somewhere in the middle of the whole stoned phantasmagoria, one tries endlessly to climb a mountain of dead, the reason
the world is not flat, one now realizes, "and see home" (161–62). And to
all of them, the dead in memory, the dead imagined, one only cries out,
"Don't die, don't die, goddamn it" (162). "Goddamn it, don't die," Dosier
himself cries out, to Lorenz, Corbin, Haney in the fated picture, "Teleck,"
who "just by the look of him, ain't long for this world" (162), to Willie
and Atevo and Trobridge dead also, to the brother, Eddie, alive but "stone
deaf and blind," and somehow, he already knows, to Quinn. Quinn too,
alive now, but somehow also already dead. "Just because we're standing in
a red-and-black bull's-eye and the shit is falling and bouncing and piling
close around us faster than we can catch it or shovel it aside, don't you
go off somewhere and die on me too" (162). But that is the way of it
in the mansion of death, and thus in a half-assed chapel on a firebase in
sight of Nui Ba Dinh, one scared kid hallucinates and watches and sees it,
while another one cries over a photograph and then eventually just sleeps,

"stretched out, leaning breathless and motionless, gazing north and east from our circle of yellow air at the fuzzy, silvery silhouette of Black Virgin Mountain — trying to see home," Dosier concludes, almost in benediction, "just like me" (165).

Here, so he will eventually come to speak it, in fantasy as in fact, and later in fact as in fantasy, is the secret of the mansion of death, the message under the sign of the GI cross. "Nobody goes home from here," Dosier writes (278). "The war has swallowed me, it has clamped off all the veins, and I'm high on dope and Darvon and mo-gas and sick and tired of the fucking footrace, so I jump down in front of the track, with the bowie knife between my teeth, and snarl." He goes on:

> How did I come to love it so? What evil taller than myself did I grapple and wrestle and throw to the ground? Subdued. Did it come with a night moon, or is it something inside, this pain in my chest? Did it enter quickly, leaving this crablike scar on my eye, or does it hover here like a poltergeist, whispering?
>
> I can never go home. I just want to see it. I won't say a thing, cross my heart. I just want to see it one more time. I want to smell it, touch it ever so lightly, put my ear to it and hear it tap, tap, tap. (279)

And later, even as one can hear the phone ringing on the other end, the call from the phone booth in California to the place that used to be called home, one begins by wanting to say perhaps, "Hi, somebody, I'm home," but then realizes, in fact, that it is, no, not home, not ever, really, not home, just here:

> I have traveled to a place where the dead lie above the ground in rows and bunches. Time has gone somewhere without me. This is not my country, not my time. My skin is drawn tight around my eyes. My clothes smell of blood. I bleed inside. I am water. I am stone. I am swift-running water, made from snow. I am stone, chipped from giant granite boulders, small shards, jagged and sharp-edged, sliding down the rockface past the timberline. Chips and flakes break away from me, and sparks sometimes. I have not come home, Ma. I have gone ahead, gone back. There is a glass between us, we cannot speak. I hear voices, I have seen a wraith, Ma. He wore black boots and britches and strange livery. He talked to me, he whispered, he laughed. He

touched my stomach with the back of his hand, like people will put an arm on your shoulder when they speak, and it burns. (307)

That, as *Close Quarters* reveals from beginning to middle to end, and as *Paco's Story* on the landscape of aftermath will begin to reveal all over again, is the first clean fact, spirit and letter reified in one inflexible iron law, fact as true as whatever standard of verification comes along. It is fact, as in fact of life, spoken in death's old embrace. Nobody goes home. Dosier lives. Quinn dies. But nobody really goes home. There is ritual and there is reality, the shadow taken for the act, the act always speaking the memory of the shadow. One takes a wife, works at climbing down. One honors memory, watches old slides with a friend's parents: " 'This is Suoi Dau,' I say, 'Just after Quinn transferred in. . . . This is Tay Ninh Base Camp. That's me and Quinn and Stepik, the medic, and the seven-three. . . . That's the Nui Ba Dinh. The Black Virgin Mountain. . . . This is the Truce Day body count. . . . And this is Quinn's girl friend from Tay Ninh. . . . This is a body count I do not recognize' " (332–33). One remembers that and all the rest and Quinn's saying right out one night "No, I ain't going home, it don't matter what I do, I don't care anymore." And one realizes that "he knew it way back then, that he had changed, and laid himself out for it and gathered it in and worked on it with his arms in a hug, hands fisted, grinning that grin of his" (335). One visits at the end the newest room in the mansion of death and says just, simply, "God-damn you, Quinn," the curse that is the profoundest cry of memory and love, the quick honoring the dead in a day's muttered version of the awful judgment, Dosier and Quinn and America and Vietnam and the burden of nothing less than history itself.

This function of *Close Quarters* as at once personal odyssey of sense making and imaginative reinscription of collective myth is further extended in the complex experimentalism of Heinemann's second novel, the tale of a wandering, crippled veteran entitled *Paco's Story*. The epigraph to that first text has been the Shakespearean "Buzz, Buzz." It is from act 2, scene 2, where Hamlet, feigning madness and having cryptically hinted to his old friends Rosencrantz and Guildenstern the design of his imposture, responds to the old time-server Polonius's news of the entry of the actors soon to conduct the play-within-the-play. ("Upon my honor — " Polonius has protested. Hamlet has replied, quickly silencing him, "Then came each actor on his ass — .") And appropriately, Philip Dosier in his war story has proved "a true son of the empire" (53), going sweet prince–like into the full murder madness that is history. The epigraph to the second work is from *Black Elk Speaks*. "Then I heard a cry in our own language," the narrator tells us, "and it said: 'Do not touch me! I am Crazy Horse!'" Out of the ongoing murder madness of our wars and through the very cry of language itself, Paco Sullivan the American in his peace story now attempts to make a return.

"Let's begin with the first clean fact, James: This ain't no war story. War stories are out — one, two, three, and a heave-ho, into the lake you go with all the other alewife scuz and foamy harbor scum" (1). Thus the complex design of memory and art in *Paco's Story* encodes itself from the first sentences onward. Who is speaking? Who is listening? What, then, in this "Vietnam" novel we have opened, if not a "war" story, is the real story to be? All these questions we ask at once as we are plunged posthaste into what is in fact surely one of the most grisly, graphic, and one-pointed war stories ever recorded. Specifically, it is the one about Paco Sullivan's participation in and sole survival of the battle in Vietnam of Fire Base Harriette, a massacre so complete as to have ended in a holocaust of friendly fire claiming his entire infantry company. "Oh, we dissolved all right, everybody but Paco," the narration tells us; and in that moment as well, it goes on,

> our screams burst through the ozone; burst through the rags and tatters and cafe-curtain-looking aurora borealis, and so forth and suchlike; clean as a whistle; clean as a new car — unfucked with and frequency perfect out into God's everlasting Cosmos. Out where it's hot enough to shrivel your eyeballs to the shape and color and consistency of raisins; out where it's cold enough to freeze your breath to resemble slab plastic.
>
> And we're pushing up daisies for half a handful of millennia (we're *all* pushing up daisies, James), until we're powder finer than talc, *finer* than fine, as smooth and hollow as an old salt lick — but that blood-curdling scream is rattling all over God's ever-loving Creation like a BB in a boxcar, only louder. (17)

Who is speaking? Quickly we have learned *that* unnerving answer: they are the dead, speaking to us from the country that is the war. As might be expected, however, handling the idea remains another matter. Brash, insistent, alternately menacing and chummy, the narration here struts its slangy bravado like some voice-over bad dream that won't go away. And so even as the war story at hand does yield to the new drama of loneliness and pain now being played out by Paco Sullivan back in the world, that other story remains as well, a primal text of memory now set forth in endless self-inscription upon waking consciousness at large.

Who is listening? Larger responses to that begin to come upon us only at painful length. Who is listening, this James? Is it, as Heinemann himself has suggested, James the disciple, James the brother of John, King James, Henry James, James Joyce, James Jones, James as in "Hey Jack," as you say in asking for a cigarette or a light?[14] The narrator is at pains to explain to James about things, especially concerning Vietnam, that the average person might not know—tactics, nomenclature, soldier slang, etc. "You James," he says often, in one combination or another. For a good while in the book, one is repeatedly inclined to ask, "Who is James?" Then, at a certain point, one realizes that the proper question is, "Who are you?"

What, then, is the Vietnam story at hand? It is exactly the story that takes place at the site where all these vectors of narration converge. It is a war story that becomes a peace story and in the same moment a peace story that can only be so by remaining a war story. It is a tale told by people who by definition could not possibly tell it to people who by consensus could not possibly wish to hear it. It is in sum the newest version of the oldest Vietnam story in the world: a war story that is a peace story; a Vietnam story that is an America story; a true story that is unrepentantly false; a false story that is heartbreakingly true. Here once again, in newest form of narrative experiment, sense making after our war seeks to recover the old, lost site of historical-mythic transaction, the original discourse of the tribe. And so, accordingly, even as we struggle to situate ourselves amidst the terms of the discourse, this one, like all good Vietnam stories, has already begun to spin meanings out of its own impossibility, to become *Paco's Story*. A triumph of creative falsehood, it becomes in fact such a "true" story as to inscribe itself into consciousness with all the power that can be summoned up only from the deepest springs of collective mythic imagining.

*Paco's Story:* it is the story, then, of all the stories, of what happened to the Americans and Vietnamese in Vietnam, of what must now continue to happen in America if any of that is to be understood. It is a novel (after the story of chapter 1, entitled, appropriately, "The First Clean Fact") about a returned veteran, the only survivor of the battle of Fire Base Harriette, saved by "God's Marvelous Plan," (the title of chapter 2), riding a bus and about to encounter his share (the title soon to come of chapter 3) of "The Thanks of a Grateful Nation." Scarred, broken, bent, his legs a patchwork of bone fragment, steel rod, pin, bolt, he gets off a bus near a town (the narrator calls it Boone) somewhere vaguely in the middle of America.

It is the story of "Paco Coming into Town." It is also the story of "The Texas Lunch," a place run by Ernest Monroe, a marine veteran of Guadalcanal and Iwo Jima, where Paco gets a job washing dishes. By day he works until his bones ache. At night, he lives alone in the seedy hotel across the street, with his booze, his pills, his pain, his memories, his bad dreams.

It is the story also of the stories of Ernest Monroe of his old war (stories, it turns out, very like Paco's, displaced to the experience of another American boy in another time and another place [125–31]). It is the story of Jesse, another Vietnam vet wandering America "looking for a place to cool out" (155); of his plans for a *real* Vietnam monument (one would move past the names of the honored dead to a giant cauldron full of money floating in a mixture of every kind of shit and pollution known to man [158–59]); and of his departing as air on a hitchhiker's whistle of "The Emperor Waltz" (164).

It is the story of Paco and the college girl, Cindy, who lives in the room next door in the Geronimo Hotel. Sometimes at night, back across the street in the Texas Lunch, when he is working late and the light is on in her room, Paco watches the girl. Sometimes, when the light is off and he is working late in the Texas Lunch, the girl watches Paco. She teases him sometimes when he comes home, leaving her door open a crack and showing herself to him. He scuttles crablike up the stairs and always just misses getting in. It is the story about the way he often lies there in his room and listens to the girl having sex with her college-boy boyfriend. It is the story of his lying there nights and often thinking about having her himself.

In this connection, it is the story as well from the chapter entitled

"Good Morning to You Lieutenant," which also comes to him sometimes in his bed, the one about how they captured the woman VC ambusher who killed two of their friends and how all of them, Jigs, Jonesy, Gallagher, and the rest, rapists, ambushers, ear collectors, American boys, endlessly gang raped her from behind and then watched while Gallagher executed her by scalping with a .357 magnum. It is also the one about how Paco killed a man in hand-to-hand combat, his adversary feeling the point of the American's long sharp filet knife twisting at his heart, crying out in the passion of his dying, "I pray you, please don't kill me. Oh God! Please do not do this, I beg you" (195). And it of course is the one about the dreams Paco has endlessly, the ghost whispers the old buddies bring around at night, the escape dream, the waiting room dream, the execution dream, the going home dream.

It is finally also the story entitled "Paco the Sneak" about how, one morning, Paco steals into Cathy's room, finds a diary, and reads in it and about how then, that same morning, he climbs aboard the westbound bus at the Texaco just outside town, the place where he arrived, and is gone. Most specifically, it is the one about the story that occurs within that story, the one in the diary itself. For there, in one last crucial version, we find Paco's story inscribed out of nightmare memory of self into a larger and corresponding nightmare domain of nothing less than national consciousness at large.

It begins harmlessly enough, this glance in someone's day in the life of America book, here that of a girl named Cathy, a student at Wyandotte College scribbling about family happenings, her brother's new bimbo girlfriend, fucking her own little Marty-boy. She mentions the new guy working at the Texas Lunch, "good-looking with nice tight buns, . . . cute, you know, but covered with scars. Wounded in the war, Unc says. Scars everywhere." She ponders the attraction, wonders about "sleeping with two guys at once" (202).

Suddenly things begin to go hard and garish. Within further entries on the imagined relative sexual merits of the two men of her dreams, she begins to envision and describe Paco exclusively and obsessively. She imagines him, sees things that happen but that she could not possibly see. She sees him in the room after work with his fatigue, the scars, the pills, the cheap booze. She sees him arising from his bed, unable to sleep in

the heat, getting drunker and drunker and gimp-dancing about and shouting things like "Come on, hit me! Hit me! Hit me!" and "Bang! Bang!
Bang-bang-bang!"

"And his room is so depressing," she goes on. "Fading wallpaper, no
telling what the motif was, and that tacky, shabby linoleum, and he's a
dingy, dreary, smelly, shabby, *shabby* little man" (205).

The entries continue: "He gives me the creeps. He has such a dogged
way of working. He gets up in the morning, dresses. Clean, dirty, it's all
the same to him. Goes straight to work, doesn't talk much with anyone.
He gets this set look on his face. Gives me the creeps. Unc says he wonders
if the guy knows where he is half the time."

And further:

"Aunt Myrna says he has a way of stiffening up and staring right
through you. As if he's a ghost. Or you're the ghost."

"How could I have ever thought it might be fun to sleep with him?
Unc says that creeps like him are best got rid of, and is going to start
working on him (206)."

She records things he cries out, lines from his dreams. She imagines
his waking up, his falling back in the bed, "rubbing his back, moaning"
(207). Shortly her imaginings of him come to inhabit her imaginings of
herself. She records her dream that he comes to her room (as he himself
has dreamed of doing) and takes her finally, a hard, angry, somehow (as
he too has imagined it) brutal coupling. And now in the dream, suddenly,
hideously, he "begins to peel the scars off as if they were a mask . . . as if
he's unbuttoning the snaps of a jacket . . . like you'd see somebody pull up
dried spaghetti from a kitchen table" (208). And now, she goes on, "he's
holding me down with that hard belly of his, and lays the scars on my chest.
It *burns* . . ." (208). He pulls them all off, making sounds like "screams,"
"stitches ripping," and now, she writes, "he lays them across my breasts
and belly—tingling and burning—lays them in my hair, wrapping them
around my head, like a skull cap. And when each scar touches me, I feel the
suffocating burn, hear the scream" (208–9). Then the dream has ended. "I
just shuddered," she puts in a last line of entry, recording the aftermath.
"It made my skin crawl" (209). Paco closes the book, goes and packs his
AWOL bag, leaves a short note of thank-you for Ernest Monroe, cadges
a ride out to the Texaco, and waits for the bus. At last, "he climbs aboard,

pays his fare, and the bus departs — coasting down the long incline of the entrance ramp — and is soon gone" (210).

What we have been reading, we see as Paco vanishes, is the confluence of the last and latest versions of his Story, the genetic text, experience, memory, dream, imagining, diary record, commonplace recital of visible event, a day in the life of America after the latest of her wars. And of this confluence of "stories" — no single one of them more true or false, real or unreal, than any other — an experienced totality called *Paco's Story* inscribes itself like a ghost whisper into the consciousness that is our own. It is the teeming burn-scar-fragment hieroglyph we ourselves must take on and wear in emblem of our dread, rapt attention, the puzzlement, fascination, guilt, attraction, loathing, the wish that it would go away and leave one in peace or that one could escape it somehow and go live one's self some-where in peace. We are in fact mightily relieved when it is ended, not unlike the curious, fascinated, horrified girl from a new, essentially memory-less, Vietnam-less generation, whose diary, since we have now pried into it along with Paco, the record of innermost thoughts and confessions, is now also our diary and thereby a precise measure of the price exacted by the Paco Sullivans of this world upon the post-Vietnam American soul.

Paco Sullivan. In the very name itself, even, is the measure of the whole business, a war story that tries in literally every way imaginable to make itself into a peace story, and in the same moment a peace story that cannot help being an endless war story. The last name, it may be remembered, is a family name familiarly celebrated in myth from Ernest Monroe's old American war: the Sullivans, five brothers serving aboard the same ship, nearly an entire generation wiped out in an old war of brav-ery and sacrifice. The first name, on the other hand, Paco, is distinctly a given one of those who have this time borne the burden in a new war of needless slaughter and uniform pain and waste. It is a veteran's echo here, particularly, in memory of a war fought often by boys with such jivelike and street-sounding names. And it is also an echo of the single word — peace — that is always, of course, the last one in every veteran's prayer.

# AMERICAN DRAMATIST

## David Rabe

MRS. HUMMEL. No, you had many fathers, many men, movie men, filmdom's great—all of them, those grand old men of yesteryear, they were your father. The Fighting Seventy-sixth, do you remember, oh, I remember, little Jimmy, what a tough little mite he was, and how he leaped upon that grenade, did you see, my God what a glory, what a glorious thing with his little tin hat.

PAVLO. My real father!

MRS. HUMMEL. He was like them, the ones I showed you in movies. I pointed them out.

—David Rabe, *The Basic Training of Pavlo Hummel*

All I knew in Vietnam were facts, nothing more: simple facts of such complexity that the job of communicating any part of them accurately seemed impossibly beyond my reach. So I kept no journal and even my letters grew progressively more prosaic, fraudulent, dull, and fewer and fewer. Cliches were welcomed, as they always are, when there is no real wish to see what they hide.

—David Rabe, Introduction to *The Basic Training of Pavlo Hummel*
   and *Sticks and Bones*

Of the three major American dramatists of the Vietnam era whose works came to public prominence during the 1970s and eighties—David Mamet, David Rabe, and Sam Shepard[1]—Rabe is always likely to be thought of, whatever the course of his career, as the "Vietnam" playwright. On the basis of the two controversial, original, and highly acclaimed works whereby he made his entry into national prominence—*The Basic Training of Pavlo Hummel* and *Sticks and Bones*—the treatment of the experience of Vietnam in popular drama was certainly the crucial ingredient in the establishing of his critical reputation. And with the addition of a third "Vietnam" play, *Streamers*, and the further establishing thereby of the critical mythos of a prizewinning Rabe "Vietnam" trilogy (and far in advance, as N. Bradley Christie has noted, of any Vietnam novel's winning a National Book Award or any Vietnam film's winning an Oscar [105]), the centrality of the war in his work has become the major basis of his reputation in academic criticism and scholarship as well.[2]

But as with many of his counterparts in the novel, in poetry, and in the literature of witness, the Vietnam dramatist David Rabe is now also an American dramatist in his generation and in this case the author of seven major American plays.[3] He is to be sure the young Vietnam veteran of indisputably original genius and the instant protégé of Joseph Papp who literally burst upon the scene with two dramas of the war so complete and arresting in their creative power as to become instant canonical texts in our dramatic literature. He is also the figure, however, whose third play, *The Orphan*, extended the concept of the family drama of violence begun in *Pavlo Hummel* and continued in *Sticks and Bones* into a cosmography of families gone wrong all the way from Agamemnon to Manson. A fourth important work, *In the Boom Boom Room*, next moved again, explicitly, to contemporary family matters of violence in America and specifically to the violence done to women. And only then, finally, in a fifth major production,[4] *Streamers*, did Rabe return to the particular matter of Vietnam, this time in a barracks drama perhaps ostensibly reminiscent of *Pavlo Hummel* but now again further expanded to confront issues of racial and sexual violence in American domestic culture as well.

After *Streamers*, certainly the culmination of a complex early development, the House of Rabe has continued to enlarge its precincts. In *Goose and Tomtom*, perhaps the most eccentric of the plays, the dramatist lets us in on a highly experimental jewel-thief comedy caper set in the back rooms of contemporary urban life. And in *Hurlyburly*, once again clearly an attempt to mark the newest intersections of sexual power and violence in American popular culture, the site is moved to the tract communities of southern California, full of creative types and failed Hollywood dreamers of the dream, latest pure precinct of quotidian national despair.

> I knew instantly the set-piece sequences that could be lifted and knew also the kind of surreal play that would result. Sensing the pressure of Joe Papp's position and power, I felt a real anger beginning. Not because I had some fixed theory of realistic theater that I wanted to protect, but rather because *Sticks and Bones* with its nonreal style was already written and *The Orphan*, a third play, which moved even further into fantasy and "theatricality," had been drafted. As a result,

my need was extreme for *Pavlo* to put down roots in the real. It would be the base from which I moved outward with other work." (*Pavlo Hummel*, xiv–xv)

So Rabe, even as his first play, *Pavlo Hummel*, remained in initial production, outlined the reflexive architecture of reality *and* imagination that would also become the architecture of a career. And so now, to attend even to that early play is to wonder at the power of its unfolding. What happens when Audie Murphy moves to the six o'clock news? What happens when Gomer Pyle shows up drunk and dinky dow in a Saigon dive? What happens when we find out this time that both are dead before they are alive, fragged, blown apart (and only later we learn from a grenade thrown by an American soldier), and like the eternal GI in all the stories, stone dead and just too dumb to lie down? What happens, in sum, when a whole tradition of popular myth goes to Vietnam and back as our worst American rerun?

In the immediate text before us, it must be admitted, such issues of complex mythic design often seem largely subsumed from the outset in the tiresome, even sordid details of the commonplace. Yet as imaged in its very title, the drama already prepares its own explosion of larger resonances. *The Basic Training of Pavlo Hummel*: in testimony to the suggestiveness of the phrase itself as encapsulated myth of American manhood, the first serious review article about Vietnam drama at large, by Robert Asahina in 1978, was in fact entitled "The Basic Training of American Playwrights." And here, moreover, the titular character *is* Pavlo the Pavlovian. He is Pavlo Hummel, a funny name to go along with funny behavior. He is the platoon numbnuts, the dufus, the American boy whose father ran out on him (45–46), trying to fit in. He fabricates the mythic genealogy of a gangster uncle executed at San Quentin and a personal history of car stealing (23). He listens breathlessly to a corporal's Vietnam stories about having to shoot old farmers and baby girls with satchel charges strapped to them (40–43). He is the oddball, the short round, literally asking to get beaten up (41), the one who pisses people off and then berates acting squad leaders for not doing their duty in stopping the trouble he creates (55). He is the goofy one who somehow takes the training seriously, tries to learn something, excels at furnace fireman duty, finds a future in the old Queen of Battle. "I get made anything but infantry," he tells his buddy Hinkle, "I'm gonna fight it, man. I'm gonna fight it. You wanna go infantry with me, Hinkle?

You're infantry and good at it too, you're your own man, I'm gonna wear my uniform everywhere when I'm home, Hinkle. My mother's gonna be so excited when she sees me. She's just gonna yell. I get nervous when I think about if she should hug me. You gonna hug your mother when you get home?" (48).

And this truly is the up-front dimension of the play, for anyone who knows anything about the army, about American boys, how incredibly real it all is, how incredibly it strikes us here as being *for* real, the whole cacophonous, claustrophobic boot camp spectacle, maggots in the shit, dipsticks in the slime. There is the sergeant, Tower, that face always in your face, screaming the argot, the cadences, the incredible litany of insult, "slits," "pussies," "ladies," "scumbags," "lower than whaleshit on the bottom of the ocean"; the hypnotic lectures, the endless nomenclatures, the canned orientations, the mindless formulas of the endless recitations of petty authority. "NOW YOU ARE TRAINEES, ALL YOU PEOPLE, AND YOU LISTEN UP," the voice screams. "I ASK YOU WHAT IS YOUR FIRST NAMES, YOU TELL ME 'TRAINEES'!" "TRAINEE!" the men shout back. "TRAINEE, SERGEANT!" the voice screams back at them. "TRAINEE SERGE—," the men attempt to reply. "I CAN'T HEAR YOU!" the voice interrupts. "*TRAINEE, SERGEANT!*" they now correctly reply.

This is the life-world of basic training, the "world" of the army, the "world" of American boys as real as any we can know. Yet it is also, quite literally, as we see from the play's first scene, a death-world as well. If Pavlo has one drill sergeant in life, Tower, who speaks incessantly in his face, he is also supplied with one from the outset in death, Ardell, who speaks incessantly in his soul. The former becomes a guide to death in life; the latter, as I have described him elsewhere, a kind of GI Virgil, becomes a guide to life in death. The point is that "reality" *in* the play is constantly filtered through the basic structural metaphor *of* the play as its own other, of a here that is already there, as there is already here; of a life that already awaits a death, as death already awaits a life. That is, we are made to see from the outset that for all our sense of the incredibly absolute "present" reality of the play, it is in the same moment a work of immense imaginative otherness. It is the drama of an American boy who lives to fulfill the structural destiny of being already dead, to meet his great last scene in the first scene, born in the U.S.A., born in Vietnam, born from the outset, like Ron Kovic's Fourth of July firecracker, into the national mythography of the grave. It is the drama, finally, of an American boy who finds his basic training literally in every way imaginable, a whole spectacle of dread reifications.

For Pavlo, in a word, is one big bad American movie waiting to happen, a walking mix-up of memory and cliche, his brother calls him, "a fuckin' myth-maker." "I gotta go to Vietnam, Mickey," Pavlo says. "Vietnam don't even exist," Mickey replies. "I gotta go to it," Pavlo persists. "Arizona, man," Mickey replies; "that's where you're going. Wyoming." Pavlo protests. The army has made something of him. "Look at me!" he shouts. "I'm different! I'm different than I was! I'm not the same anymore. I was an asshole. I'm not an asshole anymore. I'm not an asshole anymore!" (66). "You're a cartoon," Mickey replies, "you know that" (69). The characterization could not be more apt. A model of goofy bravado, he makes his way toward the inevitable confrontation with his American fate. And concurrently, the play itself, at *its* sundry levels of design, moves to a similar and awful converging. The scene with Mickey yields to close order drill with Tower and instruction on battlefield first aid, which in turn merges into a phone call to an old girlfriend and a fantasy conversation with his mother about another mother with a boy dead in Vietnam, about the father that ran away, about all the fathers in all the old movies. Now he is in a bar in Vietnam that is somehow for a moment a hospital ward and then again a bar. He is in bed with the bar girl Yen. He is in drill formation with Tower shouting commands. He is supposed to love his rifle like a good woman, like his own pecker. He humps Yen and marches to the old Jody song, the one about "JODY GOT YOUR GIRL AND GONE/ JODY HUMPIN' ON AND ON" (83). "Something of Pavlo's making love to Yen," we are told in the stage directions, is supposed to be "in his marching" (83).

Now he is in it for good. Dead once already, he is now back in Vietnam, in the hospital as a corpsman, then transferred to combat, wounded once, twice, getting further in. "I'm diggin' it man," he is soon telling Ardell. "Blowin' people away. Cuttin' 'em down" (95). He lives out the scene he has heard about with the old man and the satchel charges, himself now, even twice wounded, in it mainly for the killing pure and simple. "They're sayin' you can go home when you been hit twice and you don't even check," Ardell admonishes him. "You wanna go back out, you're thinkin', get you one more gook, get you one more slopehead, make him know the reason why" (99). "That's right," Pavlo shouts, scooping up his rifle, "They're killing everybody!" By the time he has recovered from a third wound, the carnage is out of everyone's control. He is in the killing and he is in it for good, full and regulation. "Hummel," asks the officer to whom he is referred about any possibility of leaving, "wouldn't you be home if you were eligible to be home?" (102).

Home now indeed can only be the final scene that has been the first scene and somehow all the other ones in between. Pavlo is in a bar getting in a quarrel with a lifer, Sergeant Wall, over Yen the whore. Back in basic training, a lifer, Sergeant Tower, is beginning to lecture on knowing the enemy. The fight escalates in the bar. Tower switches over to a lecture on grenades and how to use them and what they can do to a man (105–6). Meanwhile, back in Saigon, an actual grenade rolls stage center, the ultimate training aid, so to speak; and suddenly, the lesson objective becomes the random death that has been waiting all along. One scene completes itself in the other, grenade orientation with a vengeance, the latest national nightmare in a nutshell: a lifer and a kid, two GIs and a bargirl, a fragging incident in Saigon, America in Vietnam; or, how to get blown away in one easy step in the country called the war.

Thus the basic training of Pavlo Hummel: the short, happy life of your basic American fuckup. "Soooooooo . . . that about it. That bout all I got to say," Ardell thus concludes. "Am I right, Pavlo? Did I tell you true? You got anything to say? Oh, man, I know you do, you say it out?" "You tell me," he exhorts the corpse, "what you think of the cause? What you think a gettin' your ass blown clean off a freedom's frontier: what you think a bein' R.A. Army lifer?" And one last time Pavlo does say it out, does say it out in a single word. "Sheeeeee . . . ittttt," he begins, almost embarrassed. "Shit!" And how about "all the folks back home?" Ardell prods. "They shit!" Pavlo returns. "It all shit." "It shit." Ardell now coaches, Pavlo again his "*main* man," his "main motherfuckin' man" (106). "SHIT!" Pavlo shouts. "OH, SHIT! . . . SHIT." Now he howls it into silence, "SHHHHHHHHHHHIIIIIIIIIIIITTTTTTTTTTTTTTtttttttt!" Pavlo in death has the final word on the basic training that has been his American life, and the final word is shit. "I'm dead," he utters, in final recognition. "You *home*, Pavlo," Ardell returns, beginning the new cycle of orientation. Appropriately, the play ends as it only can, with Pavlo present at his own funeral and one last close order song, about soldiers and leave and girls and screwing and Jody and misery and death, the new basic training song of Pavlo Hummel and the old love song of American boys in the army.

> Saw some stockin's on the street
> Wished I was between those feet
> Once a week, I get to town.
> They see me comin', they jus' lay down
> Sergeant, sergeant can't you see
> All this misery's killing me
> Ain't no matter what you do
> Jody done it all to you.

The funeral formalities are completed. "Lift your heads and lift 'em high," the play concludes, the kid in the coffin and the coffin center stage: "Pavlo Hummel passin' by" (109).

So, with Pavlo at the conclusion, we have come to the dead end of all the mythic convergences: Pavlo in America; Pavlo in Vietnam; Pavlo as America; America in Vietnam. Of the hero-victim here, Rabe himself has written, he must possess "a certain eagerness and wide-eyed spontanaeity, along with a true, real, and complete inability to graph the implications of what he does." He "is in fact lost," but "has, for a long time, no idea that he is lost." Some of this yields to basic training. "His physical efficiency, even his mental efficiency increases," Rabe goes on. Still, "real insight never comes." He concludes: "Toughness and cynicism replace open eagerness, but he will learn only that he is lost, not how, why, or even where. His talent is for leaping into the fire" (110).

In *Pavlo Hummel* the setting is described as "The United States Army, 1965–67." In *Sticks and Bones*, it is described simply as the family home. The dates will be supplied by events, which begin to appear shortly. For the moment there are family slide pictures, a visit by the local priest, reminiscences on an old and valued friend. Shortly, something of more particular history obtrudes. The "Government" has called. "No, he's all right, he's coming home," the father, Ozzie, reassures the family (122). The family, Ozzie, Harriet, and Ricky, are about to receive a delivery. The delivery is David, Ozzie's and Harriet's son and Ricky's brother. He has been wounded in Vietnam, made blind. The war has come home with a vengeance, a major effort. It is being delivered to America's doorstep. "I've got trucks backed up out there for blocks," announces the Sergeant Major in charge.

> Other boys. I got to get on to Chicago, and some of them to Denver and Cleveland, Reno, New Orleans, Boston, Trenton, Watts, Atlanta. And when I get back they'll be layin' all over the grass; layin' there in pieces all over the grass, their backs been broken, their brains jellied, their insides turned to garbage. One-legged boys and no-legged boys. I'm due in Harlem; I got to get to the Bronx and Queens, Cincinnati, Saint Louis, Reading. I don't have time for coffee. I got deliveries to make all across this country. (131–32)

Now the time has been specified. It is the time of Vietnam and the time when Vietnam comes home to America. The play is to be a historical case study, the basic training of an American family, so to speak, of people investing themselves in "an image of how the perfectly happy family should appear," as Rabe himself has put it, and now having to deal with a son who has been to Vietnam and who now "has come home to behave in a manner that makes him no longer lovable" (225).

Yet by now we have been gripped by an equally arresting "other" reality as well. For if the show before us is the one so described above, it is also, equally, *the* Ozzie and Harriet show. It is *about* Ozzie and Harriet and Ricky and what happens to the Nelson house when David comes home from Vietnam, blind, haunted, ungrateful and mean, in many ways in fact the hateful little boy he has always been yet now strange and mumbling and always attended, somehow in vision *and* mysterious presence, by a woman named Zung, a yellow Vietnamese whore. Again, as in *Pavlo Hummel*, we are afoot on a landscape at once so familiar and so utterly defamiliarized as to challenge our very categories of recognition, *The Adventures of Ozzie and Harriet* now packaged back at us as Vietnam-era America in the gross plenitude of its pain, confusion, and waste.

The reality of the play, in short, is measured exactly against the centrality of the Nelson family mythos *as received and popularly constituted cultural fact*. The Nelson family here, indeed, as Pamela Cooper shows us in her excellent discussion, is in a single moment appallingly yet simply what passes for reality in America. It is the pure abstract or epitome of " 'instant culture' " born of a media-made "consumer society" with its

"various forms of quick and easy gratification" and now forced to encounter "the wreckage created by its sanctioning of the war in Vietnam"
(615). As Rabe himself seems to have suggested indirectly by offering at
least one production with other names, it could as easily perhaps be the
Cleaver family or the Anderson family (not to mention, at a deeper dramatic level, as various commentators have noted, the Loman family or
the family of *All My Sons*), a media-generated image of happiness reified
as mass-cultural perception into assumed cultural fact. Exactly, then, presented *on a stage* as drama of life itself reflexively generated by drama of
popular myth, *Sticks and Bones* quite literally becomes its own site of origin, existing "in a middle ground between what is thought of in theater
terms as 'realism' and 'fantasy,'" with "precise stylization" thus "a crucial
production factor." "Though it is set in a living room," Rabe tells us, "the
play is primarily taking place in theatrical space" (xxii). The language of
production, of origination, of autonomous dramatic or theatric reification
is crucial here. Creating a double or reflexive middle ground, a theatrical
site of infinite self-supplementation, the scene before us becomes a place
at once as thoroughly real as it is ineluctably mythified, and as thoroughly
mythified as it is ineluctably real.

In this case, "here" is the quintessential fifties happy family plunged
into the quintessential unhappy American family drama of the sixties, the
family plunged into the abyss that was America in Vietnam and later Vietnam in America. It is what happened to all the happy families after they
have been touched by the experience of Vietnam—when it has come into
their houses and across all the myth-media wherein they have been mainly
used to seeing only their own happy selves—like a bad child one no longer
knows, can no longer handle, full of strange gibberings and guilts. It is
the realization of terrible American child latencies. "I . . . seen him do
some awful, awful things, old Dave," Ozzie tells Ricky, even as they have
awaited David's arrival. "He was a mean . . . foul-tempered little baby"
(126). It is that realization now, there, downstairs, upstairs, in the hall, on
the stairs, in all the old familiar places in the house.

Thus we are seized upon by the central dramatic figuration of *Sticks
and Bones*, the seamless structure of a dramatic reality aping a perceived
reality of American lives that is itself a pure function of popular dramatic
myth. The "Ozzie" character is, in fact, an "Ozzie" character, played by
an actor who may or may not look like, sound like, act like Ozzie, but *is*

Ozzie—now constituted at the level of cultural reality, and precisely to that degree, now for good and ill, precisely Ozzie (and not to mention, again, particularly in his puzzled late soliloquies, Willie Loman). In many ways, of course, he is always the old Ozzie. One can almost hear the voice, "Wellll, David . . . gee, I. . . ." And the fact of the matter is that one often does hear the voice. Even as things go increasingly badly with David in the house, Ozzie rationalizes, smooths it over with the old fatherly banalities. "Yes, sir," he calls out helpfully, guiding David down the stairs, "I think, all things considered, I think we can figure we're over the hump now and it's all downhill and good from here on in. I mean, we've talked things over, Dave, what do you say? The air's been cleared, that's what I mean— the wounds acknowledged, the healing begun. It's the ones that aren't ac-knowledged—the ones that aren't talked over—they're the ones that do the deep damage. That's always what happens" (152).

Similarly, Harriet is invariably a Harriet (and at concurrent and re-lated levels, Linda Loman, doting on her men, and Mrs. Krebs, beseeching Harold to pray with her) (136). She is incessantly offering new snacks and drinks, clearing away old, running to whip up something else in the kitchen. "Ohh, it's so good to hear men's voices in the house again, my two favorite men in the world—," she chirps brightly even as things near their terrible end, bustling around cleaning up party leftovers; "it's what I live for really. Would you like some coffee? Oh, of course you would. Let me put some on. Your humble servant at your command; I do your bidding, bid me be gone" (203).

Ricky throughout is relentlessly Ricky, full of gee-whiz and sitcom teenage imperviousness, hopping about with his flash camera, gorging himself on fudge and snacks, always ready with his guitar and a song. And David is David with a vengeance (even again, at the same time, Biff to his brother's Happy), the thoughtful one, the one with difficult questions, problems, girl trouble, the tough asker. Only now the questions and prob-lems have to do with what he has done and what has happened to him in Vietnam. And only now the girl is Zung the yellow whore. "They are the color of the earth, and what is white but winter and the earth under it like a suicide?" he intones. "Why didn't you tell me what I was?" (145). And again, one keeps wishing just to hear Ozzie, "Wellll David . . . gee, I. . . ." But now, amidst the wash of familiar illusion, we continue to attend to new, ugly factualities that no amount of stylization can contain. "Normality" keeps on going from bad to worse and beyond for this family that is its own mythic-cultural cliche, this objectification of social desire so powerful and redundant as by some invisible transference to be accepted as a standard of reality. And it is because the "norm" seems so normal that the truth and reality of things keep getting so ugly. It's the "buddies left behind," Ozzie says brightly in an attempt to account to David for the latter's dark mutterings. "Men serving together in war, it's a powerful thing—" he speculates, reflecting on his own remembered buddy lore of the home front, "true comradeship" (143). And this girl David keeps mentioning, Harriet chimes in, she was "a nurse, right . . . David?" Or perhaps, Ozzie adds hopefully, "one of them foreign correspondents, English maybe or French." Harriet: "A Wac or Red Cross girl?" Ozzie: "Redhead or blonde, Dave?" But everyone knows better. Ozzie fumbles on a bit, jokes about soldiers and their screwing, "glands and secretions" and the like; and soon the real shouting has begun, shouting about "a yellow whore. Some yellow ass. You put in your prick and humped your ass. You screwed some fucking yellow whore" (144). Harriet stands there and vomits through her hands (144–45). Now there is no time for smoothing over, the offer of a cigarette, some scrambled eggs, a call to the priest, the old charade of the family, small talk, reminiscences, slides, snacks. It is time for the real Nelson family to stand up.

Increasingly, Ozzie spews out his rancors, jealousies, unfulfilled dreams, his hoarded discontents with himself and his kind. "I'm tired of hearing you, Dave," he cries out. "You understand that? I'm tired of hearing you and your crybaby voice and your crybaby stories. And your crybaby slobbering and your . . . LOOK . . . AT . . . HIM! YOU MAKE ME WANT TO VOMIT! HARRIET! YOU!"—and now he has turned on his wife—"YOU! Your internal organs—your internal female organs—they've got some kind of poison in them. They're backing up some kind of rot into the world. I think you ought to have them cut out of you. I MEAN, I JUST CAN'T STOP THINKING ABOUT IT. I JUST CAN'T STOP THINKING ABOUT IT. LITTLE BITTY CHINKY KIDS HE WANTED TO HAVE! LITTLE BITTY CHINKY YELLOW KIDS! DIDN'T YOU! FOR OUR GRANDCHILDREN! LITTLE BITTY YELLOW PUFFY— . . . creatures! . . . FOR OUR GRANDCHILDREN!" (174). Harriet, too, possessed by the venom and David's own strange, insistent, even sexual presence, has stopped the pretense of understanding and family reintegration. "The human face was not meant to be that way," she blurts out. "A nose is a thinness—you know that. And lips that are not thin are ugly, and it is we who disappear, David. They don't change, and we are gone. It is our triumph, our whiteness. We disappear. What are you doing?" David's blind-man cane presses against her. "They take us back and down if our children are theirs—," she protests, "it is not a mingling of blood, it is theft" (208–9). Soon, it all comes down in America as it did in Vietnam to pure, racial murder, and now Ozzie, the man of the house, performs it in front of all of them. This American man, father of his returned American son, murders Zung, the son's yellow whore, screaming, "Oh, what is it that you want? I'm tired. I mean it. Forgive me. I'm sick of the sight of you, squatting all the time. In filth like animals, talking gibberish, your breath sick with rot. . . . And yet you look at me with those sad pleading eyes as if there is some real thing that can come between us when you're not even here. You are deceit." His fingers close around her neck. "I'm not David," he says, asserting his own old manhood. "I'm not silly and soft . . . little David. The sight of you sickens me. YOU HEAR ME, DAVID? Believe me. I am speaking my honest true feelings. I spit on you, the both of you; I piss on you and your eyes and pain. Flesh is lies. You are garbage and filth. You are darkness. I cast you down. Deceit. Animal. Dirty animal" (216).

Now, suddenly, Ozzie, having stepped fully out of TV character and into reality character, speaks his true lines and does in reality the terrible act of sexual-racial murder; and now, suddenly, strangely, the myth-charade is magically able to reassert itself. Ricky chirps up about a "really funny movie" he has just seen last night, "this really . . . funny, funny movie, . . . really funny" (217). Harriet tries to drum up a grocery-shopping expedition. Ozzie joins in, offering to do the groceries, talking about the movie. Now they can turn to the real question. What to do with David? And Ricky the ringleader, the bringer of family joy, has the answer. "Hey, Dave, listen, will you. I mean I know it's not my place to speak out and give advice and everything because I'm the youngest, but I just gotta say my honest true feelings and I'd kill myself if I were you, Dave. You're in too much misery. I'd cut my wrists. Honestly speaking, brother to brother, you should have done it long ago" (218). It is a great idea, family truth and honesty, and they all join in to help, even as one last time David attempts to obtrude his hurt, family fun. They soothe, deny, explain, comfort. Ozzie and Harriet give final instructions. Rick pops up for a last flash picture—it is a slide, we suddenly realize, that we have seen in the family amusement with which the play has opened, the one on the screen someone has described as "somebody sick." "Mom, I like David like this," Ricky says. "He's happier," Harriet replies. "We're all happier," Ozzie adds. "Too bad he's gonna die," Ricky interjects. "No, no," Ozzie explains, "he's not gonna die, Rick. He's only gonna nearly die. Only nearly." On the old, soothing, paternal non sequitur, the play ends. "Ohhhhhhhh," Ricky responds, satisfied. "Mmmmmmmmmmmmm," Harriet adds, satisfied too and happy. Ricky begins to play David a song on his guitar. "The music is alive and fast. It has a rhythm, a drive of happiness that is contagious. The lights slowly fade" (223).

Thus we witness the restoration of the quintessential American happy family, at once a function of utterly quotidian reality and of collective myth. Thus the play departs from and returns to a single horrific surface, having in the process, however, worked its way fully through the depths, ultimately, the layering, the levels of myth, the intersections of consciousness and existence in this work, all the planes of knowing and being, the purest family drama drawn from the deepest memory of the tribe.

And now we see in the same moment how thoroughly this central experiential-mythic synthesis in the play has in fact been imaged from the outset even in its very title. "If I could be bone, Ardell," Pavlo Hummel has exclaimed in his play, wondering at the horror of the corporal who has shot the old man and the little girl, "if I could be bone. In my deepest part or center, if I could be bone" (56). Here bone has come home, as in flesh and bone, and now refigured also in a familiar children's nursery taunt. Sticks and Stones has become Sticks and Bones. And in that vast spiritual nursery that is America, names of course are exactly now what will hurt us. The recourse here, for the ideal American family, is finally the old, characteristic one: to continue the avoidance of historical naming, to channel the presence, even within the house of domestic history itself, of the horror named Vietnam, back into the newest TV fantasy, the story absorbed into the Orwellian media resolution, the happy embrace of the massage, a warm collective fade. Indeed, as James A. Robinson notes, this is the most absolutely terrifying feature of the ending as written, with David "only nearly gonna die": that David will in fact *not die* but instead suffer some dreadful vegetable reintegration with his family (137). The old war story has come home as American family nightmare fantasy, our worst media imagining, our favorite TV show gone horribly wrong. And it is a TV nightmare finally with a TV resolution: to go out where we came in, in the happy middle of the ultimate serial, soothing euthanasia of memory, making it not exactly die perhaps, but nearly, nearly, popular amnesia.

Of Rabe's third play, *The Orphan*, the author himself noted at the time of its production, "There's no reference to Vietnam in the play, not specifically. There may be one. But if I hadn't been there I wouldn't have written it" (Kollin, 54). Yet five years later, he would insist with equal vehemence, "*Streamers* is not the conclusion of a trilogy that began with *Pavlo Hummel* and *Sticks and Bones*. The conclusion was, whatever one thought of it, *The Orphan*. *Streamers* may be interrelated to these plays, but *The Orphan* caps the trilogy. I just wish critics would get that straight" (Kollin, 66).

To read *The Orphan* itself, and particularly the various staging preliminaries and the long first act, is to understand the confusion. In contrast to its predecessors, this play, on a highly abstract stage of nets and bars and scaffolds, eschews even a minimal "symbolic" realism. It is filled with time and space, gods and messengers, omens and catastrophes, a whole vast apparatus of planetary design. Heroes and heroines include Agamemnon, Clytemnestra (or, more specifically in this case, Clytemnestra 1 and Clytemnestra 2, the two figures roughly fifteen years apart in age, "the same person," we are told, "at two different points of time in her life" [8]), Aegisthus, Iphegenia, Orestes—all of them lifted more or less whole out of an Aeschylean-Sophoclean-Euripidean stock company, complete with masks and stylized destinies and lofty speeches of cosmic explanation. Mixed with them are other personages such as the Figure and the Speaker, fond of more modern excursuses on cosmic matters large and small, history and eternity, relativity, simultaneity, the unfolding universe, the space-time continuum (an early title for the play was, in fact, "Orestes and the $E=mc^2$" [Kollin, 51]), brain impulses and neuro-synaptical-chemical pathways. And walking in and out as well are various other characters simply styled "Family Members," one of them Pylades, a classical messenger, but the others hip young sixties-style females with names like "Becky," "Sally," and "Jenny." The plot is a large, groaning metaconstruction of the various remembered plots, the old Greek family affair writ large: Agamemnon, his brother Menelaus, the latter's wife Helen, the war, the problem with the ships at Aulis, the Iphegenia business, which in turn leads to the Clytemnestra and Aegisthus business (with some brief mention of the Cassandra business), and which will of course lead to the Electra and Orestes business. And mixed with all this business of history, of course, is all the other business of philosophy as well, a kind of general treatise on the mythic provenance of violence at large. Meanwhile, one of the girls chimes in every so often with some talk of other, more familiar murders, a Manson-like bunch of freaks, a leader called by the Biblical-Miltonic designation of "Abaddon" and later "the Lieutenant," and of some victims they call "gooks" (16, 22). And later the Speaker makes some explicit connections between the classic history of human sacrifice and a new philosophy of history called body count (43). Yet at the end, with the arrival of Orestes and a new history about to be born, the whole affair seems thus far to have been mainly a kind of extended metaphysical parable: "It is time that Orestes arrive with his story . . . understanding nothing" (47).

What is clearly being attempted, then, is basically an abstract mythography of violence, "a unified design in man's history of slaughter," writes Kollin exactly (53), a fated plot brought out of old tangled motive barely understood yet bloodily enacted and reenacted, with Charles Manson and his lot simply the latest of a long line of foreordained ritual killers. But for the most part it all thus far seems quite operatic and vain — an overblown, obscure, and perhaps even fuddled conceit. An elaborate mythic-experimental apparatus conflates various levels of action, history, time, and space, but as yet to what seems mainly the end of an aggressive and preening theatricality.

In the second half, however, we quickly see that more immediate and concrete drama for which the first half has been necessary preparation. We see the real family drama of Orestes here, the family drama of nothing less than the family of man. Orestes arrives center stage and becomes, finally, the figure imaged in the title: the Orphan trying to unwrite the sundry myths of his historical genealogy of death. "Son of Agamemnon, Atreus, Tantalus," the Figure calls him. "You move away from them. You progress" (51). Yet even now, the "classic" myth of genealogy being enacted in this drama of family bloodletting is also getting more and more familiar. One of the families here is clearly the Manson Family (54–55). Aegisthus suddenly sounds a good deal like an American president named Macbird. Electra has been involved in demonstrations (58–59). In sum, all the lines of murder are starting to converge. Pylades rushes into the room with the latest news from History:

PYLADES. Orestes! Orestes! He slaughters the Vietnamese.
ORESTES. They are good gentle people.
PYLADES. He burns their villages.
AEGISTHUS. In addition, who are these people the notes left by the vandals all say I am slaughtering?
SPEAKER. The Vietnamese. (62)

Shortly, disorder is the whole radical scene, strobe lights and all. Orestes the student pores over books, notes, papers, a journal. He teams up with Pylades and the girls, takes bread, wine, cheese, smokes a hash pipe. "Tell Aegisthus of crimes," they warn him, "and he will call you criminal" (66). He plans a lecture series entitled "What is the basis on which people do cruel things to one another? And how it can be stopped" (67). He moves on to magic mushrooms (68). He devours the papers on the origins of the revolution. He is newly politicized to his native myths of exceptionalism. Through the Speaker, he is made to comprehend the true secret history of the empire: "Or do you think the enormous wealth of this land all came since Aegisthus or from goodness? Has it ever been that any land ever had such power because of goodness, because of virtue?" (71).

Fully radicalized, Orestes relentlessly searches for explanations. How, he asks, on the telephone to Iphegenia, does such a good family fail so badly? (78–79). Shortly he finds the answer, and the answer he finds, of course, concerns the nature of explanations themselves: of how always, exactly, in the name of goodness and wisdom, wisdom and goodness (79), they relentlessly offer instead only "motive—alibi—and excuse" (81–82). This, he sees, is what the "myths and structures" do, are by their nature meant to do: they are basically logical explanations for "the way we let one another die." They are, he goes on, "like flood-lamps in the night—and they show you directly where to look while making it impossible for you to see anything should you look in another direction." And this is the reason

why Clytemnestra and Aegisthus ought to die—because they believe in the myths that make you blind to all they do not show—they believe in the structures and myths, and so they think that they are

sane and civilized, king and queen, with more right to slaughter Electra than I have right to bring killing down on them. I mean, what
would it be? What, brain? What, Gods? The measurable difference
between motive—alibi—and excuse. Used of course as man applies
them to himself and others apply them to him? Nothing! Science
doesn't know. Not Pythagoras or Herclides; they haven't the means.
There is only the air in which we float and talk. (81–82)

Quickly the high recognition recasts itself in hip sixties update: "What
goes round comes round" (82). The speaker is the Girl, quite fresh, insofar
as we can tell, from the murder of Sharon Tate. One family drama begets
another. The utter senselessness of his history of slaughter is recapitulated
in the utter senselessness of hers. And her explanations, it turns out, are
but the latest vapid reinscription of his own. "Aren't we all just natural
things in God's world? Is a person less a natural thing than a hurricane or
an earthquake or pneumonia in the air of God's world? We went in there
with knives as natural as the wind or rain or old age, O. They'da never
survived My Lai, or your, O, or God's earthquakes or floods, anyway. If
they weren't supposed to die we wouldn'ta been there" (84).

Now Orestes finds at last his own freedom to wreak vengeance upon
the genealogy of violence that is the "system" itself, to enlist violence
against violence even at the expense of bringing down the whole Family
and the whole House. Apace, all the myths and violences converge. "Rich
fucking pig!" (90) Orestes shrieks at Aegisthus as he and the Girl prepare
to kill him, with an apple in his mouth. "Think of yourself," he goes on to
his victim the murderous tyrant, "as a Vietnamese! . . . WE WILL GET
INTO YOU," he howls, "ALL PARANOIA!" (90).

Anointed of his newest missions of impending murder, he comes forth
in his heralded and true lineage. "Son of Man," the Figure has called
him, always in the same moment in the "army" of that other, the "issue
of your dreams," "Apollyon of the Pit" (67). He kills Aegisthus. He kills
Clytemnestra 1, his mother, heavy with himself as yet unborn. He kills
Clytemnestra 2. Abaddon, angel of the abyss he becomes, Charles Manson
Lucifer, "O" who writes " 'Helter Skelter' in blood" (94).

Then it is done, and with appalling ease. "I thought it would take
longer . . . be harder" (94), he tells the Figure. No, the latter tells him,
and here neither will there be furies. It is just the end: he has killed his

mother, and he has seen "the nothing that it means." Orestes responds that we have no need of children for we are ruining the earth. He is correct. "What need of children?" the Figure asks. "No need of her; no need of children. Orphan, you are all, first and last." In the completion of all the great cycles of myth, Dionysus finds Apollo, and the vision of both is the horror of an all-consuming cosmic solipsism. "I look at you," Orestes tells the Figure, who is now in the guise of the latter, "and you seem many shells of skin behind which you recede from me to a center I have never seen . . . a hideous lunatic eye." The Figure replies, "Sometimes you seem exactly that way to me, Orestes" (94).

Our final vision in the play, appropriately, is of "Orestes, Orestes, Great, Great Orestes" (96), alone among the planets, in the empty eternities. We go out where we have come in, in the middle of a tour of a planetarium. And up there with the rest, Orestes now represents, among the planets, earth. It is the planet about which, as is well known, the Speaker tells us, "Mercury completes its journey around the sun in far less time than Pluto" (97).

Here is history, then, rendered as the genealogy of its own endless patterns of mythic self-inscription. Like Pavlo (and in the same moment also more generally like "the youth of today," as Rabe described him in an interview [Kollin, 52–53]), Orestes is born of the pure historical lineage of death. Like Pavlo or like the feckless sixties radical he turns into, he is dead before he begins, walking dreamlike in his appointed role in the violent and deathly history of things. Like the upheavals of *Sticks and Bones*, the events of *The Orphan* are essentially those, rendered large, of a family situation drama, the family being the family of man, equally at home in Mycenae, My Lai, or Los Angeles. As Rabe observed about the play's classical origins, "I just used the myth . . . but what concerned me was certain things about generations, about idealism and the lack of it, about the betrayal of the young by the old, and then the vengeance of the young on the old. It's basic to all families" (Kollin, 55). The basic myth here, then, is the primal myth of human culture at large, a myth of life enlisted in the worship and ritual enactment of ever-advancing death. This becomes the myth according to Aeschylus, according to Einstein, according to Lyndon Johnson, according to Charles Manson, and now, most lately, according to David Rabe. Writing a multilayered history of violence, the playwright at the same time unwrites at each remove one further part of an enabling history of mythic justification. The result, particularly in the second act, becomes increasingly the dramatic actualization of that single, naked truth, a real Orestian bloodbath, so to speak, with a genuinely Einsteinian metaphysical chill. Dionysus confronts Apollo and finds only the dumb blankness that is in his own eye. And so we ourselves sense fully our own cosmic orphanhood, our aloneness among the violent eternities.

As contrasted with *The Orphan*, in his two immediately subsequent plays, *In the Boom Boom Room* and the much-acclaimed *Streamers*, Rabe attempts, if this does not seem too much a contradiction, a more straight-forward experimentalism. To be sure, he retains the signature of a characteristic stagecraft. As is always the case in Rabe, the dramatic site remains at once itself and a field of overarching mythic possibility as well—myths of genealogy, authority, cultural origin and their vindications of institutional and cultural violence. But now in the fourth and fifth plays also come extreme simplifications in character, action, dialogue, and theatrical construction. The dramatic strategies overall come to resemble a kind of minimalist realism, not unlike the neorealism of much contemporary fiction, the horror of things lurking just behind the face of things, just beyond the banal, the utterly quotidian surfaces of everyday American life. To cite a contemporary analogue, it is Pinter's old comedy of menace (Esslin, 46) but now nestled amidst the imagings of peculiarly American dreads—gender, sexuality, violence, power, race—and with such dreads now serving as prime indices of the cultural malaise spreading across the national life in the latest decades of our century.

As mentioned earlier, David Rabe himself—in salutary rebuttal, one might wish, to critics in the habit of finding three works of art more or less "about" something and declaring them a trilogy—has suggested that *The Orphan* be considered the real work in his canon where the early "Vietnam" project undertaken in *Pavlo Hummel* and *Sticks and Bones* is carried to its natural completion.[5] In a similar regard, however, it has never to my knowledge been suggested to locate discussion of Rabe's fourth major play to be formally produced—*In the Boom Boom Room*—within this same area of preoccupation. Yet I would now suggest that it too should be considered very much a Vietnam play, and one particularly in the provenance of the first. Again, Vietnam is offstage, indeed, *quite* offstage (as it will be, moreover, in *Streamers* as well, thereby further distinguishing that play significantly from the other two with which it is often grouped). In fact, the war explicitly announces itself only once, in the recollections of the play's protagonist, Chrissy, of a date she has once had with a Vietnam-bound soldier. Yet the particular details of the seemingly incidental scene carry a literal signature of connection. The boy, it turns out, has been scared but has tried "actin' other"; in kissing, therefore, she has put her tongue "real deep into his mouth," she recalls, "till I felt him turn on" (75). The scene is indeed, we are moved to remember, a mirror image of a similar incident recalled in *his* play by Pavlo Hummel (75).

It is in fact the figure of the mirror image that quite accurately defines the status of *In the Boom Boom Room* in Rabe's ongoing attempt to inscribe the experience of Vietnam into the body of post-Vietnam American myth. The play, one sees from the outset, is set in America in the age of a go-go. Yet this is exactly so only as it is also set in America in the age of Vietnam. To be specific, it is very clearly "about" what happens to women in America precisely to the degree that it is also very much about what happens to women in Vietnam.

The key to the explicit "Vietnam" connection is contained specifically in the title—first, "The" Boom Boom Room and then later "In" the Boom Boom Room. It recalls the age of the go-go lounge, the age of the topless bar, the age of the frug, the monkey, the hitchhiker, the jerk. It recalls what happens to women in America in the Boom Boom room, which here, by virtue of explicit stagecraft and thus thematic and stylistic extension, turns out to be everywhere—a bar, Chrissy's apartment, the house she grew up in, an array of sordid hotel rooms in the cities of America. Yet as the title itself indicates, and in fact could not do so in a more explicit way, everywhere also includes Vietnam. It recalls what happens to women in America by concurrently recalling what happens to women in Vietnam—like the American women we see here—bar girls, whores, short-time experts, trying to give whatever seems to be wanted to American men very confused about who they are and what they are doing: scared boys on the way to a war in perhaps some instances; but in the main just American men in this general drama of female subjugation, degradation, depersonalization—the father Harold, now getting old with his prostate trouble and his concern with function; the boyfriend Eric, anxious heterosexual full of his fears and his analysis; the streetwise Al, Nathan Detroit revisited with a vengeance; the gay man downstairs, Guy, himself described explicitly as "a Damon Runyon character," with his anguish and his wit and always on the way, in delicious, vengeful irony, to the sperm bank to flesh out the "straight" families of a barren land. Here obviously there are "Guys and Dolls" and "Guys and Dolls." All the men are "guys," and Chrissy is a "doll." And to all the American "guys" in her life, in echo of her Vietnamese sisters, Chrissy seems to say "I give you number-one short time." "I give you number-one boom boom." "I love you too much, GI," Chrissy seems to say to Harold, to Eric, to Al, to Guy, to the unknown soldier, to all the unnamed others.

The stage directions of the play make it clear that it is supposed to take place within the dominant "metaphor of the bar" (12). The first scene makes the metaphor clear. As the background music of the jukebox plays Ruby and the Romantics doing "Angel Baby," the bar is also Chrissy's apartment. The man in her arms, the current man in her life, gives way to another man in her life, in this case Harold, her father, prating of all the boys she is going to have now that she has a place of her own and complaining about his own troubles with his prick. The scene dissolves into the first actual scene in the bar, Big Tom's Boom Boom Room, with the bored girls, the bunny costumes, their act, the Hugh Hefner narration announcing their "turn-ons" and their astrological signs (20). Here is America in the Age of Aquarius indeed. The first two scenes establish the basic architecture and rhythm of the play. Henceforth, the "scene," in both the technical or dramatic and the suggestively more immediate vernacular sense, will dissolve in and out, always, in one form or another, from the recurring locus of the Boom Boom Room, the bar-apartment-whorehouse America where the big question seems always, as announced early on to Chrissy, whether she plans to "hook on the side" or not ("Not me — no. I'd never do that," she nervously answers. "I'm a dancer" [30]). And within the "scene" will likewise fade in and out the men in Chrissy's life — the characters by which the play itself is finally defined because they are finally the characters by which Chrissy's American life is defined. Out of Damon Runyon comes Guy, the gay-guy sperm donor, feeling in his own fear and loathing her similar degradation. "I'll fuck queers," he proposes by way of a pact. "You will fuck straights. And we'll come back here to tell one another of their stupidity — their peculiarity" (60). Out of therapy comes Eric, with his analysis, his narcissistic playing at "false insights," his impotent, psychic scab picking, making her the quintessential therapeutic fulfillment of his plans. Off the streets come swaggering, priapic

Al and his buddy Ralphie, American street savant. Out of the past comes Daddy Harold, still with the prostate and the bad prick and now also with vague denials about some primal memory of child violation that Chrissy herself has dreamed. "I think somethin' bad was done to me when I was little," she tells him. "I think you did something to me when I was little" (102). He cannot speak for "Uncles Billy and Michael," Harold nervously explains to his wife, albeit admitting that "they may have found the temptation of her irresistible—it is not impossible—for she was a lovely little woman always AND"—he now suddenly finds himself screaming—"YOU COULD SEE HOW SHE WANTED IT!" (109).

Meanwhile, Chrissy puzzles over it all, the men, what they want, what she wants, if anything at all. There are times, Susan tells her early on, as a preface we later see to a confession of her own lesbianism, when the sexual revulsion has been so great—"when I let them do whatever they wanted, bangin' away on me"—that the customary cleaning of her insides in the bathroom afterwards has hidden her secret nausea (43). And so Chrissy herself reflects on her own status as basic receptacle for men's masturbation in her short soliloquy on a diaphragm, that thing she is always rummaging about for or running back to get to facilitate her couplings with the men in her life. "Never think about what it's for," she says. "All those funny little things bangin' up into it. Lookin' for me. Poor little things. Findin' it" (49). She is her own history of planned promiscuity, and in this, she finds presently, she assumes her place in a long tradition, where the only change has involved the means of women's use by men and their concomitant anger and self-loathing. She is herself, she finds, the offspring of that lineage of use and abuse even down to her own mother's attempted abortion (90). "They don't mean to hurt us," she says acutely at one point. "They just don't know how not to" (78). In her life, she inscribes the whole catalogue of violation, forced contraception, abortion, new violation, a long spectacle of use and abuse that begins for American women even before birth and extends to become the pattern of their American lives.

This is domestic melodrama with a visceral bite. And it inevitably comes to the customary ending in some very bad ways. A go-go wedding for Chrissy out of the worst rock and roll movie imaginable (112) yields to Ralph and Alice Kramden with all the latent texts of horror and violence written back in. The lines of sexual force converge. She accuses Al indirectly of needing a faggot. He makes insinuations about a girl in his house with lesbian tendencies. Accusations fly about the way Al looks at other women on the subway; about the way he looks at niggers; about how Chrissy has in mind to start balling niggers; about how if she can't get it from Al she will get it from them; about how she will pursue him with evidence of his humiliation (116–24).

Now all the hoarded violence in the play erupts in domestic cataclysm. Al gives Chrissy a savage beating. "You been hurtin me!" he screams. "You been hurtin' me!" (124). "Don't hit my face!" she calls out in return, screaming now in the dark. "Don't hit my face, don't hit my stomach. Don't hit my face, don't hit my stomach, don't hit my face, don't hit my stomach." Boom-boom. Boom-boom. It is happening before our eyes, in the boom-boom room, sexual violence, sex and violence, what men and women do to each other in the Age of Aquarius, in the Age of Vietnam, in the Age of America.

Suddenly the lights go back up and there now stands a man spot-lighted, a man looking very like the man in the opening scene who turned out to be Chrissy's father. Now he is the announcer.

We are regulars indeed, in the boom-boom room. In whatever city, it is our choice, we are told — face or boobies. Accordingly here, the audience has chosen: it is not the face we now see but the boobies. Now Chrissy waits, as she has always waited, to dance. The announcer continues: "Now, she's been workin' real hard all her life to get this just right. You give her your undivided attention" (125). The lights go down in America and Chrissy dances. In obedience to the master of ceremonies in America, the regulars watch and are entertained.

When *Streamers*, the third play in Rabe's popularly known Vietnam trilogy, did finally appear in formal production in early 1976, critics were drawn to obvious major connections with *Pavlo Hummel*, a play which it thematically, stylistically, and even physically resembles (if such an expression is not too bold in discussions of dramatic art), and also, for equally obvious reasons, with *Sticks and Bones*, and particularly in its prescient vision of Vietnam as mythic-cultural inscription "back in the world." For here Vietnam in all its pain and hurt — as in roughly contemporary works of Robert Stone and Ron Kovic and later those of Stephen Wright, Philip Caputo, Bobbie Ann Mason, and others — truly does begin to spill itself back out across the domestic landscape of America. Where they still might have looked with commensurate rewards of insight for "big" connections, however, was equally to the two plays immediately preceding. In the context of *The Orphan*, for instance, *Streamers* announces itself clearly a further step in Rabe's inquiry, albeit focused on the specific historical-cultural phenomenon of America in the Vietnam War, into the mythography of historical-cultural violence at large. And in the context of its succession after *Boom Boom Room*, we may put the matter of *Streamers* and its putative status as "Vietnam" drama in even more direct focus as to its place in the evolution of Rabe's art of cultural mythmaking and mythic reinscription. To put it simply, *Streamers* is "about" Vietnam, but it is so by being more directly and explicitly, as is *Boom Boom Room* directly and explicitly, "about" American sexuality and particularly about its role as a source of social and political violence. In *Boom Boom Room*, the violence happens to be directed mainly against women, although we see it significantly implied, amidst a welter of epithets and angers — queers and straights, whites and niggers — as always ready to break out imminently among men as well. In *Streamers*, the violence of war depicted (whether the old one recalled, the Korea of the aging NCOs, or the new one prefigured, the Vietnam waiting offstage to claim them and the new batch of scared young boys in their charge) is directly against small yellow people of one nationality or another. Yet here it is American men themselves, in various explicit sexual and racial roles (and also, importantly, in their response to other implied sexual and racial roles), who become at once the chief perpetrators and victims *among themselves as well* of an inevitably ensuing and horrific carnage. To put this another way, *Streamers* is about American manliness, precisely to the degree that *Boom Boom Room* is about American womanliness, and with similar effect. The violence and domination Chrissy finds at the end of the play — and it is a sexual violence, one sees, prophetically presided over by the shades of the nigger and the queer who will take actual shape in *Streamers* — can be the only outcome of her quest to know what men want of her femaleness; for what she fails to see throughout the play in all her puzzling over it is that it is not her own femaleness at issue, but rather a femaleness, within the bars of the cage where she goes relentlessly to a go-go or the room in which she relentlessly gives number-one boom-boom, which is a social and political construction of various forms of American maleness, all of which take as their primary form of social control a long accredited tradition of American violence. In *Streamers*, it is thus almost possible to say that we have essentially the same issue with a male cast — manliness in its various social, political, cultural constructions; in that bastion of American maleness, the military; and now with the special ingredient thrown into the witches' brew, the curse of the Vietnam army that was race. The old GI rhythm of jibes, challenges, and shit-laugh tensions now flowers into military violence in the purest sense, self-hating, self-lacerating, self-annihilating violence, the violence of the barracks drama that was America at large in the era of Vietnam. The presence of the war itself is suggestively offstage, literally manifest only in the old NCOs and their stories and in the political pronouncements of the black draftee, Carlyle; but at the same time, its real ominousness *is* this very offstage-ness, its status as mute and presiding and simply there, waiting to claim its price of violence in dead, old and young alike, one by one, and beyond as well in the all-consuming agony of the national soul. (Indeed, when it comes, James A. Robinson insightfully observes, as in each of Rabe's Vietnam plays, the death that comes here will again be significantly "non-combat" [137].)

Onstage, the sense of being present in a world on the eve of disaster is inescapable. We find the army from the outset an incongruously domestic enclave amidst some vast maw of suspicion, doubt, fear, and violence yet already partaking of the tensions of its unspoken presence. And the primary terms of this cataclysm waiting to happen are embodied in its major figures: Billy, the basic army white boy, government-issue, complacent, curious, just dumb enough to be fairly happy in the green machine; Roger, the basic army black boy, long and amiably schooled to the terms of the American game, doing an inside job of being a credit to his race; Richie the bitch, the self-styled barracks queen, arch, full of ironies, suggestive, strutting his sexual mystery, inviting others to guess for themselves and in the process guess *about* themselves as well. Moreover, now also insinuating yet another disturbed presence from the transient barracks into the domain of the settled, albeit uneasy domesticity of the other three, comes Carlyle, black, angry, aggressive, relentlessly sexual, inevitably violent. And it is he, finally, as I have written elsewhere, who catalyzes the dark latencies of all of them and ultimately of the whole war-breeding system in which they must finally play their appointed parts.

Carlyle is a born agitator. Billy and Roger worry and wonder endlessly about Richie and "that stuff" (35), "the fag stuff," whether it helps to be around "normal guys" (37). Carlyle, in his first encounter with them, gets it up front, opens Richie's locker with its Playboy pinup and pronounces him "a faggot" (19). Soon Billy himself is more direct. He has told Roger what is easy to see about Richie, he says, "that you go down; that you go up and down like a Yo-Yo and you go blowin' all the trees like the wind" (27). Richie alternately responds by begging understanding ("Honestly, its not such a terrible thing. Is it Billy?" [28]) or flaunting arch aggression ("He's just my Bill," he vamps, in one last golden moment at the beginning of scene 2, fey premonition of a terrible end [63]). It is all there waiting to happen.

As with the drama of sexuality, so with the related drama of blackness. Carlyle's first meeting with Roger is a running jive on an army "short on soul," of "few brothers," "a whole bunch a pale, boring motherfuckers" (20). "And this whole Vietnam THING—," he emphasizes, "I do not dig it." "It ain't our war, brother" (23). Roger, too, is already being forced to choose. And, not surprisingly, choices converge. In a spree on the town (and a visit to a black whorehouse) Carlyle gives Billy the opportunity to be a straight man and Roger to be a black man. Increasingly, it is them against Richie. Yet precisely as their distance grows so grows Carlyle's own perverse affiliation. This is a family drama of ritual bonding with a vengeance. This fraternity of men, in which each lives by commingled love and fear of the other, grows increasingly at once apart and together. Then, suddenly, the crisis is there before them all. Carlyle and Richie lounge about, sharing a bottle. "Richie first saw me," Carlyle says, "he didn't like me much nohow, but he thought it over now, he changed his way a thinkin'. I can see that clear. We gonna be one big happy family." Richie responds: "Carlyle likes me, Billy; he thinks I'm pretty" (81). Billy and Roger look on. Suddenly, the two dread versions of the other, the white queer and the black firebrand, are quite literally playing footsie. For Billy, it is the utterly inconceivable, the union of the black and the homosexual. "You rode in my car," Carlyle appeals to him. "I showed you a good cathouse, all that sweet black pussy. Ain't we friends? Richie likes me. How come you don't like me?" (84). Billy blurts it all out straight, " 'Cause if you really are doin' what I think you're doin', you're a fuckin' animal." Weapons are about to appear. Roger protests. His world is coming down too. "Man, we live here," he says. "It's my house, too, Roger; I live here too," Richie returns. Moreover, he says, "Carlyle is my guest" (85). It is all coming down now, in one dread compression of all conflict; and each in his turn now turns on all the others in a literal chain reaction of awful release. Carlyle tries to throw the other two out, shouting, "Don't you got no feelin' for how a man feel? I don't understand you two boys. Unles'n you a pair of motherfuckers. That what you are, you a pair of motherfuckers? You slits, man. DON'T YOU HEAR ME? I DON'T UNDERSTAND THIS SITUATION. I THOUGHT WE MADE A DEAL!" Turning to Richie a moment later he commands furiously, "YOU GET ON YOUR KNEES, YOU PUNK, I MEAN NOW, AND YOU GONNA BE ON MY JOINT FAST OR YOU GONNA BE ONE BUSTED PUNK. AM I UNDERSTOOD?" (87). Quickly it comes to a knife. Carlyle slashes Billy on the hand. He continues to dart the knife, cutting more. Now Billy too is armed, holding a razor and shouting in incredulous recognition of the walking nightmare he himself has become. "I'm a twenty-four year old goddamn college graduate," he shrieks, "—intellectual scholar type—and I got a razor in my hand. I'm thinkin' about comin' up behind one black human being and I'm thinkin' nigger this and nigger that—I wanna cut his throat. THAT IS RIDICULOUS. I NEVER FACED ANYBODY IN MY LIFE WITH ANYTHING TO KILL THEM. YOU UNDERSTAND ME? I DON'T HAVE A GODDAMN THING ON THE LINE HERE!" In almost sure suicidal freedom now he embraces it all, this business that has been waiting for him. He flings away the razor. "You gay little piece of shit cake—shit cake," he hurls at Richie. "And you—you are your own goddamn fault, SAMBO, SAMBO!" he taunts Carlyle (92). Shortly he lies stabbed and quivering on the floor, cold and dying. "What did you do," Roger cries when he has seen the finality of the wounding. "What did you do, nigger— you slit him or stick him?" (95). Richie sobs and yells. Quietly, Billy lies on the floor and whimpers. "Don't stab me anymore, Carlyle, okay? I promise I was dead wrong doin' what I did. I know that now. Carlyle, promise me you won't stab me anymore. I couldn't take it. Okay? I'm cold . . . my blood . . . is . . ." (97).

Yet even now it is not finished. Drunken old Sergeant Rooney, still playing kids' games, as in an earlier appearance, full of old soldier bravado and blather, bursts in, looking for his buddy, good old "Cokesy wokesy." And he too, now, with the beer bottle his old weapon of choice, the old airborne yell his courage, finds death on the end of Carlyle's knife. "No fair. No fair!" he says as the knife goes in again and again.

Now the Vietnam drama is complete, the army bloodbath, old soldier, new soldier, white soldier, black soldier. "Ohhhhhh, how'm I gonna get back to the world now," Carlyle moans, "I got all this mess to—" (99). The cleanup squad arrives, the MPs and an officious lieutenant intent on getting all the facts and answers. "This is my house, sir. This is my god-damn house," the apprehended Carlyle protests as he is dragged back into the scene in cuffs (103). "This is my place, not your place." Meanwhile, with the forms and the jargon, the lieutenant and his minions stay hard at work at getting "to the bottom" of it (105).

When "it" has been cleaned up, all that are left behind are the walking wounded and war haunted. Roger and Richie sit adrift in numbed, linger-ing accusation. The found Cokes arrives, sees Richie crying, and wants to know why. Roger tells Cokes disgustedly, "cause he's a queer" (112). Cokes scolds Roger. Everybody's got problems, he says. His leukemia, for instance, is plenty worse than being a queer. And maybe if he'd been a queer, he goes on, he might not have his blood disease. And maybe there are a lot of ways in which his own American life might have come out dif-ferently, less drinking, more Kraut or gook-killing, maybe a wife and kids, but now it has all come down to leukemia and this strange vision somehow he can't shed of a gook in a spider hole, a battle scene like something out of a Charlie Chaplin movie, where the gook is in the hole and he is sitting on the lid, and the gook is underneath like in the familiar movie scene, the kind with "everybody fallin' down and clumsy, and him in there yellin' and bangin' away, and I'm just sittin' there lookin' around. And he was Charlie Chaplin. I don't know who I was. And then he blew up" (113). "I mean, he was like Charlie Chaplin," he repeats, "and then he blew up." Roger's reply is acute: "Sergeant . . . maybe you was Charlie Chaplin too" (114). Cokes has passed this off. "No, no," he says, "I don't know who I was." But Roger persists. "You think he was singin' it?" he asks. "What?" Cokes replies. Roger repeats the question. "You think he was singin' it?" And Cokes gets the idea. "Oh yeah, oh yeah," he says. "He was singin' it" (114). And now he too once more begins to sing it, the old song of fatalism and bravery. The sergeant now begins to sing it, but in a makeshift language, we are told, imitating Korean. Which one was Charlie Chaplin, indeed, we now ask? Who was singing the song? In what language was it, is it, this song of American manliness?[6]

The answer is suggested by the fact that the title of the song is also the title of the play. ("Beautiful Streamer, open for me./The sky is above me with no ca-no-py.") It is everyone's song. Beautiful Streamers are banners of battle and empty parachutes. Beautiful Streamer is the song sung by the sergeant and the gook of this war and now sung here also in the gook language of the last gook war. It is sung in the barracks of the gook killers and the American gooks: the nigger out of the America of Stephen Foster's melody "Beautiful Dreamer"; the queer who has prided himself on being the beautiful screamer. The song belongs to all the boys, the Americans.

At the end of the drama, we thus witness a scene of dramatic consummation inscribing itself out of the whole abounding provenance of popular history and myth: American ballads, marching songs, the caricaturing enactment of sexual and racial stereotypes, old men's war stories, silent movies. Moreover, it is also a poetic valedictory turning the affair into a ballad, the signature of an older literary drama as well. And that drama, of course, is an old American barracks drama by the name of *Billy Budd*. Indeed, one sees now, at the end, that the two texts are composed of almost identical conflicts of force. As military chronicles, both are about the cultural politics of violence. As metaphysical disquisition, both concern the insistency of evil and the vulnerability and impotence of good. In each, the psychomachia of manhood is posed as the scene of the garden recast and manifesting itself specifically in the world of men at war in the peculiarly sinister and ominous form of homoerotic threat—of threat, that is, to the very conception of *maleness itself*. Indeed here, as there, cataclysm thus grows out of what is basically homoerotic vignette, the claustral dance of fascination darkly flowering into obsession, aggression into violent consummation. And now, the new inscription of the basic motif is suggestively tripartite. Carlyle, in the Claggart imaging of the dark insinuations of sexual violence almost as pure essence of our common natures, is a stroke Melville himself surely would have loved, perhaps the most slyly menacing black character in our white literature, at least since Melville's own Babo. Richie, on the other hand, while becoming a homoerotic object of such violence, at the same time represents as insinuative presence throughout the play that side of the Claggart nature that is also homoerotic desire. Billy here in the new triangulation thus becomes that other Billy in the fullest sense, with Richie the mirroring of the fears of his own dark sexual latencies and Carlyle the final flowering of his own nature into violence for which he must stand as culpable as any other. Once again, accordingly, the play is set in a world of war, a martial arena, the war offstage but coloring all events and actions. The conflict is the old one, a natural law of relations versus a punitive military code. Once the cataclysm has occurred, the officer and his minions work by the book in the official business of restoration of the general order. The common soldiers remain at the last simply puzzled survivors, stunned interpreters of what they have witnessed. Finally, as in Melville's concluding melody, here too, in the words of one of them schooled in the common experience of their lot, the affair is finally turned into a soldier song, sad and funny at once and seemingly as old as the service itself.

Yet the chief function of myth here, as throughout Rabe's work, is our own final sense of the experience of it *as drama*, of the utter reification, that is, of its newly inscribed presence in the dramatic actuality of our own lives. The primal scene here is no mythographic conceit but rather, in utter dramatic concreteness, the scene of a knife fight and a shocking, repellent bloodbath. (Indeed, as Kollin tells us, accounts of the initial New Haven production noted numerous responses of physical revulsion to the violence of the culminating scenes [70].) Billy's terror and incredulity, even unto death, are our own. And they are our own because, like Billy, we know, deeply, inescapably, that Richie is for real; that Carlyle is for real; that the cultural pathologies of gender and race are for real; and that together they constitute here the very fabric of our lives — the cultural pathology of violence, that is, at once making America, and thereby Vietnam, possible. And it is umistakably clear to us throughout the play that Vietnam is the realest thing of all. For it is clearly the Vietnam Army we have before our eyes, black versus white, grunt versus housecat, draftee versus lifer, fresh young American boys and tired old American men. "All wars are boyish," wrote the war poet Herman Melville, the "classic" American author who already presides here as spirit-dramatist as well (Cohen, 9). Here old men returned (and some of them more than once, now) from the land of the shadow play at boys' games. Boys, preparing to go there, already play at the deadliest of the games of men. They are all proud members of the proudest of our institutions of American violence, with its battle streamers trailing the campaign record of our own history and myth. For that is the way the national song goes:

> Whose broad stripes and bright stars
> through the perilous night

o'er the ramparts we watched
were so gallantly streaming.

They are the inhabitants, along with the rest of us, of that greatest of all American institutions, at once the Republic militant and the country that remains the war.

Following upon the popular and critical triumph of *Streamers*—with its winning of virtually every major contemporary dramatic award and its general acceptance as the completion of an important cycle of "Vietnam" writing by the only major dramatist to emerge from the war—Rabe's sixth play, *Goose and Tomtom*, remains in many ways the most enigmatic and elusive of his works. (Its theatrical history is certainly the most controversial, with a short, troubled period of actual production and current availability only in a Grove Press text.) On one hand it seems almost a *jeu d'esprit*, described matter-of-factly by one writer as a rendering of "the mishaps of two small-time jewel thieves whose own pirated loot is stolen by a rival gang" (Kollin, 83). And up front, it does seem a gangster play, albeit with something of the existential menace of the Gus and Ben show of Pinter's *The Dumb Waiter*, written at the same time in an almost Damon Runyon spirit of self-parody. ("I am not at liberty to say" [11], the characters are fond of remarking, or, "I ain't sayin', except he ain't on the earth with us anymore, and when the appropriate time should come I will explain not that I am losing any such thing as you might call sleep over it" [90].) On the other hand, with its paraphernalia of dreams, enchantments, prophecies, curses, kidnapped maidens awaiting heroic rescue, talismanic jewels, alien desperados from other forsaken cosmic precincts, it clearly possesses something of the metaphysical abstraction and mythic portentousness of that perhaps most metaphysical of the earlier plays, *The Orphan*.

As is customary in Rabe's plays, however, we do not have to wait long for a conception of the basic theatrical metaphor. "TIME," the first page instructs us—"This was recently." "PLACE," it goes on—"An apartment in the underworld." As we quickly see, both sets of instructions are quite literal. This is an "underworld" play in the most immediate sense conceivable. The main characters, Goose and Tomtom, are tough guys, hardboiled types, with their talk of broads, guns, assholes, turds, "fuckin'" this and "fuckin'" that. Attended by their gun moll, Lorraine the hooker,

Tomtom's woman (but also, we find, not above fucking Goose's brains out and stealing his liver and bragging about it), they have tough-guy contests, getting pins stuck in their arms to see if they can take it. They swear revenge on Bingo, who has had "Fuckin' Eddie iced," and chortle over Bingo's sister, "keepin' her in the goddamn closet" to "take her out, pump her, man, put her back" (18). They make tough-guy plans for killings ("You wanna go shoot somebody?" [10]), capers, heists. Tomtom persistently shoves, whacks, bullies Goose, as Goose will later do in the second act to the captured rival Bingo. They are paranoid, fearful of being watched (20), always nervous, suspicious, checking each other out (23).

Yet at the same time, they speak of dreams, visions. Goose tells of his nightmare of the green witch and later his dream of the ghost who comes and tells him the secret of his once being a frog. Tomtom tells of a miraculous sunrise, "red as a wheel of blood slippin' up outa the earth to light down this tunnel I was standin' in, these chambers of cloud" (9). In the midst of their tough-guy talk, they slip into infantile profundities. "I wish I was a happy person," Tomtom says to Goose. Goose replies, "I wish I was a happy person too, Tomtom. I wish we both was. You wish we both was? Or just you was." Tomtom: "I wish we both was." Goose: "Me too" (28). Damon Runyon toffs, they are also in their way Vladimir and Estragon waiting under that tree. When we hear the thunder and witness their quarrel over explanations, we see that they could have as easily been cave men (47–48). We sense indeed their wonder as, arising among them, there now comes Bingo's kidnapped sister Lulu, blindfolded, dreaming, speaking charms and portents of the mighty hero who will come to rescue her (60–61).

All this has occurred in the first act, which is in fact nearly exactly the first half of the play. In the second, the basic "plot" is continued from the first. Bingo, who has been suspected of stealing the jewels which Goose and Tomtom have stolen for Lorraine, and which they must now either replace or duplicate by stealing enough money to buy comparable ones, comes around the apartment and is captured. Under interrogation, he tells the story about his kidnapped sister and his search for her. He is a bad guy, he says, but he has a right to his sister (80). Under further interrogation, he also goes into his earlier history about a bad partner, "the instigator," Tomtom calls him, "the party of responsibility in this problem we have

here" (88), who has put him up to stealing the jewels and then has made off
with them. Bingo tries to phone this "Bill" but has no luck. Lorraine, using
her magic crystal ball, and Tomtom, who has been the phone interlocutor
with Bill, persuade Goose that he must take Bingo out and kill him. Bingo
takes it more or less philosophically, bids farewell to Lulu, tells the others
he has no hard feelings, and goes out with Goose. When Goose returns
and the others realize that he has actually murdered Bingo, they are at
first outraged. Then Goose shows them the bloody bag of diamonds he
has taken from Bingo's belly. They are suddenly all happy. Just then, other
figures break down the walls, the doors, figures in a cosmic heist with a
spokesman, Man 1, giving the account of their own cosmogony, creation,
the sexes, life, their belief that there must be a design to things, the bar-
barians who came to corrupt them, their own subsequent wanderings, and
their attempts to explain themselves to people they now barbarize. They
leave, taking Lorraine.

It is a rival gang raid in the fullest sense possible, a bunch of guys,
no doubt, Tomtom tells Goose, the two of them now alone again as in
the beginning, from "some other neighborhood." Fondly they remember
Bingo, who perhaps has given them the diamonds, Goose speculates, "in
commemoration of his dying" (120). They remember his lack of "hard
feelings"; they see themselves as "two Bingos" now themselves. Trying to
sleep, however, they also see vengeful, monster Bingos. Now Lulu awakens
again. While she prophesies relief by Good Goose and Good Tomtom,
they both sleep and awaken to screams. They untie her. Suddenly, the
walls fade. They hold the diamonds and look up at the stars and "other
cosmic objects." Finally, "the light of the diamonds is the light of the
stars, and then more fragments of this light appear on the floor, the walls,
everywhere throughout the gigantic dark" (124).

At the beginning of the play, the two basic metaphors of local criminality and cosmogony are conflated in the enclosure of the apartment.
At the end, with the release of Lulu, the metaphor of local criminality
within cosmogony expands to become congruent with the night sky of
creation itself. Again, the localized dramatic cliche has become imaginatively the stuff of eternal myth; and again, as throughout Rabe, this has
largely been a function of structure in its largest sense—of structure, that
is, as some overarching problematic of representation. Yet here too, it has
clearly become a more immediate issue of language as well; and thus now,

as in *Hurlyburly* to come, we find Rabe's newest embrace of postmodern implication.

In the work at hand we see this most directly through the rendering of a palpable and insistent paranoia. People endlessly repeat themselves and each other in conversation. They tell themselves and each other exactly as they are doing it exactly what they are doing, as if they are trying to get a handle on it, on themselves (22–23, 104–5). They rehearse over and over what has already happened, like an alibi, testing hypotheticals, getting it straight, ordering testimony (55–56, 98–100). At times they resort to auxiliary media, such as Tomtom's incessant line drawings of scenarios as they are being talked out (81, 100–101) or Lorraine's conjured visions of the crystal ball (102–3). And so, in the recitations of dream, prophecy, vision, we see the same impulse operating at the level of the eternal and mythic and finally made explicit in the dimension of the cosmic "other" as a function of the old, old story told by the dark aliens of the conclusion and of their eternal desire for "design" and the understanding of it.

Thus, for all the manic hilarity, the desperate playfulness of hard-boiled cliche, a drama of throwaway lines becomes no throwaway drama at all. Rather, it becomes again the old drama of eternal myth, of the "stories," as Joan Didion has said, that "we tell" ourselves "in order to live" (11). The dramatic subject represented here is the cosmic caper of the eternally stolen and re-stolen treasure, the one endlessly deferred from our grasp, our sense of an ending. We are all tough guys, gun molls, jewel thieves and receivers of stolen goods, kidnapped princesses and would-be rescuers, involved in an unending series of heists, wary, paranoid, at the mercy of the guys from the next cosmic neighborhood. We hold in our hands the stolen diamonds of the theft infinitely repeated and deferred — the ones ripped from our rivals' and victims' and brothers' bellies, the ones we steal as tribute for the favors of our women — and hold in the same moment the very stars.

All this cosmic implication notwithstanding, after the dramatic turmoil and cataclysm of *Streamers*, *Goose and Tomtom* seems a kind of retrenchment of economy and focus. *Hurlyburly*, on the other hand, even by the very magnitude of theatrical allusion embodied in its title, suggests an attempt once more to construct the consciously comprehensive vision. And despite Rabe's disclaimers of the Hollywood mythos here — justly and sincerely, he has warned us with good reason about merely "pushing the implications of it into some quarantined region or eccentricity ('the West Coast') so that it need not be considered as personally pertinent" (164) — from the outset we see that it *is* fully, can only *be* fully, *the scene*.[7]

In the opening moments, for example, we watch Eddie and Phil discuss Phil's fight with his estranged wife Suzie and how he has hit her while he has been stoned because she has not made at least the pretense of paying attention to a theory of his about breaking the bank in Vegas, a theory in turn which has also been tied up with some master insight he cannot remember into global politics. By 8:45 in the morning Eddie and Phil (in a "Hollywood" manner exactly reminiscent of Robert Stone's *Children of Light*, where a chief character opens the book by consuming a breakfast of cocaine, valium, alcohol, and B vitamin) have done a number of lines of cocaine and smoked a number of joints. They complain about the entertainment industry. Phil's career as an actor depends always on the physical type of the lead (28). Eddie, a writer, says it is all Phil can expect from a career with people whose whole purpose is making something look real and serious when it is "total shit" (29). Eddie himself is bent out of shape by recent TV where visions of geopolitical madness ("not only are we headed for nuclear devastation," he complains, "if not by the Russians then by some goddamn primitive bunch of middle-eastern motherfuckers") combine with local disaster ("this accidental electrical fire in which an entire family is incinerated, the father trying to save everybody by hurling them out the window, but he's on the sixth floor, so he's, you know — they're like eggs on the sidewalk") and then top themselves off with a phone call from his loathsome and despised ex-wife (26). Shortly, Mickey joins them from the bedroom after a date with Darlene, who is supposed to be Eddie's new serious love interest, and the two quarrel over what seem to be the protocols of "relationships" but in fact come down mainly to the fine points of fucking rights (31–35). Next, Artie, an agent, arrives with Donna, a teenage runaway. He and Eddie quarrel over the former's attempt to slice deals for the two of them with a "KNOWN ANACONDA" of a producer (42), Eddie calls him, "legendary among snakes," "permanently enshrined in the reptilian hall of Hollywood fucking fame" (43). Artie gives Donna to the other boys ("She worked last time I used her," he leers [39–40]). The other boys decide that Mickey is not allowed to share, since he is now in a "serious relationship." As the scene ends, Donna is going upstairs with

Eddie. In the background, Willie Nelson is singing "All of Me." As the lights go down, Phil is exclaiming, "So this is the bachelor life" (48).

The Southern California of the entertainment industry has clearly become here the representative and mythic "scene"; and appropriately, given the proneness of the characters here and throughout the play to speak their characteristic California-speak, we also see from the outset that the domain of relentlessly superficial relationship it comprises is also almost exclusively a language "scene." We are told from the very beginning that "it is worth noting," for example, "that in the characters' speeches phrases such as 'whatchamacallit,' 'thingamajig,' 'blah-blah-blah' and 'rapateta' abound." The directions go on: "These are phrases used by the characters to keep themselves talking and should be said unhesitatingly with the authority and conviction with which one would have in fact said the missing word" (13). In short, language is not simply the way people talk here but, as we have seen, the way they act. That is, it is exactly for the most part (save perhaps for the troubled, impulsive Phil and on occasion some of the women) what passes for something called life here, what people more or less "do" most of the time in the tract houses of the Golden Land, off Mulholland and Sunset, in the Hollywood "area" as the locals are fond of saying. Their language is as transient, superficial, treacherous, self-deceiving, jargonish, and analysis-ridden as their lives—is, in fact, those very lives. Talk talk talk. Rapateta, rapateta, rapateta. Blah, blah, blah. It is the living totality of what people do. Here it is all of a piece, this talk, appearance, event, entertainment, catastrophe. An especially soulful and sensitive reconciliation, for example, occupying all of scene 2, between Eddie and Darlene and significantly mediated by Mickey and filled by everyone with an avalanche of linguistic sensitivity and sharing and space making, ends with Eddie's sublimely human "so you wanna go fuck?" (57). (Meanwhile, in the background, it is Willie Nelson again, doing "Someone to Watch Over Me.") The absolutely most meaningful dialogue in the play, on the other hand, takes place while Eddie does a monologue to the TV screen on which Johnny Carson conducts *his* nightly monologue, the two neck and neck on who can package the most standup humor out of human hideousness (153–55). In the long, oppressive haggling and analyzing and quarreling and blah-blah-blahing of it all, *Hurlyburly* is in sum the most incredibly and depressingly lifelike of Rabe's plays and thus the one most recently full—like the novels of Joan Didion and Robert Stone, which it often greatly resembles—of our hoarded mythic dreads. It is the working out of Rabe's essential creative formula with a vengeance. Here, the most familiar, commonplace, even offhand sort of cliche is capable of becoming truly and convincingly myth in its largest sense, even as that myth re-imbeds itself leadenly, refusing to rise out of its own sullen reification, in the dreadful behavioral and linguistic formulas of our actual lives. Indeed, if anything, the play is a language play about some ultimate crisis of myth, about its total absorption, as the writer Eddie phrases it, into "THINGS" in their relentless power to effect the general thing-ification of our lives. Our problem exactly, he screams, is that we have run out of even mildly entertaining visions of any kind of mythic transcendence, of "a view of the heavens as inhabited by this thoughtful, you know, meditative, maybe a trifle unpredictable and wrathful, but nevertheless UP THERE— this divine onlooker." Instead, he goes on, "we have" only "bureaucrats devoted to the accumulation of incomprehensible data—we have connoisseurs of graft and the filibuster—virtuosos of the three-martini lunch for whom we vote on the basis of their personal appearance. The air's bad, the water's got poison in it, and into whose eyes do we find outselves staring when we look for providence? We have emptied out the heavens and put oblivion in the hands of a bunch of aging insurance salesmen whose jobs are insecure" (118).

Amidst newest crises, however, we also find old Rabean continuities. Like the military plays, for instance, the site here is clearly a bachelor household. Accordingly, as dictated by the main occupants, the play is again inescapably about American men. Specifically, as Rabe himself has put it in an after-commentary, it was at least meant to be about how some of them

> were paying from within their varied armored and defended stances
> —the current disorientation and accompanying anger many feel at
> having been flung out from the heaven of their sexual and marital
> contexts and preconceptions. Whether they were right or wrong was
> not at all my concern, but the fact that they had been raised in a
> certain manner with certain obligations, duties, and expectations (all
> defined as natural) which, though they led to privilege in the social

order, carried with them certain hidden but equally inevitable effects of personal and emotional self-distortion, a crippling. (161)

So within the play, Phil, especially, who increasingly becomes Eddie's center of dramatic interest, is described by the latter in basically these terms, in a way thus, given Eddie's own analogous situation, defining the necessity and inevitability of that interest as an imaging of his own predicament as well. "You're right on schedule, Phil, that's all," Eddie tells him (the problem has been Phil's anguish over how his and Suzie's desire for a baby will alter the divorce picture). "You're a perfectly, rapateta, blah-blah-blah, modern statistic; you have the baby, you get the divorce. You're very 'now' is all, but not up to it. You're the definitive representative of the modern male in this year, but you're not willing to accept it" (81). And so, in basically these terms, do all the men in the play, Phil, Eddie, Mickey, Artie, become representatives of a common predicament, their individual dramas all versions of this larger cultural drama of self-recognition and confused, angry defense.

It should come as no surprise, then, that American women here, in ways especially reminiscent of the earlier Chrissy, fare predictably hard as a consequence. Again, as noted by Rabe himself, they are the representation of a vital energy, "a state of disruptive emotion" (167). All of them— Darlene, Donna, the wives somewhere out there, Suzie and Agnes—even as they are vilified and incessantly abused—exert among men immense power. They exercise it in their own vital sense of sexual presence. They exercise it in their procreative power of bearing children, and particularly of bearing female children. Phil, at the end, on his way to suicide in the despair over the divorce that has taken place precisely after his daughter has been born, kidnaps the child as a final act of self-assertion. Eddie admits at length that his own "little girl is a factor in every calculation I make— big or small—she's a constant" (131). (In significant contrast, Darlene, in her ensuing confession to an aborted pregnancy, imagines the living child as a teenage boy [131].) Indeed the play's archetypal scene of aggression— one so vividly presented even as verbal anecdote that we are stunned at its commingled horror and hilarity—is constituted as an almost inconceivably grotesque assault upon the humanity of a woman and her female child.

The anecdote concerns Bonnie the whore. In this case the sources are

Eddie and Mickey, who have been trying to connect her up with Phil, who needs badly, they have decided, "to get laid" (84), and who have therefore been trying to describe her skills. This leads to the story, recounted by the two of them in giggling antiphony, of how they have been delegated to pick up at the airport Robbie Rattigan, the star of a new TV pilot. They take along Bonnie, who is a TV freak and has seen the star on several "cop shows" (90). They also take along Bonnie's daughter. They put Bonnie up to giving the star a blow job in the car on the way back. While the blow job is taking place, Eddie and Mickey entertain the child with fairy tale and cartoon imitations, "making up this story about elves and shit," Eddie recalls, "and this kingdom full of wild rabbits, and the elves were getting stomped to death by gangs of wild rabbits." "Jungle Bunnies, I think, is what we called them," Mickey offers (92). "The kid was catatonic," Eddie chortles. And that, moreover, he tells Mickey, as they both collapse with laughter, "was it," the place where "we turned the corner in this venture." "Right," Mickey says. "What venture." Eddie clarifies: "Life. That was the nose dive. I mean, where it began. We veered at that moment into irredeemable depravity" (93). Thus language, as it often does in this play in the most arrant moments of men's self-scripting, speaks God's own truth. And thus persistently here the play at large speaks nothing less than "the immensity of the effort of the men to trivialize, categorize, and imprison the force they felt to be in the women" as "a measure of the fear they had of the chaos they felt to reside there—though it no doubt resided at least equally, if not predominantly within themselves, then 'Phil'" (167–68).

The quote indicates the ceaseless channeling of momentum in the play into a long, dismal version of what must pass for us here again and again as our only meaning or moral: that men in their dealings with women and women in their dealings with men are a mess; that, at some profound level of insight, often beyond articulation, they know it; and that they thus spend most of their lives fumbling hopelessly with their inability to handle it. Among the men in particular, it is a real contest to see who is the biggest mess. As to the issue of manly desire, however, there can be no question of its primary focus on Phil, described by Rabe as "the shadow, the prisoner, the outlaw, the ex-con of vanished passions" (167). And although there is truly, as Rabe again asserts, "no exact 'mouthpiece' character in the play, its psychological focus comes to lodge increasingly in Eddie's attempts to deal with "the 'Phil' in himself, the forces of vitality and disorder" (167), while at the same time not embracing another extreme of Mickey's cerebral gift for analytical, even cynical insulation and detachment. To this degree, the play truly is, as Rabe recalls himself describing it in an offhand moment, about how Eddie through the eventual death of Phil was saved from being Mickey. He is saved, in fact, as the play's last scene makes clear, by grief, by his capacity at least to feel something. In the nature of things, of "SO MUCH TO FIGURE OUT," as he shrieks near the end, there is at least this. Here, then perhaps, even the idiot-wisdom of a Donna, the last character left on stage with him, can begin to make at least a rudimentary sense. She has lied, she confesses to Eddie, about a trip she has been describing on which she has gotten a lot of souvenirs. Actually, she says, "I got no further than Oxnard." "I know where Oxnard is," Eddie replies. "Great!" she responds, "with immense enthusiasm." "What's so great about people knowing where Oxnard is?" he asks, "laughing," we are told, "a little." "It's great when people know what each other are talking about, right, isn't that what we been talking about?" She natters on about love, in this version a brief fling with a Mexican, how it was mainly "a mess." She decides she is sleepy, and shortly Eddie lies down on the couch, where he says she can join him. She makes a last offer of a fuck. He says no. He wants to know if she needs "a lude or anthing," maybe a "Valium." She says no. They both say goodnight, and Donna wishes him "pleasant dreams." We doubt that these will come. But maybe, just this once, we are encouraged to believe, there will be some sleep (159–60).

At the end, as often throughout, the available meanings here seem almost too up-front and obvious: that grieving is at least better than feeling nothing; that some communication is better than no communication; that sleeping in a house is better than being on the street; that, in the gospel according to Donna, "it's all part of the flow of which we are a part, too, and everything pertains to everything one way or another, see what I mean" (156). But that after all *is* exactly the point. Precisely to the degree that the ritual formulas of our language do constitute the primary actions of our lives, we must thus take our large mythic meanings there where they are truly lodged, in the linguistic surfaces of the commonplace and even the cliche; and thus, of its own linguistic surfaces as well, the play creates itself throughout as at once both parable and enactment of its own figuration.

"You know, we're all just background in one another's life. Cardboard cutouts bumping around in this vague, you know, hurlyburly, this spin-off of what was once prime time life; so don't hassle me about this interpersonal fuck-up on the highway, okay?" (112–13). Thus one voice of authority, speaking the latest confusions, names the drama from within; and so also another, speaking by Shakespearean invocation an ancient dramaturgy-thaumaturgy, names it equally from without.[8] So here again, even down to a title, Rabe continues to write American drama as its own mythic accounting. "Blah-blah-blah"; "rapateta-rapateta-rapateta"; "thingamajig-whatchamacallit-hurlyburly"; in a bar or a barracks or a living room; in an apartment or a tract house or a cosmos; somewhere indeed, exactly between latest nonsense and oldest magic, David Rabe continues to write the sundry dramas of language that are our common American lives.

# POETS AFTER OUR WAR

*John Balaban, W. D. Ehrhart, David Huddle,*

*Yusef Komunyakaa, Walter McDonald, Bruce Weigl*

We have been Democracy on Zippo raids,
burning houses to the ground,
driving eager amtracs through new-sown fields.

We are the ones who have to live
with the memory that we were the instruments
of your pigeon-breasted fantasies.
We are inextricable accomplices
in this travesty of dreams:
but we are not alone.

We are the ones you sent to fight a war
you did not know a thing about—
those of us that lived
have tried to tell you what went wrong.
Now you think you do not have to listen.

Just because we will not fit
into the uniforms of photographs
of you at twenty-one
does not mean you can disown us.

We are your sons, America,
and you cannot change that.
When you awake,
we will still be here.

—W. D. Ehrhart, "A Relative Thing"

American Eagle beating its wings over Asia
  million dollar helicopters
  a billion dollars worth of Marines
     who loved Aunt Betty
       Drawn from the shores and farms shaking
  from the high schools to the landing barge
  blowing the air through their cheeks with fear
    in *Life* on Television
Put it this way on the radio
Put it this way in television language
       Use the words
          language, language,
           "A bad guess"

—Allen Ginsberg, "Wichita Vortex Sutra"

Much like the Anglo-American experience of World War I, the experience of Vietnam brought forth the work of combat poets speaking the nightmare of war with a new wisdom of horror and abandonment. And so too, for other poets of the era, the war similarly came to pose a problem of sense making often challenging anew our ideas of the very media of poetic representation themselves. The works of veteran-poets were anthologized in two important early collections, *Winning Hearts and Minds: War Poems by Vietnam Veterans*, edited by Larry Rottmann, Jan Barry, and Basil T. Paquet, and *Demilitarized Zones*, edited by W. D. Ehrhart and Jan Barry; and more recently they have been assembled in a major university press anthology, *Unaccustomed Mercy: Soldier-Poets of the Vietnam War*, and also reunited with other responses from the poetic community in *Carrying the Darkness: American Indochina—The Poetry of the Vietnam War*, both edited by Ehrhart. They also were represented in major early collections by individual poets such as Michael Casey's *Obscenities* and D. C. Berry's *saigon cemetery*.[1] Emerging most significantly, however, as poetic voices from the experience of the war were six writers, John Balaban, W. D. Ehrhart, David Huddle, Yusef Komunyakaa, Walter McDonald, and Bruce Weigl, who have now also gone on to become significant poets of their American generation as well. They are poets after our war who, even as they continue to speak its memory, now trace out in addition the patterns of its broader mythic configuring within our life and culture at large.

With the appearance of *After Our War*, John Balaban announced clearly his sense of the crucial role of the Vietnam poet as new cultural mythmaker, as centralizing agent in the large work of necessary cultural revision. His attempt, as I have suggested elsewhere, was to project memory into the grand contexts of imaginative and mythic comprehension that have traditionally marked the major poetic art of a given age. He has been, truly, the figure of the poet after our war.

Balaban's vision of the war itself has been colored throughout by a distinctly original sense of experiential perspective. Although he survived as much military violence and saw as much of war's carnage and horror as most actual combatants, he experienced the Vietnam conflict specifically through civilian alternative service during 1967–69 as a conscientious objector, first as an instructor in linguistics at the University of Can Tho and later as a field representative of the Committee of Responsibility to Save War Damaged Children. He also returned to Vietnam in 1971 to spend nearly another year traveling the countryside and recording Vietnamese folk poetry. Indeed, along with the novelist Robert Olen Butler, he is one of the few American writers to come out of the war—and the fact will be crucial both to his poetry and to his subsequent work as a novelist, memoirist, and chronicler of cultural myth—to possess a fluency in Vietnamese. Coupled particularly with his training as a linguist, it allows him as a poet to extend in radically original ways an already complex sense of the possibilities of language, particularly of languages non-western. As a consequence, moreover, it also propels his writing into broader questions of language, representation, and linguistic referentiality often aligned with those of contemporary critical theory at large.

The originality of experiential vision and commitment which grounds Balaban's work as poetic and cultural mythmaker inscribes itself in an equally original literary career of suggestive range and eclecticism. His books of poetry include *After Our War*, *Blue Mountain*, and a third, *Words for My Daughter*, forthcoming. He has also published *Ca Dao Vietnam*, a collection of Vietnamese folk poetry in translation. As a novelist, he published in 1985 the highly regarded *Coming Down Again*, a Conradian adventure of quest and return, the basic structure imaged in its doubled title, set in the opium triangle of Southeast Asia in the last days of the Vietnam war. He has also published a children's fable, *The Hawk's Tale*, and has most recently written the narrative for *Vietnam: The Land We Never Knew*, a book of photography by the veteran Geoffrey Clifford.[2] Forthcoming is a memoir entitled *Remembering Heaven's Face*. Finally, in an extension of literary enterprise suggestively uniting him with the other poets discussed here, all of whom either currently teach or have taught literature and creative writing, he is a university professor of English.[3]

As I have suggested elsewhere, Balaban's first volume, *After Our War*, both in the title itself and the long single poem from which it derives, defines from the outset the essential character of his career as post-Vietnam cultural mythmaker. His purpose is to reinscribe the old high modernist project of *kulchur*, to reconstitute an idea of something like poetic tradition as a newly possible context of value and meaning. At the same time, the enterprise is also the familiar one of the old high modernist project in suggestive postmodern formulation, the text often as collage, collation, and even mass-media montage. In this, one of his guides is clearly T. S. Eliot. Another, of prime importance in his extension of poetic rangings into everything from the Greek and Roman classics and Anglo-Saxon to the popular idioms of a London newspaper or the songs of Elton John, is clearly Ezra Pound. And in his broadening of poetic reach explicitly into the Orient—in the present case, that particularly of Vietnamese folk poetry—one senses the distinct provenance of the Pound tradition as well. So in direct generational legacy Lowell also would often seem to speak here of the individual poet's quest toward faith in a possible recovery of history and of sustaining historical myth in the face of an annihilating techno-culture. And so likewise in Balaban's darkly powerful imagings of nature and of recuperative natural growth are enacted new versions of Roethke's related project of mythic recovery as well.

In "After Our War" alone, for instance, all of these would seem to mingle with Thomas Nashe, Thomas Kyd, John Milton, and an original Vietnamese cast literally beyond description, "all the old folks—Slit Eye/and Spilled Guts, Fried Face and Little Missy Stumps" (4). Kyd's Hieronymo, who has become Eliot's Hieronymo, now becomes Balaban's Hieronymo:

> Morally quits, Hieronymo gnashes off his tongue,
> spits out the liver lump to a front-row lap,
> but wishes, then to explain; even: to recite poetry.

Meanwhile, in the same mythic precincts, we are told,

Yesterday a pig snouting for truffles uncovered
moles, blind and bellyful of *Paradise Lost.*
Gleeful, let us go somewhere to curse God and die. (3)

The text, in sum, is a whole, dreadful, ferocious landscape of war: "When
we blighted the fields," the poem begins,

the harvests replied:
"You have blighted your flesh." Muck-marrowed,
bones ungluing like book paste; nerve hems
shredded or grimed in something foul, leaking,
we visit each other like a plague. Kiss-Kiss.
Intelligence is helplessly evil; words lie. (3)

But in the same moment, words are all we have, the poet's words, the
other poets' words, the words of the other poetries, something like what
remains of poetic myth, after our wars. And from that, we somehow begin
to piece back together some sustaining vision of the world and of our relationship to it. We take the words where we can get them, with our own
words often in the process themselves returned to us in newly signifying
reecho. In "Along the Mekong," for instance, the poet is first Balaban,
among the rich, odorous, noisy hubbub of life, while reading a *New Yorker*
article, something by a

Thomas Whiteside.
2, 4, 5-T teratogenicity in births;
South Vietnam 1/7th defoliated; residue
in rivers, foods, and mother's milk [;] (12)

but now, suddenly, in the same moment, he is also somehow Walt Whitman, stunned into a rapt attending at the teeming wonder of it all. "Why,
a reporter, or a cook," he marvels,

could write this poem
if he had learned dictation. But what if I said,
simply suggested, that all this blood fleck, muscle rot, earth root and
    earth leaf, scraps
of glittery scales, fine white grains, fast talk
gut grime, crab claws, bright light, sweetest smells
—Said: a human self; a mirror held up before. (13)

In "The Gardenia in the Moon," the poet again himself speaks first, walking alone "In Pennsylvania Woods" with sudden visions of

> A machine gun . . . cracking like slapping sticks.
> A yelling man smacked into the smooth canal. (26)

Apace, out of that memory of old death speaks anew, in the text of the reinscribed report of a slain U.S. agricultural field worker, a brave voice of moral objection from beyond even that final fact of death. "I'm not satisfied that this is true," the latter protests of events reported to him, military-bureaucratic excuses for occasional destruction. "I have the following facts and questions in mind" (30). The two voices in the poem have become one voice, and it is the voice of history now posed as ongoing mythic self-inscription and critique. "Gitelson, do-gooder? a fool?" the poet cries out at the end.

> Am I a Christer and your corpse-monger?
> Dead, I am your father, brother, Dead, we are your son. (37)

We make our poems after our war as we find them: in the mistypings of a Saigon bargirl (make . love . not.. war ........," she concludes, "fuck....you" [60]); in an Old English riddle ("The anwer to the riddle is: Riddle" [57]); in a Vietnamese proverb ("Birds have nests; men have ancestors" [81]). We find them quite necessarily "On a Photograph of Schoolchildren Wearing Gas Masks. Rheims. World War I" (70). We see there a war, Rheims, 1916; a war, Rheims, 1940; a war, Japan, 1945; a war, Dien Bien Phu, 1954; a war, somewhere else in Vietnam, "April, 1965." We see children and terrible weapons and murder and the conscience-salving communiques of commanders. We hear the voice of the poet, recorder, myth-inscriber and new mythic creator, the voice of the ongoing attempt at human sense making attempting to speak after our war. And again the voice speaks in itself *and* in the conscious project of mythic recovery and revision, forging the forms of traditional poetic statement into creative union with ongoing inscriptions of memory, even as that memory in turn becomes the basis of new poetic myth for other times and better. (As might be expected, given Balaban's own sense of poetic-cultural context, this is itself a very "Vietnamese" idea. So he writes, for instance, in the preface to *Ca Dao:* "For the Vietnamese, as for the Chinese whose language bears

similar timeless traits, a poem is a pre-existing eternality which becomes
a personal event in which the reader is allowed to dwell for as long as
he can maintain the reverie. This makes sense of the Chinese aphorism
'and there's a poem to prove it too' — which as an appeal to authority is,
for us, absurd" [17].) And thus, as I have suggested elsewhere, even down
to the last poem of this remarkable book, in the memory of one more
dying friend there comes a new gift of high imaginative insight as well,
the human example translated into the possibility of transfiguring poetic
myth that might yet allow one to ride out the dominion of the world. The
poet sees him, the friend, and precisely as he does see him sees him also
beyond, at once here and there, in "the condition," as Joseph Campbell
has called it, "of the god" (15):

> Ehrhart, diving and flying in a whirl of methadone
> and realization, watches for star-nesting birds;
> spies a man-bird; beaked, crimson-winged,
> with a body of gold — Garuda,
> who routed the gods, their wheel of blades,
> who severed the snake guard, spat back its poison,
> whose wing-beat rush could stop the world.
> Who spat back the poison. Who dwells in the sun.

"Keep moving," the poet exhorts his friend, himself, and *our*selves, "and
don't look down" (135).

In *Blue Mountain*, the enterprise of post-Vietnam poetic-cultural
mythmaking and remaking is clearly continued, even now to the poet's
significant reconstitution in major poems of his own textual structures
in attempts at clarified and enlarged mythic postulation. He essays not
only the inscription and reinscription of poetic myth but now also self-
reinscription as well, the revision of the cultural project and experience
of becoming the poet after our war into itself the substance of new myth.
Moreover, as with many second and third works by Vietnam writers, the
focus of the enterprise of sense making after our war is now both there
and here and specifically here, now, back in the world, in our place, the
place here that, every bit as much as there, was also the war and in great
degree remains so.

In "April 30, 1975," for instance, peace finally sounds throughout Vietnam. The bells ring in America as well, but as the poet and his wife sit on the porch, what they in fact now look out over is the spectacle of a nearer land, their own, in which

> City lights have reddened the bellies of fumed clouds
> like trip flares scorching skies over a city at war.

There has become here; here is now there. In traffic, cars screech, their brake lights crimson, to near misses. A girl maces a mugger.

> *Some kids have burnt a bum on Brooklyn Bridge.*
> *Screaming out of sleep, he flares the causeway.*

Poisoned vapors, hellish light, rapes, assaults, immolations, all blend here and there, there and here, into composite specter of memory and present consciousness. "The war returns like figures in a dream," the poet concludes. Still, perhaps, now, at home, a return may also be at least the start of a new going. "In Vietnam," the poet writes at the last, in literal mythic transport,

> pagodas chime their bells.
> "A Clear Mind spreads like the wind,
> By the Lo waterfalls, free and high,
> You wash away the dust of life." (43)

A similar doubled vision, "there" and "here" at once cast upon a single terrain of poetic mythography, characterizes "In Celebration of Spring." "Our Asian war is over," the poet says. At the same time, he adds,

> others have begun.
> Our elders, who tried to mortgage lies, are disgraced, or dead, and
>    already
> the brokers are picking their pockets for the keys and the
>    credit cards.

And now, he goes on,

> In delta swamp in a united Vietnam,
> a Marine with a bullfrog for a face,
> rots in equatorial heat.
> An eel slides through the cage of his bared ribs.

Meanwhile, back in the world, "all across the U.S.A./the wounded walk about and wonder where to go." Can an old swamp become a new garden? we are asked. Can the world once again be made at one, our world of the war miasma of self-destruction, be it military or ecological, with the great cycles of nature? It is a vision, the poet tells us, the mood shifted explicitly in the last stanza to a stern and moving imperative, to which we must commit our fullest resources of experiential will *and* collective mythic imagining. "Swear by the locust," he commands,

> by dragonflies on ferns,
> by the minnow's flash, the tremble of a breast,
> by the new earth spongy under our feet:
> that as we grow old, we will not grow evil,
> that although our garden seeps with sewage,
> and our elders think it's up for auction — swear
> by this dazzle that does not wish to leave us —
> that we will be keepers of a garden, nonetheless. (48)

So we continue to enact the poet's work of the world, the complex poetic process of mythic revision upon the landscape of culture after our war. And so particularly here, in the at once new and old poem bearing that title, "After Our War," we now make that process an ongoing exercise in poetic self-revision as well. "After Our War": in structure, it strikes us as having been radically compressed; yet in vision, it strikes us as having been massively enlarged. How this is done comprises a case study not unlike comparable revisions to be undertaken by Balaban's important contemporary, Bruce Weigl, of poetic self-reinscription as itself a significant step in the larger progress toward major poetic myth. In the first half at least, "After Our War" still seems in many ways very much the old poem, a vista of carnage, butchery, befoulment, miasmic filth and stink, a collection of gibbering horrors. "After our war," the poet now begins,

> the dismembered bits,
> — all those pierced eyes, ear slivers, jaw splinters,
> gouged lips, odd tibias, skin flaps, and toes —
> came squinting, wobbling, jabbering back.

Yet now, if possible, as the poem moves into an essentially new second half, things have also taken even a more imaginatively terrible new turn.

"There" has again become "here" with a vengeance, and, as it turns out, also with a grotesque form of domestic justice.

> Since all things naturally return to their source,
> these snags and tatters arrived, with immigrant uncertainty,
> in the United States,

he tells us. "It was almost," he adds, "a home." The result, the vision of it here now, as well as there, is a stunning original horror: a new mirroring of ourselves, after our war, now with spare parts of terrible memory, now ourselves imaginatively wearing the carnage. "So, now," we are informed,

> one can sometimes see a friend or a famous man talking
> with an extra pair of lips glued and yammering on his cheek,
> and this is why handshakes are often unpleasant,
> why it is better, sometimes, not to look another in the eye,
> why at your daughter's breast thickens a hard keloidal scar.

And it is the new idea of the horror endlessly revisited upon itself that poetry and language are now asked to bear. "After the war," he asks, defining that quest for meaning that unites us,

> with such Cheshire cats grinning in our trees,
> will the ancient tales still tell us new truths? Will the myriad world
>   surrender new metaphor?
> After our war, how will love speak? (37)

In large degree, the search for such speaking remains Balaban's on-going project. It is always the work of the poet after our war, he seems to tell us, after this war in particular, the media war, the celebrity war, the lost war, the war of American virtue and befuddlement, a kind of news update on the latest desolations. In the *Centre Daily Times*, we find an account of ourself, we are told,

> written up in the local small town press
> for popping a loud-mouth punk in the choppers

on the obverse page, "back to back," with the victims of the old war, "the page one refugees." "Familiar faces," the poet writes.

We followed them
through defoliated forests, cratered fields,
past the blasted water buffalo,
the shredded tree lines, the human head
dropped on the dusty road, eyes open.
the dusty road which called you all to death.

Macbeth-like, we strut and fret, play the poor player. When we speak, we
speak the names of the dead themselves, and we recall ourselves and others
from that place that is now somewhere else. There is Page, now "with a
steel plate in his head," and Gitelson, whose "brains," the poet remembers,
"leaked on my hands and knee," and the poet himself, "me, yours truly,"
he says,

agape in the Burn Ward in Da Nang, a quonset hut,
a half a garbage can that smelled like Burger King,
listening to whispers and nitrate fizzing on flesh
in a silence that simmered like a fly in a wound.

Thus we try to make new consolidations of the old hoarded texts. But
now, we have only the latest news of separation between ourselves and the
world, of desire only and of our eternal wish to connect. "Oh," the poet
concludes, "big sighs. Windy sighs. And ghostly laughter" (59).

So the ghost laughter of memory coupled with the desire for new
imaginative connection persists in the latest news from the home front for
Balaban, "Words for My Daughter." And again, appropriately, the setting
is quite domestic. A poet recalls his childhood: his fat friend Reds, defending his beaten mother with a hammer, running from his old man and not
looking

back across the thick swale
of teasel and black-eyed Susans until it was safe
to yell fuck you at the skinny drunk
stamping around barefoot and holding his ribs;

"the Connelly kid" who "came home to find/his alcoholic mother getting fucked by the milkman" and who "broke a milk bottle and jabbed the
guy humping on his mom"; the nameless frightened girl running past the

porch with the dart stuck in her back, and then later the offending brother
the kids tried to hang from an oak ("Before they hoisted him, yowling
and heavy/on the clothesline, they made him claw the creekbank/and eat
worms."). "So these were my playmates," the poet tells his daughter.

> I love them still
> for their justice and valor and desperate loves
> twisted in shapes of hammer and shard.

He goes on:

> I want you to know about their pain
> and about the pain they could loose on others.
> If you're reading this, I hope you will think,
> Well, my dad had it rough as a kid, so what?
> If you're reading this, you can read the news
> and you know that children can suffer worse.

Worse indeed. Among the American children remembered now comes
the remembered Vietnamese child as well,

> the nine-year old boy, naked and lacerated,
> thrashing on his pee on a steel operating table
> and yelling "Dau. Dau,"

—it is the Vietnamese for "Pain. Pain,"—

> while I, trying to
> translate
> in the mayhem of Tet for surgeons who didn't know
> who this boy was or what happened to him kept asking
> "Where? Where's the pain?" until a surgeon
> said "Forget it. His ears are blown."

Now, years later than any of those childhoods, there has come an
American holiday, a daughter's first Halloween. And now also, on that
night when we dress up in costumes designed to haunt, there has come
this: "a tiny Green Beret" who

> was saying trick or treat and I thought *oh oh*
> but remembered it was Halloween and where I was.

Now, at the end point of remembering, has come a literal déjà vu. Yet now, at that awful terminus, has come exactly a new point of possibility as well. And that new possibility, of course, is the shared experience of words themselves which the poem even now has begun to complete. Words for his daughter: "I want you to know the worst and be free from it," he writes; "I want you to know the worst and still find good." And words now also, clearly, for himself: "Day by day," he concludes,

> as you play nearby or laugh
> with the ladies at People's Bank as we go around town
> and I find myself beaming like a fool,
> I suspect I am here less for your protection
> than you are here for mine, as if you were sent
> to call me back into our helpless tribe. (42)

There is a poet here who writes. There is a daughter who may read. There is the old human pull, memory and desire commingled, of the whole helpless tribe. What we have left to us at least for the sake of ourselves and our children are words, albeit only words, yet words nonetheless— words perhaps finally not so much about what we can teach our children but what our children can possibly teach us. They are Halloween words indeed: magic words; words of incantation and spells; words that can make tonight the most haunted night of the year or the old promise of the saints renewed. They are at once all of these and more: words of memory, words of desire, words for his daughter, words for himself, and now somehow also words for us all.

While beginning his career as a poet and most recently celebrating a poetic culmination in the emergence of *To Those Who Have Gone Home Tired*, an edition of his collected poems, W. D. Ehrhart has also paralleled John Balaban in his wide-ranging experiments in literary enterprise—as poet, critic, cultural essayist, memoirist, novelist, samizdat publisher, veterans' activist—and in forms cross-literary, transgeneric, multimedia, including a significant role in the production of Stanley Karnow's *Vietnam: A Television History*. His first works included several early volumes of poems as well as *Demilitarized Zones*, already noted as an important edition of early writings about Vietnam by veterans of the war. Subsequent writings have included a memoir of the war, *Vietnam-Perkasie: A Memoir, Going*

*Back: An Ex-Marine Returns to Vietnam*, and *Passing Time*, a further account of combat and return.[4]

Like Balaban's, however, Ehrhart's most sustained gifts of vision and voice have clearly been those of the poet after our war and one specifically, as noted by Lorrie Smith, connecting "two converging continuums: his personal coming of age and the destructive flow of history" (14). Like Bruce Weigl's, she goes on, his is a major body of work refusing "to recuperate a past before the war or a poetry untinged by its anguish," a poetry that grounds itself "in the immediacy of the war" yet at the same time travels "beyond a mere litany of atrocities to imagine the war's continuing and palpable presence in American life," to create a "range of responses which measure and connect the war's psychic, cultural, political, and literary costs" (14).

As might be expected of the American soldier poet of this generation after this particular war, in Ehrhart's early work, there is a distinct cultivation of the voice of the poetry of the Anglo-American generation of that other war which this one, in both nature and impact, seemed so closely to resemble. He is at once the rude, angry soldier poet, early on attempting to find a voice,[5] and the spiritually chastened culture hero whose odyssey out of memory toward imaginative sense making becomes the quest for new myth and better. Poems such as "The One That Died" and "Hunting" are characteristic in their GI bluntness as well as their Owen-Sassoon-Hemingway precision and control. Of sorting the personal effects of the dead man that "isn't welcome anymore," because "he could too easily take our place," he concludes,

> We'll keep the cigarettes;
> divide them up among us.
> His parents have no use for them,
> and cigarettes are hard to get. (10)

Of the boyish epiphany, in the latter poem,

> that I have never hunted anything in my whole life
> except other men,

he remarks with a veteran's discipline,

But I have learned by now
where such thoughts lead,
and soon pass on
to chow, and sleep,
and how much longer until I change my socks. (13)

Yet even here, in "A Generation of Peace," as the early collection was named, there are pointings in new imaginative directions as well. In memory there is also imagined futurity.

Do they think of me now
in those strange Asian villages,

the poet asks in "Making the Children Behave,"

where nothing seemed
quite human
but myself
and my few grim friends
moving through them
hunched
in lines?

"When they tell stories to their children," he concludes,

of the evil
that awaits misbehavior,
is it me they conjure? (20)

Old horror becomes strange new admonition of common myth. There are stories, the poet imagines, that others will tell about us to explain evil; and to know them, he imagines further, would be to gain an explanation of our own.

Sometimes the appeal to mythic self-reconsideration is more direct and even, as Smith notes for instance, consciously polemic (14–15). The war has truly been "A Relative Thing," the poet admonishes. The old well-documented brutalities, the mangled pregnant women with stillborn children, the terrorized old men, Hue City, "Democracy on Zippo Raids": these have been truly collective endeavors. As to the soldiers, he writes, "We are inextricable accomplices in this travesty of dreams: but," he goes

on, "we are not alone." There is the larger business of relative things
as well.

> Just because we will not fit
> into the uniforms of photographs
> of you at twenty-one
> does not mean that you can disown us,

he writes. "We are your sons, America, and you cannot change that." So
it always is with true relatives: "When you awake, we will still be here"
(17–18).

The appeal of sense making can likewise be made abroad to those
others who have borne the battle, perhaps in other uniforms, yet poets also
with their visions of the quest, he imagines, the hunger that they likely
share. To the man who tried to kill him, for instance, he writes in "Letter,"

> What's it like back there?
> It's all behind us here;
> and after all the years of possibility, things are back to normal.

Moreover, he goes on,

> We just had a special birthday,
> and we've found again our inspiration
> by recalling where we came from
> and forgetting where we've been.

Once again, he tells his war brother, Americans have found the old silent
habit:

> Oh, we're still haggling over pieces
> of the lives sticking out
> beyond the margins of our latest
> history books—but no one haggles
> with the authors.

In contrast, he exhorts, firmly, "*Do better than that.*" At least, in spite of
what is happening here, he tells him,

> remember where you've been, and why.
> And then build houses; build villages,

dikes and schools, songs
and children in that green land
I blackened with my shadow and the shadow of my flag.

"Remember," he begs:

Remember Ho Chi Minh
was a poet: please,
do not let it all come down
to nothing. (34–35)

Meanwhile, back in the world, at whatever the cost, new authors must continue to haggle with the margins of history, must continue to speak of old goings and new possibilities of departure. At home, now, later, camping with an old friend wounded in the war amidst the great mountains of the Klamath Indians, the poet recalls, in "A Confirmation," "the day you went down screaming,/angry." Then, he adds, "Two months later I went down." He goes on:

We all went down eventually,
the villages aflame, the long
grim lines of soldiers, flotsam
in the vortex of a sinking illusion:
goodbye, Ginny; goodbye, John Kennedy;
goodbye, Tom Paine and high school history—
though here we are still, you and I.
We live our lives now
in a kind of awkward silence
in the perfect stillness of the shadows
of the Klamath Indians.

Yet at the same time, there is also a new kind of camping the "High Country," as Ehrhart concludes in the poem by that name, and one in which memory of loss and silence may yet be possibly redeemed. Ironically, the "camping" here is itself remembered from a time during the war; and the memory is of the wonder of how such peace and purity of life— "so close" among "the stars," the poet remembers, that

we climbed the Milky Way with our dreams
and stalked the Bear with Orion

—could have gone on amidst such horror, a world where

> calculating
> men in three-piece suits and uniforms
> with stars called firestorms down upon
> the heads of people with conical hats
> and spoke of Peace with Honor.

And further, he goes on,

> Calculating men in three-piece suits
> and uniforms with stars are calling down
> firestorms upon the heads of peasants
> in Central America now.

Yet for the poet, there can still come the old best trick of memory, that trick being the one of imaginative reconstitution. Boys grown older, some of them gone to doctors, others gone to soldiers and then teachers, can still remember camping the high country and now imagine anew, imagine once again, as the poem tells us in conclusion, of bathing deep at sunrise in the currents, amidst the movement of things and the world,

> the water rushing among the rocks,
> and over our bodies, and on. (72)

Although David Huddle has become best known as a writer of short fiction, with several major collections, now including *A Dream with No Stump Roots in It*, *Only the Little Bone*, and *The High Spirits*, he has also revealed himself as a war poet of distinctive voice and evolution. In "Words," for instance, he literally recreates the babble of moral and cultural confusion that was Vietnam in the language most familiar to virtually any GI, that of the young girls of that tormented nation who often bought and sold themselves in image of its own ceaseless rape. "What did those girls say," the poet begins by asking,

> when you walked the strip
> of tin shack bars, gewgaw stores, barber shops,
> laundries and restaurants, most all of which
> had beds in back, those girls who had to get up
> in Saigon before dawn to catch their rides to Cu Chi,

packed ten to a Lambretta, chattering, gay
in their own lovely tongue, on the dusty
circus road to work, but then what did they say?

We will never know that old, lovely, unheard music. Rather, one will be condemned to hear in memory just the late dreadful caw and cackle, the argot of the old profession:

*Come here, talk to me, you handsome, GI*
*I miss you, I love you too much, you want*
*short time, go in back, I don't care, I want*
*your baby, sorry about that, GI,*
*you number ten.*

Yet the poet's task must still be at once to remember and inscribe anew. Now, even "a history away," he concludes, "I translate dumbly what those girls would say" (145–46).

Similarly, in "Vermont," he continues still the process of somehow putting it back together, finding some current equilibrium of old memory and new imaginative desire. "I'm forty-one," he begins. "I was twenty-three then." Now, he goes on, "I'm here with what I've dreamed or remembered." Specifically, there have been "the Grand Hotel at Vung Tau one weekend" and

the most delicate
sixteen-year-old girl who ever delivered
casual heartbreak to a moon-eyed GI.

He is "trying to make it balance" now, he tells us, "but I/can't. Believe me, I've weighed it out." There has been the particular matter of memory, all the way back on the flight to Cu Chi as "the green land moved in its own dream down there." It is of

a girl turning her elegant face away
after all I had to say.

Again, it is the silence here that speaks in fullest poetic resonance, the vision of a gesture at once remembered and preserved. "This was in Vietnam," he concludes. "Who didn't love me" (147).

In addition to these poems of explicit response to the experience of the war and its American aftermath, so also for Huddle, in the cycle of poems entitled *Paper Boy*, the rewriting of American memory becomes the subject of new domestic myth as well. Paper boy. He is, of course, in the small-town context, a most familiar figure. He is the industrious one on the bicycle, the one trusted enough to learn and complete a route, the one out in all the weathers, the one who can be counted on, in an adult responsibility beyond his years, to deliver the news. And here what he delivers, of course, is the history of ourselves. "*Tell about [that place]*," the book's Faulknerian epigraph commands, in new inscription of an old literary-cultural question. "*What's it like there. What do they do there. Why do they live there. Why do they live at all.*" So, in response, the paper boy begins his rounds.

There is the opening poem, "Town History, 1917," of the murdered grandfather, founder of

> a livery
> stable, a funeral
> parlor, a watch repair
> shop, and a general
> store,

and shot down in the street (3). The genealogy of odd violence here, it turns out, moreover, is also something of a family affair at large. The poet's own father has also been there, almost murdered himself at age seven when

> Aunt
> Elrica, in her teens,
> went into shock
> and clasped her hand
> over my daddy's mouth
> to stop his crying.
> She almost smothered
> him before he could
> get her hand pried
> loose. (3)

There are specific poems of family life, of the poet's growing up; of an angry, somewhat quixotic father; a sensible, firm-willed mother; odd feckless neighbors; schoolmate twin brothers who drown while swimming; and the queer child-memory of funeral and aftermath. There is the account, in "Delivering the Times, 1952–55," of the poet as paper boy, the four and a half-mile walk, the three dangerous dogs, "Crow Jim King," he recalls, who "broke me in" and

> showed me
> how to blow snot
> out of one side
> of my nose holding
> the other side shut
> with my finger. (7)

After two years have come savings of ninety dollars,

> for that gold-plated
> trumpet Daddy
> had to teach me how
> to play.

He concludes:

> And even
> though Sunday
> was a heavy load,
> I walked that route
> every day until
> I had to start
> catching the bus
> to the consolidated
> high school. (7)

"Miss Florence Jackson" has been the stern old spinster of a sixth-grade teacher, "old goose bosom," James Newman has called her, who has sent the poet to the principal over his telling of a joke he overheard from his grandfather but

> hadn't understood
> about a cow and a bull
> and a preacher,

and who has explained "birth control" by saying angrily that

"People have a choice
about whether or not
to have children." (15)

We meet the much-admired "Jeep Alley, Emperor of Baseball," and a first
love, Janie Swecker, too smart in schoolwork for her own good, who loans
the narrator her mother's copy of *Gone with the Wind* and therein figures
grandly in a dream he has where

Miss Jackson was marching
through Georgia,
Atlanta was burning,
and I was riding hard
to pull Janie
out of the flames. (18–19)

We hear accounts of a hapless storekeeper, nicknamed "Geronimo" after
murdering an employee in self-defense, and of a schoolmate's ferocious
mother whom even the district agent can't collect on for back newspaper
subscription. Bill Dalton's daddy gets his head split down the middle with
an axe by Phoenix Hill over a moonshine operation and lives. The further
adventures of the paper boy lead him to friendship with Deetum Dunford,
six months AWOL from the army and

hiding out back
in the mountain
near Billsby

and also to a crush on "a pretty woman just married and in shorts" (29).
He goes crow shooting with his grandfather, listens to his stories at table
about being a train fireman and about

how at mealtime Uncle Dave
and his daddy had had terrible
arguments about that war
the one had fought in
and the other hadn't. (32)

He rejoices in local oddities, Monkey Dunford and Dude and their sister,
Hat, and Hitler, who missed shooting his wife and ruined their new re-

frigerator. He tells, as he himself has heard it, while home from college, from Otis Shannon the barber, "What Finally Happened to Pete Bushey," son of mean Fay, after he has cut Billy Mabe's throat:

> Otis said Pete stood
> and watched awhile,
> then walked on back home
> to wait for the deputy
> to come and get him. (43)

His brother learns to fly in the military, buzzes the hometown and becomes the stuff of local celebrity. He and his father visit Aunt Inez at the Old Lawson Place one last time before her passing, she who was "the baby of the Lawson family," and

> had been good at calligraphy,
> astrology, fixing watches,
> and auto mechanics.

At the auction afterward, we are told,

> Aunt Inez's 1928 Chevrolet,
> locked up where she'd parked it
> one morning thirty years ago, went for sixteen hundred dollars. (47)

And now suddenly, there has arrived the business of "Going, 1960–1970." He travels off to college in Charlottesville, has a roommate whose parents take him to Farmington Country Club and drive him

> home once
> in a Cadillac, first one
> except Barrett's hearse
> that'd ever been in our driveway. (48)

He rides his first airplane to Fort Jackson, South Carolina, for basic training, rides a train back to Baltimore ("and I was used/to that" [48]). He dances with a Polish girl in Stuttgart, rides a ferry to Denmark from Sweden, is spending Thanksgiving in Luxembourg City where he sees skinned rabbit and deer carcasses outside a butcher shop and gets a letter saying that his grandfather is sick. He suprises everyone at home "on his way west of Hawaii" and wears his uniform to see his grandfather, and then shortly flies in by helicopter

> to an old, cracked
> French-built tennis court
> near the capital city of
> Binh Chanh Province
> so that one Asian
> could beat up
> another one
> under my
> super-
> vision. (50)

Drunk in Tokyo, he is cussed out in English by a beautiful whore. He hears incredible woman stories about Bangkok, plans his own woman deals for his first night in San Francisco ("laying down $100 for some/good-smelling California girl"), but instead goes

> straight to the airport
> and caught the first
> flight home. (51)

His grandfather is still alive, barely, but enough to want the five fifths of I.W. Harper the poet gets for him only to have his grandmother methodically smash every one of them. His father dances at his wedding "the first two times in his life, first with my bride and then with my mother." "I felt/like kissing him," the poet tells us,

> because I'd been through enough of a
> war to know courage
> when I saw it. (52)

Then he is

> up there
> going to Columbia
> and drinking cocktails
> with writers who knew my name

when it finally happens to the old one, who falls, trying to take a pee,

wedging his head
between the bathtub and the wall,
my father working
almost an hour getting him out,
knowing all that time
his father was gone. (53)

The poet gets a haircut, goes down as he knows he must, sees his father
weep and then

felt a hurt snap
through my whole body,
wanted just for that instant
to plunge down with him
into that grave, going down
into black dirt, keep going
down with him the rest
of my life. (54)

He comes home again with his wife and a baby girl; his wife and his
mother get

busy doing whatever
it is two women
and a baby do
upstairs in a bedroom;

he talks mortgage with his father, and the two of them go over to get some
things from the grandfather's old tool shop. The poet looks

for the glass
with the dancing girls
who took off their clothes
when you filled it
with water or whiskey,

and "the naked woman/paperweight," can't find them, gets exercised

into discoursing
on why the hell
anybody would live

in a place where
people stole
anything of value,
the human condition
was unbearable
enough, even in
civilized towns. (56)

His father only half-listens, instead sees to it that the poet finds

a wrench,
a saw, some wire pliers,
a couple of screwdrivers.

"Then," we are told in conclusion,

He picked out
the oldest hammer there,
offered it to me,
and I took it
from his hand. (57)

The paper boy has grown up, taken his own place in the train of generations, been to Vietnam and back, become another kind of paper boy,
a known writer, found his way through a fair-sized sample of the human
condition, come home one last time to find out what he has always known:
that good tools are hard to come by and are best passed on by family,
elders of the tribe, and hand to hand.

Again for the poet, amidst all the old contextualizations, Vietnam remains the secret crux. It is the long foregrounding of a departure. It is the
latest ritual of return. Somewhere in between, in "Going 1960–1970," a
paper boy saw a war and became a writer. Now, in "Gifts," he begins anew
the old mythography of the tribe.

Like John Balaban's and W. D. Ehrhart's, then, to borrow the latter's
phrasing, David Huddle's vision of the the poet after our war remains "A
Relative Thing." It is the old family affair of common meaning, at once
the photographs we keep and the stories we tell about them to live by after
our wars. "I grew up staring at the picture of him": the poet begins, the
poem itself simply entitled "Cousin":

oak leaves on his shoulders, crossed rifles
on his lapels, and down his chest so many medals
the camera lost them.

And in person, it turns out, he is the stuff of legend as well, in stories where "World War Two/exploded" for a listening boy "on the front porch/when he'd visit and talk," in being "wounded twice" and knowing "he'd almost died." "Courage rang in his voice," the stanza concludes.

Now, the poet goes on, "ten years from my war, thirty from his," there is a new visit, more stories, many of them the old ones. "He remembered names of men," the poet recalls, "weapons, tactics, places, and I could see/his better than mine." Indeed, we find out, "He'd known Hemingway!" The literary trump card is the clincher. "I tried hard couldn't find a thing to say," the poet says simply in abrupt conclusion (146). And he says it, one notices, with studied illiteracy, a simple run-on. The men of the old wars knew Hemingway. The men of this one are still trying to find a syntax, let alone a myth.[6]

Like the work of David Huddle, that of the veteran-poet Yusef Komunyakaa likewise often seeks new understandings of the meaning of Vietnam in American lives not so much through the direct poetic address of the war as through various other forms of historical and mythic contextualization. (Indeed, notable about both of his first two important collections, *Copacetic* and *I Apologize for the Eyes in My Head*, is the suggestively explicit absence of the war itself as a topic of poetic inquiry.) And the particular forms, moreover, of that contextualization encountered here, in early poems published elsewhere directly addressing the war and also in more recent Vietnam poems comprising the bulk of a newest collection, entitled *Dien Cai Dau*, are those that in addition enlarge importantly our particular vision — one that continues to be lamentably underrepresented in our public literature of the war and of postwar experience — of the black American in the Vietnam era and its aftermath.

As noted above, Komunyakaa's initial poetic mythmaking after our war, particularly in his first two books, tells about Vietnam mainly by telling about America, and particularly about black America, and the tradition of what Houston Baker has called the "long black song" of African-American experience in the New World. The first half, for instance, of *Copacetic*, subtitled "Blackmetal Blues," seems devoted to an odyssey of

black consciousness ranging from the teeming hustle of contemporary life
to the old dream of the origin, "Back Then," "a bridge into the morning,"
a place and time

> when gold
> didn't burn out a man's eyes
> before auction blocks groaned in courtyards & nearly got the best of
> me. (23)

The present is the domain of "Slick Sam the Freight Train Hopper" in the
swamps (3)

> & Anna, that beautiful girl
> you once loved enough
> to die over & over again for,

who

> now lives in New Orleans
> on both sides
> of Bourbon Street. (6)

The past is a journey back through the windings of

> Family tree,
> Taproot,
> genealogy of blues. (19)

The echo of an old forgotten music,

> Across the cotton field
> Muddy Water's bone-song. (17)

mingles with visions of "Uncle Jesse (R.I.P.)" (18) with

> A Prince Albert
> cigarette between two fingers,
> Old Crow on his breath, that .38 Smith & Wesson
> under his overalls jumper,
> & the click-click of dice
> & bright shuffle of cards
> in a game called "coon can"
> still in his disposition. (19)

"Untitled Blues," indeed, becomes the master iconography of it all, after that curious photograph by Yevgeni Yevtushenko of

> a black boy
> behind a laughing white mask
> he's painted on. (13)

"The boy/locked inside your camera," the poet speculates,

> perhaps he's lucky—
> he knows how to steal
> laughs in a place
> where your skin
> is your passport. (14)

In the second half of the text, entitled "Mojo," the poet himself increasingly takes center stage, so to speak, as black personality. He inventories ideas of "Safe Subjects," knowing still that

> It's truth we're after here,
> hurting for, out in the streets
> where my brothers kill each other,
> each other's daughters & guardian angels
> in the opera of dead arrival. (32)

("Say something that resuscitates us," he commands himself, "behind the masks, as we stumble off into neon nights/to loveless beds & a second skin/ of loneliness" [32].) He apotheosizes "Villon/Leadbelly," "Two bad actors canonized by ballads" (37). He sings "Elegy for Thelonious" (40), runs "hard love" with "Copacetic Mingus" (41). "Woman, I Got the Blues," he says in his own music,

> Sweet Mercy, I worship
> the curvature of your ass.
> I build an altar in my head.
> I kiss your breasts and forget my name. (43)

He is "crazy nigger" in "Newport Beach, 1979" (45), "street nigger" in "Addendum" (I'm a womb-scratcher./I'm a double-dealer./I'm the chance you take/with the past tonight" [50]). He is the walking, talking "Blues Chant Hoodoo Revival," composed of "my story," "your story," "this story," "my story," "our story" (56). "Let's pour the night/into our stone water jars," he sings, adding in refrain, "bad luck isn't red flowers/crushed under jackboots" (56); then "pain isn't just red flowers/crushed under jackboots" (57); then finally, "this song isn't red flowers/crushed into silence" (58). It truly is the long black song, untitled blues in the key of history, "Epilogue to the Opera of Dead on Arrival." After singing "Ain't Goin' Down to the Well/No Mo' like Leadbelly," after trying to wish the woman named "Sweet Luck" back from the murdered dead, the poet cries out to his tormentors,

> Handcuff me, slam my head
> against bars of the jailhouse,
> use your blackjacks,
> zero in on my weaknesses,
> let enough melancholy
> to kill a mule
> settle into my lungs. (52)

In *I Apologize for the Eyes in My Head*, the opera of blues continues, at once hard, poignant, menacing, joyous, incredibly painful, outrageously exuberant. There are poems of self, of personal pain, loss, questioning, such as "Insufficient Blue," "After the Heart's Interrogation," and "The Heart's Graveyard Shift." In "Happy-Go-Lucky's Wolf Skull Dream Mask," the poet instructs himself in adaptation:

> OK, lift this mask
> up to your eyes, over your face
> a perfect fit.

> Well, Mr. Magnifico,
> what do you see? How's your world? (14)

Afoot on the landscape as well are figures of pain and memory such as "The Thorn Merchant," "The Thorn Merchant's Right-Hand Man," "The Thorn Merchant's Wife," "The Thorn Merchant's Mistress," "The Thorn Merchant's Son." Larger mythic memory also takes its shape in "1984" in "the ghost-catcher's madrigal":

> The end of what? To count disremembered years
> we say Gandhi, JFK, King, leafing through names and faces. (39)

The question remains.

> We can transplant broken hearts
> but can we put goodness back into them? (39)

We contemplate nature in a "Dreambook Bestiary," a strange, diminished memory of the garden (45–47). We ponder "Jonestown: More Eyes for *Jadigwa's Dream*" and subtitle our efforts "*After Rousseau*" (49). Amidst the spectral panorama, in "For the Walking Dead," there are for the first time whispering images of a familiar war, "Veronica" with her death cape in the bar where

> White phosphorus blooms
> five miles away, burning sky
> for a long moment, mortars
> rock in iron shoes cradled
> by earth, within earshot
> of carbines stuttering through
> elephant grass. (63)

She "counts the unreturned/faces," the poet tells us, "pale beads on an abacus," and

> lets them work her into the bar's darkest corner.
> They hold her, a shield against everything they know. (63)

But for the most part the mythic-poetic world of *I Apologize for the Eyes in My Head* continues to be the larger dominion of "The Beast & Burden," the place of "Seven Improvisations" still danced and sung by the old contrarieties, "Arm in arm & slipknot. Birth, death, back to back—silent mouth against the other's ear. They sing a duet, *e pluribus unum*" (73).

As noted earlier, Komunyakaa at the same time he was publishing his first two volumes also did publish poetry explicitly about the experience of the war. And here too came an art at once of utter concretion and strange mythic otherness conjoined in new imaginative authority of vision and voice. In "Somewhere Near Phu Bai" we stand guard at night and

> count the shapes ten meters
> out front, over & over, making sure
> they're always there,

remember Charlie's reputation for switching the direction of claymores, wonder

> If I hear a noise
> will I push the button
> & blow myself away? (149)

In "Starlight Scope Myopia," we sit in the eerie haze of night vision and imagine the enemy speaking as they go about their work:

> Caught in the infrared,
> What are they saying?
>
> Are they talking about women
> or calling the Americans
>
> *beaucoup dien cai dau?*
> One of them is laughing.
> You want to place a finger
> to his lips & say "shhhh."
> You try reading ghost-talk
>
> on their lips. They say
> "up-up we go," lifting as one.
> This one, old, bowlegged,
>
> you feel you could reach out
> & take him into your arms. You
>
> peer down the sights of our M-16,
> seeing the full moon
> loaded on an ox cart. (151)

We learn of the "Tiger Lady," the Viet Cong "dressed as a drag queen/with a .45" who

> glides along
> air, on magic, on his Honda
> shooting American officers [,] (152)

and "The Dead at Quang Tri," who most spookily "get up from/our ambushes and walk away" ("Like bygones," he writes, "if only they'd be done with,/the body counts would mean something" [153]). And later, "After the Fall of Saigon," we envision the old "Pearl of the Orient" and the great hasty discardings,

> Bandoliers, miniskirts, tennis shoes,
> fatigue jackets, combat boots—
> the city's color bruised, polyester
> suits limping down sidestreets. (154)

We see an old "mama'san," "Cowboys" parking "new Harleys/along Lam Son Square" and getting into "their disappearing act," and Dzung, the girl leaving the Continental Hotel, practicing on not

> mixing up the words to Trinh's
> "Mad Girl's Love Song"
> & "Stars Fell on Alabama,"
> trying to bite off her tongue. (155)

The vision of the experience of Vietnam itself at last presented by Yusef Komunyakaa, the poet after our war, as the subject of a book of poems, his third and most recent, is imaged suggestively in the powerful and wide-ranging resonances of its title: *Dien Cai Dau*. Di-en Kai Dow. Din Key Dow. Dinky Dow. Obviously in transliterated formal Vietnamese, suddenly the phrase has also become what it has been all along, the pidgin Dinky Dow, among the most familiar of all phrases known to those who served in Vietnam. It is the phrase for crazy. It was also, for a Vietnamese, the phrase for "American soldier." It is language itself, that is, with the ancient quite precise music of its enunciation (something a non-Vietnamese would in fact require considerable study and instruction to learn) transmuted to the ugly slang of soldier throwaway that was the war.

Not surprisingly, in contrast to the quite musical quality of a great deal of Komunyakaa's poetry in the first two collections, the poems here are for the most part basic and ugly. Some of them are already familiar, including all of those mentioned earlier, such as "Somewhere Near Phu Bai," "Starlight Scope Myopia," "Tiger Lady," and "After the Fall of Saigon" (now entitled, in suggestive abridgment, simply "After the Fall"), as well as related ones from previous work such as "The Dead at Quang Tri" (although now significantly rewritten), "A Break from the Bush," and

"Boat People." And virtually all of the rest are notable for their work-manlike concentration, across the space of years, on the experience itself as the basis of new poetic myth only now and in the most painful and rudimentary fashion beginning to be recorded.

The poems are as hard and direct as "Roll Call," a Vietnam photo-graph, largely intact except as marked by certain old griefs ("Only/a few lovers have blurred/the edges of this picture") of soldiers standing forma-tion over M-16s, each of them

> propped upright
> between a pair of jungle boots, a helmet on its barrel,
> as if it were a man (15)

in memory of their recent dead; or "Fragging," the murderers of a too-aggressive lieutenant pulling lots for the duty

> as they single out each other,
> pretending they're not there. (16)

One poem creates, out of a conjoined hellish burning of memory and new fire of imagination, as does a related and important one by Komun-yakaa's contemporary Bruce Weigl, a song of napalm. In " 'You and I Are Disappearing,' " the poet writes,

> The cry I bring down from the hills
> belongs to a girl still burning
> inside my head.

She burns in every place in every way—"like a piece of paper," "like fox-fire," "like a sack of dry ice," "like oil on water," "like a cattail torch/dipped in gasoline,"

> like the fat tip
> of a banker's cigar,
> silent as quicksilver.
> A tiger under a rainbow
> at nightfall.

Thus he concludes, in a new Vietnam scripture of horrific, even apocalyp-tic invocation:

She burns like a shot glass of vodka.
She burns like a field of poppies
at the edge of a rain forest.
She rises like dragonsmoke
to my nostrils.
She burns like a burning bush
driven by a godawful wind. (17)

The poems deal directly with the experience of black and white soldiers in Vietnam in the unwritten war that was often as much of the horror
as anything else. In "Tu Do Street," he writes of the bar girls of Saigon,
of their brothers the Vietnamese in the jungle, of the Americans black
and white who come to them seeking love. It is as much hell, he says, as
one need find in either country, America or Vietnam, that is the war. The
tunnels are everywhere:

Back in the bush at Dak To
& Khe Sanh, we fought
the brothers of these women
we now run to hold in our arms.
There's more than a nation
inside us, as black & white
soldiers touch the same lovers
minutes apart, tasting
each other's breath,
without knowing these rooms
run into each other like tunnels
leading to the underworld. (29)

In a similar vein, another poem, "The One-Legged Stool," is not
exactly a poem, or even a prose-poem, as it is rendered, so much as a
one-act drama, the badass soliloquy of a black prisoner to his Vietnamese
captors spoken out of solitary confinement. He won't believe their lies,
he says, about Dr. King's death, about what they say the white prisoners
are saying about him. In fact, they cannot break him precisely because he
has already, he tells them, seen worse in his own land. "Yeah, VC," he
says. "I've been through Georgia. Yeah, been through 'Bama too. Missis-

sippi, yeah." To the end, there is at least the uneasy marriage of terrible truth with this small comfort. "With your eyes pressed against the face-window," he taunts them, "you're like a white moon over Stone Mountain. You're everywhere. All I have to go back to are faces just like yours at the door" (42).

Toward the end, there is a homecoming of sorts, in poems such as "Thanks," for all the bizarre escapes and in wonderment at whatever "something" it was that

> stood among those lost trees
> & moved only when I moved [;] (45)

in "To Have Danced with Death," where the poet gets off the plane behind "the black sergeant first class" with one leg ("I wanted him to walk ahead,/to disappear through glass,/to be consumed by music//that might move him like Sandman Sims,/but he merely rocked on his good leg/ like a bleak and soundless bell" [46]); in "Report from the Skull's Diorama," where the memory of VC pamphlets on who *"didn't kill/Dr. Martin Luther King"* (47) now mixes with the helicopter vision of "the men left below" (47),

> the leaflets
> clinging to the men & stumps,
> waving to me across the years. (48)

The poems also eventually come home in both a figurative and the most utterly literal sense. We hear the story of the soldier bilked out of his allotment for another boyfriend at home in "Combat Pay for Jody." We are forced to look back also at Vietnam in "After the Fall," "Saigon Bar Girls, 1975," "Boat People." In "Toys in a Field," we see Vietnamese children playing among old gun mounts, all of them silent at their play

> except for the boy
> with American eyes
> who keeps singing
> rat-a-tat-tat, hugging
> a broken machine gun. (56)

We hear of the poet's own possible reunion back in the world with his own possible child with American eyes, *"Dui Boi*, Dust of Life" (58). We see one who came back in "Losses," now the old story of one who lives with ghosts,

> turns in a circle
> until a few faces from Dak To
> track him down,

recedes further and further to that place

> away from car horns & backfire
> where only days are stolen. (61)

We see one who waits for one who did not come back, now in an eternity only of "Between Days" (62). We at last go to the wall, again figuratively *and* literally, in "Facing It," the wall itself, that ultimate Vietnam text of memory buried in the Washington, D.C., earth for all to read by walking down into its grave. And there we find more of the old bewilderment and loss, now focused in the strange confusion of one who has come back reading the names of all those who did not and yet who are also with him here ever as there.

> My black face fades,
> hiding inside the black granite,

the poet begins.

> I said I wouldn't,
> dammit: No tears.
> I'm stone. I'm flesh.

Inside the wall, the place, the memorial, the text, one goes down the names, "half-expecting," the poet writes, "to find/my own in letters like smoke," sees an old name not his own and "the booby trap's white flash." Yet at the same time one feels one's own old becoming of a piece with what is within the wall; the wall itself seems to enact its own new becoming of a piece strangely with what goes on without. Sometimes, it is pure illusion. "Names shimmer on a woman's blouse," the poet writes, but "when she walks away/the names stay on the wall." Sometimes, however, the reflections also seem to be working the other way, back perhaps toward something like life. "Brushstrokes flash," he writes,

> a red bird's
> wings cutting across my stare.
> The sky. A plane in the sky.

The war tugs, still, in strange recurrent imaging and reimaging of conflict and loss, black and white as the wall itself and all the history whereof it speaks:

> A white vet's image floats
> closer to me, then his pale eyes
> look through mine. I'm a window.
> He's lost his right arm
> inside the stone. (63)

Then the image is replaced, and in some sense reversed, by a final one, perhaps equally ambiguous as to our sense of the conflicting surfaces of reality yet unequivocal in the reality of vision that, for some moment of imaginative respite, at least, seems to get the final word. "In the black mirror," the poet concludes,

> a woman's trying to erase names:
> No, she's brushing a boy's hair.

The conclusion is an abstract or epitome of the poet's continuing quest after our wars. There can be no erasure of old *or* new texts of grief. What there can be, however, is at least some new imaginative attunement to images of possible renewal where we find them in the surfaces of life after our war. Here the surface at hand is that newest of incredibly complicated texts of experiential memory called the Vietnam wall. Yet it is also, in this same sudden moment, the reflection of some deeper mythic remembrance as well, some oldest of home-gestures imaged for the very eternities in a woman's brushing back of a boy's hair. The true work of the poet after our war will be the work of "Facing It," the continuing search amidst the texts of the world for such moments of reflexive epiphany. And it will be the attempt to articulate out of such moments the new text of creative supplementation wherein the imagings of history and myth can be contained within some new order of redemptory vision, some whole new poetry of ongoing life.

The genesis of Walter McDonald's career as a Vietnam poet after our war may be fairly summarized in the title of his first collection: *Caliban in Blue*. He is a former career air force officer, a pilot, and a veteran of combat aviation in the war, but now also the warrior become an American poet, a rude but sinewed voice, bearer of a primal wisdom, the new man from the New World after the latest extension of the colonial enterprise.[7] He is also the author of subsequent collections including *Burning the Fence*, *The Flying Dutchman*, *After the Noise of Saigon*, and, most recently, *Night Landings*. And in these titles also we see imaged again one more version of the Vietnam writer's sense, in his generation, of the particular mythic dimension of his enterprise. Besides *Caliban in Blue*, he is also the westerner, the Texan, of *Burning the Fence*; he is *The Flying Dutchman*; years after the old fact of the war, he attends deeply and tries to tell us what America sounds like now, still, *After the Noise of Saigon*; and so, in *Night Landings*, he is the once-young pilot now looking beyond the middle of life toward increasingly final tests of hard flying to come.

Like David Huddle's and Yusef Komunyakaa's, many of McDonald's poems from the outset, and even those roughly contemporary with his own experience of the war itself, speak not so much of that experience directly as of the ways in which it is reconstituted through the medium of other mythic contexts. In "The Winter Before the War," a quite conventional poem of leaf raking, a first snowfall, ice fishing, and hot chocolate around the fireplace, Vietnam emerges as subject in the way people watch each other's eyes during the nightly news. In another early work, "Missing in Action," the measure of the loss in combat of a friend named Kelly is rendered through a memory of their common love of James Joyce.

"Caliban in Blue," in contrast, *is* about flying in a war over Asia. But it is also mainly about a new kind of mythic American man, a flying man, Shakespeare's Caliban, then Browning's Caliban, now this Caliban. He is worshiper and minion of a new Setobos, the old anthropomorphic god of the Browning poem now become something more like the name for an inertial guidance system, programmed to the formulas, in the "blue skies" of "orient west" of something called "air power." "Air power is peace power,/his motto catechizes," the poet tells us,

as we, diving, spout flame from under,
off in one hell
of a roar. (188)

It is a war of pure Pavlovian hard-on, discipline, aggression, "pulsing orgasm" of reward. "His arms like radar/point the spot," the poet says.

> For this, I trained to salivate
> and tingle, target-diving,
> hand enfolding hard throttle
> in solitary masculine delight.

Soon comes the moment itself, and

> savage release;
> pull out
> and off we go again
> thrusting deep
> into the martial lascivious blue
> of uncle's sky.

Caliban has transferred his fealty and employeeship from Setobos to Uncle Sam. His song is the love song of Caliban in Blue, the new song of pure military sex, with the sky the limit and the target nothing less than the very destruction of the earth whence he came.

Moreover, "Once You've Been to War," McDonald writes in a related poem, this sense of fundamental wrench and solitary displacement from earth remains the abiding fact of consciousness and the basis of any of its possible or necessary imaginings. We "plant at night in dreams" that which

> by dawn has rooted, ferns like veils,
> orchids, fuchsia tendrils reaching for trees,
> my secret back yard dense as the front,
> three canopies of rain forest
> chittering with spider monkeys,
> toucans, orange and black minahs,
> birds of paradise. (50)

But there are also "times," he goes on,

> deep in my pillow below three canopies
> of rain forest that I did not plant
> but helped to burn, the sand bags burst
> and sand blows over everything.

Concertina wire can't hold it back.
Roaches blue-bronzed and emerald,
the size of condors,

tweezer their way over dunes
the winds shuffle and fold like cards.
Rockets slam down beyond the trees,
fall-out clatters the leaves
like hail. In parched riverbeds

fish keep flopping,
jets diving are lightning without rain,
and in the distance, bombs explode so long
the hollows of my knees flutter
like flutes whittled from bone. (50)

Of old fire and noise—in a vision reminiscent of John Balaban's similar imagings of natural apocalypse—comes the permanent price of vision for those who try to reconceive the world after our war, possible nature gone forever alien and grotesque, monstrous and blighted.

Yet here also again, as with Balaban, and imaged in the enactment of the poetic process itself, the poet does not yield victory to the endlessly annihilating vision of the war. Rather he begins, at least, by simply learning to live with it as the banner of his disposition. "Whoever loses a war wears a white flag/forever," he writes.

We climb like anyone step by step
away from what we have done and didn't do.
We mean nothing and no one harm.
We kill to live.

And out of such acceptance, the poem makes clear, we find new ways to learn to live, breathe clean, fish deep:

Hearing a roar
lower than wind in the needles, huffing,
our rod tips springing each booted step
over stones, we rake in deeper breaths
of nothing like air near timberline,
shift our creels and backpacks

and lean into the last steep mile
where the river starts, where cutthroat
and rainbow trout have spawned
and started in shadows pool by pool downhill
where nothing but dark flies can trick them. (51)

And live one does, McDonald says *and* does, the poet after our war, and attempts to indite what can be recovered of full visions of life, born equally of old memory and new imagining. He writes, in the main body of his work, of the rhythms of life in the Southwest, "hardscrabble" country, to use an adjective of which he is repeatedly fond, plains, canyons, desert, ridgeline. He writes of farming, of children, of the seasons. He writes, in the fullest sense, of the elements, "where we live," as he puts it in "Getting It Done,"

only brown earth and sky
and in between, all that matters. (69)

But life in McDonald's poetry, as it is in that of his Vietnam contemporaries, is always life in context, the context of new and necessary myth born in what W. D. Ehrhart calls "The Awkward Silence," the condition of living, as McDonald phrases it, "After the Noise of Saigon." Ever in such context, it is the portion of the poet after our war to see his children being admonished to clean their plates as he has once seen food pickers working over the dump near Tan Son Nhut, reminding him at the time, he says, of "bears at Yellowstone" (5). It is also to see them in that moment as forever other children, once himself perhaps, once Vietnamese children quite other from all of them, yet now every bit as much as these children, his own, part and fabric of the poet's life. "I call them back/and growl," he tells us in conclusion, "I can't help it. It's like hearing/my father's voice again." He goes on:

I never tell them
why they have to eat it. I never say
they're like two beautiful children

I found staring at me one night through the screen of my window,
at Tan Son Nhut, bone-faced. Or that

when I crawled out of my stifling monsoon
dream to feed them, they were gone. (6)

It is the poet's portion after our war to see one's world always, in sum, as
*exactly* here and other, as itself eternal suspension of memory and dream,
history and myth, fact and imagination. This price of vision itself as ghost
palimpsest, for McDonald, as for his contemporaries, often becomes the
highest one of all exacted by this war upon its poet-survivor. Yet it remains
one, he insists, as do they all, that he must continue to be willing to pay
for the new visions of myth required to sustain us after our war. "If where
we hunt defines us," he writes,

then stalking this steep hillside dark with spruce makes sense,
more than the dreams I've floundered in
for years, trying to fathom signs
all night and wading ashore
disgusted.

For indeed to remember the old war anger, now reimaged in the solitary
hunt, is also to know finally that "These blue trees have" at once

nothing
and all to do with what I'm here for
after the noise of Saigon,
the simple sap that rises in me
like bad blood I need to spill
out here alone in the silence

of deep woods, far from people I know
who see me as a friend, not some damned
madman stumbling for his life. (65)

Thus we continue to measure the price of stumbling passage, the lonely
charade of composure often masking the desperate, even mad quest of
poetic consciousness after sense making. Yet the fact remains, in the evolving body of McDonald's work, that such odysseys of consciousness toward
experiential and imaginative reconstitution continue to get made and that
the attempts at their poetic accounting continue to get written. McDonald, imaging the quest at large of the Vietnam writer in his generation,

insists that this is a price worth paying for himself and people he knows and thus presumably also for ourselves and people we know. It is indeed more than worth paying, he seems to tell us, to hear what the poems of the world continue to sound like after the noise of Saigon.

*Night Landings* constitutes the most recent set of exercises in the pilot's training of Caliban in Blue that has served as McDonald's central metaphor of poetic enterprise throughout his career. And, not surprisingly, like the latest works of contemporaries considered here, it too proves in distinctive ways an exemplary text in the ongoing evolution of the poet after our war.

Predictably, given the figure of continuing flight and of education in flight, the Caliban we meet here is in many ways the old Caliban. The entire first section of the book, in fact, entitled "Hazards of Flight," is devoted mainly (albeit with one crucial inclusion entitled "Marriage") to a record of training and military initiation. And now such an accounting culminates again, in poems such as "The Wild Swans of Dalat," "The Last Days in a Bunker," and "The Children of Saigon," with an old memory of war updated to latest visitation of nightmare imagining.

But the Caliban we see here is also most decidedly now Caliban, as indicated by the major bulk of the book's four other sections, in the middle of life and career and looking beyond. We find recapitulated, for instance, virtually all of the familiar themes and topics of the earlier "middle" books. In "Building on Hardscrabble," the section's title poem and others such as "Splitting Wood for the Winter," "Witching," "The Wind's a Hawk," and "Living on Open Plains" tell us again of farming and of new attunements with the rhythms of nature and the cycles of the seasons. In "Things About to Disappear,"[8] again through the title poem, now used as a conclusion, and others such as "The Digs in Escondido," "Settling the Plains," "Wild-catting," and "Torching Grandfather's Weed Fields," we note the passages of history and the changing face of the western landscape. In "The Songs We Fought For," the passages of life we celebrate—again in the concluding title poem and others such as "What We Did in the Willows," "Owls and Uncle Bubba," "Honky-Tonk Blues," and "Perpetual Motion"—are the closer ones of sexual initiation, courtship, family. Finally, in "All that Aches and Blesses," in a series beginning with "Finding My Father's Hands in Midlife" and moving on through the crucial title poem to conclude with "The Middle Years," we come to the life passage as well of a new preparation and a looking beyond.

To be sure, throughout this most recent mythic installment in the imaginative evolution of Caliban in Blue, the war and its memory remain profoundly present and often as matters of explicit reference. Yet poetic treatment of the war as direct subject, as may already have been noted, is confined basically to the work's opening section. And references in succeeding poems, while often quite explicit in their way, reveal themselves increasingly contextualized as never before into larger patterns of life and evolution of consciousness. Caliban has become progressively adept at "Living with Nightmares." "At night," he tells us,

> I dream my life ends
> at Saigon, but here I am,
>
> watching my wife make breakfast for children who weren't born
> overseas.

He goes on:

> What am I, a ghost? Safe
> on this side of morning,
>
> no rockets, I've stopped
> reaching to check
> for wounds, I'm reaching
> to lace my shoes,
> my own shoes. (28)

Accordingly, a subsequent contemplation entitled "After the Rains of Saigon" is rendered largely apropos of the weather rhythms of western farming. "The Songs We Fought For," from "Willie and Waylon, Hank and Loretta," are explicitly those same ones, he tells us, that

> could break a man's heart
> with the draft and a war in Vietnam
>
> drawing him closer daily.

Yet they are profoundly subsumed, in the poem they inspire, into the larger rituals of love and war, as indicated by the doubled title itself, played out by men and women in bars across America,

> slow-dancing
> close as we'd ever be to another in clothes,
> lost in a sad, sweet fiddle-rhythm,
> sliding on polished boots
> and humming softly to ourselves. (63)

Indeed, as *Night Landings* unfolds its new poetic evolutions, the war fades eventually altogether from explicit reference, becoming an uninscribed presence, always, somehow, ineluctably there, yet depending for its meanings on all the broader contextualizations. It fades so overtly, in fact, that we are surprised, then, when we actually do encounter it explicitly once more only as we come to the work's final poem. Yet there, in "The Middle Years," amidst all the rest, again we see it. "All day," the poet writes,

> we take turns holding hands and counting
> the years we never believed we'd make it —
> the hours of skinned knees and pleading,
> diapers and teenage rage and fever
>
> in the middle of the night, and parents
> dying, and Saigon, the endless guilt of surviving. (79)

He goes on:

> Nights, we lie touching
> for hours and listen, the silent woods
>
> so close we can hear owls diving.
> These woods are not our woods,
> though we hold a key to dead pine planks
> laid side by side, shiplap like a dream
> that lasts, a double bed that fits us
> after all these years, a blunt
> front-feeding stove that gives back
> temporary heat for all the logs we own. (79–80)

Amidst all the rest, there it is. But that, now, is just the point. For the point is also that the poet goes on. Vietnam remains a thing, a fact of life and consciousness, but it has also become a part of things. It has become a part of things amidst all the other things, a piece of "The Middle Years."

More explicitly perhaps than that of any poet after our war, the body of Bruce Weigl's work—again, as with McDonald's, even down to the titles of his major texts—may be said to chart the enactment of a poetic career as an evolution of mythic consciousness distinctly tied to the American experience of Vietnam. As Lorrie Smith writes, "Weigl's poems begin at the point of assimilating the war into large historical and imaginative constructs." Over the course of a career, they range from specific memories of that war to visions of "midwest factory towns whose slag heaps, smokestacks, bars, and graveyard shifts recall the gray landscapes of James Wright and Philip Levine." And "whether viewed from Vietnam or Ohio," she goes on, "the war penetrates all of Weigl's observations. Linked by peculiarly American brands of violence and pathos, the two places are not so far apart. The dark underside of Vietnam is finally, as in Ehrhart, a monstrous exaggeration and a logical extension of the more banal forms of violence and moral depletion of home" (15–16). Moreover, such a linkage, writes Vincente Gotera, enlarging on Smith's insights, is one that the poet will allow neither himself nor any of us who may read him to relinquish. Weigl's work is indeed a continual dismantling, says Gotera, in direct echo of Smith, of "the popular myth that we have regained our national innocence [by confessing] that U.S. involvement in Vietnam was a mistake" (160).

Accordingly, as readers we witness just such a combined evolution and continuing insistence, as early chapbooks such as *Executioner* and *A Sackful of Old Quarrels* find their culmination in *A Romance*, a first work eloquently invoking its mythic provenance even as it subjects the very idea of romance itself, the whole tradition of the visionary quest and particularly its historical American postulations, to virtually every possible form, sublime and ridiculous, of radical mythic self-critique. Out of "Monkey," a long poem of experience and visionary myth lodged at the center, both formal and thematic, of *A Romance*, comes the genesis of a subsequent major volume, *The Monkey Wars*, a continuation of the quest through the new contextualizations of myth now arising from the memory of the war in its historical aftermath. Out of the last poem of that book, "Song of

Napalm," flowers in dreadful turn the title of a succeeding one, the prior text re-written both as itself and as larger composite text, *Song of Napalm*; and now also, the process of poetic inscription here continues, as with Balaban, Komunyakaa, and others, to include self-reinscription as well, art as cultural revision enacted upon the cultural text that has become one's own body of experiential-poetic myth.[9]

"All wars are boyish": As noted in an earlier discussion of the dramatist David Rabe, with this line from "A March into Virginia," Herman Melville supplied a definitive American gloss (and one later to receive the imprimatur of our own century, of course, from Robert Lowell) on a vision of war extending from his poetry of the cataclysm of 1861–65 all the way to his final masterpiece, *Billy Budd*. In Bruce Weigl's *A Romance*, that concept of war as archetypal ritual of American boyishness, at once innocent and terrible as only American boys can be innocent and terrible, may be said to supply the fundamental energy of vision inscribing itself at once within the text as experiential design and beyond the text into the structures of contemporary American myth at large. It is that "romance" of vision, as it might be called, that becomes at once both theme and form in the text: a continuation of the old American myth of the quest, at once ecstatic and giddy, brave and horrendous, sublime and idiotic. "Sailing to Bien Hoa" is the "dream" of a "hydroplane," all racing speed and power, but also of driving now with "shrapnel" in one's "thighs/like tiny splinters." Memory is a vision, part hallucination, part cartoon, of

> a flower
> a kit, a mannikin playing the guitar,
> a yellow fish eating a bird, a truck
> floating in urine, a rat carrying a banjo,
> a fool counting the cards, a monkey praying, a procession of
>     whales. (3)

Yet out of the very procession of dream and memory and perhaps dream again in all its teeming grotesquerie, "far off," just beyond the whales, arises something else now as well: something like, in fact, Vietnam as it must have been once, "two children eating rice, speaking French—I'm sure of the children, their damp flutes, the long line of their vowels" (3). Out of the cockeyed American quest-conjunctions of dream, memory, and language has come anew the old, full, sweet music of life itself.

In most cases, the idea of romance so conceived—the twinned quests of vision and language in their possible issuings out of memory into new redemptory myth—takes a decidedly more mundane and literal path of turnings and vain repetitions. In the work's title poem, it confines itself to the tawdry martial feats of honky-tonk men who want to be lovers and always wind up being fighters instead in order to become lovers. "It is always this way with me in bars," the poet writes,

> wanting women I know
> I'll have to get my face
> punched bloody to love.

It is in fact the way of it with men, he likewise concludes, him with his

> giant lies to women
> who have heard them from me,
> from the thousands of me
> out on the town with our impossible strategies
> for no good reason but our selves,
> who are holy.

Such old foolishness of boy-men also can be a Romance, must be a Romance, he seems to say, like the stories, perhaps, Joan Didion tells us we make up in order to live: lies we tell because we have to "for no good reason but our selves,/ who are holy" (6–7).

*A Romance* is likewise telling the story of "Monkey" over and over again, in the hope, as the epigraph from James Wright puts it, that "Out of the horror there arises the musical ache that is beautiful" (15). If it helps to remember we are alive, we start out with pure, simple conjugation.

> I am you are he she it is
> they are you are we are,

the poet begins.

> I am you are he she it is
> they are you are we are.
> When they ask for our number
> pretend to be breathing. (15)

We then enter the jungle, the place, Vietnam. We live the experience then:

Those small Vietnamese soldiers.
They love to hold your hand.
Back away from their dark cheeks.
Small Vietnamese soldiers.
They love to love you. (15)

We live the memory now:

Good times bad times sleep
get up work. Sleep get up
good times bad times.
Work eat sleep good bad work times. (16)

We meet the monkey:

My monkey from Vietnam.
My monkey.
Put your hand here.
I beat the monkey.
I didn't know him.
He was bloody.
He lowered his intestines
to my shoes. My shoes
spit-shined the moment
I learned to tie the bow. (17)

We see the men:

There is a hill.
Men run top hill.
Men take hill.
Give hill to man. (19)

We see the particular man and the monkey, now back in the world:

Me and my monkey
and me and my monkey
my Vietnamese monkey
my little brown monkey
came with me
to Guam and Hawaii

in Ohio he saw
my people he
jumped on my daddy
he slipped into mother
he baptized my sister
he's my little brown monkey
he came here from heaven
to give me his spirit imagine
my monkey my beautiful
monkey he saved me lifted
me above the punji
sticks above the minds
above the ground burning
above the dead above
the living above the
wounding dying the wounded
dying. (19)

Eventually, through the words of death and the pull of old memory they inscribe, we see the monkey poem dissolve back into the same old business, now again back in the war:

Men take hill away from smaller men.
Men take hill and give to fatter man.
Men take hill. Hill has number.
Men run up hill.
Run down. (19)

The poem ends. But it ends not with an ending but rather, as an echo of the work's larger structure, with what is essentially a revised transition. It thus ends also with the distinct sense (in fact fulfilled through its reinscribed form in its final reappearance in a later text, *Song of Napalm*) that it could keep going, trying to get finished, mark the end of the quest with some new musical ache that is beautiful. Here, and in ensuing works, as Lorrie Smith writes, for Weigl the war truly is "a monkey on his back—tenacious memory, potent and insidious as a drug, a carnivalesque *Doppelganger*, both intimate and repugnant; a symbol of man's unregenerate brutality" (16). The point remains as it does in *A Romance* at large (and eventually, as we will see, beyond in the body of Weigl's work) that our only hope of shaking the brutality is to keep trying to tell the monkey poem for as long as it takes us to get it right. Boyishly, heroically, romantically, in all the possibilities of those old adverbs both sublime and ludicrous, *A Romance*, even as it becomes repeatedly an ironic critique of its own forms and processes of sense-making, insists that the impossible can at times be made strangely possible. In "Executioner on Holiday," we can at least envision a dream in which

> one day I'm back in the army,
> a nameless private in a crack
> platoon. We never see the enemy
> yet we have wonderful statistics.
> Next day a crippled friend
> walks across the room,
> tells me his paralysis was unreal,
> thin steel sliver. (38)

We can re-write the war and the statistics and even perhaps the face in the mirror, "gaunt but interesting," the "eyes . . . innocent without passion or desire," the "smile slightly twisted" (39). In "Him, on the Bicycle," we can indeed go even further to transform the worst old dream of aerial murder, Vietnam-style, into a new ecstasy of flight. Now, in *A Romance*, as before in life, the "he" who was the enemy rides the bicycle again on the Ho Chi Minh Trail. And now likewise, as before, the "I" who is the poet rides the American "liftship" (30). Yet now also, suddenly, *as never before*, the war itself gets re-written. "He pulls me out of the ship," the poet tells us,

> there's firing far away.
> I'm on the back of the bike
> holding his hips.
> It's hard pumping for two,
> I hop off and push the bike.

And now also, suddenly, miraculously, he goes on, something *truly* impossible happens:

> I'm brushing past trees,
> the man on the bike stops pumping,
> lifts his feet,

we don't waste a stroke.
His hat flies off,
I catch it behind my back,
put it on, I want to live forever!

Like a blaze
streaming down the trail. (30)

Most of the time, *A Romance* is not nearly this wondrous or ecstatic.
More often, it is an attempt, and in itself enough of a romance even at
that, to try simply to remember something of "Life Before Fear." Or it is
enough perhaps, at least, to go back to the old fear and face it and know
it for what it is, to walk it, as in "Mines" ("Here is how you walk at night:
slowly lift/one leg, clear the sides with your arms, clear the back,/front,
put the leg down, like swimming" [33]) with something of a new bravery
of caution and resolve. A Romance is a foolish thing, an outworn kind of
poem, not to mention an idle imagining, a lie even, but it is still something, used rightly and known for what it is, that we can use to tell stories
to live by. A Romance is working toward getting the monkey poem right
for as long as it takes.

The evolution of Weigl's sense of the poet as post-Vietnam American mythmaker continues in the appropriately entitled *The Monkey Wars*,
poetry writing itself now enlarging itself out of the old conflicts of self and
individual consciousness into new visions of the conflicts of sense making
in the life of culture at large. At times the poems are of significant personal
history, poems of family and origin and self-recontextualization such as "A
Childhood," "The Town Inside," "Song for a Lost First Cousin," "1955"
(the altar boy down at the rail next "To the next mouth/Open in the O of
acceptance/So much like a scream/That can't get out of the lungs. . . ./
I don't know why my hands should shake,/I'm only remembering something" [12–13]). At times they seek the contextualizations of other lives, as
in "Hope," "Letter to X," "Elegy for A," "For the Wife Beater's Wife,"
"Homage to Elvis, Homage to the Fathers" ("He changed us somehow: we
cleaned up,/We spun the 45s in the basement,/danced on the cool concrete
and plastered/Our hair back like his and twisted/Our forbidden hips./
Across the alley our fathers died/Piece by piece among the blast furnace
rumble./They breathed the steel rifted air/As if it were good" [40–41]).

For a moment, in "Vaudeville," the old monkey himself, no other, finds a sudden domestic contextualization, in a bar, taking "a long drink" and fixing his gaze on the poet,

> Rolling back his eyes
> As if remembering another place.

And so, he continues,

> the air around me seemed a membrane
> Enfolding the sensible world
> And something came from inside me
> to hug the body so terribly like mine.

It is the old familiar specter with a home truth, he assures us, now real as the next drink or the next breath,

> The monkey, no myth this time,
> Grinning, howling, never letting go. (38)

Most often, however, it is that other place itself that becomes the real and abiding ghost presence embodied in these new monkey poems entitled *The Monkey Wars*, that other place still inscribing itself first, last, and at every point in between into this place that we now call America after our war. It comes first (and as the first poem in the text) as something like "Amnesia," an old hypothetical almost. Imagine, the poem seems to begin:

> If there was a world more disturbing than this
> Where black clouds bowed down and swallowed you whole
> And overgrown tropical plants
> Rotted, effervescent in the muggy twilight and monkeys
> Screamed something
> That came to sound like words to each other
> Across the triple-canopy you shared,
> You don't remember it.

But now think also, it seems to continue:

> You tell yourself no and cry a thousand days.
> You imagine the crows calling autumn into place
> Are your brothers and you could

If only the strength and will were there
Fly up to them to be black
And useful to the wind. (1)

For the most part, though, when the monkeys speak, there is nothing
of amnesia putative or otherwise but rather return of experiential memory
quite sensible in the fullest degree. It is a vivid snapshot in the eyes, such
as "The Girl at the Chu Lai Laundry." In "Burning Shit at An Khe," it is
a stink in the nose and a long befoulment, an attempt to flee memory and
"olive drab" and

everything Green as far from the shit
As the fading light allowed,

but

Only now I can't fly.
I lay down in it
And finger paint the words of who I am
across my chest
Until I'm covered and there's only one smell, one word. (11)

It etches itself like a burn of shame into moral memory in "The Last Lie,"
"Temple near Quang Tri, Not on the Map," "Surrounding Blues on the
Way Down." It threads itself through the fabric of our lives, in sum, as that
which will not allow "Amnesia" as a first word nor will allow anything but
itself as the last, the eternal "Song of Napalm." Back in the world, with a
wife, after a storm across the horse pasture, in the quiet, even there the
picture persists, the famous one,

the girl
Running from her village, napalm
Stuck to her dress like jelly,
Her hands reaching for the no one
Who waits in waves of heat before her. (46–47)

"So I can keep on living," the poet goes on:

So I can stay here beside you,
I try to imagine she runs down the road and wings
Beat inside her until she rises

Above the stinking jungle and her pain
Eases, and your pain, and mine.

But as with most monkey poems in the long run, as opposed, say, to "Him, on the Bicycle," here will come no ecstatic levitation act. The "Song of Napalm" will itself become the last word, the one we learn simply, somehow, to live with. Always, the poet concludes, "the lie swings back again":

The lie works only as long as it takes to speak
And the girl runs only as far
As the napalm allows
Until her burning tendons and crackling
muscles draw her up
into that final position
Burning bodies so perfectly assume. Nothing
Can change that; she is burned behind my eyes
And not your good love or the rain-swept air
And not the jungle green
Pasture unfolding before us can deny it. (47)

So Bruce Weigl's poetic texts, individual and collective, continue now to detail the evolution of his career as poetic mythmaker after our war. *A Romance*, by way of "Monkey," inscribes itself into *The Monkey Wars*; *A Romance* and *The Monkey Wars*, with the latter now the echo of its own last poem as last word, inscribe themselves into *Song of Napalm*. The re-writing of one's own experience becomes the re-writing of one's own body of poetic myth; and so, with Weigl, as with Balaban, especially in the case of early poems, some of them become significantly not so much different versions of themselves as themselves different poems. Accordingly, again as with Balaban, the chief subject of poetry increasingly becomes poetic process itself.

From its dark scream of a dust jacket onward, *Song of Napalm* images all these trajectories and more. As Russell Banks observes on the jacket, for instance, it is surely a major novel of the war, at once a descent into hell and a harrowed passage of return. And like Michael Herr's *Dispatches*, a work whose twofold rhythm of remembering and narrating it deeply inscribes, it likewise becomes a newest "classic" text of Vietnam witness as well. "Each captured fraction of experience is subjected to ruthless scrutiny," writes Robert Stone in an introduction; and so, he continues, personal sense making becomes communal experience as well. "Again and again," says Stone, Weigl "brings us to the outer limits of our reference point, to that dread zone of the spirit where wars are fought and survived" (no page).

"Breathing In," then, for Weigl, to borrow Herr's analogous figure, becomes again "Sailing to Bien Hoa." It is "Girl at the Chu Lai Laundry," "Temple Near Quang Tri, Not on the Map," "Him, on the Bicycle," "Surrounding Blues on the Way Down," "The Last Lie." And it is also, of course, the old "Monkey," now increasingly become something like the reality of its own poetic content.

Newly and strikingly, however, "Breathing In" is now also, in important addition, "The Way of Tet." It is a story of love, about "the boy who came ten thousand miles" and "the girl whose words he can't understand, their song a veil between them" (6). And it is also, of course, as its title insists, a story about war, about "Year of the monkey, year of the human wave," year where it all began to come down and the long walk out of tragedy would begin. "Tomorrow blood would run in every province," writes the poet.

> Tomorrow people would rise from tunnels everywhere
> and resurrect something ancient inside them.

Yet now, still, for a moment, it all waits; and

> he need only touch her, only
> lift the blanket from her shoulders
> and the automatic shape of love unfolds,
> the flare's light burning down on them,
> lost in a wave that arrives
> after a thousand years of grief at their hearts. (6)

Breathing In in turn becomes Being There, first "Song of Napalm" itself and then a host of other now-familiar imagings as well: "Burning Shit at An Khe," "Mines," "When Saigon Was French," "Mercy," "The Snowy Egret." But now too come "LZ Nowhere," "Dogs," "Breakdown." Now too indeed comes an endless dream of memory,

> a lousy, worthless
> sleep of strangers with guns,
> children trapped in the alley,
> the teenage soldiers glancing back
> over their shoulders
> the moment before they squeeze the trigger. (47)

It is Vietnam now increasingly as eternal present, a waking bad dream against which we can only continue to make vain incantation. "I am going to stay here as long as I can," the poet writes. "I am going to sit in the garden as if nothing has happened," he continues, repeating, "and let the bruised azaleas have their way" (47).

"Breathing Out," finally comes for Weigl here in "Amnesia," "A Romance," and the old poem of homecoming, "Ana Grasa." To be sure, *it* also remains as well, the vision of a dream-tossed morning in bad echo of Emily Dickinson, "not excellent and fair" (54). "Inside me the war had eaten a hole," the poet tells us, speaking now "On the Anniversary of Her Grace."

> I could not touch anyone.
> The wind blew through me to the green place
> where they still fell in their blood.
> I could hear their voices at night.

"I could not undress in the light," he confesses, "her body cast in the dark rented room" (55). He goes on:

> I could keep the dragons at the gate.
> I could paint my face and hide
> as shadow in the triple-canopy jungle.
> I could not eat or sleep then walk all day
> and all night watch a moonlit path for movement.
>
> I could draw leeches from my skin
> with the tip of a cigarette
> and dig a hole deep enough to save me
> before the sun bloodied the hills we could not take
> even with our lives
> but I could not open my arms to her

that first night of forgiveness.
I could not touch anyone.
I thought my body would catch fire. (55)

Yet now also "Breathing Out" becomes, finally, "Dialectical Materialism," "The Kiss," and "Elegy." All three might be most accurately termed acts of supplication. All three indeed pursue the prayer of language whereby old pain and loss may yet continue to be redeemed.

The first, inscribed "*Hanoi, December 1985*," addresses an old man whose "small stone and stick/ house" still standing somehow "beyond the dikes" recalls, amidst the new life and hubbub of a city reborn, the vision of a family gathered against "our great planes" with their terrible bombs.

> He doesn't say
> how he must have huddled
> those nights with his family,
> how he must have spread himself
> over them
> until the village bell called them back to their beds,

the poet writes.

> There are questions which
> people who have everything
> ask people who have nothing
> and they do not understand. (67)

"The Kiss," in contrast, describes another father, his own, on the day that the poet himself has gone to war. It comes back now, part memory of departure ("From the cold I was shaking and ached/to be away from the love of those waving through the frozen window"), part some half-imagined dream of childhood rescue ("Out of that black air of debris," he writes, "out of nowhere, my father bent down, lifted me and ran/to the house of strangers" [68]). Now the two merge again, memory and dream-parenthesis, newest imagining of the old generations of love:

> And again that day on the plane
> he appeared to me,
> my forgotten orders in his hands.
> He bent down to put the envelope on my lap,

on my lips he kissed me hard
and without a word he was gone
into the cold again.
Through the jungle, through the highlands,
through all that green dying
I touched my fingers to my lips. (69)

Finally, in "Elegy," "Breathing Out" now also becomes benediction for the young Americans as well. "Into sunlight they marched," he begins,

into no saints day,
and were cut down.
They marched without knowing
how the air would be sucked from their lungs,
how their lungs would collapse,
how the world would twist itself,
would bend into cruel angles.

Deeper and deeper, he continues,

Into the black understanding they marched
until the angels came
calling their names,
until they rose,
one by one from the blood.
The light blasted down on them.
The bullets sliced through the razor grass
so there was not even time to speak.
The words would not let themselves be spoken.

"Some of them died," he concludes. "Some of them were not allowed to" (70).

It is for the dead of Vietnam that the poet has returned to speak. But it is in the same moment clearly for the living of Vietnam as well. After our war, in sum, it is for the poet to speak first and last for those who died and for those who were not allowed to, for all those who were there in Vietnam and America when

the bullets sliced through the razor grass
so that there was not even time to speak.

It is for the poet to speak, that is, for those who were rendered speech-
less in all the ways Vietnam made speechlessness possible for all of us,
for those who died and for those who continue to suffer that other death
which Weigl's brother poet after our war, W. D. Ehrhart, has called in all
the simplicity of mythic exactitude "The Awkward Silence."

# THE LITERATURE OF WITNESS

*Gloria Emerson, Frances Fitzgerald,*

*Robert Stone, Michael Herr*

"I suppose the question about Cole," Holliwell said, "is who he thinks he is and what he thinks he's doing."

"Do you mean does he think he's Regis Debray?"

"No," Holliwell said, "I mean beyond that."

"Beyond that?" Zecca asked. "Beyond that isn't necessarily my business. Beyond that he's a Vietnam burn-out. A pilgrim."

"There's a lot of us," Holliwell said.

"You see yourself as a burn-out?" Marie asked. She turned to her husband. "I wouldn't have described him that way."

"Maybe just badly seared," Holliwell said.

—Robert Stone, *A Flag for Sunrise*

At dusk the Luminists walk
toward home and chromatic dreams
of their ancestors—the glowworm,
lightning, the aurora borealis—
in full display. Let the French
rise from the water lily,
American light is no less.
Luminescent, it will flourish.

They were not wrong. Everywhere
you see their descendents—
red neon signs of bars and motels,
televisions emptying blue snow
into silent bedrooms.
Other nights you wake to stare

at the yellow-green faces
of alarm clocks, radar screens,
x-rays of your bones. Their light
is the light you live by,
the Luminists in their graves
are satisfied: cool to touch
and to the eye, fluorescent
lamps glow in museums above
their canvases, the sky above all,
all with their glossy finish.
—Michael Pettit, *American Light*


This chapter considers the work of four writers closely associated with the literature of the Vietnam war yet not technically "veterans" in the direct sense that might be applied to most of the figures discussed earlier. Yet each of them, by virtue of major literary witness to the experience of the war, came to prominence as a "Vietnam" writer; and each continues to explore the possibilities of a literature that, in response to the memory of Vietnam, might extend such witness into new and major forms of creative statement about American life and culture at large.

The distinguishing feature of the literature of witness, its dominant, even obsessive concern, has been its identification of the true locus of the war and its cultural legacy as at once the landscape of historical experience *and* of collective national imagining. Accordingly, its chief contribution to historical-cultural argument has been its equal insistence on the status of the discourses of experience and myth not as oppositions or polarities but rather as reciprocities—and with each requiring the other, in fact, for its own ongoing inscription. This is to say that they have made explicit the recurrent discovery of virtually all the major veteran-novelists, playwrights, and poets of the war as well. And that is the discovery of their enlistment, of course, in the great literary project of the postmodern, the project of *writing itself*; of writing, that is, as a conscious and constant de-centering of vision and language; of writing, in sum, from within the very dialectic of culture at large.

Given this new character, then, of postmodern witness, it should not surprise us that, out of a vast body of journalistic response to the American experience of Vietnam and its aftermath almost exclusively by men, works by two women, Gloria Emerson and Frances Fitzgerald, may be seen now to speak with particular authority of insight as few others have managed; and they do so in large measure, I would propose, through their function as exemplary feminist texts, as texts, that is, which attempt to re-write our vision of that experience from within a specific critique of the essentially male structures of consciousness that shape it. Here I should also say at once that I mean to use "feminist" in a context of general definition that goes beyond any localized politics of sexuality toward issues of language, authority, and power in their largest sense: feminist, then, in that as texts by women they elect not to center themselves within various established value and meaning systems of a dominant culture. Moreover, in the cases of the "classic" Vietnam texts in particular for which the two authors are best known, I would obviously wish to distinguish them as well from exercises written during the war and its aftermath in what might be called the "pop-macho" vein of myth-critique, which from the earliest days of writing about Vietnam became a literary journalistic commonplace, and which, carried to its creative limits, could produce, in texts such as Norman Mailer's *Why Are We in Vietnam?*, William Eastlake's *The Bamboo Bed*, Gustav Hasford's *The Short-Timers*, or Michael Herr's *Dispatches*, works of indisputable genius. The "genius" of *Winners and Losers* and *Fire in the Lake*, in contrast (and it is a structure of approach that would also characterize postwar texts on other subjects, such as Emerson's *Some American Men* and Fitzgerald's *America Revised* and *Cities on a Hill*), while often producing comparable insights, would lie rather in their capacity to address the experience of Vietnam from within the configurings of American institutional thought at large and thus also on a ground of inquiry extending backward from the domain of the battlefield and command post through intermediate structures of language, administration, and control to the most fundamental assumptions of culture itself.

Accordingly, one is not surprised to find that Emerson's classic study of the experience of the war and of its aftermath in American lives, *Winners and Losers*, begins, for instance, not in Vietnam but at home, back in the world; and it begins also, despite an early and quick disavowal of interest in particular concerns of the domestic women's liberation movement (7), with an immediate sensation on the author's part of old, unwelcome recognition and return, of being and writing once more from somewhere that might be called "woman's place." "Getting back was not good," Emerson writes. "In New York a pleasant woman asked me what I had worn to officers' dances; the question did not make me smile. There were none; in any case, I would never have gone. Others asked me how I had dressed, what I had eaten, what war I would cover next, if I had seen anyone killed. 'You will never, never regret the experience,' a lady said as we both waited to have our hair cut in a place on 62nd Street. 'It's a once-in-a-lifetime chance'" (5). "No one meant to be cruel," she goes on. "I did not want people to tell me over and over to have a nice day, to take care, to have a nice day." Nonetheless, she concludes, "It was all I heard" (5–6). Here, on her return from the male world of Vietnam, where she has been "an equal," albeit in ways "often it was too much to bear" (7), she comes back to the discursive terms of an old familiar formula. Yet "here," we quickly learn, is in its own way but a version of "there," "there" but a version of "here": "We are their women. They've got us" (7). The quote is the first in the book she cites as having heard from an American GI in Vietnam. The speaker has been an average field soldier, a mortar man, referring to his relationship with his officers. "He meant the enlisted men," she goes on, "and he was right. I had always known how women were leashed, confined, made so small and uncertain. But in Vietnam, among the most helpless and humiliated were the soldiers themselves" (7). (Or, she might have added, as her text itself will quickly show, not to mention Fitzgerald's, the Vietnamese.)

So, in these repeated figures of reversal, we quickly come to feel the sense of new narrative positionment underwriting the peculiar authority of this big, wise, angry, intensely moral book.[1] It is a book that relentlessly locates the tragedy of Vietnam for Americans and Vietnamese alike within a structure of dialectical consciousness essentially playing variations on its near-infinite possibilities as a formula for oppression, a formula basically reworkable to suit the needs of any given institutional definition of authority at hand. Authority indeed: "Winners" and "Losers." Who is a "Winner," and who is a "Loser"? The new answer suggested here becomes apparent in the double play we quickly see Emerson to have worked even on the figure of her title. It obviously depends, she makes clear from the outset, on who is writing the "game." So accordingly, on a scale commensurate to the horrendous stakes of the one in question, she undertakes nothing less than a kind of revisionist post-Vietnam census of the American soul, an unwriting of an old false dialectics of received cultural definition and explanation toward a full, bitter, and true accounting of tragic cost exacted by the war upon every person it may have ultimately touched and beyond.

Appropriate to the overtly nontraditional position of inquiry it establishes for itself from the outset, *Winners and Losers* throughout makes not even the barest pretense to "balance" in any known conventional sense of that journalistic term. Indeed, as a "survey" of the national character, it makes no claims to be anything other than vast and jangling, calculatedly eccentric and even heterotopic. Accordingly, most of the chief "chararacters" we meet in the course of the narrative, for example, seem frequently in fact to be chosen for mention because of their distinct status as sociocultural caricatures: the young regimental surgeon and West Point regular, son of the academy and of the tradition of George Patton, the father, who writes a prayer for war ("God Our Heavenly Father, hear our prayer. . . . forget not the least of thy children as they hide from us in the jungles") in the name of his Vietnam commander George Patton, the son (21); Kingman Brewster, president of Yale, who can somehow square his own vociferous opposition to the war with a defense of an old friend named McGeorge Bundy as being well motivated but deficient in "judgment" (34); the veteran, Cyclops, screwed and confused, with his vague admiration for an ex-enemy, his regrets, his VC skull and picture of the Vietnamese woman with the shot-up legs, his letter about a dead wife signed " 'Love, Mike,' with a peace symbol by his name" (73); the smiling sexist judge in Tennessee, insistently referring to the author as "honey," "my friend," "my little queen," and describing his position in support of the war as that of a "typical pacifist" — against "wars" and "fighting" and "feuding" — yet convinced that "one of the worst problems we have today in this country is not teaching young people to have proper respect for conventional authority" (174–75); a woman protestor who has splashed blood on the State Dining Room at the White House and remembers being asked during her arrest by a Secret Service agent whether "she meant to embarrass the President" (209); a chief of army chaplains who defends his choice of duty with the pious observation that "a man of discernment has to give his government the benefit of the doubt" (211); a returned veteran and antiwar activist whose reports of witnessing repeated atrocities in his infantry company have been ultimately dispensed with and dismissed in a CID after-investigation letter thanking him "for his interest in the military" (215); the senior officer at a military and press symposium at the Naval War College who has wanted to know if Seymour Hersh is a "queer" (246); the scion of a great publishing family who can recount the sad wisdom gained of his youthful adventures with the "Mission" with something close to the intellectual nonchalance of a drama critic or a wine snob (317–26). (After all, as the author remembers the boy's mother remarking once in Saigon to a stunned army gunship pilot, "Every man should have his war" [328].) To be sure, most of the caricatures wind up on the predictable side of the political accounting. Yet at the same time we see that the real challenge posed here is to our very conceptions of a "side" or an "accounting." How, in particular, and why, we find ourselves asking, should we expect a book of unrelenting moral inquiry into a whole history of "balanced" or "objective" justifications for an evil war to give us even a single balanced or objective portrait of someone interested or otherwise implicated in perpetuating such an enterprise of justification? Indeed, it is precisely to that end that Emerson insistently pushes us beyond conventional example to reexamine our very assumptions of "balance" or "objectivity." Without significant explanation, she privileges the depiction of an ex-POW turned moral collaborator, even down an almost too touching final word. (Did he win or lose the war, his son has asked. "I told him," he says, "I was on the side of the winners" [235].) And so, as if in equally calculated and glaring obverse, the reflections on the war of an old friend and Asia hand she similarly redacts as a spluttering collocation of playing-field cliche: "I'm sorry we got beaten so badly" (295); "I just don't like to be really involved in anything that is a failure" (296); "I mean, for Christ sake, I don't really see that we're the bad boy" (297).

"I have made many people angry," Emerson says openly in midtext (241). Yet that is ultimately what impresses us as just the point, the attempt to strike repeatedly a place of calculated unpositioning, of angry challenge and offset, with the categorical notions themselves of slant or bias, objectivity or equipoise, equally to be damned. If this is what it must take, she seems to say to us throughout, then this is what it must take if we are to refashion nothing less than a whole new structure of vision, a structure at last allowing us to see through a whole fabric of misperception, immoral assumption, and failed expression to a uniform tragedy of suffering and pain and waste. The queer or extreme example is the exact example, she persistently seems to tell us. It is the one that precisely in its queerness or extremity, and thus also, precisely in the queerness or extremity of its newly engendered and engendering relation with all the others, returns us to ourselves most fully in new contexts of illumination and insight.

"We are an odd people with odd playthings," Emerson has observed, for instance, midway in the text, "odd ideas of what is good for our male children." She has been writing specifically about a television commercial she has recently seen that depicts two men playing a game called "Tank Command," described as "the strategic military game from Ideal." The two men shoot it up and "make a lot of faces to show that it is an exciting, tough game." Finally, when one wins, "the man who has just been outsmarted looks up and says: 'War is Hell'" (195). The commercial has reminded her of some frightened superstitious boys she has known in an armored unit in Vietnam and of their refusal to eat apricots. A sergeant of theirs, it turns out, has hit a mine after eating apricots. After that, the rule has become, "If a guy eats apricots, he is not coming with us" (194). It is her reflections on all this that have led her to the remarks cited above. These in turn now lead her to a description of a survey conducted "in June 1968, after the great Tet offensive in Vietnam, when American and Vietnamese casualties rose," by "George Gallup, founder of the American Institute for Public Opinion," who has subsequently "concluded in an article called 'What Combat Does to Our Men,' that combat was beneficial." She goes on: "The Gallup Poll had analyzed the answers of 140 veterans of Vietnam in a survey to find out how they were affected. Mr. Gallup wrote, 'In summary: These 18- to 25-year-olds command respect because they respect themselves. They have gained self-confidence, firmed up their goals. They have learned to follow and to lead, to accept responsibility and to be responsible for others. While only 26 wanted to go to Vietnam in the first place, 94 percent, having returned, say they are glad for the experience. What kind of citizens will they be? Judging from the cross section we talked to, the answer is: superior'" (195–96). This is Emerson's method throughout. Old thoughts of some strange boys in a place of suffering and death called Vietnam get mingled with new thoughts on a bad commercial. In turn, and through the unlikely medium of a Gallup survey, these thoughts then unfold themselves into larger and illuminating general reflections on a place of toys and polls called America where the vision of war gets lost somewhere between the game and the game cliche. Odd enumerations in the general accounting, it is these, she relentlessly demonstrates to us, that must and ultimately do tell us the truer truth. And they do so, moreover, precisely in their crowdings and odd compoundings, in the teeming jumble of activity that is the operation of moral consciousness itself. Only in this fashion, indeed in the logic of *moral* association as it were, odd and serendipitous and often precisely against a predicted grain of argument or logic in its conventional sense, does the truer truth begin to get told at all.

Overall, the method is also imaged in the structure of the book at large and even in the titles of individual chapters. The one, for instance, from which the above examples are drawn, in its way the formal and thematic hinge of Emerson's design, is entitled "Odd Things Not Forgotten." The first two in the text have been "Endings: One Kind or Another," and "Families: Together and Not Together," and another just preceding, "Small Places." Next will come "Experts": reflections on sundry pilgrims and burnouts, engineers, victims, academic purveyors and apostles of policy, heroes and fools; the ex-Harvard liberal tourist, his chastened insight full to the last of shopworn good motive; the old friend from MAAG with his memories and excuses and his head full of mission-speak. And at the last will follow as well, at once in summary and in microcosmic after-image of all that has gone before, "Winners and Losers." To the end continue the odd enumerations: the story of Don Luce, the man who gave his career for the sake of getting out the truth about Con Son and the tiger cages and the best years of his life for the sake of peace for his beloved Vietnamese, all the while never giving up on the hosts of fellow Americans who came to number themselves among "the people who despised him" (355); that of Mr. Bao, the old translator with a new name, the compromised poet and mystic making a bad go of it in the country of the people he used to work for ("I wished him well," Emerson writes, "but I felt no pity for him, no real interest, no pleasure at the reunion. He was as he had always been" [363]); that of Mrs. Ransom, Louise, Vassar 1942, trying to redeem some particle of good out of the death in Vietnam of a fine son through the quest after amnesty for his fellows who chose to evade the draft or desert ("How can a generation continue to struggle, with no victories?" she keeps asking herself. "They've known nothing but losing" [368]); that of Mr. Norton, the man who saw the Vietnamese who shot him and does not blame, the paraplegic in the VA who now spends his days there trying to prove mostly that he is not malingering. (In the wards, we are told, "they were always on you, they used to keep at you, telling you what you could *really* do if you felt like it." In the land of the college try, he remembers a friend telling him, "Everyone knows how to be a paraplegic, don't they?" [380].) So, to the end, the odd enumerations continue; and so to the end the odd enumerations themselves become the general accounting, each making its fullest and truest meanings precisely in the new and ever-enlarging structure of vision founded of its relation to all the others. The odd enumerations, she seems to tell us, are all we have, "Battles, Retreats, Gains, Losses, and Ruins," names and stories from a place that was the war. The fullness of their significance must now continue to be measured, even as the book itself concludes, in the new order of our attending.

"People will always be kind," Emerson has remembered telling the paraplegic at the last. "He smiled," she has gone on to conclude, "and knew exactly what that meant" (380). So at the end, as in the beginning, *Winners and Losers* continues to probe relentlessly beneath the horrific commonplaces of what continues to pass in post-Vietnam America as cultural conversation and to extend the work of journalism toward a form of cultural discourse that would call for an ongoing angry critique and revision of its own most seemingly benign assumptions of meaning and value. A second, more recent book by Emerson, *Some American Men*, represents the extension of that critique, often by similar reconstitutions of traditional ideas of journalistic/analytic "structure" or "argument" into the domestic matrix of American life itself. And although she is at pains to note that such an extension of inquiry has not come of her direct experience with the American men of Vietnam exclusively or even predominantly, she does not deny for a moment the inscription of the war as a larger text of history and myth into the one here over which it often silently presides. Of the American men of Vietnam themselves, she writes, "This is not a book about them, but perhaps they are the reason I began it, for no other American men had ever spoken to me as they did. Knowing them, all camouflage between us put aside, taught me not only how to speak to other men but how to hear what once I might not have heard at all" (12). For it is in that silent dialogue, she tells us from the outset, that we must now begin to speak of American men, the one going on back behind the camouflage in what she calls the astonishing "intricacy of their memories and . . . the vast, secret ledgers they keep on themselves while often passing as plain, practical, busy men not given to introspection, one eye on the world," the camouflage behind which, in short, "some men pull off a close escape from life and know why" (14). "It is not unusual," she goes on in an early section, "for women to speak of wanting and needing happiness; that word may be used by us." On the contrary, "men, who also want and need the same, are more careful with their laments and see visible emotion as a form of surrender. They conceal and muddle and evade, turn sly or joke or provide answers that are only twigs pointing nowhere. Or they retreat. They do not wish to appear helpless or silly or as if they were men tossed about, even when their lives are hateful. And often they can be strangely fragile and cautious when a leap is called for, the cold stare and the hard question for once not excessive" (24).

The project, in sum, of this new feminist text by Gloria Emerson in the new American literature of post-Vietnam witness is to go behind that other surface of gender as a social construction, the surface of what women often do feel rightly to be very "wrong" about men, "their hardness; their lack of the generous, quick response; the distance they keep; their faces that so often seem shut; the things they find difficult to say; their tendency to tell women when a decision is required, 'We'll see.'" For that very surface, she contends, is the very other of the feminist critique, the function of "the old stances they are certain they must assume." So it can only be, she contends: "In a country whose insistence on delusion seems without clear limits, the old definition of masculinity still persists. And it persists because of hidden permission and unspoken expectations" (13).

As with "Winners and Losers," Emerson's method imaged here of reversing traditional agendas and hierarchies of culture implied in its most cherished cultural epithets, terms of privileged and not-so-privileged entitling, is again recapitulated in the title of the present work as well. "Some American Men." Not "American Men," or "The American Man," but "Some American Men." Again, she makes no pretense to dispassionate survey or comprehensive analysis. In the sample observed is noted the position of the observer, at once beyond science or objective description or analysis and somewhere precisely between experience and myth. The method overall is similarly rendered in the at first seemingly eccentric, yet later quite "rational" — albeit in a new key of "reason" — pattern of chapter entitling and arrangement. "Disorderly Conduct" contains examples of aberrant maleness, deviations from a standard which themselves increasingly become the account of an alternative vision of "conduct" or "conducts" new and better. An ex–draft-resister and expatriate teacher in his mid-thirties painfully leads his psychologically disabled writing students through eccentric projects of constructing themselves and their personal histories into new images of self-worth. A young Princetonian, class of '83, and descended, somewhere back in Oklahoma and Arkansas, as he happily tells one of his professors, "from backward people" (37), plays out the educational equivalent of guerrilla theater in a life of resolute eclecticism — the labor of the oil fields, editorship of *The Daily Princetonian*, the senior creative writing prize, post-graduate dishwashing and fry-cook work, and performance with a band "influenced by country western, the wide open prairies, and poor nutrition" (59), somehow adding up to the story of Stona Fitch, the "busiest boy of all" (51). He is the boy who will avoid, if nothing else, he avers, the horrible death of the moose with its head hung on the wall of the newspaper office, the one that "died of boredom" (43). In briefer vignettes, a twenty-six-year-old medical professional, an R.N., recalls his father's inability to bear the idea, at the conclusion of his studies, that his son would henceforth respond to the title "nurse" (34). On television, the faces of women completing a marathon attract unusual attention. "With men," however, it has generally seemed just a version of "an old story, no one cringed or turned away at the sight of a man in pain" (35).

In succeeding chapters entitled "Work" and "Duty," on the other hand, the project of envisioning and then re-envisioning categories of "normalcy" and "aberration" is continued exactly in reverse. For in their titular emphasis on their seeming broader inquiry into the conventional or traditional categories of male behavior, they describe in fact a storehouse of male cultural pathologies, large and small, so vast and various as to be almost beyond rational categorization. And again, as if to underscore Emerson's untraditional approach as a matter of method as well, the organization is not encyclopedic but rather, as in related texts such as Michael Herr's *Dispatches* and Frances Fitzgerald's *Fire in the Lake*, calculatedly heterotopic, eccentric, disparate, and jumbling, the work not so much analysis as collage or even montage.

In "Work," the nature of the pathology itself is spelled out early on. "The difference between men and women" in this regard, Emerson writes, "is only that men are expected to work faithfully all their lives, without interruption or wishing otherwise," for "having a job is not optional." Simply phrased, it is a dead metaphor in the fullest sense, a cliche that contains its own dreadful truth, "Do or Die." "It is by this means," she concludes, "they use their lives and are so judged" (65). A purveyor of up-scale American sorbet has arrived at success from a privileged childhood and supercareers in prestige car sales and music publishing and cooking and finds himself mainly still chasing the memory of an immigrant grand-father and "the happy version of the story" where "men in the Godoff family" always "sent for villages, they took children under their wings, they said 'Don't worry and it will be all right,' and made money so that those of their own blood would be safe for a certain time and know, in this way, how they were loved" (84). Another scion of wealth, and a gifted foreign correspondent, rejects the journalistic myths of masculine calling and finally finds peace and perhaps something even called "fun" (106)— and in context the word does not seem in the least frivolous—in the editor-ship of a cooking magazine that seems at last, even as its success forces its sale and his "promotion" to larger responsibilities, "something of his own" (66). A "director of loss prevention" (107) specializing in theft pro-tection for supermarkets and restaurants, a professional in the detection of "workplace deviance" (109) surveys a life and a career at some natu-ral intersection of violence and power and understands, looking back on earlier days as a sheriff's officer, how "he found a purity in all of it, and knew that it had been three and a half years exactly since he had been in a scuffle in New Jersey, this too in the line of duty" (126). A brilliant young physician, unambitious, passive, quietly indifferent to material gain, leaves even the quiet practice of country medicine to find in the Cambodian refugee camps of Thailand (and in Bangkok later, as it turns out, in the saving of the author's own life from meningitis) for once something like a doctor's true work; and then beyond he further pursues the "whispers" of self-exploration to a mountain in Kenya where he finds by natural accident the death, as one woman phrases it, of "a man so out of step with the spirit of the country in which he lived" that he "had been in danger all along and never knew it" (150). In rust belt cities across America, men *and* women lose work and do their best to find dignity, with and from each other, the ones among "the 35.3 million Americans" seen as "acceptable losses and no longer considered news" (176). A young poet (it is Bruce Weigl, one of the major figures earlier considered here) comes home to one of those places, where the U.S. Army once had sent him orders to Vietnam that had been the first invitation he had ever received to go anywhere and finds "he hoped that his father, the fathers of his parents, all the fathers, had not hated what was done to them, then knew better than to hope this but did not want them to be forgotten, pushed aside by paler men selling something. He had in mind the scented men with small and neat hands who did their drinking on airplanes and had fair skin that was finer than his own grandmother's had ever been" (180).

In "Duty," as opposed to the general tenor of "Work," we shift to that particular albeit seemingly equal and omnipresent cultural imperative imposed by the American tradition of moral manhood in war, the means of undergoing the ritual, as she phrases it, whereby the nation "decides when men must show they love it" (186). Both literally in terms of structure and figuratively in terms of outwardly ramifying significance into other aspects of the text, it is a very short chapter with a very large mythic provenance and reverberation. And the anecdotes are curiously consistent, taken as they are from various American wars, the vision of a piece of manhood, "a story, a small feather" of some trial of masculinity confronted and recorded to consciousness. Yet even here, in plumbing the caution of American veterans in revealing what they actually carry afterward from being American men in war, the curious "logic" of the text is rather one of new discovery than of old recording. What they "remember" consistently goes against the grain of the uniform horror and suffering they have often witnessed and the after-the-fact reticence and lonely caution with which it so often seems to be encompassed. Dan Loney, the man with the child deformed by the Agent Orange from Vietnam coursing somewhere in his genes, remembers the teenage VC girl, clearly enemy and armed with the SKS rifle, whom he has silently, secretly allowed to get away one Christmas. More than forty years after the Battle of the Bulge, James Finn remembers most vividly the GI from the artillery unit who looked once at his face and inexplicably stepped into the middle of a road in the Ardennes and offered him warm coffee. Jack Newcombe cherishes beyond all relics of war for reasons he can hardly remember the snapshot picture of some remembered German children. Against all predictable "logic," it turns out, something like this is what each American man in his way, one more "case study" like that recorded by a veterans' psychiatrist near the chapter's end, carries through a lifetime of trying "to be what his country most admired in its men and required of them, staying forever in a ghostly theater of war, with no one he knew to lead him out" (227). And exactly now against the same "logic," we suddenly realize, have been the answers to similar questions about this ritual of American manhood given by American boys before, in fact, they are "men." Indeed, as is often the case with Emerson, of presumed disparity of vision has come an astonishing consonance of sensibility. To be sure, in a survey she cites deriving from an actual questionnaire given to some New York eighteen-year-olds in 1980, we find that some of them, on the eve of an age of newly resurrected "Americanism," have already bought back into the old histories and myths. Others, however, answer in new versions of what their elders, now not surprisingly, have already in their ways told us. "I want to ask Ronald Reagan that if I go away in the army for two years, when I come back do I have to go to the tenth grade again?" one responds. "I just want to play the tuba," another says. Another, refusing to be photographed in "a helmet or sailor's cap" insists "any war is disgusting and terrible." He goes on, "I wouldn't go with any service. I would never go, no matter what, never." What about jail? the questioner persists. "I would run forever," the boy concludes (187).

Such, we discover, in "Duty" are the prospects for American men before *and* after the fact of the military ritual of manhood. As with "Work," so with "Duty": the truth of the experience lies there waiting before and after the mythic initiation, the experiential fall into the history of our enterprises and battles. What then are even the possibilities of alternative prospects?

A final chapter, entitled "Love and Other Great Risks," now attempts to address that issue by making the text's own larger "logic" of unwriting itself a ground of new creation. A new mythology, in short, projects its evolution out of the deconstructed detritus of the old. As imaged in the title itself, this chapter now proceeds to the new task of saying nothing less than *exactly* what it means. Apace, in the context of newly possible visions of manhood, instances of the previously eccentric and heterotopic now quite literally become the representative and even the exemplary.

In love and in all other things they do, men remain, she says, "specialists in disavowal," with "their idiocy" utterly "unknown to them" (234). They have trouble in particular with "this coarsened, short word, as if only women should come right out with it, as if leaving the mouths of men it might shrivel or defile them before our very eyes." Rather, they most often "wind stories around love. The stories contain a code you are expected to crack, no questions asked, and this is the closest they can come on ordinary days" (244). And precisely because they are most often odd, cryptic, encoded, such stories are most exemplary, she says, in their mysteries and silences, revealing again and again, as she concludes, that "not all love can be translated and there are men, and women too, who will not permit any attempt" (255).

Of individual lives come the queered, small parables. A university intellectual, a man of accomplishment and family, falls out of and into love with his remarkable wives; a black son of Caribbean immigrants with a life of welfare casework and a city crumbling down around him finds himself sustained by a marriage almost childlike in its romance; an ex–football hero and successful international journalist attempts to sort out old national myths of achievement and fair play and winning and losing— the author remembers him best from the Laotian border incursion, the notorious Lam Son 719, where at a hospital clearing station "his Vietnamese" has been "so good he could understand every word the wounded were saying in high, thin voices, what they were asking for, the soldiers who now knew no one cared about them" (301). These American men, it oddly turns out, all have one startling habit of sensibility in common: they all also think a great deal about their fathers, the men from whom they in their American manhood have come. Their stories in fact of such fathers are often their great stories of love. And so now, finally, the text also turns us to a current story of fatherhood enacted as a middle-aged history instructor, having lost his wife to cancer, tries to bring up his daughter in a world where the struggle to redefine the American woman neglects exactly that concomitant redefinition that must also take place with the idea of an American man. This father, it turns out, has just taken a big chance on tenure by speaking on the Princeton University campus where he works to introduce the Reverend Jesse Jackson. A student has asked him about the professional jeopardy in which he has seemed to place himself. He has replied, thinking of his dead wife and his living daughter, with an answer that is a definitive story of love and other risks. "The worst thing in my life has already happened," he tells the student. "What is there to be scared of?" The student has realized that this Mr. Jiminez could have made some magisterial speech on principle, has been under no obligation to speak of his own life. Yet he has done otherwise. The student has already been thinking about "how the lives of women were changing but of the thousands of nails still holding them down," but now, the work concludes, she is also "reminded that some men were changing too" (315). "Although she refused to count on such hope," the author adds, "she saw the possibility that many more men were capable of change and that someone her age might just live to see it" (315). Here, in one last enlistment in Emerson's text of a "new" journalism in the possible work of cultural revision, this concluding case study becomes no empirical last word but rather, still, at least an idea, a thought, not unlike that of Paul Berlin's old lieutenant in *Going After Cacciato*, a "maybe so," and thereby a possible history of us all.

In *Some American Men*, as in *Winners and Losers*, Emerson continues to trace out the power of myth *as* historical genealogy of culture reified into the actuality of historical-cultural fact. To examine the working of this power at quite similar intersections of history and myth has also been the project and the method of Frances Fitzgerald throughout her journalistic career. Indeed, it is just that sense of dialectical enterprise which now, for instance, almost twenty years later, continues to define the distinctly original genius of *Fire in the Lake*, that second groundbreaking feminist text about the American experience of Vietnam in its relation to the essentially male, western, rationalistic, scientific traditions of a dominant American culture. And if she would seem to undertake there the same project begun in *Winners and Losers* and extended in *Some American Men* within a broader and more theoretical and dispassionate framework of sociocultural analysis, one senses as well nonetheless a similarly intense spirit of revisionist moral commitment. Indeed, in *Fire in the Lake* one finds the work of historical-mythic reinscription in the largest sense, an attempt to trace out the tragedy of America in Vietnam through a calculated unwriting of a whole received dialectical formula of American consciousness, a formula essentially western and essentially male, and one again at the bottom of a fundamental arrogance of cultural assumption cataclysmic in its tragic consequences. So she notes from the outset:

> In going to Vietnam the United States was not only transposing itself into a different epoch of history; it was entering a world qualitatively different from its own. Culturally as geographically Vietnam lies half a world away from the United States. Many Americans in

Vietnam learned to speak Vietnamese, but the language gave no more than a hint of the basic intellectual grammar that lay underneath. In a sense there was no more correspondence between the two worlds than between the atmosphere of the earth and that of the sea. There was no direct translation between them in the simple equations of $x$ is $y$ and $a$ means $b$. To find the common ground that existed between them, both Americans and Vietnamese would have to re-create the whole world of the other, the whole intellectual landscape. The effort of the comprehension would be only the first step, for it would reveal the deeper issues of the encounter. It would force both nations to consider again the question of morality, to consider which of their values belong only to themselves or only to a certain stage of development. It would, perhaps, allow them to see that the process of change in the life of a society is a delicate and mysterious affair, and that the introduction of the foreign and the new can have vast and unpredictable consequences. It might in the end force both peoples to look back upon their own society, for it is in contrast that is the essence of vision. (7)

"States of Mind." As brilliantly figured even in the title of its first chapter, Fitzgerald's work thus locates from the outset a vision of the failure of American "mission" in Vietnam as immediate military-political enterprise within the context of a larger failure of American "intelligence" on the broadest terms conceivable. So also, in the first of what will become a series of almost countless similar imagings of linguistic reversal, it likewise announces itself from the outset as a journalistic text, quite like Emerson's, that will most often make its largest linguistic and cultural meanings through a radical critique of our fundamental categories of linguistic and cultural assumption.

On the latter count, in its careful tracing out of a fated collision between American and Vietnamese world views—one predicated on an idea of a society of "replaceable parts" (10) as opposed to an older idea of "social harmony" (23), one embracing a "national myth" of infinite "creativity and progress" as opposed to a traditional vision of "limitation and enclosure" (8)—within a meticulous rendering of the contexts of Vietnamese social history from the earliest days to the present, Fitzgerald's text brings us ultimately to a vision of tragedy near all consuming, with its victims, like Emerson's, mainly those who did the suffering and dying, the young American soldiers and, especially, for Fitzgerald, the Vietnamese:

> Young men from the small towns of America, the GIs who came to Vietnam found themselves in a place halfway round the earth among people with whom they could make no human contact. Like an Orwellian army, they knew everything about military tactics, but nothing about who they were or who the enemy was. And they found themselves not attacking fixed positions but walking through the jungle or through villages among small yellow people, as strange and exposed among them as if they were Martians. Their buddies were killed by land mines, sniper fire, and mortar attacks, but the enemy remained invisible, not only in the jungle but among the people of the villages—an almost metaphysical enemy who inflicted upon them heat, boredom, terror, and death, and gave them nothing to show for it—no territory taken, no visible sign of progress except the bodies of small yellow men. (370)

Accordingly, across a widening abyss of language and understanding, her book traces out into new stature of monstrous relief the real villains of the tragedy, the policy makers and policy mouthers who wrote the script and effectively dictated its playing out in full horrific denouement.

Indeed, from an American cultural perspective at least, perhaps the fullest achievement of *Fire in the Lake* as text is its measuring of the human depths of the tragedy of Vietnam against the backdrop of one of the most utterly inhuman spectacles of language ever mounted, an orgy of American techno-macho-malewrite and malespeak sublimely unaware of its hidden dialectics of cultural arrogance and insistently fostering the hideous politics of its own cruel self-deconstruction.[2] "'Tough-minded' analysts" working on the basis of "'rational' calculations of United States interests," could but only see their natural task as "'containing the expansion of the Communist bloc' and preventing future 'wars of national liberation' around the world" (6). And here, as the text shows us throughout, would be but the tip of a rhetoric insistently privileging the active-aggressive over the passive-deliberative and thus always by implication as well the "brave" over the "cowardly," the "good" over the "evil," and, above all, the "winning" (342) over the "losing" (376–77). A random collocation of phrases, any phrases, could somehow always tell the whole story: "vigorously rebuilding the machinery of administration and reshaping plans to carry the war to the Viet-Cong . . . able and energetic leader . . . demonstrated his grasp of the basic elements—political, economic, and psychological as well as military" (253). In the rhetoric itself one form of consciousness simply sought to overwhelm all possible others in numbing self-reification: an ever-enlarging set of notes, one might have called it, and as Fitzgerald relentlessly shows us, toward some grand American fiction of a "free world." "If a nation had free elections," she observes simply, "it belonged to the 'free world.'" "If it did not," she continues, "it belonged to those moral nether regions inhabited by Communists, Fascists, and backward people" (329).

So on, and so on, thus interminably, she shows us, the language-mission ground forward: "Each year the new young men, so full of vague notions of 'developmment,' so certain of their capacity to solve 'problems,' so anxious to 'communicate' with the Vietnamese, eagerly took their places in this old, old, war." ("Last year's program fell short of its goal," they would always say, "but this year for the first time we've got some coordination between the ARVN, the RF-PF, and the RD. The hamlet chief here is sleeping in his hamlet. And Major Trinh, an outstanding guy, is giving us his full cooperation" [339–40].) Never mind that today or on any day the Vietnamese *xa*, the village, might remain somwhere beyond translation as "the place where the people come together to worship the spirits" (10), the religious ground of a whole world order, "an entire way of life — an agriculture, a social structure, a political system." Never mind that the prevailing "reason" thus attempted to address a world of the natural and supernatural resembling, if anything, "one of those strange metaphysical puzzles of Jorge Luis Borges" where "an entire community imagines another one which, though magical and otherworldly, looks, detail for detail, like itself" (14).

On and on the language would march beyond even any simple or obvious surface dialectics of privileging toward a monolithic absorption of all possible othernesses and dualisms, including even, by ultimate implication, presumably those for which its own "privileged" terms (What, for instance, might supply the "as opposed to" of the Vietnamese of "proper" or "harmonious" or "correct"?) could not be said even to exist. On and on it would march, in sum, toward the containment of a whole organization of mind that it had never in the first place been structured to conceive. To be sure, at the level of applied policy, the ultimate moral and ideological implications of the project would remain camouflaged within an endless "torrent of Latinisms on the subject of 'consensus-making bodies in a fractionalized political system' and 'viable institutions for power-sharing which would gradually lead to the legitimization of the entire governmental framework'" (324). And it would have been perhaps one of the chiefest blessings of the war if such gibberish had proven merely hilarious, somehow stopped in midphrase like some old and puerile freeze-frame image of "young men from RAND and Simulmatics" armed with paramilitary Swedish Ks and jaunting "about the countryside in Land Rovers studying 'upward mobility among village elites' or 'the interrelationship of land reform with peasant political motivation'" (362). More often, however, its cost would be most closely reckoned in a giddily oxymoronic poetics of disaster, as in perhaps the most celebrated case, the Battle of Ben Tre, where a young American actually declared of a village that "we had to destroy it in order to save it" (393). There indeed the discourses of the destructive and the salvific could commingle in a single seamless tragic figuration. And closer still to the action, on the true nightside of policy where most of the work actually got done, there for sure and indelibly the language-mission could show itself only for what it *really* was: pure hygenic murder, clean and simple. Out in "Indian Country," "the Viet Cong did not live in places, they 'infested areas'; to 'clean them out' the American forces went on 'sweep and clear' operations or moved all the villagers into refugee camps in order to 'sanitize the area'" (368).

In a top-to-bottom rhetoric, Fitzgerald concludes, lay language-macho once and for all writ hideous, a systematic discursive formula for cultural arrogance, political oppression, and, at bottom, even racial genocide. In language, as in action, and vice versa, "moral infallibility, military invincibility—the two went together and were not to be differentiated, not in Vietnam, in any case, where the enemy was not only Communist but small, yellow, and poor" (368). And so, as defeat became increasingly inevitable, Americans retreated even more fully than ever into a world of familiar "'tough minded' analytical terms"—"graduated escalation," "limited war" (374); "harassment and interdiction," "free fire zones," "body-count" (375–76)—convinced to the last that official terminology, gamely and insistently applied, could still somehow make it all come right. Inevitably, in language and life alike, "the American war effort" had no final recourse but to become "almost entirely solipsistic: the U.S. government was trying to save 'American prestige' for Americans alone, to convince itself of American superiority" (377).

"'It is beyond imagination,'" Fitzgerald late in the text most trenchantly quotes "Professor Kissinger" as saying "just before joining the Nixon administration, 'that parties that have been murdering and betraying each other for twenty-one years could work together as a team, giving joint instructions to the country.'" She goes on: "It may be beyond the imagination of American officials, but it is not necessarily beyond that of the Vietnamese who have come to hold the Americans responsible for those murders and betrayals. It is true that there will never be a permanent coalition in which each party joins in an amicable agreement to disagree. The Vietnamese way is not that of a balance of power, but that of accommodation leading to unity" (440). The most seemingly innocuous figure of speech from an American official, she shows us, could inscribe patternings of linguistic and spiritual difference constituting nothing less than the orbits of worlds.

In this relation, it should not surprise us that a text that persistently hovers over the later stages of Fitzgerald's own from which most of these passages are drawn is Shakespeare's *The Tempest*. A chapter devoted to the increasing resemblance of the American enterprise to previous colonialisms she calls "Prospero, Caliban, Ariel." An ensuing one, toward the last, traces out the means whereby a visionary American rhetoric of world mixing and word mixing became increasingly but a series of new names for "the unrestricted use of violence against the Vietnamese" (378). Its concluding exemplum is a treatise on comparative "terror" carrying the signature, appropriately, of that American arch-craftsman of "working definition," Dr. Douglas Pike. ("A frank word is required here about 'terror' on the other side, by the Government and Allied forces fighting in Viet-nam. No one with any experience in Vietnam denies that troops, police and others commanding physical power, have committeed excesses that are, by our working definition, acts of terror . . ." [378].) Its title: simply "Prospero." There the matter remained, in unrelenting reflexiveness of word and deed. Precisely as the experts continued their vain, cruel, self-comforting attempts to engineer the discourse of mastery, Brave New World it had truly become.

As if to this end of realization, it turns out, in the epigraph to an introductory chapter entitled "Nations and Empires," Fitzgerald has already recorded by way of prophetic context a dialogue between an emissary of the ruler of Wei and an unnamed Master who has been asked for his assistance in the administration of "government." "What," the emissary asks, "will you consider the first thing to be done." The Master replies, "What is necessary is to rectify names. If names be not correct, language is not in accord with the truth of things. If language not be in accord with the truth of things, affairs cannot be carried on to success" (33). Such an epigraph, we see in retrospect, could now be read as an almost exact measure of the degree to which an arrogant western nominalism had attempted to unwrite and foreclose a whole counterposing tradition of linguistic and cultural assumption in something like a dialectics of pure reversal. So at the end, as in the beginning, the lesson of power could be read precisely in the lesson of language and in this case specifically in the blindnesses, avoidances, and monolithic certainties of a discourse of oppression rooted in the most fundamental assumptions of the American character. The price of failing to learn that lesson, Fitzgerald shows us, in an enlargement on Emerson's analogous figure, would be a broken conversation on a scale of cataclysmic geo-cultural proportion, the tragedy of America in Vietnam; and the ongoing expense for those unwilling to learn it then or now would be the attempt to continue to cast language across an ever-widening abyss of consciousness—an abyss of irrelation that, had it been crossed, might have opened the way toward a new thinking and writing of nothing less than history itself.

Transferred to the realm of American public education, the idea of the inscription and reinscription of "official" history as enabling myth of culture also becomes the subject of Fitzgerald's second book, *America Revised*. Most specifically, her subject there becomes history itself as quite literal textual production or commodity, with responsibilities of authorship and authority distributed among a variety of political, economic, and educational interest groups and with the idea of writing itself subject to a process of ongoing "revision" persistently relocating the intersections of history and national myth according to their various assertions of corporate power.

Appropriately, then, for a study of the ideas of history, historiography, history as historiographic and textual myth, all reduced to terms of purest production, the text at hand, *America Revised*, opens with a vignette from the "history business" it will proceed to anatomize and analyze. In telling anecdotal flurry, we go to the book shows, find out how in an almost dizzyingly brief span of recent development a "hot" historical-commercial-textual issue such as civil rights is quickly succeeded by ecology only to come back as black culture only to be succeeded by drugs. "Some companies" we hear the narrator's informant breathlessly concluding, "have gone out of business trying to keep up" (4).

Such an exemplum configures from the outset the basic moral of the story about history in America. In response to a bewildering collocation of trendy imperatives, it has of necessity become "Good-bye Columbus" with a passion *and* a vengeance. Major actors have become bit players. Some have simply vanished. Others, predictably, from groups previously marginalized or excluded, have appeared. Some players have remained, with their roles being that which has changed. Teddy Roosevelt trades the heroism of San Juan Hill for that of a prophetic environmentalism. Thaddaeus Stevens exchanges low political vindictiveness for high moral sincerity. Various basic myths of terminology have been altered beyond recognition. Progress now equals simply "change." The past is a confusion. The present is a tangle. Various texts traverse a full array of varieties of political diversity. They glory in pedagogical pluralism. Social science "concepts" vie for the spotlight with triumphs of contemporary design art. Texts become demonstrations of "polymorphous perverse," American history not as the old familiar homogeneous bland boredom but as "sensuous experience" (16). Moreover, as if all this, alternately encouraging and confusing as it might be, were not enough, we come to the real crux of the business, the business of historical revision and the revision of history in the particular context of the education business, and signaled by the word peculiar to that business (often, as the book will subseqently reveal, a code for sundry forms of the most arrant sort of censorship), "adoption." One keeps up with history only in fact as one keeps up also with the myth-endorsing and myth-censoring power of school district committees. "Should students read histories written ten, fifteen, thirty years ago?" the author asks. Obviously, she concludes, "In theory, the system is reasonable — except — and here is the crucial inclusion — except that each generation of children reads only one generation of schoolbooks" and further, therefore, "that transient history is those children's history forever — their particular version of America" (17). And while the facts demonstrably have never stuck in any particular way, and do so even less than they minimally had before, there is still, therefore, in whatever American histories may be remembered, "a tone of voice, a definition of the register" that is nothing less than the sound of national myth (19). This is particularly so, she adds, because uniquely as books they are almost always "consensus documents," in several crucial respects. First, "many people have a hand in writing them"; second, "they are tailored to please a public that extends even beyond the vast educational establishment." They are thus, "consensus documents" in the largest sense of mythic consequence: "they are themselves a part of history, in that they reflect the concerns, the conventional wisdom, and even the fads of the age that produced them" (20).

Such texts we learn shortly, as we get into technical matters of production, are often written by dead people. Authorities or scholars pair on title pages and spines with various specialists and editors and consultants. In fact, such texts are really not so often "written" as, in the argot of the trade, "developed" (22). Textbook editors in trade houses thus become nothing less than "truth givers," "the arbiters of American values," with "the publishing companies the Ministries of Truth for children" (27) while at the same time "trying to make money in one of the freest of free enterprises in the United States" (28).

Yet their constituencies are not consumers in the normal sense. There are state and local adoption boards. There are political action groups whose pressure and power change with the political times. Political and social change itself as a function of words, pictures, type-setting, format-devising, becomes an insurmountable problem of book technology. The artifact itself becomes the bizarre hybrid, the most bland result of an excruciating art of political compromise (46) coupled with an incredible political self-consciousness and (in an age of litigation) political hypersensitivity (42).

And all this is so frightening because these texts are of course working history in the fullest sense, the medium of its direct mythic implantation in average people's lives. That is, they are inherently, as opposed to more "academic" or "critical" texts, by their nature "nationalistic histories," written "not to explore but to instruct—to tell children what their elders want them to know about their country." They are vessels of "the truths selected for posterity" (47). Thus the very idea of revision becomes the crux, the site of mythic crisis, the problem of "writing" and "truth" itself. For "what changes," as Fitzgerald tells us, "is nothing less than the character of the United States" (59). The result, she goes on, especially given the historical and educational turmoil of recent decades, can only be a centralizing "sense of uncertainty" deriving both of historical flux itself and of multiple countervailing images contending for contemporary consciousness as both past and present projections of national character and myth.

Nowhere, she goes on, is the current welter of confusion more clearly demonstrated than in the major strain of historical mythologizing that might be entitled, perhaps, "the Americanization of Americans." The nineteenth-century version of that, she shows us, was essentially a conservative process, basically an attempt to write a history of assimilation, something like the Americanization of ourselves. The twentieth-century version of the project, on the other hand, what might be called eventually the Americanization of "others," likewise begins in the same conservative vein but then in our own era quickly explodes, particularly in the wake of the 1960s, into a disparate panoply of "blacks, 'ethnics,' Indians, Asians, and women" (93). At its silliest, such a trend has generated and continues to generate, she shows us, the most idiotic sort of tokenism. A stranger to our nation in the sixties, for instance, given the high historical profiles of Booker T. Washington and Ralph Bunche, would think that much of the present republic was founded on the combined miracles of peanuts and the United Nations. At a deeper level, the same trend yields the worst sort of ethnic pandering. To use a simple example here, contemporary Hispanics are now treated in many progressive texts to a wholesale re-writing of the villainy of the conquistadores. The cumulative effect of all this, she concludes, is a unity-multiplicity dialectic gone wild: old images of false American homogeneity born of heterogeneity now yield to a new false heterogeneity born of homogeneity, to the suggestion "that Americans have no common history, no common culture, and no common values, and that membership in a racial or cultural group constitutes the most fundamental experience of each individual. The message would be that the center cannot, and should not, hold" (104). Yet in the face of this, she goes on, we find nothing on the larger forces of *actual* decentering addressed in any coherent way. A rhetoric of chauvinism has simply been replaced by one of analytic bewilderment. Earlier critical ellipses have simply been replaced by fuddled evasions. The texts of our history thus work their way out of the prison house of context into a progressive and absolute decontextualization (145).

Arising out of the account of such decontextualization, the final critique of American public-education historiography and historiographic myth offered by Fitzgerald is at once the most seemingly paradoxical in base of argument and concomitantly the most original and even revelatory. After all the demonstrations of its ellipses, omissions, avoidances, evasions, substitutions, she tells us, what we really come to identify as the distinguishing defect of our curricular history is its stultifying concreteness. In its very there-ness, she shows us, is the index of its greatest avoidance: the absence of anything like intellectual history, the history of thought itself, not simply ideology but the ideas that make ideology. What our students read instead is history, to use Herbert Marcuse's figure from "The Closing of the Universe of Discourse," written in an educational version of the discourse of the purely "operational," history devoid of dialectical openings for critical judgment (*One-Dimensional Man*, 84–120), a history where analysis, thinking about thinking, is at the very most simply moral editorializing according to current fashion (153). In such history we find nothing like "character." We find total absence of "conflict," especially the unthinkable "class-conflict." It is all history writing in the "Tinker Bell mode" (155), bland, uninsulting, and utterly—and this is the really astonishing feature of its concreteness—without, as any writer even remotely aware of the act of writing would at least think of it, *content*. Especially for the history writer, it is history with no conflict, no confrontation, no sense of the dialectical play of forces that is nothing less than history itself (156–57). As to historical "problems," no one is really responsible for them (158). If known at all, they are indeed known after the fact only as their "solutions" (157). The result, appropriate to the age of the operationalists who gave us Vietnam, is the perfection of value-free technology, the "natural disaster" theory of history (158). Of course, since it is American history, it is still full of the ideas of a historical moral imperative (160) or of a cherished dream of progress (161), but now it is one with no sense whatsoever of moral agency inscribed in its putative moral connections. It is at best a mosaic with a moral overlay. And even when it generates a contemporary alternative, in the genre known as the "inquiry" texts, the questions themselves of moral or political analysis are for the most part often "irrelevant, fallacious, or just plain stupid" (164).

In all their contemporary versions, such texts thus mainly perpetuate the old legacy of John Dewey (174), with relevance as a function of utility, utility as a basis of uniformity, and accordingly, in its ongoing larger politicization, the tradition prevailing to this day of civics as history, history as civics, social reform through education, education as social reform. What is needed with "history" in this definition, Fitzgerald asserts in contrast, is a new contextualization as "old," she reveals to us, as the prescient work of researchers of the 1930s such as George S. Counts of Columbia Teachers College, work revealing that American high schools for instance could only be counted on to reflect "the external social structure and its values" and thus "that teachers could not hope to change society in any fundamental way—They could merely hope to humanize it" (203). This call to work from within what might be termed the structuralist freeze she also suggestively connects with another older voice of this century from almost exactly the same year, Bertrand Russell, who "once wrote that 'the whole conception of truth is one which is difficult to reconcile with the usual ideals of citizenship,' if only because 'it is impossible to instill the scientific spirit into the young so long as any propositions are regarded as sacrosanct and not open to question'" (209). The old tyranny of unexamined assumption, she concludes, has simply now been replaced by a new version of itself predicated on an insistent "ahistoricism and dullness" (210).

Of necessity, the book ends not with answers but with questions. "Why is it that the school-reform movements have all been so intellectually reductive? Why in the profession most directly concerned with education should there be a level of anti-intellectualism and sheer mindlessness found in few other professions? And, finally, why is it that schoolteachers and parents make no protest against all the gimmickry and the bland Socialist-realism-style writing in the books that children have to read?" (213). And of necessity as well, in concrete imaging of new possibility, Fitzgerald's own responses work inward from such questions to comprise a virtual inventory of post-structuralist critiques of systematic education itself: that as a discipline, pedagogy is essentially self-defining (214); that education thus considered as "discipline" or "social therapy" is too easily confused with social control (215); that confusion of the "schools" with some ideal vision of "the world" invests the whole of social reform in a rather small area of society and thereby invests our own children with something like "the psychology of laboratory pigeons" (218). The design of Fitzgerald's text, the quest after a new design of American history in education, flowers ultimately into a quest also for a new design of American education in history.

The inscription and reinscription of American civic history and of history as American civics through the forms of argument called cultural myth—and in this case a particularly cherished civic figure of the myth of national exceptionalism—becomes both the further subject and textual enterprise of Fitzgerald's *Cities on a Hill*. Although subtitled "A Journey Through Contemporary American Cultures," it is also more directly characterized, at least on the cover of its mass-market paperback version, as "A Brilliant Exploration of Visionary Communities Remaking the American Dream." In this case, oddly, the piece of publisher's hype would seem the more accurate, for it does describe the book's unique positioning as a study of the ongoing reciprocity in American life of lived history and endlessly self-recapitulated and self-recapitulating myth. It is in fact a study of "visionary communities," ones imaged in particular in the old civic-utopian figure of the "American Dream" offered up by the puritan patriarch John Winthrop aboard the sailing ship *Arbella* even before he had reached the shores of the forbidding New World: "For we must consider that we shall be as a city upon a hill. The eyes of all people are upon us, so that if we shall deal falsely with our God in this work we have undertaken, and so cause Him to withdraw His present help from us, we shall be made a story and a by-word throughout the world." "The remarkable thing," Fitzgerald notes at the end of her introduction, "was that four centuries later Americans were still building cities on a hill." What the book reveals further is how fully the enterprise remains in mythic context, the context of providential election and mission and thereby of exceptional and even millennial destiny. In the era that people would come to recall as post-Vietnam, she shows us, Americans of incredibly vast differences of age, sexual preference, religion, politics, and economics and across an array of permutations of democratic ideology too vast to be reckoned would reveal one thing in common: they would still be attempting to inscribe history as the American millennium.

Again, as in her foregoing texts, the particular method of inscription here is that of the calculatedly eccentric or even heterotopic. Indeed, as the author announces from the outset, her entire method of "choice"—which will eventually incorporate major analyses of the gay community of the Castro District of San Francisco; the Protestant fundamentalist enclave centered on Liberty Baptist Church in Lynchburg, Virginia; the retirement community of Sun City, Florida; and the "New Age" cult of Rajneeshpuram in Oregon—will create itself from the outset not in an idea of representative collocation but of intentionally eccentric and creative juxtaposition. The whole idea called "this book," she begins, has its genesis in "a story I heard about the mayor of San Francisco making an appearance at a drag ball and of a chance visit I paid to Jerry Falwell's church a year later. It began with a sensation—in both cases the same— of strangeness inside the familiar: a kind of shock of non-recognition" (11). Pursued further, the disjuncture itself assumed its own dimensions of myth. In San Francisco, she writes, at the end of America, the dream of the west, first the Gold Coast, Barbary Shore, then City Lights Bookshop and North Beach, the mecca of the counter-culture, then later Haight-Ashbury during the summer of love, the gay community had literally taken the old dream and had literally made it wear some flowers in its hair. "The Castro—or what they called their 'liberated zone'—was a kind of laboratory for experimentation with alternate ways to live. It was also a carnival where social conventions were turned upside down just for the pleasure of seeing what they looked like the wrong way up" (12). Yet to see that in fullness of recognition, she goes on, would be achieved only in her own case by being plunged into another experience of "straight" living that in an instant now seemed as otherworldly as the Castro seemed normal. In Lynchburg on a new assignment, convinced that she was going to find some imagined idea of "real Americans," she writes, "The people in Falwell's church looked so much like those television-commercial Americans it was as if the images had walked off the screen twenty-five years later." The problem of dialectical recognition is, of course, "only now it was they who looked exotic" (13).

So, in turn, dialectic breeds dialectic. After this particularly radical experience of juxtaposition, she writes, "I began to look for other communities—or cultural enclaves—that had taken shape during the sixties and seventies to explore" (19). Not surprisingly, one of the most "radical" versions of new enclaves was one formed almost exclusively of conservatives, the retirement community called Sun City. "These communities were not, of course," she writes, "ideological or programmatic; many of them had been conceived and built by commercial developers. But they were radical in the sense that never before in history had older people taken themselves off to live in isolation from the younger generations" (20). The other, Rajneeshpuram, completing a kind of "parallelogram," she writes ("two religious movements and two social groups; two sixties communities and two groups with conservative views"—although even at this stage such distinctions are already starting to blur and break down), would be something very "new" looking for something very old, a "New Age" community itself, in the wake of the sixties, become a kind of cultural troglodyte and curiously in its way oddly moving toward an archaic radical separatism as fast as Falwell's anachronistic fundamentalists seemed to be struggling back toward modernity (22).

Again, the seemingly odd and heterotopic becomes the exemplary and representative. And much of what Fitzgerald discovers about the contours of contemporary American utopian thought is already figured in her conceptions of structure itself. In every instance, she writes, "The people who joined such groups had the extraordinary notion that they could start all over again from scratch. Uncomfortable with, or simply careless of, their own personal histories and their family traditions, they thought they could shuck them off and make new lives, new families, even new societies. They aimed to reinvent themselves" (23).

Yet the oddly disparate stories become far more than structuralist accounts of a monomyth. Rather they become accounts of how a given monomyth always becomes the account of its own dialectical contrarieties and of how the playing out of those contrarieties as history must somehow become in the form of historical accounting an inquiry into the ongoing dialectic of history and cultural mythmaking at large. To be sure, there is in each case something like a recapitulated structure, scenario, even choreography. Anywhere in America where utopia rears its banner and creates a myth of history that by historical enactment becomes a new text of myth, there comes inevitably the text of counterinscription, the myth-history of apocalypse. In the Castro, it is imaged first in various forces of social repression, then later, in the murders of George Moscone and Harvey Milk, in full-fledged reactionary violence, and thereafter finally in the specter of AIDS, true visitation of the end, Biblical plague, God in the whirlwind, the mythic consummation of the whole theology, utopia, love, civic virtue, divine wrath, punishment. In Lynchburg the church and university militant become the church and university embattled, the neofundamentalist rewriting of Winthrop's Boston and Harvard, with their enterprise the inscription of American history backward into the image of "Falwell's contention that separation between church and state did not mean separation between church and government" (181). A civil pietism called the "moral majority" thus becomes the full metaphysical analogue of the forces of light cast in some last pitched battle with the minions of darkness. At Sun City the radical construction of a civic-cultural icon called old age or senior citizenship ironizes beyond belief the old American myth of civic-utopian resurrection. The eminence of old age establishes itself *at* the fountain of youth, Florida, itself, from Mr. Flagler's filled-in swamp to the latest version of the Magic Kingdom, a complete American creation. The utopia of old age is thus created in the land of youth, age honored as never in our history or any history—("no society recorded in history," she in fact writes, "has ever had whole villages—whole cities—composed exclusively of elderly people" [212])—only to situate Americans already weakly contextualized by egalitarian blankness with "no jobs, no families around them, and not very much future" in a community newly chosen "already so homogeneous as to threaten the boundaries of the self" and place them in a world of totalizing artifice. Old age finds the new American millennium/apocalypse indeed, "in a town without any history on the edge of a social frontier, inventing a world for themselves" (232). In Rajneeshpuram—really no more odd, the author finally discovers, in its combination of apocalyptic moral earnestness and homey plasticity, than Liberty Baptist—we arrive at what seems at first some newest intersection of American charlatanism, lubricity, and pure energized avarice, only in the same moment to find it as old in fact as Aimee Semple McPherson or Elmer Gantry (one or the other of whom, the point would seem to be, was "real," and the other "fictional"). It is a place that ultimately "bore rather more resemblance," she brilliantly notes, "to Cam Ranh Bay in the mid sixties than to any hippie commune of the same date" (261). And there we find enacted as wondrously melodramatic and colorfully etched a morality play as any native Manichean ever dreamed, one conducted in the West at the pure far eastern merging of loopy American spirituality and American commodification, of utopian faith at the end of the burnt-out sixties commingled with the most cynical involvements imaginable in local politics, property, and commercial enterprise. Apocalypse becomes a tragicomedy of sex, greed, power, and betrayal nestled in a blissed-out looneybin of leftover Human Potential therapies and Aquarian moonshine, all going down to a Bagwan absconditus and a morass of debt, disillusionment, and moral disarray.

But here, finally, as in all of Fitzgerald's work, one must not be tempted by the genius of particular analyses to misread her larger project. For given even the essentially structuralist tradition of social anthropology into which the text obviously situates itself, the chief achievement of "structural" inquiry throughout, and the source of the work's profoundest insights, is precisely its creative enlarging or multiplication upon traditional structuralist logic, reason, argument. Thus finally, we must insist, we are by exact intention *not* talking simply about four versions of a mono-mythic story. The "story" of *Cities on a Hill*, if one may be said to exist, is again rather, as with the work of so many other Vietnam writers in their generation, the story times four of the dialectical forms and processes of historical-mythic consciousness itself. To put this another way, a text entitled *Cities on a Hill* is thus formed of four discrete versions of the text that is at once American history and American myth at its moment of perpetual intersection in American lives, the perpetual historical "starting over," in this case, of the mythic idea or possibility of "starting over" itself. Yet what must be insisted on is the image not of a bringing together, a reconciliation of diversity into unity or structural consistency, but rather a shaking out, a fourfold unwriting, as it were, that would be a fourfold new writing. And it is this project of poststructuralist recontextualization here that makes Fitzgerald's project truly "contemporary" in the largest sense, an enterprise partnered newly with the idea of the American vision as an ongoing conversation of history and myth, a domain, somewhere at once beyond and within dialectic, where the nation perpetually attempts to inscribe itself anew and where now the accountings of its history and its myths must again begin to be written.

The visionary pilgrimage of American consciousness, at once self-unfolding and self-enfolding, out of apocalyptic myth into history which becomes new projection of myth-apocalypse: this is similarly the enterprise recorded in the major fiction of a third figure associated, like Emerson, Fitzgerald, and, as we shall see, Michael Herr, with a celebrated "blockbuster" text of Vietnam witness; and that figure is of course Robert Stone, the author of *Dog Soldiers*.

So completely has Stone come to be associated with the literary legacy of Vietnam, in fact, in his sundry inscribings of his vision of the war and its aftermath across the twinned landscapes of contemporary history and myth, that he should probably be now considered the novelistic laureate of the post-Vietnam American soul. For indeed, throughout the expanse of his works, surely no single author in our time has created a collocation of Americans so completely haunted by such particular history and particular myth in their perigrinations across the dream-nightmare landscape of the late twentieth century. Yet any American reader conversant with his first work of fiction, *A Hall of Mirrors*, might have anticipated the possibilities of such a career in the power of that first novel's achievement as a inscription of national life at the intersection of contemporary history and myth in postmodern crisis, its calculated depiction of subterranean New Orleans, as Stone himself has put it, as urban microcosm of our collective spirit, "a city in which the American condition is driven to extremity" (Wood, 1). Then, of course, came that second, highly celebrated work tracing out the war's immense purchase on American lives, the account of a doomed, violent heroin adventure-scam revealing, in Thomas Myers's graphic formulation, "that Vietnam is only the most visible promontory of a transformed American cultural landscape, that the indiscriminate violence, moral decay, and social fragmentation that fester behind the seamless official narrative of the war have become principal features of life in the United States as well" (198). Next, there followed, in *A Flag for Sunrise*, an equally celebrated third chronicle of "lost Americans," as Michael Wood described them, pursuing their post-Vietnam destinies amidst the political turmoil of contemporary Central America. And most recently, in *Children of Light*, Stone's pursuit of our collective national passion for spiritual extremity has led him now to contemporary Hollywood, the illusion factory where the American dream has always gone to mythologize itself into forms of dread, vulgar apotheosis. In sum, these works constitute a career that has now placed him, along with other chief fictive practitioners of the literature of American witness such as Norman Mailer, Joan Didion, and, most recently, Don De Lillo, at the forefront of inquiry into the essential forms and processes of American life and mythmaking in the last half of the twentieth century. From the outset he has been a political novelist in the most traditional sense; and in the calculated re-writing of the representational novel in its various political genres — the historical novel; the gothic or psychological tale of terror; the thriller; the novel of detection and intrigue; the existential fable; the novel of revolution; and (a most significant American addition) the novel of Hollywood and of the movies—postmodern realistic fiction in America finds its new flowering of mythic forms. It traces out the full range of political vectors and congruencies, the currents and interflowings of power and desire, with individual lives, in their broken circuits of meanings and value, becoming sign and index of collective national crisis of spirit. To this degree he speaks thus with the darkly discrete strain of national personality that has always habited the American sense of the modern: that strain of E. A. Robinson, who in a sense became our nineteenth-century "laureate of failure" (Dickey, xx) in its grim visitations in individual lives; or that more recent updating, as Kurt Vonnegut, Jr., has observed regarding the work of his contemporary Joseph Heller, of obsessive concern with the essential "pain and disappointments experienced by mediocre men of good will" (1). But here is it also failure on a scale of both the individual and the consciously national and even geopolitical, the grandeur of the dream and the fall from it now beckoning down the long, dark, claustral road of a uniform national "spell," as one of Stone's characters puts it, "of existential dread" (298). For if he is among our most seemingly mimetic of major novelists, he is always, it must be remembered, among our most hallucinatory as well. In postmodern variation of distinguished American forebears such as Brockden Brown, Hawthorne, Melville, Twain, Faulkner, and others, he writes from within the very dialectic of consciousness itself, reminding us persistently of the dream-likeness of our lives and the life-likeness of our dreams. His characters live amidst a chaos of drugs, alcohol, random violence, hoarded madnesses. To make moral choices in their worlds is an attempt to walk a thin line between acceptable and unacceptable pathologies. (In a story entitled "Helping," to choose a most recent example, an alcoholic social worker employed counseling veterans, confronted by a client specializing in a dementia of phony Vietnam flashbacks, is thrown out of recovery and back upon the already-shredded resources of his wife's dying love. By the end, he is separated from madness, we must infer, and perhaps even murder or suicide, only by the possibility that she will appear at a window in their house and make some sign acknowledging his needful presence.) It has been fashionable, in talking about the work of Stone and his contemporaries, to say that they are writing about "paranoia" at the level of national and geopolitical myth, about "paranoia" become as much as we know in our lives of what passes for reality. For Stone, this is true only at its most inclusive: he is in the largest sense nothing less than our great fictive mythologist of American dread.

The burden of American reality inscribed in *A Hall of Mirrors* (and noted again, one should add, in exact titular echo in Stone's newest novel as well) is in large degree figured in the epigraph, from Robert Lowell's poem "Children of Light." Here we are, already, on the terrain of American myth at large, the New World and its dream of moral vision, possibility, and hope. The novel is, truly, even before it has begun, of Americans in ancestral image, "Pilgrims unhoused by Geneva's light," holy would-be millennialists cut loose from the ancient comfort of sacraments, questing believers looking for a reason to be so. And truly they carry likewise the burden of the first planting, of "the Serpent's seeds of light," carry it on the American landscape upon which now, still,

> light is where the ancient blood of Cain
> Is burning, burning the unburied grain.

In *A Hall of Mirrors* the harvest of the fields of America is one of uniform failure. The scene is America on the verge, sordid apocalypse, modern-day New Orleans, site of dreams, the Big Easy, ripe with decadence and possibility. It is the place where American dreams empty out, the alluvion receptacle of the heartland where promise is drawn and voided. Here it is a scene of racism, right-wing paranoia, capitalist greed and media-sell, righteousness and power commingled in a dreadful evangelism, stoned apocalypse. Amidst it walk, moreover, the literal detritus of the land, high and low, powerful and dispossessed, the rapacious would-be masters and the walking prey. And riding all the convergences of force are three particular Americans on the edge. First, there is Rheinhardt, the ex-Julliard musician, failed virtuoso, Mozart-loving pilgrim and all-purpose burnout, the drifter, the drunk, protean man. Clearly formed already in the image of a host of mythic others, he is Django Reinhardt, jazzman; he is Ellison's Rinehart, Rinehart the runner, pimp, lover, holy-con; most currently, he is also Norman Mailer's D.J./Deejay gone far-white and far-right, full practitioner, as he terms it, of "sheer existential amorality" (250), and now in the employ of M. T. Bingamon's new Voice of America, WUSA. It is "the voice of Almighty God in this part of the forest," Rheinhardt proclaims, the one where he gets "to call the faithful to prayer" (134). It is indeed, as it bills itself, "The Voice of an American's America — The Truth Shall Make You Free" (103). Second, there is the woman, Geraldine, the West Virginia hill girl, wounded, wearing to the world her scarred beauty of a face, done in with a carpet knife by one more jealous drunk of a man. ("Soft Girl. Soft. Soft. Tough," Rheinhardt remembers after she is gone [395].) She can hold on for a moment with Rheinhardt, lover and fellow soul-survivor, against inevitable calamity, while even in that moment stalking the death that is her destination. Finally, there is also Morgan Rainey, scion of benighted white southern history, Harvard intellectual social worker, pain-devotee, bleeding-heart eccentric and isolato. He is, in his own despicable misery, the patron saint of wretched suffering humanity.

The world they inhabit is afoot with horrors and cons. Rainey, employed in some vague capacity to survey welfare recipients of public assistance, finds himself embroiled in a racist power-grab predicated on the exposure of welfare chiseling among the black community. Apace, Rheinhardt's employer Bingamon and a collocation of right-wing nuts, all convinced of the "pattern," the conspiracy, the communist-negro-jew-liberal combine, as well as corrupt local officials large and small, plot a right-wing apocalypse. It is all of a piece, black and white, powerful and dispossessed, large and small, and everyone is implicated. Individuals work their way amidst the currents of manipulation and force. Rheinhardt defends his compromises with stoned, easy skepticism. "Unusual times demand unusual hustles," he says (250). "My conscience is clear. . . . It's bone dry." "I'm an honest workman, making my workmanlike way" (301). The passion of Morgan Rainey plays itself out in feckless self-torturing nightmare, his determination to bear the suffering of the least of God's children the expiation of some ancient curse of family and region. "I want to find out about humanness," he has explained to Rheinhardt (175). To this, the latter has replied, with implications far beyond the local, "Very shortly you will belong to pathology" (179). Meanwhile, Geraldine holds on, hopes against hope in that sense to which a cliche is always, at the last, tragically true. "I love you Rheinhardt," she cries out at one point, "because you're a flyer. You're up in the air" (225). "I'm a person with sublime needs," he has shortly replied (226). But as she knows, it is all going down. "And fears shall be in the way," she remembers from an old Bible verse as forces converge at the last in a floodlit, packed stadium, searching amidst the garish noise and confusion of right-wing political-religious spectacle and freak show for the lover of her spiritual abandonment, "scared, scared, scared" (330). The forces gather indeed. Morgan Rainey, himself making his way into the stadium and the rally, now works against nothing less than "powers" and "principalities." (321). "I'm going down on them," he has phrased it in the moment of pathetic, absurd decision ("Who do you think *them* is?" his incredulous listener, one more old black who knows the way of things, has interrupted) "I have to. For myself. For life" (312–13). ("God's skunk" [255], Rheinhardt has called him all along, the "athlete of perception" [251] with the reek of "conscience" [255].) And so Rheinhardt, to the end, plays *his* appointed role, as he has called himself, "the evil fool of the air" (254).

Now, at the last, the evil fool of the air has the air to himself, stands at dead center, works the stage, the emcee-deejay in charge. In the final shameless scam, the ultimate cynicism, comes the newest text of protean man, unhinged, unmoored, afoot, afloat, and utterly amoral, the pure stoned survivor. Events move to the inevitable moment of cacophonous horror: the national anthem plays to Rheinhardt's voice-over now conjoined with the distant rising of Geraldine's own final outcry of her lonely fear and pain. "While the band played and the people above her started to sing, Geraldine decided to try screaming. When they came to 'so proudly we hail,' she screamed until they had sung 'the twilight's last gleaming,' holding the scream long enough to hear it ring against the walls, and all through the end of the song she screamed as loud as she could and she did not stop screaming until she heard Rheinhardt's voice, a hundred times magnified say, 'Patriotic Americans — your attention, please!'" (333). Meanwhile, amidst the whole paranoiac calculation — the menagerie of right-wing nuts on the stage, an admiral, a general, a geriatric cowboy star, local racist political hacks by the handful; the attendant charalatans, survivors, and hangers on; the lurking disaffected and dispossessed waiting just outside the security net on the fringe — Rainey approaches and joins forces by naked circumstance with Prothwaite, the mad, old-line IWW internationalist, leftover radical, widower of the revolution, now come to *his* moment of illumination (352). In a two-man, one-truck dynamite mission, it literally all goes up in a gust of high explosive disorder, American entropy, last visitation of leftover radical history, final collision of all the currents of force.

It is all, at the end, as Rheinhardt's old friend, Farley the Sailor, Father Jensen, holy-con, and fellow survivor puts it, the whole scam, "a perfectly marvelous long-term hustle rotten at the core" (359). Rainey is simply absorbed into the vast maw of chaos he has embraced. Geraldine winds up dead, pure, sordid, and simple, a suicide in a holding cell, hanged by a cold bed chain, given up on her search for her lost cynical man, busted after the night of right-wing apocalypse over an unused cheap handgun and a forgotten joint. And amidst all this Rheinhardt, even as the apocalypse nears, plays to the last the emcee, the holy-con deejay with the music in his head, the stoned fool, the survivor, broadcasting God's truth back at itself in ghastly parody. "Fellow Americans!" he cries out over the loudspeaker. "Let us consider the American way." He goes on:

> The American Way is innocence. . . . In all situations we must and shall display an innocence so vast and awesome that the entire world will be reduced by it. American innocence shall rise in mighty clouds of vapor to the scent of heaven and confound the nations!
>
> Our legions, patriots, are not like those of the other fellow. We are not perverts with rotten brains as the English is. We are not a sordid little turd like the French. We are not nuts like the Kraut. We are not strutting maniacs like the gibroney and the greaseball!
>
> On the contrary our eyes are the clearest eyes looking out on the world today. I tell you that before our wide, fixed blue-eyed stare the devious councils of the foreign horde are confounded as the brazen idolators before enlightened Moses.
>
> No matter what they say, Americans, remember this—we're OK! Who else can say that? No one. No one else can say—we're OK. Only in America can a people say—we're OK. I want you to say it all with me. (366–67)

The voice of WUSA becomes the voice of America, leading the pep rally. And, not surprisingly, the subject now turns to the newest American adventure in empire, the one in Asia, the one that has been in the newspapers all along, the one that presides here, even as it will throughout Stone's writing: Vietnam. "Americans," he resumes, "our shoulders are broad and sweaty but our breath is sweet. When your American soldier fighting today drops a napalm bomb on a cluster of gibbering chinks, it's a bomb with a heart" (367). On across the landscape of patriotic consciousness, the speech inscribes itself as pure, stoned, scabrous fantasia, Nathaniel West by way of Norman Mailer, conjuring up all the old shibboleths, the old fat lady, somebody's aunt or grandmother, on the bus, going to the world's fair, Columbia the gem, the gigantic leering coon-rapist, homo erectus, wearing the cap with the red star. "The fiend stirs!" he shrieks in giddy non sequitur. "Iowa's never so pretty in May" (367–68). It is the ultimate cynicism, and it brings down the house. Now, in the deepest fantasy of the national unconscious, newest version of the dread, lurid apocalypse that is postmodern America, the time has come to run. Or, as Farley the sailor puts it, himself in the midst of flight and delivering the blow that crushes M. T. Bingamon's skull in a last confrontation in his stadium redoubt, "survival time. . . . No amenities" (378).

That is the way of it in America. At the end, there is again only Rhein-hardt, at work again on being the New Man, the mutation, the man for cold weather (397). And this is the survivor's wisdom, his knowledge of what must be, even as he looks at a corpse upon a slab, a woman once named Geraldine, an old part of old him now gone the way of him, the way of things. "No Help." The book ends as it begins, with a drunk in a drunk, the language of pain. "Defend me friends," he has intoned to him-self in the odd, vulnerable moment, "I am but hurt" (181, 251), but then still with sly cynicism his blanket, his field dressing, his cover. Now it is the language of pain itself that speaks, pain only. "One more time," he cries out. "I'm a survivor. I love you, baby—No Help."

"I love you baby—No Help."

"I love you baby—No Help" (405–6).

"I am but hurt," he says now and says it "out loud" (398). But now is also another time and another bar, and time and place for a new dream, a new speech, another attempt for the "new man," "the man for cold weather," to play the deejay, to be the Voice of America. Rheinhardt now, he says, is Denver bound (Denver—the old goal of the new pilgrims, the beats, the most recent generation of American saints—Sal Paradise, Dean Moriarity, Carlo Marx) and going there to look down from "the highest point in the city" upon "all the things this breathing world affords." For, he continues, "this is a wonderful Republic to be a young man in, and don't you forget it" (407). Yet in the same moment, there are the lower frequencies, the words of pain that work and will out in endless refrain. As the novel closes, he continues to shout just, "They killed my girl I'm gonna bust up the bar." At the conclusion, broadcast news to the contrary, he is only Rheinhardt, in the end as in the beginning, alone, drunk, looking for a lost clarinet. " 'They killed my girl,' Rheinhardt said, walking down the street. 'I'm gonna bust up the bar' " (409).

At the end, he is only again Rheinhardt the drifter, Rheinhardt, pure-heart, hard-heart, pilgrim, back in the canyons of America, the streets where he has lived from the outset by the motto of the visionary drunk, always himself and other, the hallucination that he is and will be. "Now you get the fears, kid," the faceless derelict specter of the streets has told him early on. Now he still looks for the clarinet, listening for the signature, the time, the "invisible notation" (363). But now is no time for Mozart, only time now for the new music of the land, the song that he and Geraldine and everyone else in the book have heard playing forth from all the jukeboxes in all the honky-tonks, America's dread melody: "Walk Don't Run."

With his second novel, *Dog Soldiers*, Stone wrote in that very key and image of American virtue in flight the Vietnam book that made him, and, in great degree, Vietnam books themselves, famous; and he did so by writing, as is well known, a Vietnam book not so much about Vietnam as about America—from Saigon to L.A. and back ultimately to the seared unreal edge of the national landscape at large; and about the immense purchase made by the war upon the American souls upon which it made its grim inscription. Yet precisely as it traces out a heroin scam run by two Vietnam survivors and amoral adventurer-burnouts amidst a world of paranoiac congruencies, thugs, junkies, stoned crazies, agents without portfolio, America at the strung-out end of the sixties and now entering a new decade for the playing out of the accumulated madness—"an arrow of death," as I have called it earlier, "pointing the war back to its spiritual heartland" (109)—he did truly tell nearly as much about the American experience of Vietnam as there was to know.[3]

From the outset, there is here, here is there. The reversal inscribes itself "there" even as, for instance, John Converse and Frank Hicks plot their deadly run against the fates. In Vietnam, they talk about Vietnam, and inevitably they talk as well about "back in the world":

> "It's a funny place," Hicks said.
> "Let smiles cease," Converse said. "Let laughter flee. This is the place where everybody finds out who they are."
> Hicks shook his head.

"What a bummer for the gooks."

Converse looked at his watch and then rubbed his shoulders as if he were warming them.

"You can't blame us too much. We didn't know who we were till we got here. We thought we were something else." (56–57)

Yet from here, now, there is no going back "there" in any sense. For "here" has in fact become there, if anything, with a vengeance, the special American madness of history that became Vietnam now working its way back across an old, innocent, hopeful republic.

"You'd better be careful," Hicks told him. "It's gone funny in the states."

"It can't be funnier than here."

"Here everything's simple," Hicks said. "It's funnier there. I don't know who you're running with but I bet they got no sense of irony" (57).

And so back in the world, when it has all eventually come, on a mountaintop redoubt, to the newest version of a terrible end, with Hicks, Converse, his wife Marge, entangled with various narcs, feds, rival dealers, agents, and enforcers, all waiting for the final explosion of horror, the other half of the connection is similarly encapsulated in the words of a mad, fraudulent, leftover hippie guru: "there" is but the domestic extension of the general scene, uniform craziness gone bad that is the signature of an age. (And as if to cement the design of mythic interface, as Michael Herr might have called it, America coming back the other way, the whole stoned continuum that was the sixties, the fictional locus here is clearly Ken Kesey's La Honda.) "Innocence. Energy," he expostulates (272). "Myths, . . . Phantasmagoria, Projections" (273). On this side of the water as on that, the why of things in America has gone on pure indeterminate. Or, as Thomas Myers has put it more directly, "Vietnam" here "not only has informed American sensibility of the blacker aspects within the national soul, but also has enhanced and legitimized them" (198). Of his buddy Ray Hicks's determination to see the violent adventure through to what can only be for him a deadly end, Converse admits, finally, "I don't know what that guy did or why he did it." Accordingly, of his own role he contines, "I don't know what I'm doing or why I do it or what it's like." Surely it must all come to "something simple," Marge interjects. On the contrary, Converse concludes: "Nobody knows." He goes on, "confidently": "That's the principle we were defending over there. That's why we fought the war" (307).

Throughout the book, it is all of a piece, America, Vietnam, America and Vietnam, America in Vietnam, Vietnam in America, the whole mythic apparatus in endless self-inscription. So Hicks suggests, by word and gestural embrace, as he stares down with Marge Converse from the Hollywood Hills, newest word for Babylon, Saigon East, the City of the Angels, the City of Man: "'The big ones eat the little ones up here,' he said. He flung his free arm toward the hanging gardens of the canyon householders" (164). The motion itself now comes as clear domestic after-image of the mad missionary widow he has once encountered, on the day that this whole dreadful business has been launched, in Saigon—"He saw her gesture with her hand toward the moneychangers and the arcade and the *terrasse* of the Continental Hotel. It was a Vietnamese gesture. 'Satan,' she called to him, 'is very powerful here.' 'Yes,' Converse said, 'he would be'" (9). It has all come home indeed. He goes on now: "'All summer these people sweat fire, all winter they sweat the floods. Shit creeps out of the night under those sundecks, and they know it.' He was shouting at her over the wind and the engine. 'Fucking L.A. man—go out for a Sunday spin, you're a short hair away from the dawn of creation'" (164).

And the devil-motive here is the the chief character, the heroin, the binding force, the connection. It is the ultimate embodiment of American high, stoned on Vietnam, the source of the amoral adventure, the risk, the power, the greed. The dope itself is the abundance, the sheer overload of pleasure, pain, and waste, the dread plenitude of the war (229). It is, as old sixties burnout Dieter puts it, latest version, here as there, of the "American dream": Walk out with "innocence," "energy," wind up "Doctor Dope" (272). It is the new allegiance, the latest and greatest American trip, "walking with the King," Hicks calls it, "the big H" (171). And here, in latest and greatest adventure, are the true soldiers of the empire. Converse, the scaredest man in the world, the writer who went to Vietnam to see it and got eaten by his subject. ("You hear stories over there," he tries to explain. "They say everybody does it. Being there fucks up your perspective." Probably, moreover, he tells his father-in-law, old-line radical, gone to seed in the tabloid business, connoisseur of American bad-taste bizarrerie, the present horror show is probably just his version of a classic American destiny. "I've been waiting all my life to fuck up like this," he

says. "Character is fate" [124, 126].) As with the foolishly encountered passion of Converse, so must likewise play out that of Hicks, his zen brother
in Vietnam and amoral American adventure: Hicks the "samurai," the last
true "Lone Ranger, the great desperado." "It may not be an original conception," as Dieter puts it, "but he's quite good at it" (272). He is a man,
as the latter has said, who "takes his history seriously. He takes his people
seriously. . . . He takes everything seriously. He's a serious man, like your
President — *un homme serieux*, a total American" (270).

So for everyone involved, at the end, it has indeed, somewhere out
at the edge of America, truly all become of a place, of a piece, a great,
lurid spectacle of firepower, noise, pain, explosion, light. On a mountain
firebase, frontier redoubt, surrounded by border waste, the war literally recapitulates itself amidst rock, forest, and cave, a Day-Glo landscape crazily
strung with illuminating devices and wires and speakers, a cacophony of
American amplification. Apace, Hicks becomes "the little man in the boonies . . . on the right side for a change" (296). He is the new Robert Jordan
(284), this time with the rifle grenades and the sound effects. And the
landscape on which he operates, out of T. S. Eliot by way of Ernest Hemingway and B. Traven and now filtered through the garish sixties light of
more recent mythic memory — over "there" the war, over "here" Kesey,
La Honda, the Pranksters — becomes the latest word in cultural culmination. It is "Disneyland" (316), the great American theme park. Across the
whole possible range of literary-historical figuration that may be said to
constitute national myth, the war has truly come home. It is all completely
inscribed. Hicks is back in the corps, back in the Nam, playing to "the Big
Sound of Charles" (322). Dieter, attempting one last "gesture" of exorcism of the heroin-demon, dies by friendly fire (315). Converse surrenders
by Chieu Hoi (328–30). All that is left now is Hicks, the pain-carrier, the
Nietzschean, and his progress toward a death, an expiation. Shot up, stag-
gering onward in final flight, seeing it through to the end, he cries out to
all of them from within, "I don't want to see all you people so scared, it
drives me nuts, it makes me mad. I'll take it" (328). He is carrying it all,
the pain, the smack, the weapon, all of it, toward the rendezvous, the final
field-stripping of illusion: "The answer is the thing itself" (330).

At that rendezvous, Converse and Marge find only a big bag of heroin
worth abandoning and a corpse. To use an old word from the war now
configuring new spectacle as well, the waste is complete. And so ends this

American anecdote of waste, a war story. Yet if it has been but merely an anecdote, a war story, it has also had to it, as Converse realizes at the last, all the fatedness of nothing less than History itself. "The thought came to him," in fact, "that if, years before in the Yokuska geedunk, they had been able to see how everything would end, they would probably have done it all anyway. Fun and games, amor fati. Semper Fi" (337). "Peace," he has said to what is left of Hicks. It is an old soldier blessing, a benediction on all of it that Hicks has named once, simply surveying, in the midst of the adventure, the impedimentia of drugs and death on a dingy YMCA-room table: "Uncontrolled Folly" (90). Yet in the same moment it is also, in a word, the signature, Vietnam-vintage, of new myth for our times. "B. Traven," one of the characters in Stone's ensuing novel — Frank Holliwell, himself a Vietnam survivor-ghost — will reflect as he considers his own place, amidst the welter of postwar Central America, as American pilgrim in History: "south of cliche." So we must echo the lost Americans of *Dog Soldiers* in the similar vein of Michael Herr, in a word completing the latest mythic circuit of literary-historical figuration: "Vietnam, Vietnam, Vietnam, we've all been there" (260).

The subject of *A Flag for Sunrise* is, in a related word — it is, in fact, the single word that repeatedly fills and informs the book, even down to its literal word of benediction — History. It is specifically, in this novel of intrigue, adventure, ideas, and revolution, history in the contemporary Americas in the last days of American empire; and thus inevitably in addition, it can only be history of America in Vietnam as well. Indeed throughout, as the protagonist, the American cultural anthropologist Frank Holliwell, ultimately comes to see, Vietnam presides over the book as abiding signature of history in the minds and spirits of everyone it has touched. It is a "dreadful nostalgia" (119) of failure and waste, curse of "pilgrim" and "burnout," and of others, like Holliwell himself, "badly seared" (165). It is a requiem for American virtue, a word for the death in ways one must now know and labor to understand of an idea called America in the minds of men. It is surely this in a proximate sense for Americans who, in the words of a brilliant, hard-eyed realist of a revolutionary, "of all people, should be aware of how it's going in the world" after a place where "a lot of gringo asses got kicked forever" (206). But in a larger and more important sense, Vietnam is nothing less, as Michael Wood put it when the book first appeared, than the whole "secret anterior horror in this story." He goes on: "It is where people have been, what they remember, history's madness clinging to their skin, a 'special lunacy,' in Stone's words, a world of 'excuses and evasions,' of 'lost dreams and death,' the world of our wars" (1). It is the secret anterior horror in particular here of, among others, Frank Holliwell, the American who has once worked on his government's service in Vietnam and now finds himself on the verge of facing that history once again in the latest "American-sponsored shithole" (170), bloody, tortured, nightmare Tecan. And it is Holliwell who now becomes our chief focus of understanding on that same history about to be newly enacted.

Indeed, on the eve of his departure for that land of passion and blood and his own eventual involvement in love and revolution, Holliwell already glosses such history in the latest version to come as he begins a friendship lecture he has been invited to give at the national university of neighboring Compostela. His disquisition on comparative culture, of course, is to be appropriately academic. He is drunk, however, and the lecture becomes as a result its own subtext. Its subject becomes in fact not culture in the traditional vein of political-academic euphemism but rather the particular "secret culture," as he calls it, that has always been America's finest export. "It's a wonderful thing," he tells a stunned crowd, " — or it was."

> It was strong and dreadful, it was majestic and ruthless. It was a stranger to pity. And it's not for sale, ladies and gentlemen. Let me tell you now some of the things we believed: we believed we knew more about great unpeopled spaces than any other European nation. We considered spaces unoccupied by us as unpeopled. At the same time, we believed we knew more about guilt. We believed that no one wished and willed as hard as we, and that no one was so able to make wishes true. We believed we were more. More was our secret watchword. (109)

"More." In Tecan he will find, among squalor, fear, blood, and revolution, also the latest American version of that at once dread and wondrous utopian imperative. Specifically, he will find it embodied in the Devotionist nun and medical missionary May Feeney, called Justin. "*More* was what drove her," the narrator tells us. "Whatever the world afforded in the name of virtue, sacrifice, good works — she wanted more, wanted it all, as though she deserved it. She could be clever, she could play a little homely poker but she had never learned to trim the lights of her pride" (342). So in Tecan now, already, awaits the American Justin with "her hunger for absolutes" (343). And so also to her now must come Holliwell, post-Vietnam emissary of their shared history, left only with what she will come astutely to call his abiding "faith in despair" (368). Bound up in a drama of political intrigue and violent revolution, they come to stand finally at the deadly ground zero of three interwoven plottings of relationship among Americans and sundry political others, all converging in a nexus of inescapable force. The first centers on Holliwell, the anthropologist and reformed spook now once again become unwilling emissary of mission, and a host of shadowy "contacts": Marty Nolan, the old friend and Vietnam agency hand; Oscar Ocampo, erstwhile colleague but now doomed *maricón* and double agent; Tom and Marie Zecca, U.S. Army consular officer and wife Vietnam nostalgics of hard, good intention on newest versions of their government's service. The second focuses on Justin and the drunken gnostic priest, Egan, and their involvement on one hand with the forces of radical upheaval, led by the romantic revolutionary cleric Godoy, and on the other with the darkly sadistic Campos, Guardia lieutenant of the local government detachment of thugs and torturers and eventually the agent of Justin's own revolutionary martyrdom. The third, and the wild card in the equation in every sense, includes Pablo Tabor, half-breed psychopath, American Coast-Guard deserter, homicidal speed freak, as well as his equally unhinged and amoral employers, Jack and Deedee Callahan, old-line Central American smugglers and general hedonists, holiday gun-runners off on a political spree this time beyond their control or anyone else's. Meanwhile, swirling about amidst the action are a collection of larger forces, vectors, congruencies—American, third-world revolutionary, Catholic liberationist, old-line Communist international. Shadowy figures obtrude at will: a leftover British agent, now in the employ of international business-resort interests; a right-wing expatriate Cuban; an aging Central American patriot-revolutionary, fresh from Prague with his old memories of struggle and faith; a homicidal Mennonite pilgrim and serial killer of children.

Thus History presides over all, while Holliwell and Justin, partaking of the wild currents of force and upheaval, pass to the fated moment when she must become his lover and he her lover-betrayer. It is History as pure existential adventure, "a ride on the edge." Yet even now, as Holliwell sees especially, it is but the latest version of the old American plot. It may be in fact the newest wind of God from the ocean; yet in that same moment it also remains one carrying "an iodine smell, a smell of jacaranda, of flowers he knew to be half-forgotten, six-toned names from across the world— *me-iang, ving, ba*—the smell of Villes in Ban Me Thuot, cooking oil, excrement, incense, death. The smell of the world turning. War" (338). It is history, America in the end of the twentieth century, latest version, he knows, of the old "abridgment of hope" (430). And always, brooding over it all like a foetid stink, remains Vietnam and its Americans and what it has made of them and left them. Vietnam: "A great deal of profoundly fractured cerebration had gone down in Vietnam. People had been by turns Fascist mystics, Communist revolutionaries and junkies; at certain times certain people had managed to be all three at once. It was the nature of the time—the most specious lunacy had been conceived, written and enacted on both sides of the Pacific. Most of the survivors were themselves again, for what it was worth. No one could be held totally reponsible for his utterances during that time" (28). They are now all at best simply trying to live all of that down, trying to come to terms with those days when they could actually believe, perhaps, in something like "total vindication" (25).

Here, accordingly, like Vietnam but now only worse, the drama ends badly and bloodily for everyone. The uprising succeeds, but locally it has been only a diversion. Justin dies brutally by beating and electroshock torture at the hands of Campos, who himself will be undone, one is allowed to hope (and to the degree he has already been "taken out" at least in a spiritual sense, as Jean Strouse has observed [24], by Justin in the bold example of her dying), by new historical masters. Pablo, who has in the course of the gunrunning expedition killed his amoral violent company only to wash ashore in the midst of revolution, is in turn murdered by Holliwell, with whom he has again been set adrift in escape. Indeed, of the principals, it is only the latter who survives to tell the tale, lives to see the sunrise. But here surest of all there is no drum roll either, no flag, no rush, no one playing the sunbeam for Jesus. There is only the old lesson of murder, the one the murderer himself reads in the face of the victim, latest version always of the true "abridgement of hope" (430). So Holliwell now contemplates the visage of the late Pablo Tabor:

He was at a loss now to find the shimmering evil he had seen in it before. The stricken features were like a child's, distorted with pain and fear yet still marked with that inexplicable flicker of expectation. It was a brother's face, a son's, one's own. Anybody's face, just another victim of ignorance and fear. Just another one of us, Holliwell thought.

I get the joke now, he said to himself. We're all the joke. We're the joke on one another. It's our nature. In the same moment, he thought of May. What a misfortune, he thought, that we only have each other. (430)

One reads the face of death here and reads as well the death of the large view itself, vintage American, last decades of the twentieth century. "Positive Thinkers," a major in Saigon has once called the idea, "beyond good and evil in five easy steps—it had to be O.K. because it was them after all. It was good old us, Those Who Are, Those Who See, the gang" (244). And now it has all gone "B. Traven" with a vengeance, "south of cliche" (245). "We're at a very primitive stage of mankind," Marty Nolan has insisted, "that's what people don't understand. Just pick up the *Times* on any given day and you've got a catalogue of ape behavior. Strip away the slogans and the excuses and the verbiage, the so-called ideology, and you're reading about what one pack of chimpanzees did to another" (26).

Whatever the text, we see along with Holliwell at the end, Marty Nolan has been right, just as he has also been right with that single sentence left in the typewriter one day back in the Central Highlands: "The Jew is at home in the modern world" (19). Old or new, the text at hand *is* always just some latest version of the old big one "about the Demiurge and the Abridgment of Hope" (439). What remains only, a chastened resolve at best, is some small choice of making one's peace with it. "She has her sunrise," he thinks, "and I have mine." And then, the text concludes, "Holliwell knew that he was home; he had nothing to fear from the sun. A man has nothing to fear, he thought to himself, who understands history" (439).

"History," the old-line revolutionist Aguirre has said. "She's a cold bitch" (210). Or, as the ancient, dying criminal-Jew Naftali has put it to Pablo, "History will turn you around, sailor" (252). It is all of a piece, muses the priest Egan in drunken epiphany, the stuff of some great, dark gnostic gospel, the great impassive slidings and convergences of "the world moving in time" (372). And it is always, as Holliwell finally realizes most fully of all, just the latest word in predation. It is in fact what, of an afternoon's diving, he has known down under the reef in the shudder that has passed over the sea, "an invisible shadow, a silence within a silence" (227):

> Whirl. People disappeared and were said to have died, as in war. Or their contexts changed like stage flats leaving them inappropriately costumed, speaking the wrong lines. Some disappeared in place, their skulls hollowed out by corrosive spirits or devoured by parasites.
>
> The world and the stations of men changed ruthlessly; the funhouse barrel turned without slowing. The fall of last week's airplane sends amazed salesmen down the ledge. The coral polyps and sawfish receive a dry rain. In suburban shopping centers the first chordates walk the pavement, marvels of mimesis. Their exoskeletons exactly duplicate the dominant species. Behind their soft octopus eyes — rudimentary swim bladders and stiletto teeth.
>
> Just out here. Each one alone. The rest is fantasy. (246)

In the very stars that come out at night, one reads the emblems of fear, "rags in the wind, the taste of a tannery." And through it all, he rightly sees, "one is only out here in this, whatever it is" (246).

Yet on the textual landscape in which Holiwell serves as prime historical actor, it is finally most important for us to note that he also serves out his quest for a new, chastened American vision of history on that ground of provisional sense-making, now familiar in Stone's work, charted out by the complex reinscription of literary-historical myth. In fact, it is crucial to Stone's meanings here that the drama of history played out in *A Flag for Sunrise* must also persistently announce itself as well as the drama of history as textuality, the old modernist literary project of History as *kulchur* brought back to us in explicit and complex postmodern formulation. It is precisely for this reason that the text of the novel announces persistently, for instance, its attempts to strike explicit "literary" positionings amidst various structures of major tradition. It appropriates emphatically the whole mythic provenance of the political novel of Dostoevsky, Conrad, Greene, Malraux, Mailer, as well as that of the novel of ideas from Tolstoi, Stendhal, Melville, Mann, Faulkner, Joyce; and it accommodates them both in the same moment to the sharp, familiar unfamiliarities of neorealism in the various postmodernist styles of Vonnegut, Styron, Mailer, Pynchon, Heller, Didion, Hunter S. Thompson, and Michael Herr. Throughout, we are confronted with a near-inexhaustible play of such textual reference, south indeed of cliche, east *and* west of allusion, a large master text (much in the vein of Styron's *Sophie's Choice*, of which it frequently reminds us) that is itself a collocation of master texts, high and low, sublime and ridiculous, lofty and banal, all the way from a Dantean horror through a Kafkan nightmare to the latest familiar hustle. ("Coca Cola" reads a sign welcoming Pablo Tabor to his assignation with Central American politics, "Bienvenidos a— LA COLONIA PENAL" [174].) Much has been made in this respect of Joseph Conrad, of course, and Graham Greene. But one must reckon importantly also with T. S. Eliot and Malcolm Lowry, not to mention, in a single short passage, for instance, near the end — the one depicting Holliwell's murderous interlude at sea with Pablo just prior to his rescue — Ernest Hemingway (*The Old Man and the Sea*), Stephen Crane ("The Open Boat"), and that earlier devotionist of sunrise epiphanies upon the deep, Samuel Taylor Coleridge ("The Rime of the Ancient Mariner").

And, presiding over all, we attend also finally to those two distinctly American voices, at once both in the text and above it, that quite literally have the first word *and* the last, define more than any others its explicit structure of literary-cultural provenance: the structure of nothing less than American visionary myth itself. "A Wife — at Daybreak, I shall be — Sunrise — Hast thou a flag for me?" (381). Thus Justin has recited from Emily Dickinson upon rising from the place of purity and blood where she and Holliwell have become lovers. "To struggle unceasingly in the name of history. Gimme a flag, gimme a drum roll, I'm going to be there on that morning, yes I am" (265). Thus earlier she has also invoked equally that other native poetic celebrant of flags and sunrises, Francis Scott Key. "American": a single word, in sunrise greeting, is what Holliwell calls out to his rescuers at the end. "That was a good enough word for his purposes," he reflects. Like Walt Whitman's grass, it is the flag of his disposition, a Logos in the blood. What Americans always see by the dawn's early light, the book tells us throughout, is the banner of their own apocalyptic Americanness. Meanwhile, the last word in the text remains not America but History (439).

As with subterranean New Orleans and the blighted southern California moonscape of Stone's earlier novels, the real secret domain of bloody, forsaken Tecan is nothing less than History; and now, explicitly, history is bananas. "It's a banana republic," Justin has told Holliwell in a merry moment. "I'm sure that's in the papers." Holliwell replies with appropriate academic levity. "Strategic considerations aside," he tells her, "bananas are worth fighting for. Any nutritionist can tell you that." The conversation continues:

> "Really?"
> Holliwell stood up, his eyes on hers. There was clear light there, when the film dissolved. The film of weariness or fear.
> "If you don't eat your bananas, you don't get enough potassium. If you don't get your potassium, you experience a sense of existential dread."
> "Now I'm a nurse," she said, "and I never heard that."
> "You can look it up. One of the symptoms of potassium insufficiency is a sense of existential dread."
> "You're the scientist. I'm supposed to believe what you tell me."
> "Certainly. And now you know why Tecan is vital to the United States."
> "The United States," she told him, "may be in for a spell of existential dread." (298)

It is the litany of American dread that presides over all Stone's texts. "Now you get the fears, kid," speaks the drunken faceless oracle encountered by Rheinhardt on the New Orleans streets of *A Hall of Mirrors* (25). "I am afraid," intones John Converse of *Dog Soldiers*, "therefore I am" (42). And so in Stone's latest novel, *Children of Light*, we now also come upon Gordon Walker, actor and screenwriter, in a sunlit American first scene of a California morning where, within a few waking moments, he has already ingested Valium, vitamin B, alcohol, and cocaine: "He was about to be afraid" (4). Stone is the the chief novelistic exegete of that particular fear that might be called postmodern American dread. It is the fear, in the apt phrasing of Hunter S. Thompson, that accompanies not trembling but loathing, the American sickness unto death. It is a morning in California, a weekend in Vegas, a trip to the Republican or Democratic National Convention, fear and *loathing*—fear and loathing of the sheer earnest vulgarity of it all, earnest and vulgar in a way that only the world's greatest consumer nation, the greatest capitalist democratic society in history can be earnest and vulgar. American fear and American loathing, it is a ticket to ride, in Jean Strouse's adept formulation, on "The Heebiejeebieville Express" (1).

And *Children of Light* takes us now to the place where American dreams and American nightmares all go to die: Hollywood. As the title alone suggests, here, from the outset, is the American scene indeed. It is a figure from the Gospels, describing the inheritors of the Kingdom. It is a poem by Robert Lowell, recalling an old dream of American mission. It is a novel by Robert Stone, becoming the account of its own mythic provenance: America at the movies, pilgrims afoot on the old geography of dreams, last vision of the Logos, word democratic en masse. ("Courage," the protagonist Walker warns a Mexican painter in the midst of a lavish location party. "There are people at this table who can vulgarize pure light" [213].) These then are the children of light come home, at once in oldest and newest fulfillment of the American scripture: the history of faith now become pure industry of dreams.

Thus Stone aligns his vision, to use some analogous wording he himself has more recently supplied in introduction to a foregoing Hollywood "classic," *The Day of the Locust*, with that of his distinguished predecessor and connoisseur of American dreads, Nathanael West, who "recognized something in the bewildered, jilted crowd on the streets of Los Angeles that triggered an ancient recognition" and accordingly "always imagined the worst." "Out in the mysterious heartland," Stone continues, "who knew what stirred? Anything might set it off. It was the more dangerous because people were so fascinated by movies. And indeed they would always be out there: congressmen with subpoenas, the Legion of Decency, the Manson family. Eventually someone would shoot the president just to impress an actress. The movies made them crazy" (no page).

To be sure, the direct line of genre here is so well established as to require a certain mocking of its own availability. The whole scene, exults Walker to his actress-lover, the doomed, crazy Lu Anne Bourgeois, imagining their latest desperate coupling now blazoned before the world, is a walking West Coast tabloid special: "two of the principal artists in bed, apparently in the art of scoffing I know not what, tooting up, coke and the movies, sordidness and blackmail, Hurray for Hollywood, movies as metaphor, crazy California, decline of the West, *ad astra ad nauseam!*" (190). It is a tired trope, and the text tells us so. Yet here now, that is just the point, the very American obviousness of the figure, so to speak, that must yet make its truest meaning. The movies simply enact as mass-cultural production and iconography what we have left of self-fashioning. In latest garish consummation of all the old American reciprocities—life and art, memory and imagination, history and myth—we are all these texts of culture and more. Soon to be a major motion picture, we are *Children of Light: The Movie.*

We are all, always, at best *and* worst, the quintessential history of the scripts of ourselves, Stone relentlessly tells us; and so his text itself here enforces the point by becoming incessantly the account of its own almost incredibly complex intertextualizations. Walker the screenwriter-actor, it turns out, has just finished playing Lear. Lu Anne Bourgeois, known to the world as Lee Verger, has come to her career from a triumph, never since equaled, as Rosalind in *As You Like It.* Now, for both of them, Walker, the broken-down hack, and Lu Anne, the schizophrenic crazy with the Long Friends, as she calls the attendant spirit-imagings and presences of her madness, the patterns of inscription that are their lives become conflated in a last creative gamble. He has re-written Kate Chopin's *The Awakening*— lately come on the scene of American myth in the garb of liberal-academic high fashion—for a film in which Lee Verger becomes Edna Pontellier.

Meanwhile, and presiding over all, a host of sundry other texts of the movie novel itself play out *their* various dreadful reifications as well. The terrain of the text becomes the terrain of the genre, a complex reconstruction of those similar "worlds" of Fitzgerald, West, Mailer, Budd Schulberg, Harold Robbins, Jacqueline Susann, Joan Didion, and—especially in the intertextualizing of reality and illusion that itself becomes the novel's great theme—John Fowles. An election of formal design again becomes an accounting of the larger idea of formal provenance itself; a particular myth-text of culture becomes an inquiry into the forms and processes of cultural mythmaking at large.

Again, as always in Stone, the newest intertextualizations of history, genre, and myth can in the same moment only embrace the oldest. Here we reencounter nothing less than the movie as the most ancient sort of morality play (a working title, in fact, was "Summoner's Grace"). As with all of Stone's work, it is about the postmodern idea of the holy, pilgrims, burnouts, those badly seared, those who would serve errands of the spirit in some fashion afoot among the minions of darkness on the old geography of the quest. On location (in this case, arid Mexico grotesquely made lush and passing for nineteenth-century Louisiana), two more American pilgrims, Walker and Lu Anne Bourgeois, come to a fated last lovers' meeting with their destiny on a moonscape of humanoid grotesques where the name of the game is uniform predation. It is an all-star American cast: the terrifying, almost surreal (in this incredibly druggy book) Drogues, directors, father and son, the elder a Hollywood legend, the younger assuming the mantle, dominant males circled in a scrabbling simian tribe; Joy McIntyre, well-used "body double," spreading it around with the wizened old jade of a great man in a last chance on the scene; Dongan Lowndes, the drunken, one-shot novelist, writing hyena on the latest magazine debacle; Billy Bly, worn-out stunt man gone bisexual, eunuch and protector to the queen; Axlerod, the unit manager; Howard, fresh from the investors in Vegas; Jack Best, the blackmailer-flack; the attendants, the gofers, the coordinators, the nonpeople in nonjobs. (Here, as with Didion, one is often moved to ask, what, exactly, is an "agent," a "publicist," a "producer," a "director," a "key grip," a "best boy," a "body double," a "unit manager?") Into this ape-world walk Gordon Walker, Lu Anne Bourgeois, people who only want to have love, be good, hang on to each other, mad and feckless as that may seem. They are simply people, to borrow Stone's own expression of the issue, trying to face "the tremendous difficulty of setting out to act decently" (Bonetti, 95). Gordon Walker: drunk, coke ridden, tired, pointless, sick unto death. Lu Anne Bourgeois: schizoid, mad, compatriot of the Long Friends; once Rosalind, now Lee Verger waiting to be Edna. ("She finds out who she is," the script tells us, "and it's too much and she dies" [132].) The two of them, drugged, hurting, panic ridden (his wife has left him; her husband, for convenient measure her psychiatrist-companion, Leonce Pontellier and Doctor Mandelet rolled into one, has just done likewise with her) now come back for one last desperate round of Bats or Birdies, something like the old bedtime game they once played in first love as crazy overgrown children of the dream industry. Now it is the most desperate play of all, endgame, simple and pure, yet in the same moment still somehow breathless melodrama of illusion, maybe still not quite for real or keeps. "I would die for you" (231), he tells her in a crucial moment, knowing even as he speaks the high cinematic falsehood of it: "It was true, he thought, but not really helpful" (235–36). And so in the same scene, she replies in similar knowledge and in kind: "I don't require dying for" (236).

Likewise, the high drama at hand is not so much fated, he knows, as "on a whim." "On a whim," indeed, "he had come to a place where he was without friends to see a woman whom he had no business to see. There were no other motives of consequence behind his journey" (138). So also, for Lu Anne, it is not fated either but only necessary. If it passes for high romance, just as well; but it is also, she sees, for women in their forties, a piece of the way of it. In Hollywood and in America, today's great love is always mainly just a matter of somebody's departed wife and an actress he wants to take her place. "Connie and I, Gordon mine, we're confronting hollow-eyed forty-odd," she explains. "We've been screwed, blued and tattooed. We've been put with child and aborted, hosed down ripped open chewed and spat out seven ways from sundown! We've been burned by lovers, pissed on by our kids, shit on by mothers-in-law, punched out for laughing and punched out for crying and you expect us to sit still for your romantic peregrinations? Foolish man!" The script remains the common one, she says. "The girls get shriveled and the boys get soft and sentimental. That's how the world goes" (176). It is not fated, destined, only inevitable, necessary.

Thus the modest attempts at self-understanding of people who try to live with at most modest illusions in a world where the industry is illusion and the bigger and more immodest the better. As put to them, their correspondingly immodest choice is to play or die, join the hyenas, eat shit (42). These two make a last valiant effort not to die. The price comes high, however, as it always does for those who will not accept the forms of illusion that the world brings ready made, in the special agony of isolation that is madness. But here now as well, as is so often the case in Stone, out on the edge of illusion itself, it is at last madness wherein also may lie the possibility of grace.

Specifically, the crisis comes as Walker and Lu Anne have attempted flight and made their way back to an old familiar place, a remembered scene of life and art, on a mountain, the set of an old B. Traven remake, an abandoned shack once envisioned by a demented mogul as a shrine commemorating the triumphs of the silver screen and now just a pigsty abandoned to elements and space. And there, we truly have it all in living color, the total playing out of fractured lives, Lu Anne in the frenzy of final abandonment to psychic disintegration, Walker at the strung-out end of his own cocaine-alcohol ride with her into final insanity: storm, stigmata, ritual cleansing, gadarene swine, rainbows, epiphanies, blood and filth. We are present for "the pigshit at the end of the rainbow" (245), movies to the last. ("You know what I bet?" Walker has called out. "I bet it's a sign from God." If so, Lu Anne responds, "God's telling us we really fucked up" [242].) Yet in that moment, we also do witness something like true epiphany, or at least as true as any we are likely to see amidst mortal travail. "Ah, Christ, it's dreadful," she says. "It's dreadful we have spirits and can't keep them clean" (244). Here is the last round of Bats or Birdies, no time for Shakespeare: a blasted heath, king of the intellectuals, Lear *and* the fool; to him, Lu Anne, Rosalind, Edna, Lee from Hollywood. "This is the scene they left out of *Porky's*," Lu Anne shouts, hands full of filth. "The pigshit fight scene. We should have one in *The Awakening*" (246). They have and do. It is in *Children of Light*, the new cinematic text, playing toward its final scene.

Walker, to the end, works for time, cleverness, wit, the cynic's old self-insulating excuse for sanity and control. But now Lu Anne cries out, "Walker, when will it cease, the incessant din of your goddamn speculation? Will only death suffice to shut your cottonpicking mouth?" "Merciful Heavens! Show the man a pile of shit and he'll tell you how it works." Rubbing filth into his forehead in the sign of the cross, she declaims: "In the name of pigshit and pigshit and pigshit. Amen. Let us reflect in this holy season on the transience of being and all the stuff we done wrong. Let's have Brother Walker here give us only a tiny sampling of the countless words at his command to tell us how we're doing." "Not well," he replies. "Yeah, we are," Lu Anne tells him. "We're going with the flow. This is where the flow goes" (245).

He has lost her. It all ends, back at Bahia Mar, after the futile escape of flight is concluded, in the fated swim that has been in the script all along, the final take of *The Awakening* (and newest version of *A Star is Born*), with the main question being how to play it. She is Edna at the end, but also somewhere back there with Rosalind at the Yale Rep, and maybe Norman Maine and Lupe Velez, whichever of them was in a movie and which was real, and at the same time not Lee Verger, just Lu Anne Bourgeois on a twilight beach, running toward the sea and death:

"See the world, Walker? How it goes? . . . Give me my robe," she calls out. "Put on my crown. Hey, it's Shakespeare, Walker. . . . Want to marry me, Walker? I see a church." It is all coming now, "immortal longing" she calls it. "Give me your answer do!" she cries. "I'm half crazy, all for the love of you!" (251).

"Come with me, Gordon. This is best" (251). "Come," she has called at the last. "Or else save me" (252). As he has proven himself throughout, Walker in the crucial moment is capable of neither. In a final scene, we see him alone, back in Hollywood, dried out, nursing hepatitis and a Perrier, after the memorial service for a lost body and a lost soul that he has pointedly had the manners to be absent from; and he is only Walker, "the thing itself," unaccommodated man (4) once again among the jackals reassembled. At a table in Joe Allen's sit Shelley, the old druggy bedmate and agent's girl Friday now set up on her own; the actor Jack Glenn, most recently Lu Anne's cinematic Robert Lebrun; and, for amusement, presumably, a Frenchman named Celli; and as they work over the leavings of the latest disaster, they begin again the newest scripting of Walker, his role, his failure. Come on Gordon, they taunt, quote something from the Bard. Literature, they say, that ought to make it right.

" 'When she died, Gordon, did you think of any great quotes from Shakespeare? . . . He can quote Shakespeare from here to Sunday,' Shelley explained to her friends. 'He's a walking concordance. So was she. Come on, Gordo,' she insisted. 'You stood on the shore when she went down for number three. What did you say?' " (256).

Walker, in his fatigue and shame, demurs. She persists. "Too much of water hast the maid," she suggests, pouring Walker's Perrier into his lap. "How's that grab?" (257). To the end, the lines persist. "Sweet are the uses of adversity," Jack says. He asks, "That's *As You Like It*, right?" "That's it," Shelley says. "Men have died from time to time and worms have eaten them, but not for love."

"Great line," says Jack Glenn (258).

This is the new version of an old secret that resides at the heart of Stone's literary-cinematic fashioning of American myth for our times: we live and die by the lines. The lines are nothing less than ourselves inasmuch as we may be said to exist at all. They are the openings in our fuddled lives of what we have of history and myth and their ceaselessly inscribed dialectic of relationship, and we are the project of those inscriptions.

As the lines go, so is constituted a life. *"How strange and awful it seemed to stand under the sky!"* Lu Anne reads in the *Awakening* script, in direct rendering of the original, *"how delicious"*:

*"She felt like some newborn creature, opening its eyes in a familiar world that she had never known."*

*"The touch of the sea is sensuous, enfolding the body, in its soft close embrace"* (133).

And later: *"They need not have thought that they could possess her"* (196). Acting it out, she makes a line of it herself—"the old nothingness and grief routine" (97)—and a commentary: "Edna was independent and courageous. Whereas, Lu Anne thought, I'm just chickenshit and crazy" (98). She reads the margins: "All suicides died for life more abundant, Walker's notes said" (98). "Life more abundant," she repeats to herself, "that's the ticket. That's what we need" (99). She prays. "My God," she begs, "be there for me. So there is something there for me. So I am not just out in this shit lonely, deluded and lost" (146). In these lines, born of sundry texts and urges, we read the passion of Lu Anne Bourgeois, known to the world as Lee Verger, actress, creation of America at the movies. She is the object-lover-muse complete. "I was your Eve," Lu Anne tells Walker. "I was your actress. I lived and breathed you. I enacted and I took forms. Whatever was thought right, however I was counseled. In my secret life I was your secret lover" (235). "I'm your actress," she vows to him repeatedly, "I'm your actress, that's right" (235, 236), and to that conception she is faithful to the end.

"If a hart do lack a hind," Walker recites to her near the last, "let him seek out Rosalind."

> She smiled distantly. The lightning flashed again, farther away. "What good times we have on our mountain," she said. "Poetry and music." She closed her eyes and passed her bloody hands before her face, going into character. "If the cat will after kind, so be sure will Rosalind."
>
> Walker took a deep breath.
>
> "But it never worked out."
>
> "Things don't work out, Gordon. They just be." (236)

All the stories we tell in order to live are all there in the playing out of the drama. The oldest myth-script reprises itself down through all the literary-historical successions into the latest Hollywood version of the newest. That is the current story of the lines out here in America. "What we need here is a dream," Walker has observed to himself of that first California morning early on, "a little something to get by on" (5). "We need a plan, he thought. A plan and a dream, somewhere to go. Dreams were business to Walker, they were life. Like salt, like water. Lifeblood" (8). "A dream, he thought. That's what we need" (9). The need for a dream: It is what we have, one assumes, in a phrase that is a great favorite of Walker's, in place of "inner resources" (9, 42, 68). (And as a legendary drunken writer-histrio, we suddenly realize, how could he have been anything *but* a great reader of John Berryman?) Here, in the script-world of Stone's literary-cinematic text, we have simply ridden the Heebiejeebieville Express to the latest stop on the old passage of *kulchur:* final western landscape of performance and witness, dream capital of the world, destination and endplace of American Light.

American Light that once proposed to become the new light of the World; American Light that became eventually instead, in Vietnam, the Light at the End of the Tunnel; American Light as Hollywood hallucination of post-Vietnam memory and myth; American Light as Las Vegas glow of neon apocalypse in the western sky; American Light as The Great White Way: these are the imagings of American Light in related forms of literary-mythic projection to be found in the works of Michael Herr. The sense of the almost infinite suggestability of such a figure as corporate mythic inscription of national energy and belief radiates throughout the body of his work, and it may also be said to be inscribed most crucially in the evolving *character* of that body of creation itself—beginning in the postmodern triumph of journalism and art in *Dispatches*, continuing in major work on the scripts of the films *Apocalypse Now* and *Full Metal Jacket*, and extending along the way, in new domains of the verbal and visual, the narrative and documentary-cinematic, into the further mixed-media experimentation of *The Big Room* and, as mentioned earlier, *Walter Winchell*—and in its challenge to our very ideas of genre, medium, authorship, and textual authority, and indeed finally to our very ideas of symbolic representation themselves. As fully as for any Vietnam author in the generation of the war, in the work of Michael Herr, the re-writing of America becomes a conscious revision of nothing less than the idea of *writing itself* considered at the very limits of textual understanding at large.

It is exactly American Light in this complex figuration that lies at the heart of Herr's incomparable *Dispatches*, still in many ways the ultimate Vietnam experience *and* myth-text; and it remains even now the generative principle of ongoing historical-mythic inscription that continues to make it so. "There was such a dense concentration of American energy there," he writes, in perhaps the most crucial sentence in the book, "American and essentially adolescent, if that energy could have been channeled into anything more than noise, waste and pain, it would have lighted up Indochina for a thousand years" (44).

To "light up": as anyone who knows much of Vietnam will recall, in the domain of the concrete and experiential, the figure has a quite immediate significance. To "light up": to grease, ding, wax, waste, blow away. (And it is, for instance, with the most dreadful and unsettling familiarity, that twenty years after Vietnam one now often hears television baseball announcers talk about someone's hitting a home run as "lighting one up.") Yet in the particular context at hand, *then and now*, it also inscribes the larger sense of grand enterprise that was Vietnam in the mythic or political abstract: to "light up" as in light up with energy, light up with faith, light up with all the joy of the great American jubilee. And it is the almost infinite creative reflexiveness of such figures throughout Herr's work that often comes literally to embody what has been called here the spirit of witness, the sense of writing from within the sundry dialectics—life and art, experience and imagination, history and myth—that make writing itself possible.

Indeed, as to *Dispatches* in particular as Vietnam "classic," a chief fascination and perplexity in this respect for many readers has continued to be its status, in one way or another, precisely as a work of "witness" rather than of more direct experiential participation. Yet in a certain sense, one now sees, to raise such a question here, at least in such limited terms, is to ignore the crucial issue of textuality, the question's final identification, so to speak, not as principle of life *or* art, but rather as principle of life *and* art. That is, it is not simply a question—although as Herr makes explicit, for himself it surely begins there—of the authority of "witness" of the combatant versus that of the journalistic-literary onlooker, but one extending to include further, by ultimate implication, that of the essentially "removed" imaginative artificer as well.[4] It is a question, finally, of writing itself in the largest degree, not a matter of "being there" in any particular sense at all, so much as a matter of being one's self, a writer, an American in the last half of the twentieth century trying to make sense of a collocation of experience and myth called Vietnam. For writer and reader alike, then, "witness" *becomes* "being there" in *Dispatches* exactly as it becomes new inscribing of the word's old etymology, sense making itself as at once experienced and narrated event.

Thus throughout *Dispatches*, Herr stands in this largest double implication of "witness" as participant and mythic interpreter and does so to the degree that the act of writing so defined becomes in fact as much a "subject" of the text as any other it can claim.[5] Accordingly, the work locates the scene of writing itself in something like a consciously Heisenbergian formula of relationship: a relationship at once of pure reciprocity and pure destabilization between the structures of experience on one hand and the structures of mythic consciousness on the other. "Witness" then becomes the enabling act of conscious and creative mediation between the thing experienced and the thing mythologized, the means whereby reality itself is *realized* by honoring the role *myth* plays in its creation, just as myth is *mythologized* by honoring the role *reality* plays in its creation. So Thomas Myers in his discussion of such issues in the work cites crucially Gordon O. Taylor's use (in the latter's own discussion of the way personal narratives of Vietnam such as *Dispatches* measure themselves against preexistent fictive models) of the word "witness" in just this comprehensive sense: the sense of " 'the protagonist more as witness than as hero,' the recorder who willingly enters the historical bargain of enduring and recreating for the reader 'self-encounters enforced, in landscapes of the mind, by the environments of war' ("American Personal Narrative," 300)" (*Walking Point*, 151). And it is exactly the matter of "witness" so designated that becomes the key to the new historical-mythic grammar of *Dispatches* and indeed makes it a kind of master-grammatology at large of the Vietnam author's re-writing of America: the insistent and creative identification of its own textual positioning (and hence its own new cultural status) *in or at the place of historical-mythic intersection itself*, somewhere between fact and fiction, experiential memory and imaginative art.

Thus, the site of writing itself, in this, what Fredric Jameson has called "the first terrible postmodernist war," becomes "the space of postmodern warfare," of "the breakdown of all previous narrative paradigms . . . along with the breakdown of any shared language through which a veteran may be said to convey such an experience." And it may thus "be said to open up the place of a whole new reflexivity" ("Postmodernism," 84, cited in Myers, *Walking Point*, 151). Indeed, a recurrent litany in the book is of the degree to which one in Herr's particular position had to resist repeatedly getting lost in the abyss, being simply pulled into the garish experiential-literary-mythic ecstasy of it all. Virtually all readers are familiar with his famous quote: "I went to cover the war and the war covered me; an old story, unless of course you've never heard it." What most have failed to read carefully in addition is a contextualizing supplement which follows concerning witness itself as a form of action, of seeing for the purpose of saying, so to speak, as a form of moral and cultural complicity. "I went there behind the crude but serious belief," he goes on, "that you had to be able to look at anything, serious because I acted on it and went, crude because I didn't know, it took the war to teach it, that you were as responsible for everything you saw as you were for everything you did" (20). And taken *together* then, the two sentences image what is in fact Herr's chief work in the book, which is the work of keeping his moral and mythic bearings in a world of war, at once phenomenon of history and enterprise of narration, seemingly designed at every turn to deny an identifiable structure for either, let alone both. Throughout, we do our best to remain suspended somewhere in the dialectical middle of it all, history and myth, life and art, experience and text sliding in and out of each other in giddy reciprocity of total defamiliarization. "You'd stand there nailed in your tracks sometimes," he writes, "no bearings and none in sight, thinking, *Where the fuck am I*, fallen into some unnatural East-West interface, a California corridor cut and bought and burned deep into Asia, and once we'd done it we couldn't remember what for" (43). "Anyhow," he tells us,

> you couldn't use standard methods to date the doom; might as well say that Vietnam was where the Trail of Tears was headed all along, the turnaround point where it would touch and come back to form a containing perimeter; might just as well lay it on the proto-Gringos who found the New England woods too raw and empty for their peace and filled them up with their own imported devils. Maybe it was already over for us in Indochina when Alden Pyle's body washed up under the bridge at Dakao, his lungs all full of mud; maybe it caved in with Dien Bien Phu. But the first happened in a novel, and while

the second happened on the ground it happened to the French, and Washington gave it no more substance than if Graham Greene had made it up too. (49)

"Straight history, auto-revised history, history without handles" (49), he calls it, but "for all the books and articles and white papers, all the talk and the miles of film, something wasn't answered, it wasn't even asked. We were backgrounded, deep, but when the background started sliding forward not a single life was saved by the information" (49). Somewhere between background and foreground, it has all simply become *Fort Apache*, ultimate American "mythopathic moment": "more a war movie than a Western, Nam paradigm, Vietnam, not a movie, no jive cartoon either where the characters get smacked around and electrocuted and dropped from heights, flattened out and frizzed black and broken like a dish, then up again and whole and back in the game, 'Nobody dies,' as someone said in another war movie" (46). It has all become indeed, simply Vietnam as latest classic text of westering American mission, "varieties of religious experience" (58) in manic blare and babble of cultural collision:

> Prayers in the Delta, prayers in the Highlands, prayers in the Marine bunkers of the "frontier" facing the DMZ, and for every prayer there was a counter-prayer—it was hard to see who had the edge. In Dalat the emperor's mother sprinkled rice in her hair so the birds could fly around her and feed while she said her morning prayers. In wood-paneled, air-conditioned chapels in Saigon, MACV padres would fire one up to sweet muscular Jesus, blessing ammo dumps and 105s and officers' clubs. The best-armed patrols in history went out after services to feed smoke to people whose priests could let themselves burn down to consecrated ash on street corners. Deep in the alleys you could hear small Buddhist chimes ringing for peace, *hoa bien*; smell incense in the middle of the thickest Asian street funk; see groups of ARVN with their families waiting for transport huddled around a burning prayer strip. Sermonettes came over Armed Forces radio every couple of hours, once I heard a chaplain from the 9th Division starting up, "Oh Gawd, help us learn to live with Thee in a more dynamic way in these perilous time that we may better serve Thee in the struggle against Thine enemies. . . ." Holy war, long-nose jihad like a face-off between one god who would hold the coonskin to the

wall while we nailed it up, and another whose detachment would see the blood run out of ten generations, if that was how long it took for the wheel to go around. (45)

Here, at the pure In-County terminus of national energy and belief came the last great American camp meeting and production number on record, the biggest noise and light show in the world, high on war: "'Quakin' and Shakin',' they called it, great balls of fire, Contact" (63). "Somewhere" in Vietnam, writes Herr, "all the mythic tracks intersected, from the lowest John Wayne wetdream to the most aggravated soldier-poet fantasy, and where they did I believe that everyone knew everything about everyone else, every one of us there a true volunteer" (20). "The mix was so amazing," he says, "incipient saints and realized homicidals, unconscious lyric poets and mean dumb motherfuckers with their brains all down in their necks" (30); "lurps, seals, recondos, Green-Beret bushmasters, redundant mutilators, heavy rapers, eye-shooters, widow-makers, nametakers, classic essential American types; point men, *isolatos* and out-riders like they were programmed in their genes to do it, the first taste made them crazy for it, just like they knew it would" (34–35). In fact, in some ways, he goes on, it could seem harder to understand those who did not give in to the whole manic spectacle of it than those who did. "A lot of men found their compassion in the war," he writes, "some found it and couldn't live with it, war-washed shutdown of feeling, like who gives a fuck."

> People retreated into positions of hard irony, cynicism, despair, some saw the action and declared for it, only heavy killing could make them feel so alive. And some just went insane, followed the black-light arrow around the bend and took possession of the madness that had been waiting there in trust for them for eighteen or twenty-five or fifty years. Every time there was combat you had a license to go maniac, everyone snapped over the line at least once there and nobody noticed, they hardly noticed if you forgot to snap back again. (58)

"Maybe you couldn't love the war and hate it inside the same instant," he goes on, "but sometimes those feelings alternated so rapidly that they spun together in a strobic wheel rolling all the way up until you were literally High on War like it said on all the helmet covers" (63). Moreover, in the midst of this, he has added, it thus "seemed the least of the war's contradictions that to lose your worst sense of American shame you had to leave the Dial Soapers in Saigon and a hundred headquarters who spoke goodworks and killed nobody themselves, and go out to the grungy men in the jungle who talked bloody murder and killed people all the time" (42).

Yet there as well was often the most terrible sense of historical-mythic recognition of all. "All those faces," he writes, "sometimes it was like looking into faces at a rock concert, locked in, the event had them; or like students who were very heavily advanced, serious beyond what you'd call their years if you didn't know for yourself what the minutes and hours of those years were made up of" (16). "They even wrote a song," he tells us, "a letter to the mother of a dead Marine, that went something like, 'Tough shit, tough shit, your kid got greased, but what the fuck, he was just a grunt. . . .' They got savaged a lot and softened a lot, their secret brutalized them and darkened them and very often it made them beautiful. It took no age, seasoning or education to make them know exactly where true violence resided" (103). Young as most of them may have been, they were the fulfillment of a family history, and now they carried that history somewhere beyond apotheosis. "Was it possible," he asks, "they were there and not haunted?"

> No, not possible, not a chance, I know I wasn't the only one. Where are they now? (Where am I now?) I stood as close to them as I could without actually being one of them, and then I stood as far back as I could without leaving the planet. Disgust doesn't begin to describe what they made me feel, they threw people out of helicopters, tied people up and put their dogs on them. Brutality was just a word in my mouth before that. But disgust was only one color in the whole mandala, gentleness and pity were other colors, there wasn't a color left out. I think that those people who used to say that they only wept for the Vietnamese never really wept for anyone at all if they couldn't squeeze out at least one for these men and boys when they died or had their lives cracked open for them. (67)

Then or now, there or here, in the far range or the proximate—indeed, in any of the senses of "perspective" or "witness" itself imaginable—the burden of Vietnam remains for Herr that there is no such thing as distance. The country that was the war remains a word that is a world, a world that is a word. "After enough time passed and memory receded and settled," he writes, "the name itself became a prayer, coded like all prayer to go past the extremes of petition and gratitude: Vietnam Vietnam Vietnam, say again, until the word lost all its old loads of pain, pleasure, horror, guilt, nostalgia" (56).

And just as there is no such thing as mental distance in making sense of Vietnam, so at the documentary close-up are there also for Herr *only* texts, and texts in utterly bewildering array of plenitude. Vietnam is an old French map on a Saigon hotel room wall, as "CURRENT," the narrator presently suggests to us, as any new attempts at inscription being enacted at that moment by armored American bulldozers upon the face of Asia itself. ("*We knew that the uses of most information were flexible, different pieces of ground told different stories to different people*," he tells us from the outset. "*We also knew for years now there had been no country here but the war*" [3].) Vietnam is a song title ("Stop the War, These Cats Is Killing Themselves"), a piece of radio traffic ("Willie Peter/Make you a buh-liever"), a throwaway line from a pilot ("Vietnam, man, Bomb 'em and feed 'em, bomb 'em and feed 'em" [10]). Like the good one the narrator hears even as the book has hardly begun ("Patrol went up the mountain. One man came back. He died before he could tell us what happened" [6]), Vietnam is a war story recast sublimely and relentlessly only as its own search for closure.

"As one-pointed and resonant as any war story I ever heard," Herr calls the one in question, "it took me a year to understand it. . . . I waited for the rest, but it seemed not to be that kind of story; when I asked him what had happened he just looked like he felt sorry for me, fucked if he'd waste time telling stories to anyone dumb as I was" (6). As Thomas Myers writes, "Like this single sphinxian riddle," so "Vietnam overall presents itself to Herr as a series of discrete images that demand individual completion, portents and promontories of historical significance that reveal their possible relationships only through a process of personal absorption, connection, and invention" (150). Throughout, *Dispatches* becomes a wonderfully American sideshow of nonstop mythopathic moments, archetypal vignettes, instant allegories, freeze-frame zingers, a text, finally, that is an allegory of its own ever-enlarging quest after historical-mythic meanings.

Vietnam as American mantra *and* Vietnam as war story eternally in search of its own missing bottom line: the two images themselves in Herr

are exquisitely conditioned to the at once real and hallucinatory landscape of *Dispatches*, of equal parts memory and imagination, experience and
myth, private epiphany and collective madness. (Not for nothing, for instance, even down to the level of functional grammar, is a work conceived
in a condition of pure overload written with almost excruciating gram-
matical exactitude in two dominant syntactical forms: the fragment and
the run-on.) Vietnam becomes *Dispatches*, and *Dispatches* becomes Vietnam, the ultimate American text: Vietnam is virtually the last word in the
book; it is an endlessly repeated word in between; and it is, even as we fix
our eyes upon the page, virtually the first ("There was a map, . . ." we are
told, and already then we somehow know we are about to hear it spoken,
the word, the name [3].) A geography of experience becomes newest car-
tography of myth, abstract or epitome of the process of sense making that
the text itself enacts.

So throughout *Dispatches*, one text of Vietnam becomes all texts of
Vietnam; one image becomes all images; one war story becomes all war
stories. Or, as Thomas Myers again puts it, "Small dispatches function
as historical poetic conceits, concentrations of symbolic energy emitting
bonds of suggestiveness that intersect with others to form a communicating network of correspondences" (154). And this is not, as I have written
earlier, to make some large formalist argument for "structure" in a work
itself first written as articles published variously and then variously revised
into a book that can be best described as "a kind of serial pastiche" (146).
It is to testify, rather, to the ceaseless operation of the work from within
as a remarkable American achievement of the poststructuralist principle
of *writing itself* as kind of expanding-universe project of cultural grammatology at large, a whole that finally is a triumph of its own "secret history"
of self-contextualization and mythic reconstitution. As text of American
Light, it is, finally, the ultimate illumination round, spectacularly self-
consuming artifact of its own brilliant incandescence. And this remains
both the secret and the genius of *Dispatches* throughout, its wondrous inscription at every turn into the very fabric of national consciousness at
large. For we all know together, ultimately, the bottom line in *that* text,
America in the last half of the century, the final word, and it is a curse,
a prayer, an admonition, a release. "Vietnam Vietnam Vietnam," it says,
"we've all been there" (260).

Mythopathic moment: In a movie about the cavalry and the Indians recalled by Michael Herr in Vietnam, "Henry Fonda as the new colonel says to John Wayne, the old hand, 'We saw some Apache as we neared the Fort,' and John Wayne says, 'If you saw them, sir, they weren't Apache'" (46). Mythopathic moment: In a movie about Vietnam for which Michael Herr has written a voice-over narration, a demented cavalry commander has confided to the narrator his sublime joy in it all. "I love the smell of napalm in the morning," he says, watching a strike going in and recalling an even more memorable one. He muses on the latter. "You know one time we had a hill bombed," he goes on dreamily. "For twelve hours and when it was all over I walked up. We didn't find one of 'em, not one stinking dink body. The smell, you know, that gasoline smell. The whole hill. It smelled like . . . victory."[6]

In Michael Herr's *Dispatches*, writing becomes historical-mythic intertext projecting far beyond conventional definitions of genre and mode toward the very boundaries of textuality itself; and so, in Herr's further career, extensions of the concept of writing so defined continue to inscribe a kind of paradigm of the Vietnam author as postmodern media experimentalist. Certainly this has been the case with his complex authorial involvements in two major film depictions of the American experience of Vietnam, the first Francis Ford Coppola's *Apocalypse Now*, cited above, and the second Stanley Kubrick's *Full Metal Jacket*. In both, across the ever-expanding domain of intertextual relation comprising post-Vietnam American consciousness, he continues to chart out new imagings of the country that was the war.[7]

From the standpoint of filmmaking alone, it has been said that the history of the creation of *Apocalypse Now* was enough like Vietnam to enact its own epic legend of imitative fallacy. The film as commercial-technological enterprise became as grand and myth-invested, and often in many of the same ways—enormous logistical complications and cost overruns, for example, coupled with natural disasters and other massive confusions of purpose—as the war it set out to depict. That part of the artistic history of *Apocalypse Now* involving the writer Michael Herr, author of the legendary *Dispatches*, would at the very least seem to support this view. For, if published records are to be believed, an "original" script exclusive of any contribution by Herr had already, prior to his involvement, been not only written but acted, filmed, and edited. To put it simply, the movie had been "made." Then, further, the story goes, Herr was asked to write a "narration" (Chaillet, 57–61). And the result was the combination acting-script and voice-over monologue familiar now to nearly a generation of theater audiences.

Whatever the truth of anecdote, the specific plot of writing at hand, one suspects, for Michael Herr, the author of *Dispatches*, is one that could hardly have been refused. For in this film, already announcing its explicit mythic provenance in a Vietnam version of what Herr himself had termed there the old "heavy heart-of-darkness trip" (8), he had been asked to add, in the new text, a "narration" of what in the older text, Joseph Conrad's *Heart of Darkness*, through the narration of one Charlie Marlow, *was* in fact the text. This is to say that the narrative, in newest creative evolution, had to become at once mythic reinscription *of itself* as text and gloss and commentary *on itself* in its corresponding filmic enactment. In the new textual domain of American film about Vietnam, the logic of the supplement, so to speak, had come full circle.

As various critics have observed, the action of the film alone conflates brilliantly the textual "plot," at once quintessential American odyssey and great, complex analogue of the earlier work as mythic template. With the narrator-protagonist, the American Captain Willard, we are dispatched upriver from Saigon to kill a renegade Green Beret colonel named Kurtz, the ultimate one-man assistance command who has taken the war into his own hands, has in fact taken command of the war and in the same moment let the war take command of him. We meet the officers and intelligence operatives as the new "managers" who speak menacingly of the danger of Kurtz's "methods" that became "unsound, . . . unsound." We reencounter Conrad's half-caste helmsman-captain in the troubled black commander of the navy river craft; and, almost unimaginably, Tim Page somehow by way of Dennis Hopper, we find the mad Russian fool on the jungle bank now come back to us as a war- and dope-addled American correspondent. We see the various outposts of "civilization" along the way reimaged in the various insertions of American presence in the war zone, the cavalry perimeters, the firebase complete with Playboy Bunny USO show, the nightmare bridge. We ultimately meet Kurtz himself and witness, now through the eyes of Kurtz's own assassin, the rapture of his dying.

What Herr's narration adds to all this, however, is the sense of a direct line of energy emanating from the older work's truest source of genius, which is of course the oracular Conradian presence itself. We see carefully reinscribed, for instance, Marlow's suggestive art of disclosure in his various textual recitations about Kurtz, from the brilliant military record, from the news media, from the latter's own letters and other writings. But most of all we feel Kurtz in the deeper tonalities, that omnipresent sense of *voice* itself. Like Marlow, Willard himself, increasingly, in fusion of word and image, becomes the other he seeks. "There is no way to tell his story without telling mine," he tells us explicitly from the beginning, "and if his story is really a confession, then so is mine." And to this design, as metaphor and action, he is more than faithful to the end. "Part of me was afraid of what I would find and what I would do when I got there," he admits, as events near their culmination. "I knew the risks or imagined I knew. But the thing I felt most, much stronger than fear, was the desire to confront him."

At the same time, however, as various interpreters have noted, Marlow is also here Marlow clearly updated in terms not only of general myth but of particular medium as well—specifically film in its debts to the hard-boiled detective novel—and thus in terms of a set of intertextual relations that often supplement in vividly American line of transmission those already suggested. For if Willard is in many ways Joseph Conrad's Charlie Marlow, he is also in many other important ways Raymond Chandler's Philip Marlow; and the landscape he surveys, as John Hellman has amply demonstrated, in its crazed, burnt-out California surrealism, is often not so much "Vietnam as a separate culture, but as the resisting equal of a hallucinatory self-projection of American culture" (190).

Moreover, it is of course here also that the narration pushes forward to complete the newest mythic circuits of California connection as well, as the new "plot," the "mission," often becomes a literal magical mystery tour of the war culture at large, complete with dope and acid rock, surfing, go-go dancing, a whole army, as Willard refers to the crew of the river craft, of "rock and roll kids with one foot in the grave." To use Herr's own figure, the movie becomes thus in its way the spectacular fulfillment of the chief defect of that earlier cinematic depiction of Vietnam apocalypse, *The Green Berets*, which in fact, as he had written earlier in *Dispatches*, had not been about Vietnam at all, but rather about Santa Monica (188). Here such reversal becomes explicit aesthetic principle, Vietnam as intertext of trans-Pacific American phantasmagoria.

And this, ultimately, beyond Conrad's Marlow and Chandler's Marlow, is what we remember most vividly about *Apocalypse Now*, our sense in the drama over which the narration now presides of the crowdings of all the hoarded mythic texts of postmodern America, the howling wilderness now truly become the jungle that has been waiting all along: "out there" the general calls it, "beyond." The old millennial visitation of fire and sword now becomes firepower played to the tune of sixties acid rock. "The End," the dreadful electric-sitar dirge of a melody with which the movie begins, signals the Apocalypse according not to Cotton Mather but to Jim Morrison. And Willard, as original synthesizing force, now truly stands where *all* the mythic tracks converge in the full intertextual authority of that marvelous figure. For if he has once been Conrad's narrator and Chandler's narrator, he has also been, one must now unmistakably see, now cannot help seeing, the narrator of one other foregoing myth text. He has also been the narrator of *Dispatches*.

One senses this often in various dramatic and visual moments in the film in utter concretion. Had we not sat with Conrad's Marlow, for example, during his sundry prefacings out of the deepening twilight off Gravesend or waited, with Chandler's detective in his seedy digs, for a new "assignment," as readers of *Dispatches* we would still somehow find ourselves prepared utterly for the opening scenes of *Apocalypse Now* in Willard's Saigon hotel room. We are ready, when it happens, to drop into the jungle places about to be turned into their own black-and-white newsreel, to meet the crazed cav commander who wants to crank up a courtesy operation for the visiting surfer, to find a Playboy Bunny helicopter descending in a blaze of floodlights upon troops somewhere out on the end of nowhere, to find a mad dopehead correspondent who talks rather like Tim Page. From the narrator's first words onward, in sum, we are prepared, in newest intertextual completion, to find the heart-of-darkness trip extended now into *Dispatches* as *Apocalypse Now*, and *Apocalypse Now* as *Dispatches*.

We are prepared, most of all, as Willard begins to tell us of himself and of his mission, to hear *that* unmistakable voice as well. "I was going to the worst place in the world," the *Dispatches* narrator begins, "but I didn't even know it yet. Weeks away and hundreds of miles up a river that snaked through the war like a main circuit cable plugged straight into Kurtz." And also in the familiar cadences of the earlier text, he persuades us from the outset to an equally familiar knowledge of the rootedness of his adventure in the darkest historic recesses of the national soul: "Everyone gets everything he wants. I wanted a mission, and for my sins they gave me one. Brought it up to me like room service." Of the nature of Kurtz's defection, he says: "Never leave the boat. Absolutely goddamn right, unless you were going all the way. Kurtz got off the boat. He split from the whole fucking program." Of the nature of his own defection from America, the "world": "Trouble is, I'd been back there and I knew that it just didn't exist anymore . . ."; and "When I was here I wanted to be there, when I was there all I could think of was getting back into the jungle." Of witnessing a surreal Wagnerian air cavalry assault against a village: "If that's how Kilgore fought the war, I began to wonder what they really had against Kurtz. It wasn't just insanity and murder. There was enough of that for everyone." Of the management of the enterprise at large: "The war was being run by a bunch of four-star clowns who were going to end up giving the whole circus away." Of what has claimed Kurtz, himself, them all: "Even the jungle wanted him dead, and that's who he really took his orders from anyway."

Accordingly, as in *Dispatches*, at times, all possible texts seem to be converging at once here in some mad genius of overload. In one particularly nightmarish scene, Willard's rock-and-roll crew spontaneously shoots up a sampan they are in the process of searching, killing nearly everyone. The hard-boiled Willard executes the only survivor, a young woman, with cold precision. "We'd cut 'em in half with a machine gun and give 'em a Band-Aid," he muses, in a line that could have literally been transcribed from *Dispatches*, and then adds in equally Conradian explicitude, "It was a lie. And the more I saw of them, the more I hated lies." Likewise, the visionary spectacle at the end of Kurtz's jungle imperium becomes by overt textual invocation a literal high modernist myth-apocalypse, Conrad by way of Eliot back to Jung and J. G. Frazer and then forward again to Kurtz as newest pop oracle and guru.

Yet the particular completion of all the texts here, it is most important to insist, lies finally not in language but in act; and the act, of course, in cold, precise Vietnam inscription, is pure and simple murder. In *Apocalypse Now*, newest Vietnam updating of the heart-of-darkness trip, Willard may honor his literary provenance by serving as the chief mythic interpreter of the plot of history before us, but he is also a historical actor in that other heart-of-darkness trip being played out by an American soldier in Vietnam who in this case, quite explicitly, is a paid assassin on his government's service. And it is exactly in this respect, of course, for Michael Herr the writer, the creator of the narration, that *Apocalypse Now*, as newest text of Vietnam witness, quite literally completes the formula of mythic-cultural complicity posited in *Dispatches:* the narrator who went to "watch" or "see" and explain and who saw as well that he could not be other than implicated in the horror, now *in fact* becomes the narrator on the mission to meet and kill the horror even as he tries desperately to witness and explain. Furthermore, the new text of film here as at once narrative and dramatic medium now also inscribes that extension of relationship as a thing itself enacted. Word becomes utterly inseparable from deed. Even as the voice attempts to render events out into some overarching text of interpretation, sense-making has become of a piece with nothing less than the thing itself, *Apocalypse Now*.

In Herr's writing for a second major Vietnam film, Stanley Kubrick's *Full Metal Jacket*, the enterprise of filmic authorship involves an even more direct relationship to a particular literary source, in this case a contemporary Vietnam "classic" (itself a celebrated text of memory and imagination, history and myth), Gustav Hasford's *The Short-Timers*. The issue further complicates itself, moreover, by the fact of Herr's explicit identification, by his own accounting, along with Kubrick himself as the coauthor of a screenplay. Thus the function of writing here, if anything, becomes even more complex than in the foregoing instance. There, at least, it can be identified in historical provenance and technical function. It is, with small exceptions that come to our attention, "voice-over." Writing here, on the other hand, has now become somewhere truly indeterminate, as has the question of authorship at large. The film is both Gustav Hasford's *The Short-Timers* and Gustav Hasford's, Michael Herr's, and Stanley Kubrick's *Full Metal Jacket*, the de-genred, de-mediated, de-authorized text.

Yet it is exactly in these new mergings and distributions of authority that the film also becomes in significant ways the newest case study of Vietnam witness as historical-mythic intertext. For now, as an issue of writing in particular, the focus of the project once more becomes language in new semiotic relation, of "voice," especially for the two distinctly "literary" writers involved, extending once again the concept of literary textuality itself into new creative dimensions.

To look at the "literary" source of the "film" project is to see the complex textual relationship in which the enterprise is already foregrounded. The epigraph to Gustav Hasford's at once dreadfully real *and* hallucinatory novel, *The Short-Timers*, reads as follows: "I think Vietnam is what we had instead of happy childhoods." It is taken, of course, from Michael Herr's at once dreadfully real and hallucinatory work of journalism, *Dispatches*. As I have mentioned elsewhere, the quote is one that has frequently been taken out of context, albeit suggestively for its wondrously American breadth of historical-mythic implication. (In the place where it appears, it refers quite specifically to Herr's comradeship with fellow correspondents such as Sean Flynn, Dana Stone, and Tim Page—the latter happening to be English.) Here, however, as it turns out, the quote is decidedly in context. For Hasford's narrator (and, in the movie, although in a rather more limited function, Kubrick's and Herr's), Private Joker, is a combat soldier who also happens to *be* a combat journalist, or rather a combat journalist who winds up knee-deep in his own desperate struggle as combatant. Thus again, and now as a function of both texts, we find ourselves in the familiar domain of witness, at once enterprise of sense making and testament of complicity. And as might be suggested in this close prefiguring, the film text that results often becomes a conscious merging of such corporate energies.

Accordingly, the "voice" we hear on significant occasions is often quite recognizably that of the narrator of *Dispatches* now itself coming back at us in strange mythic after-echo. On the flight into Hue that will become his and Rafterman's journey into hell, for instance, Joker asks a helicopter door gunner, "How can you shoot women and children?" As readers of *Dispatches*, we know the answer before we hear it. "Easy," he says, laughing. "You just don't lead 'em so much" (64–65). "You people one-one?" a lieutenant asks, echoing a remembered officer from *Dispatches*, while flagging down some newly arrived correspondents who have failed to salute him. "No sir," Joker replies, in throwaway echo of one of Herr's company on the occasion, "We're reporters for *Stars and Stripes*." Shortly the young lieutenant has metamorphosed into yet another officer from *Dispatches*, the young Green Beret captain at Soc Trang happily waiting for bad weather. "Well, if you people came looking for a story," he says cheerily, "this is your lucky day. We got Condition Red and we're definitely expecting rain" (65). And so also Herr's famed epiphany on a helmet liner—a peace sign juxtaposed to the words "Born to Kill"—is reinscribed into a scene where Joker is berated by a madman colonel for such a sin of grunt iconography (71–72).[8]

At the same time, that "voice" of *Dispatches* is also clearly assimilated to the other "voices" that are the unmistakable inscriptions of *The Short-Timers*. And here too the resultant effect is now often that of some strange, new, oracular echo. At times, it is a question of almost pure tone, a kind of eerie ventriloquism, as when Joker speaks, for instance, looking down at the graves of murdered civilians in Hue. "The dead have been covered with lime," he says, in the terrifying matter-of-factness that so often characterizes the book. "The dead only know one thing. It is better to be alive" (70). And along with him, other characters likewise speak not only in such tones but often quite literally as they have in the other text as well. "We're the Lusthog Squad," brags Cowboy. "We're life-takers and heartbreakers. We shoot 'em full of holes and fill 'em full of lead" (73). "I love the little Commie bastards, man," says Crazy Earl. "I really do. These enemy grunts are as hard as slant-eyed drill instructors. These are great days we're living, bros! We are jolly green giants, walking the earth with guns. These people we wasted here today . . . are the finest human beings we will ever know. After we rotate back to the world, we're gonnna miss having anyone around that's worth shooting" (74).

So, in the larger film text, such conflated inscriptions and reinscriptions from both narrative sources feed into a "plot" (basically derived from *The Short-Timers* itself) as familiar from low art as the Conradian one of *Apocalypse Now* is from high—the platoon movie, the old basic-training-to-combat story, but now with no "initiation," "passage from innocence to experience," "growth of character," "achievement of moral manhood," but simply the feeding of a collection of American marine boy-monsters into a Disneyland of megadeath called Vietnam during the Tet offensive. Its feeling, in fact, reinforced by camera cutting and technique, is that of almost pure documentary. Out of pop culture into the contemporary dramatic classic and now inserted back into the domain of the nightly news, the film is something like the meeting of Gomer Pyle and Pavlo Hummel at the crossroads of America and bloody murder. Accordingly, in the convergings of the various texts and, ultimately, the various media of writing, there has come something like an *enactment* of the total merging of intertextual authority, the journalist, the novelist, the scriptwriter or writers, the filmmaker. *Full Metal Jacket* thus becomes a work at once something like cinema verité carried over by the complex textual energies of its creation (and thereby extending once again the fundamental discovery of virtually all the major literary depictions of the war) into ultimate fantasy of horror, history become its absolute mythic other.

Thus we find the true "place" in *Full Metal Jacket* called Vietnam. It is a place Herr himself notes as recognizing even as he first read Hasford's book before writing the script, the domain of "the living, behaving presence of what Jung called the Shadow," the pure other. "It was everywhere in Conrad's work," he goes on, "it starred in all of Buñuel's films, and it served as my personal copilot in Vietnam, where I learned to know and respect it." Accordingly, it now inscribed itself back into his own work as well, in a film, as a newest kind of creative defamiliarization. "Almost the first thing that struck me about *Full Metal Jacket*," he records upon his seeing the finished movie, "was how little it had to do with me." On the other hand, he adds, he also found the work "very different from Gus's book" albeit "true to it." The result, in sum, was a movie itself, especially as his own project of writing was concerned, as a parable of intertextualization and necessary loss. Indeed, he goes on, "I couldn't remember for a long time what I thought had been cut—lines that had been fun to write, whole scenes, beloved voice overs, stuff that looked great on the page but couldn't be performed." Yet what remained, he suddenly came to realize, was a performance perhaps of a higher order, a heteroglossic revision of experience and myth become original creation. "I could only remember the completeness of the movie," he concludes, "and how new it looked to me" (vii).

A corresponding experiment by Herr in intertextual possibility in the domain of the book text has been his collaboration with the painter Guy Peellaert in *The Big Room*.[9] A combined media study of Las Vegas and its role in American cultural iconography, on one hand it is a work virtually unprecedented in its sheer, vulgar audacity. (One surely hesitates to call it an art book. But coffee-table book seems an equally poor choice.) Yet on the other, and in exactly these respects, it often recalls explicitly as well the related work of other well-known contemporaries such as Norman Mailer, Joan Didion, and Hunter S. Thompson (and in the latter case, along with corresponding illustrations by Ralph Steadman). For it comprises, in its visual dimension—assembled portraits of an array of American

figures ranging from legendary mobsters, tycoons, and sundry other out-
riders of the American dream to athletes, superstars, sex goddesses, and
U.S. presidents—a stunning neorealist meditation on the notion of American "personality" in virtually every sense of the word imaginable; and as
a text of writing it likewise becomes a series of minimalist vignettes, at
once comprehending the visual text as narrative history and mythic gloss,
not to mention everything in between from stand-up monologue to sales
pitch. These combined media are accompanied with a pre-text, the story
of a place and an architecture, a history and an idea; and of course, as we
must already know (and as an epigraph from P. T. Barnum should warn
us), it is our own "secret history" as well, the frontier dream of the self
now endlessly enacted back at us as the classic American art of the sell.

And there, in that pre-text, even as the book has barely begun, it rises
out of the desert before us, Las Vegas, in all the glory of a national dream of
personality and place come to its apotheosis of freakish commodification.
("What are they talking about in New York and L.A.," the narrator barks
at us in the warm-up monologue, "what do they mean, 'too Las Vegas?'
The word 'excess' doesn't even apply here" [10].) Las Vegas *is* the Big
Room, the place where only the Big Stars get to play, pure Show Business
become the quintessential American place. It is the ultimate reification of
national desire, *the thing itself*; and at the same time, it remains the ultimate projection of collective mythic fantasy, at once national dream *and*
national nightmare. Vegas rises out of the desert as the site of all possibility and gratification, the idea of possibility itself as infinitely devised
pleasure dome, a high-roller's Xanadu, a sybarite's Disneyland, the greatest American theme park ever conceived and created; and in the same
moment it rears itself as the ultimate mythic recess and repository of our
secret crimes and corruptions, the hidden chambers, the back rooms, the
exclusive penthouses, the places of brokerage and wagering and betrayal.
The Big Room as the ultimate American pleasure trip is also in the same
moment the ultimate American corruption trip, the opening to the dark
secret places of the American soul, the monochrome hells.

Now here, of course, the Big Room has also begun to be the book
text that is its precise physical and aesthetic analogue. And thus also it
transmogrifies itself apace exactly into a kind of garish, exploding Glas-
architecture as only Americans could make it, at once expansive and claustral, ecstatic and lurid, voluptuary and brooding. The portraits of sundry

personalities often come at us in a single moment as ghastly self-parody mated to some terrible poignancy of self-revelation. Meanwhile, the narrative rides along as well on the emotional roller coaster of some festive, crazed, continuous stand-up act. "Don't laugh people," we are told from the outset about this business called show business, "it could happen to you" (12).

Moreover, it is as if, the book tells us from the outset, all of this has been waiting there for us all along as some foregone locus of the American end, "this scrubby nowhere place, so totally and profoundly Nowhere that it stood as motionless and confusing as a mirror. A mirror and a mirage where the great lines of a great nation converged in the physical representation of mental American infinity and made their great run out towards vanishing point" (8). Between two valleys, there, "Paradise" and "Death" ("John Milton," we are told, "couldn't have put it any closer to the dime"), the "star psychosis" of westward movement—embodied in Kit Carson— and the big sell from the east—embodied in P. T. Barnum—converged as inevitably, we are told, as any two such forces could have ever managed, "because a big country needs a big room (Barnum)," the equation goes, "and a big room needs a big country (Carson)." And thus to enter the original Big Room, the narrator reveals to us, the Carson-Barnum museum of the class act (9), is also to find the old gateway to "the long room," the one that is "the portrait gallery of our creation." So the pre-text concludes:

> Because let's face it ladies and gentlemen, even those of us who don't think of ourselves as being particularly creative made this one, we made it all together. It's as long as our memories, and if it seems to narrow and darken at the far end, that's just an illusion, as you'll see when you've walked it for yourself. There's nothing to be nervous about, we've been working together for years, we're terrific and we love each other very much. We'll be a wonderful audience, and they'll just be what they've always been. Let's really mean it then. Let's all join in. Let's all respond. (15)

So at the behest of the new Barnum-narrator, we enter the Big Room that is the marriage chapel of star psychosis and the big shill. To our surprise, the first painting we see is FDR at Hoover, once Boulder, Dam. Quickly following is one of Bugsy Siegel at the bar in the Flamingo. To our further surprise, we see that the first prose vignette is about not either man but both, "this pair," the narrator tells us, his Vegas metaphor appropriate and exact, "dealt spontaneously from the great American deck" (16). Roosevelt is the "president by a landslide of the twentieth century" who built the dam that sent the juice that would transform the desert into the city of power and light called Las Vegas (16, 19). Siegel, in contrast, is the "practical" father of Vegas with the "outrageous plan," the one who "pointed toward the emptiness and said, fatally *insisted*, that right there in the middle of what looked just like nowhere to everyone else, he would build his fabulous Flamingo Hotel" (19) and thus who, in that moment of vision and insistence, beyond all others "dreamed up everything we mean when we say Las Vegas" (20).

And now the parade of stars itself begins. We see first Jimmy Durante, literally Vegas's opening act, the comedian who made the idea of being surrounded by assassins sound hilarious and who inscribed a career into a classic fadeout "like a man . . . practicing for his own death" (21). Next comes Hoot Gibson, the cowboy who became a star and then a faded star and then a faded cowboy. There follow Betty Hutton; Conrad Hilton; Nick the Greek; Noel Coward, down in the arena pure Mayfair, très élégant, the text tells us, up in his room dreaming redskins and covered wagons (32); Tallulah Bankhead; Walter Winchell; Xavier Cugat (and Charo); Joe Dimaggio; Milton Berle, new master of the show of shows, the biggest room of all, television. (In the painting he sits in a dressing room, a photo of his mother on a mirror blank of any other reflection.) In the text, Marilyn Monroe writes a letter to someone. "They've gone now," it says. " 'It's quite lonely here in Las Vegas. This is certainly a wild town . . .' " (47). In her portrait, she lies somewhat as she must have near the end, in bed, naked, partly under a sheet, holding the phone. Jimmy Hoffa follows, succeeded by Sugar Ray Robinson, Liberace (by his admission, a parody of a celebrity), Jayne Mansfield (by sheer presence of the divine Marilyn, a parody of a parody), Judy Garland, Joe E. Lewis, Mario Lanza, Red Skelton, Howard Hughes, Lenny Bruce, Nat King Cole, Marlene Dietrich, George Raft, Joe Louis (the quintessential Vegas story, the text tells us, heavyweight champion of the world, the all-American Negro; somebody small, brown, shrunken, the portrait tells us, lighting a cigarette at dawn after work, Official Greeter at Caesar's Palace). Then come Martin and Lewis, ultimate "partners." The written entry for Bob Hope details the author's ride with him to a Bob Hope show in a place called Vietnam. In the painting he appears, however, probably in Vegas, tuxedoed and in an appropriately star-spangled routine, chorus girls assembled and trailing brief wisps and strategic rags of old glory. Bing Crosby follows, getting off a train, looking terribly alone in a road picture; then Richard Nixon (done in the biggest room of all, the White House, and the site, the narrator reminds us, of one of the great closing acts in our history [92]); then Evel Knievel, Howard Cosell, Joe Namath, JFK (the narrative is about the senator and the Rat Pack; the painting depicts hard-looking men in tuxedos gathered around the senator and, slightly concealed beside him, the girl). Next comes Sammy Davis, Jr., protean freak, "the greatest black Puerto Rican Jewish one-eyed entertainer in the business—no, in the whole *history* of the business" (103), the text tells us, the one who even kissed Nixon in front of everybody; then Bobby Darin, Colonel Parker, Elvis Presley (alone, looking something like Captain America getting off the plane, his text entry four simple lines from "Are You Lonesome Tonight"); then Tom Jones, Johnny Carson (his portrait itself on a glowing TV screen somewhere as ever "between Cathode and Psyche" [114]), Muhammad Ali, Orson Welles.

Then suddenly, nearing the end, we encounter two more paintings and two noticeably longer textual entries that seem to be both representative personal histories and larger mythic recapitulations. The first portrait is of Meyer Lansky, guiding underworld spirit of it all, now depicted in retirement in Miami, carrying the story in his own enigmatic silence, just another old man on Collins Avenue early in the morning walking a geriatric cocker. The second is the unmistakable Frank Sinatra, sitting enthroned in the late glow of Chairman of the Board. The Lansky text begins with an epigraph from Machiavelli on the fit and unfit uses of cruelty and quickly inscribes as a culminating story of Vegas a whole American history of corruption and power, the history of a place wherein "the concept of 'crime' became as archaic as 'government for the people'" (126). Accordingly, the Sinatra text inscribes the story of a star written essentially as the obverse of the underworld chronicle we have just read, and now, as the text tells us, "no division between the singer and the song, incomparable, untouchable, singing the song of songs, the long slow ballad of money sex and power. A song from the source and the seat of the controversy, *Gee it's lonely really lonely at the top*, high teachings from the Voice, the story of a life sung softly with emotion to empty tables across the big room in the wee small hours of the Twentieth Century" (139).

Yet now further, we discover, briefly, a coda, at once recapitulation and valedictory. In a final portrait, entitled "The Big Room," we again recognize Bugsy Siegel, aged not a moment, looking as young as he probably did the day Lansky's people killed him; but now he sits not at a bar but on a flowered couch in a place that looks like a parlor or living room, not in a tuxedo but in a suit, in front of an empty fireplace, like Gatsby, waiting. The text on the other hand leaves Siegel in the underworld and comes up to offer some last words for his real mistress, the city, the culmination of the vision and dream. For Vegas, it turns out, like most of the lives it depicts, is itself aging, a fading star falling inexorably back into the desert. Maybe some mad billionaire with a passion for history will take it over, the narrator speculates, "restore and preserve it like Williamsburg, turn it into a Prosperity Museum." Or "maybe alkali, the old leveller, will make its big comeback, and it will be alkali, not silver and gold, juice, talent, buns or a fantastic body that will be the last currency here" (143). And then all that will be left is the silence and the memory of the spectacle, the Big Room, American destination and epicenter of the end.

"The night before I left Las Vegas," Norman Mailer's celebrity-protagonist Stephen Rojack tells us in *An American Dream*, "I walked out in the desert to look at the moon. There was a jeweled city on the horizon, spires rising in the night, but the jewels were diadems of electric and the spires were the neon of signs ten stories high. I was not good enough to climb up and pull them down" (251–52). And out there he goes farther "to the desert where the mad before me had come," where he finds an empty phone booth. He dials an old number. "And in the moonlight," he says, "a voice came back, a lovely voice, and said, 'Why, hello, hon, I thought you'd never call. It's kind of cool right now, and the girls are swell. Marilyn says to say hello. We get along, which is odd, you know, because girls don't swing. But toodle-oo, old baby-boy, and keep the dice for free, the moon is out and she's a mother to me" (252).

There, at the end of Mailer's book, in the glow of the neon city commingled with the old witchery of the moon, we recognize ourselves to be truly in the presence of American Light. And now also, at the end of Michael Herr's and Guy Peellaert's book, we similarly realize we have been reading *and* seeing something much the same, something of a quality, we understand, that is itself of the nature of light. In the paintings it seems to come from nowhere and everywhere, on a train, a plane, an elevator, a staircase, or a television screen; in a car, a phone booth, a dressing room, a trailer, a penthouse, a revolving door, a bus station; on the street; by a swimming pool; indoors or outdoors; daytime or nighttime. It is the ultimate Vegas effect, and it is all the same. And in the text of writing we see now that it is likewise the ever-same light, original energy of the continent, the light of empowerment and the light of annihilation, the light of dreams and the light of nightmares. We see now that it is all the same light, and so also we see now *that it never changes*. For it is the gift of spirit now once and forever commodified, pale, hard, unwavering, as purest national product. It is American Light, and we are its children.

# CODA

## The Colors of the Spirit

Nature always wears the colors of the spirit.
—Ralph Waldo Emerson, *Nature*

The country seemed so much more mysterious with no Americans in it. It seemed like a different state altogether and, without my countrymen, inscrutable. I realized then how much I had depended on the Americans for my news. Even the lies and misapprehensions were American, rising from the American character and obedient to it; the history was American. Surely the Vietnamese embraced lies and misapprehensions as gaudy and exotic as our own, but I did not know what they were. Their jinns were not mine. I had grown comfortable inside the American illusion and could not comprehend the Vietnamese, so it was hopeless weighing and measuring today against yesterday. There was no connection between them. I began to think of the war as a parenthesis inside a far-going sentence, the parenthesis in English but the sentence itself in a language I did not know and could not decipher. I understood finally that I was on my own.
—Ward Just, *The American Blues*

Nearly a quarter of a century after official American entry into the Vietnam conflict, American preoccupation with the war continues to expand in exponential proportions. The experience of the war remains a major topic of literature and film; and on television, now in strange, ironic after-image of seemingly interminable years of Vietnam via the nightly news, it now finds its regular place among the soaps and sitcoms. On the VCR market, a documentary tape series vies with more familiar video chronicles of other wars and better. For those who underwent the experience of Vietnam, such continuing developments may elicit any number of forms of response, ranging everywhere from gratitude, appreciation, and acceptance to irony, irritation, or outright anger. Of one form of response, however, there is no avoidance possible for any of them. And that is the recognition of having been present at the place where, perhaps more than at any other we will ever remember, American nature became in fact history: at once history *in* fact and history *as* fact, and thereby history also as unprecedented crisis of cultural myth. For them, the world must ineluctably wear that particular fact of American history called Vietnam as the new mythic color of the spirit.

Precisely in such imaging of national mood, Ward Just's *The American Blues* announces from the outset its primary purpose as ongoing response to the experience of Vietnam: the depiction of the continuing immense purchase of the war upon the American soul. And, appropriate to its preoccupation with a media-war imaged for more than a decade across a nation's newspapers and television screens, the text itself opens explicitly with a final media image of that war, a televised vision of the end.

An unnamed narrator sits in the cold north country of New England. The year is 1975. He and his wife and son have retreated there, he says, "refugees" (or perhaps "exiles," he corrects himself) "from wartime Washington," escaped in some "fervor to simplify" (1). ("We came to the north country to get back to fundamentals —," his wife throws up to him early in the text. "Yes," he remembers responding, "That was the trouble" [21].) For there, receiving the one television channel he can receive, he can only sit, still obsessed with his own memories of life and experience and history in that place of heat and jungle, ecstatic sacrifice and grotesque folly, sublimity and exhaustion he will call throughout the text simply "the Zone"; he can only sit and watch, mesmerized, drunk for nearly a month, the botched dismal conclusion. He sees a harried, ashen-faced diplomat, an old friend, being interviewed by a celebrated correspondent, also an old friend. "Looking back on it is something we'll do for a very long time," he hears his friend the diplomat saying on television. "It'll become an industry. There are so many of us who've been here." The correspondent presses the questioning. He wants also to know about "the lessons." "And the lessons?" he asks. "What will the lessons be?" First the diplomat counters somewhat flippantly, with a quote from Stalin, he thinks, perhaps by way of Shostakovich. "In order to sleep soundly, Americans will believe anything." The correspondent remains insistent. "But what will they be, the lessons?" The diplomat becomes mordantly serious. With a voice "soft, almost hushed," he answers, "They will be whatever makes us think well of ourselves" (4).

In this media vignette is imaged also the plight of the narrator, exactly. As a writer (he is also, we shortly discover, the author of not only the text before us but also a nearly completed "history of the war") he has in effect become the dialogue, a kind of walking war story still in search of the closure of lessons. He is a story, he tells us, at once about the war and not about the war that must somehow help us once again, if at all possible, to think well of ourselves. "This is not a story of the war," he has in fact begun, "except insofar as everything in my unsettled middle age seems to wind back to it." Moreover, he goes on, noting us, his audience, "I know how much you dislike reading about it, all dissolution, failure, hackneyed ironies, and guilt, not to mention the facts themselves, regiments of them, *armies*." Still, he concludes, "I must risk being the bore at dinner for these few opening pages, for the life of the war is essential to the story I have to tell. And that is not about the war at all but about the peace that followed the war" (1).

Those pages, of course, turn into a book. And, not surprisingly, they are something of a mirror image of that other book, the "history" stalled on the last chapter, the one, he admits, that is itself "autobiography," although, he keeps trying to convince himself, "I would appear nowhere in it. It was a history of the war pure and simple" (134). Moreover, what he concludes of the latter will of course be true of the former as well, both of them versions, to seize his own offhand phrasing, of "what happens when you get stuck in the last chapter" (177). History as autobiography, auto-biography as history: from the twinned texts that comprise the larger text of *The American Blues*, the one that we keep reading and the one that we keep reading about, the one that we read explicitly, so to speak, and the one thereby that we read implicitly as well, we attempt desperately along with the author to find an intertextualizing structure of vision that would somehow comprehend the meanings of both. "I remembered a friend say-ing once that if you were lucky enough to discover Trollope in middle age," he writes, "you'd never do without, because you could never live long enough to read all he wrote." So it is for himself and Vietnam, he goes on: "I felt that way about the war, so remarkably dense an experience, with such treasure so buried" (12). But therein also of course lies exactly now the "personal" problem of a "historical" ending, for which he says he is "obliged to depend on the recollections of others" (14). For, he goes on, "I knew that a simple reconstruction of the final battle was not enough." There must be one more way to see it for himself, to go there again, to be himself present in experiential closure that will thereby enable historical-literary completion. He tells his wife "I can't end this book." She responds by telling him that he has to "let it go." "The *book*?" he asks "incredulously." "She could not know what she was asking," he adds. She knows precisely, it turns out, what she has been asking: not the book, she has said "furiously." "*The war*" (15).

He perseveres, somewhere between amused and depressed at the old false leads rendered by the current president and familiar faces in the administration. The nation, the president insists, needs to be talked out of "a crisis of the American spirit": "There was narcissism and malaise, and the American people had to put these dark times behind them in order to advance to greatness. Narcissism and materialism threatened progress; the people had become pessimistic, they were so preoccupied by the past. The people had to be tough of mind and spirit; they had to *forget*." Meanwhile, the narrator adds simply (and at this point we ourselves would be utterly incredulous if he should express a particle of surprise), "my last chapter wouldn't come" (15).

Then, outside, amidst the cold landscape and the blue of the mountains, the narrator hears one day what "no one who has ever heard the sound in wartime will ever forget, slap*slap*slap*slap*" (16). It is a Huey, but now carrying a banker, a friend they have nicknamed "Eurodollar Ed," most likely "scouting the valley for a developer" (16). And in that moment it takes the very image of war-become-progress itself to make him see the real problem left over from the Zone, which is not, in fact, one of forgetting but rather one of insistent remembering. "I was trembling with fear and memory," he writes; "the Zone had been singular in its urgency and restless vitality." He goes on:

> I had been too long in this place, I could not see the future; the past blocked my vision. I was alone with my cocktails, my interviews, my boy, and my increasingly aggrieved wife. Now it was another late fall, with infinite winter in the sullen air, the winter that went on forever. As the sound of the chopper faded and then ceased altogether, I understood that I had been living inside my history of the war, my feverish memory of it; this year was that year relived, but in a cold and lonely climate. (16)

There is nothing left for him to do, he and his wife conclude, but to seek some solitary respite. He travels farther into the north country to an old friend from those days, now a celebrated mystery novelist with a James Bond–like protagonist whose annual appearance in print keeps enough money, women, and drink at hand to supply some version of the old excitement. As if in this recognition, the project becomes a quick trip in the mind's eye to the great times themselves, himself and Quinn and the rest back in Saigon. He writes, "I made preparations to evacuate—a temporary measure I told myself. I needed time off, some rest & recreation at Quinn's playground in the Northeast Kingdom" (22). Yet this, as even the phrasing suggests in advance, will be no going ahead but a going back, a fogged and fuddled exercise in old camaraderie, excessive drink, and middle-aged dread and reminiscence, and a prearranged ecstatic, doomed liaison with a much younger woman, a free-spirit ski instructor. The latter, of course, is now of a generation that has essentially not known anything of the war and the Zone, or, if at all, has known it as some unpleasant and eminently forgettable minor aside, a bad national adventure subsumed in the general present business of being young and self-sufficiently alive. Yet it is not so much, the novel is at pains to show us, that the girl, Marty, is untouched by the history that is the war so much as she has simply made it "history." She has made it history, that is, in the common sense as generations do— as in "well, yes, but that's history"; and she has also made it so in the more technical sense of mythic-cultural appropriation, history, so to speak, as something perhaps quite important but finally no more important or no less important than any other kind of history. And it is that deeper realism which speaks when she says, "America seems so exhausted to me now, all those old *men* with their loopy memories" (145). (Just before, when the narrator has foolishly injured himself in some over-zealous skiing, he has been offered whiskey by a military-looking type about his age, clearly "a soldier," "a drinking soldier, a soldier who knew something about casualties" (143). Later, he encounters the same man in a bar. "When were you there," he asks. "Sixty-four," is the reply, "and again in sixty-eight." "God," he calls out in parting, with a laugh, "Wasn't it a son of a bitch" [174].) Marty knows that in fact the two of them, the older man and the younger woman, "come from different ends of the earth" (162). And now, she adds, "I have to have a clear run, that's the benefit of the times we live in, one of the expected results of your history, yours and Quinn's" (163).

Indeed, we eventually discover, and we are not particularly surprised, the entire business of the liaison itself, as if matters of living and writing, autobiography and history, and all the rest, were not sufficiently confused, might itself be deemed a larger kind of writer's experiment. And it is one that has been instigated, moreover, not by the narrator but by the other writer, the novelist, the old alter ego and surrogate self Quinn, for a problem of autobiography and history he himself has been working on. Succinctly, Quinn's own young mistress (daughter, in fact, of an older one) spells it out, this business of the narrator and Marty. "So Quinn had an idea," she confesses:

> He wanted to put you two close together and into a kind of combat, it didn't matter which kind; he wanted to know which culture was the stronger and more durable, which the path to the future and which the cul-de-sac. Those seemed to be the only choices, and what better guide than a woman met by chance, a young woman unencumbered. And you know Quinn, he loves to set out mine fields and watch people move through them. He had been away from America for so long, he did not know how things were. You were his only contact. And you were obsessed by the war. And he was so interested in your response and in hers. Was there a common ground after all? And a way to prepare for the future, postwar. And how did that connect to the past, or was it only a parenthesis? It seemed an ideal encounter, a man who came from the fundamentals and a woman who was looking for them. Then—. (192)

"Then—." Of the experiment (exactly whose, whose life versus whose art, whose autobiography versus whose history, no longer an issue) for the narrator now comes the only possible conclusion, the only going back that can be a going ahead, a return to "the Zone" itself. And apace, what has seemed an insistently realistic text (albeit in relentless contemplation of its own textual status) moves into an entirely new space of figuration where it becomes something like its own metaphysical correlative. There is time and space travel (now possible by way of a "visa," of course) which enables an actual distant voyaging back to "the Zone," "the place," the narrator tells his son with visionary certainty, "where modern American history begins" (196). He literally does another "tour," this time with a guide who now likewise speaks something in a vein resembling planetary truth. "My escort was a young woman who had been successfully reeducated and wished now to join her country's diplomatic service," he writes;

"she was avid to go to America, after the normalization of relations." He goes on, "She knew the names of the various states and regions, and professed admiration for our popular culture. She had known a number of Americans during the occupation and had found them clumsy and often cruel but guileless and generous with money; ill at ease, so far from home. Americans, she concluded, did not travel well" (199–200).

So now also comes the truth of similar self-recognition from within. And, not surprisingly, the figures of such recognition now become almost obsessively those of writing itself. As Thomas Myers puts it, "What the narrator confronts in postwar Vietnam . . . is not historical clarification but new categories of mystery, additional signifiers of his aloneness" (*Walking Point*, 219). For indeed now he actually wrestles with the real secret of American presence and thus the real source of writing about what happened there, available in the Zone only *now that the Americans themselves are no longer present.* "I made detailed notes," the narrator says, "but they were unusable. The country seemed so much more mysterious with no Americans in it. It seemed like a different state altogether and, without my countrymen, inscrutable." In the Zone *without the Americans,* "Einstein's rule," as he has called it about the necessity of writing about war "from the middle," has come home with a new force of literality. For he has discovered that it is the very conceptions of language and meaning themselves constituting his own very Americanness that he must renounce before the deepest American secrets of writing about Vietnam may be unlocked:

> I realized then how much I had depended on the Americans for my news. Even the lies and misapprehensions were American, rising from the American character and obedient to it; the history was American. Surely the Vietnamese embraced lies and misapprehensions as gaudy and exotic as our own, but I did not know what they were. Their jinns were not mine. I had grown comfortable inside the American illusion and could not comprehend the Vietnamese, so it was hopeless weighing and measuring today against yesterday. There was no connection between them. I began to think of the war as a parenthesis inside a far-going sentence, the parenthesis in English but the sentence itself in a language I did not know and could not decipher. I understood finally that I was on my own. (200–201)

It is an understanding, he recognizes, at once deeply within and some-where beyond language, something as vague and portentous sounding as "*Amerikanische Kunst des 20. jahrhunderts*" (204). But words now are the only things that remain. He writes impulsively to the diplomat, the one he has heard speaking at the start. He has been wrong, he tells him, about the cherished "thesis, half a century old now," itself of another lost genera-tion's cultural mythmaking, "that the large abstract words such as glory, honor, courage, and cowardice, were obscene," and that "that which was chaste was factual, in the instance of the war, the details of the weather, the geography, the weapons, the battle groups, and the statistical appara-tus that supported it all." He has been mistaken indeed. For now he has realized that "in this war all we had were the large abstract words. It was difficult to state them without fortification, but I had a skull filled to over-flowing with facts—untainted, innocent, and none of them described the war, except who had won and who had lost and in this war that was only a detail" (203).

As such larger meditations on language strip away illusion from illu-sion, so writing itself moves toward some null point of final self-critique. Shortly, the narrator is reduced to writing personal letters, longhand (we are not sure now to whom), the solitude broken only by casette tapes, played out against the silence of Saigon, of "Tatum and Billie Holiday and Ella Fitzgerald and Fats," American blues, scribble scribble. Eventually, even these words fail. Then, finally, he tells us, "the silence was com-plete, except for the music behind me; there was no living thing in sight, only the tortured shadows of the past crowding my memory." Sleepless, haunted, he writes, "I stood naked," night after night, "sweating, hearing only the restless racket inside my own mind, and the blues on tape. How could I communicate this in a personal letter? You wouldn't understand. My imagined multitudes held me in thrall, and I would not banish them. They were necessary. They were close as brothers, my multitudes; they were mine" (204).

The "lesson" in "the Zone" is the one that has been imaged all along in the place they used to call "the World." And it is the latest Asiatic ver-sion of the American lesson that we failed to learn there the last time, the lesson of a monolithic certainty in vision and language wrecking itself against the abiding mystery of the other. It is a very Asiatic lesson indeed.

Words can only fail. Yet we must proceed in that knowledge. For the words of the world are honored most by the acknowledgment of their failure in the solitary silence, background music, unworded blues. "Do you see it now?" he asks. "I was so tired, and in order to advance I would have to travel through the multitudes, from the present into the past, counting, weighing, measuring, *listening*. They had given so much and wanted so little in return; they only wanted acknowledgment of the debt. They wanted a secure place in the public memory. None of us must be forgotten, and in that way the future is guaranteed and our sleep untroubled. So we must ask for mercy, and it was in the *asking*. . . ." Words *must* fail in this pilgrimage (and it is exactly, we will soon see, the figure of history and mythic sense-making that also concludes *Meditations in Green*) exactly that they may again succeed. The novel indeed ends by speaking out of the failure of words into an encouragement of their new comfort. "Listen," the narrator says, in a concluding sentence, to the ghosts, to himself, to us, "everything's going to work out fine" (205). They are words not so much of promise perhaps as of comfort, whistling in the dark, the old national habit among the multitudinous presences, but now at least chastened, acknowledged; they are words that are the final lesson at once of history and of sense-making itself, of failure confronted and accepted, and now merged with new songs of old wise endurance, the American Blues.

Through such complex intertextualizations, *The American Blues* thus arises ultimately out of the matrix of realism to become a highly experimental inquiry into the most profound issues of language and meaning, of myths of self and culture and of cultural mythmaking at large. In contrast, as with more explicitly experimental texts such as Norman Mailer's *Why Are We in Vietnam?*, Tim O'Brien's *Going After Cacciato*, and other enterprises in the vein of fiction that over the last two decades or so we have come to call "magical realism," a critique of mythic sense-making in Stephen Wright's *Meditations in Green* reveals itself from the outset as the work's dominant, even obsessive theme. Yet in the spirit imaged in its title, the work of such a critique now becomes projected, even as it arises out of a spectacle of horror often as graphic as any in our whole literature of the war, into new dimensions of creative possibility as well. *Meditations in Green* is at once a hideous war story and a stoned American pastorale, a general nightmare of the end which, through the shaping and transforming process of imaginative art, ultimately does come, magically, miraculously, by the novel's end, to bear also the generative promise of new creation.

As with *The American Blues*, its at first somewhat unlikely counterpart, *Meditations in Green*[1] quickly turns out to be a book that is several books, this time at the level of explicit metafictive novelistic construction, again each of which can be read only in terms of the others. It begins by introducing us into the consciousness of the protagonist, an ex-Vietnam soldier named Griffin, with one of a series of interchapters entitled "Meditations in Green," described aptly by Thomas Myers as "a high-relief map of Griffin's internalized postwar battlefield" inscribing through "a plenitude of botanical correspondences his passage from initial hopefulness through guilt, vindictiveness, and alienation to the debilitating dreams of heroin addiction" (*Walking Point*, 207). It then moves to two other narratives, one emanating from a first-person narrator and another from a third-person narrator. The former announces himself early on: "I, your genial narrator, wreathed in a beard of smoke, look into the light and recite strange tales from the war back in the long ago time" (8). It is, as we soon find out, the latest version of what Michael Herr has already pronounced to us as the most familiar of Vietnam litanies: "Dear Mom, Stoned Again" (34). His book is a book of imagination. At the same time, he is also the other narrator as well. There, his book is a book of memory. The two merge and interflow in and out of each other to form, as the interchapters remind us, a series of meditations in green, and one ultimately in which the institutional war-green, the olive drab of death and old destruction, becomes the fruitional green of promise, the peace-green of life and new creation.

In the book of memory—Vietnam—we are given the whole stoned, lurid spectacle. The setting is in a military intelligence unit engaged in everything from photo-interpretation (with specialities in bomb-damage assessment and, of course, a major herbicide program) to physical torture. The narrator-protagonist, Griffin, and his fellow draftees who work there spend their lives in a near-permanent state of drugged hallucination. The unit commander dies on takeoff in a plane most likely sabotaged by a homicidal GI. Grunts from the Spook House drive around in their jeep with decomposing Viet Cong corpses sitting in the back seat. The corpses are wearing party hats. Weird Wendell, enlisting fellow GIs and base-camp Vietnamese, makes a make-believe war movie with a true-life cast of thousands. (Not for nothing do his prior artistic credentials include, as Donald

Ringnalda points out, work as Jimi Hendrix's sound mixer for "Are You Experienced?" ["Chlorophyll Overdose," 131].) During the last scene the idiotic make-believe comes hideously real. His creative endeavors interrupted by an actual Viet Cong attack on the base camp, Wendell keeps filming. A plane takes a direct hit from a mortar round. He films the pilot being incinerated in his cockpit. He films a U.S. captain and "a genuine VC in black shorts locked in a lover's clench on the gravel outside the O club and stabbing one another at intervals with long knives" (332). In an ensuing explosion, Wendell himself falls, mangled, mortally wounded. He dies giving camera directions and quoting from a cherished copy of *Atlas Shrugged* (334) which he has been reading and then methodically destroying (and thus for good measure making a figure of Wright's own novel, as again Ringnalda points out, an experimental novel that "destroys, page by page, a conventional novel" ["Chlorophyll Overdose," 135]). Over in the chapel, a real film has been playing all the while, spectatorless. Griffin wonders how it came out. He does not know that it has self-destructed, as has Wendell's, on the last frame. In fact, as in fantasy—or, if you will, in fantasy as in fact—it is Vietnam, the movie: "The screen was blank, a rectangle of burning light" (338).[2]

Back in the world, both initially and for a good part of the novel to come, we are forced to comprehend what seems an equally nightmarish mixup of fact *and* phantasmagoria. Literally and literarily, they blend across a whole stoned, echolalic spectrum. Griffin, clearly a heroin addict, rewrites the American iconography of the veteran's poppy in ways never imagined. Trips, his old war buddy, still both here and there as well, endlessly stalks after and plots lovingly various forms of demise for a figure he takes to be his old NCO nemesis, Sergeant Antrim. Griffin finds a friend and possible soul mate named Huette Mirandella. Her nickname: Huey. More neo-Shakespearean horseplay shows up in a botanic psychologist named Arden. As in Vietnam, so back in the world, it can only get crazier and crazier. Trips continues his mad quest. Huey pronounces "all this plant jive" thus far but "words, words, words." It is time, she challenges Griffin, to "test how green your thumb really is" (264).

As the novel would have it, the exhortation is, both figuratively and quite literally, the crucial seed planted in the fertile ground of ever-creating consciousness. Out of a nightmare memory of old death comes a generative thrusting forth of imagination into imagings and envisionings of new life.

As with *The American Blues*, the sundry books of fact and imagination, history and myth, memory and invention in *Meditations in Green* merge at the novel's end, and with comparable result. Outside, nothing much probably does change a very great deal. Given the way the world goes, the operative question may well always be the one recorded at the bottom line of the last of the novel's meditations in green: "Who has a question for Mr. Memory?" (340). In life, this may indeed always be the basic issue. At the same time, however, through the generative power of art, there has now emerged the possibility that such a going back might become the stuff of a going ahead as well. And that going ahead for Stephen Wright, as with Dylan Thomas, will lie in "the green fuse that drives the flower," the vision of an art that would come to touch on nothing less than the eternal springs of creation. Here may yet reside, one may be bold enough to believe, the answer to what Griffin announces near the end as "Problem of the Age." Question: "How to occupy the diminishing interval between fire and wind and flags" (340). Answer: Imagine. Create. Make it happen. "I think my thumb has always been green" (340), he exclaims. Aborning in a new Johnny Appleseed ready to hump the American boonies with the best of them, the dream of a new imaginative possibility has come to germination:

> In the spring I'll wander national highways, leather breeches around my legs, pot on my head, sowing seeds from the burlap bag across my shoulder, resting in the afternoon in the shade of a laurel tree.
>
> At night I carve peace pipes from old cypress branches.
>
> Everywhere the green fuses are burning and look now, snipping rapidly ahead of your leaping eye, the forged blades cutting through the page, the transformation of this printed sheet twisted about a metal stem for your lapel your hat your antenna, a paper emblem of the widow's hope, the doctor's apothecary, the veteran's friend: a modest flower. (340–41)

In the play of the text, the extending of experiential and cultural memory into new dimensions of the imaginatively possible, the veteran's flower newly engenders itself out of the memorial of death into the promise of new life. Out of *The American Blues* comes *Meditations in Green*. Out of the breakdown of words come other words at once of old comfort and of new growth. Singly and together and in their sundry other textualizations, the works of Vietnam writers consistently recapitulate the cultural project of writing contained in John Balaban's eloquent admonition. "Swear by the locust," he commands,

> by dragonflies on ferns,
> by the minnow's flash, the tremble of a breast,
> by the new earth spongy under our feet:
> that as we grow old, we will not grow evil,
> that although our garden seeps with sewage,
> and our elders think it's up for auction — swear
> by this dazzle that does not wish to leave us —
> that we will be keepers of a garden, nonetheless. (48)

To use a memorable figure from the era, this is Flower Power indeed. From Ron Kovic's Fourth of July firecracker exploding in the grave, it is the new Memorial Day poppy. From Vietnam authors in their generation, it is the veteran's friend, his dream, his creation, his gift, to you.

*American Blues. Meditations in Green.* Such titles and texts from Vietnam authors in their generation continue to remind us, to return to the epigraph from Tim O'Brien with which this book began, of the things they carried. But now also they continue to command us not only to remember but also to imagine. Imagine, they seem to tell us, after a season of the American Blues a new Meditation in Green that would be the true work of cultural revision. Imagine, they say, out of the embrace of memory a re-writing of the old dream of origin that might still find its flowering in the truest of new generations, a generation of peace.

# NOTES

## INTRODUCTION

1 Pulitzer Prize winners include Frances Fitzgerald for *Fire in the Lake* and, most recently, Neil Sheehan for *A Bright Shining Lie*. National Book Award winners also include the above, as well as Gloria Emerson for *Winners and Losers*, Robert Stone for *Dog Soldiers*, Michael Herr for *Dispatches*, Tim O'Brien for *Going After Cacciato*, and Larry Heinemann for *Paco's Story*. For *Meditations in Green*, Stephen Wright won the Maxwell Perkins Prize. For the body of his achievement in fiction, Robert Stone also received in 1988 an American Academy Institute of Arts and Letters Award (including a stipend of $50,000 a year for five years). The Yale Poetry Prize was awarded to Michael Casey for his early collection of Vietnam poems entitled *Obscenities*. John Balaban's *After Our War* received the prize for the Lamont Poetry Selection. The Tony and New York Drama Critics' Circle awards have been given to David Rabe for both *Sticks and Bones* and *Streamers*.

2 Such discussions have centered, as might be expected, mainly on authors and works in the domain of what are considered traditionally "literary" texts; also, as might be expected, they have largely followed the pattern of the major awards. In narrative literature, five writers have basically received to date (and this in spite of the fact that most have produced a significant body of other writing as well) the bulk of critical attention for basically five texts: Tim O'Brien for *Going After Cacciato*; Philip Caputo for *A Rumor of War*; Robert Stone for *Dog Soldiers*; Michael Herr for *Dispatches*; and Stephen Wright for *Meditations in Green*. And now, after his unexpected National Book Award for *Paco's Story*, the "surprise" winner, as breathlessly depicted by the media, over Toni Morrison's *Beloved*, some new attention is also being devoted to Larry Heinemann. Virtually all the critical attention in poetry has been given to Bruce Weigl, with some recent increasing consideration also to W. D. Ehrhart and Yusef Komunyakaa. The playwright David Rabe has generally in academic circles been "ranked" with the two other major figures of his generation, Sam Shepard and David Mamet.

Book-length scholarly studies include my own introductory *American Literature and the Experience of Vietnam*, John Hellman's *American Myth and the Legacy of Vietnam*, Timothy Lomperis's *Reading the Wind: The Literature of the Vietnam War* (with a valuable bibliographic essay by John Clark Pratt); and Thomas Myers's *Walking Point: American Narratives of Vietnam*. Also, Michael Stephens, in *The Dramaturgy of Style: Voice in Short Fiction*, an extensive study of postmodern literature, devotes a major chapter to "voice" in Vietnam writing. Essay collections on the literature of the war include *Search and Clear*, ed. William J. Searle, and *America Rediscovered*, ed. Owen W. Gilman, Jr., and Lorrie Smith. A major bibliography of Vietnam texts in literature and the humanities is Sandra M. Wittman's *Writing About Vietnam*. Articles, reviews, review-essays, interviews, panels, and other critical discussions have appeared in virtually all major journals and quarterlies dealing with American literature and American Studies as well as in many dealing with general literature, criticism, and theory.

Oddly, one might add in this regard, in a time when radical expansions of critical theory as an academic enterprise have coexisted with the development here of a literature often literally crying out to be read through various modes of poststructuralist inquiry, critical discussion in general has remained rather traditional and conservative. Perhaps the problem is partly the one, in the case of such profoundly "written" texts, of theoretical application ascribed by Harold Bloom to that earlier, incredibly self-conscious chronicler of American initiations, Emerson, when he notes the special problematics of deconstructing a discourse predicated so completely on an awareness of its own status as rhetorical construction (*Kabbalah*, 120–21; *Agon*, 156). Partly, it may also derive from the more localized situation ascribed by Donald Ringnalda to Vietnam fiction in particular as a case of a body of rhetorically self-conscious texts "written mainly by grunts who did not go to Vietnam as writers, and certainly not as students of literary history who were cognizant of post-modern theories of the novel," and whose "post-modern novels" might thus be reckoned essentially "blue-collar revelations of a blue-collar experience" (37). Recent criticism partaking productively of contemporary conversations is on the increase and includes Myers's book, Jerome Klinkowitz's "Writing Under Fire" (in earlier form an introductory essay to a collection of Vietnam experimental fictions by that name) reprinted in Larry McCaffrey's *Postmodern Fiction*, essays in the two collections cited, and papers included in a recent special issue of *Genre* (Winter 1988). For one exemplary attempt to locate a major poststructuralist Vietnam text within a highly developed matrix of theory, see Evelyn Cobley, "Narrating the Facts of War: New Journalism in Herr's *Dispatches* and Documentary Realism in First World War Novels." For theoretically oriented feminist analyses of Vietnam narrative, see Jacqueline E. Lawson, " 'She's a pretty woman . . . for a gook': The Misogyny of the Vietnam War," and Kalí Tal, "The Mind at War: Images of Women in Vietnam by Combat Veterans." And for a stimulating and provocative feminist reading of cultural representations of the war across a broad spectrum of genre and mode, see Susan Jeffords, *The Remasculinization of America*.

## THE LIFE OF FICTION

1 Halberstam is also the author, of course, of one of the best-known journalistic analyses of the Vietnam war in the context of American policy making, *The Best and the Brightest;* and his later work, of equal interest and distinction, has covered topics ranging from, in *The Breaks of the Game,* American professional athletics to, in *The Reckoning,* the rise and fall of the national automobile industry. Bunting, a former army officer who became president of Briarcliff College and later of Hampden-Sydney College, is a well-known educator. Having made a similar transition from professional military service to the academy, Pratt, a former air force colonel now professor of English at Colorado State University, is a prominent figure in Vietnam studies and, as noted earlier, the author-compiler of the celebrated *Vietnam Voices.* Webb, as will be noted presently, one of the most highly decorated marine officers of the war, attracted great public attention during his controversial tenure as secretary of the navy. At the time of its publication, Del Vecchio's novel was compared with everything from *Moby-Dick* to *The Naked and the Dead.* It has been followed by an equally massive novel of the Cambodian tragedy, *For the Sake of All Living Things.* Hasford's became the basis for Stanley Kubrick's much-praised film, *Full Metal Jacket,* and has recently given rise to a novelistic sequel, *The Phantom Blooper.* Just began his career as the author of major works of Vietnam-era reportage such as *Military Men* and *To What End* as well as an early novel of the war entitled *Stringer,* and he has since become, as will be discussed later, one of our most prominent and prolific fictional chroniclers of the American political scene. For his efforts, Wright, also to be discussed later, won the prestigious Maxwell Perkins prize awarded by Charles Scribner's Sons for a first novel.

2 Also of distinct generational identity, albeit working out of a radically different context of "experience" in the specific sense uniting the writers in this text, should be mentioned related figures such as Barry Hannah, Bobbie Ann Mason, Jayne Anne Phillips, Madison Smartt Bell, and Susan Fromberg Schaeffer. Vietnam *as experience,* although not from a direct experiential perspective, reverberates through Hannah's much-praised fictions of the late 1970s and early 1980s including *Airships, The Tennis Handsome,* and *Ray.* Mason's novel *In Country,* following her important chroniclings of contemporary southern life in *Shiloh and Other Stories* and detailing the attempts of a young woman to reconstruct the memory of a dead Vietnam GI–father she never knew and to understand the plight of an uncle still living his own experience of Vietnam a generation later, remains one of the most sensitive depictions of the price exacted by the war upon its survivors in its domestic aftermath. In this connection, see for instance, Robert H. Brinkmeyer, "Finding One's History: Bobbie Ann Mason and Contemporary Southern Literature." Phillips's *Machine Dreams* is an eloquent chronicle of generations culminating in another young woman's similar attempts to locate the meanings of her brother's death in the war within some

larger possible sense of the continuities of American lives. In Bell's *Soldier's Joy*, two veterans of the war and former childhood friends, one white and one black, return to their separate Americas only to be forced into a new, desperate brotherhood of violence in the racial combat zone of the Vietnam-era South. A contrasting tale of Pete Bravado from Brooklyn and his attempts back in the world, day after endless day, to make some small peace with the war that keeps fighting itself in his head, Schaeffer's highly acclaimed *Buffalo Afternoon* also, as Nicholas Proffitt points out in a recent review, demonstrates the possibility of dealing with Vietnam as experiential and imaginative presence, both in the depiction of combat itself and of the war's domestic aftermath, in the work of a writer of the Vietnam generation who has not in any technical sense "been there." Exactly to this degree, observes Proffitt—himself a veteran Vietnam correspondent and author of major novels of the war such as *The Embassy House* and *Gardens of Stone*—the work becomes an exemplary revelation, through the eyes of a gifted novelist, of how completely the war has now become our common legacy of history and myth.

3 Considerations of three other major writers of fiction mentioned above, Robert Stone, Ward Just, and Stephen Wright, will be deferred to subsequent chapters. Obviously, as already noted, Stone is also thought of as a major "Vietnam" novelist. Because of his quite different "experiential" perspective from the above writers on Vietnam and the origination of his fiction in the tradition of observer-report, I defer discussion of his works to a chapter considering them, along with those of Gloria Emerson, Frances Fitzgerald, and Michael Herr, under the heading of "The Literature of Witness." The novels of Just, a somewhat older figure writing out of the "witness" tradition, and Wright, a somewhat younger figure working out of the "veteran" perspective, will be discussed in a concluding section, a kind of coda to the text at large on the history and prospects of writing by Vietnam authors in their generation, entitled "The Colors of the Spirit."

4 Curiously, O'Brien has continued to deny any sense of strongly conscious affiliation with other masters of magical realism such as Borges, Marquez, Kundera, and Calvino. About what he once called "the *New York Times*'s 'magical realism' thing," for instance, he replied to one interviewer after the publication of *Going After Cacciato*, "I haven't read any of those guys. I've since read Borges, but I haven't even read much Borges." As to Marquez in particular, he went on, "I'd feel good if that magical realism quote were directed toward Borges. But Garcia Marquez—I'm afraid that I still haven't finished anything he's written. Maybe I'll give *One Hundred Years of Solitude* another shot. Everybody says it's a real modern classic" (Schroeder, 139). To another interviewer's question of whether he had read Marquez at the time, he replied, somewhat in contrast but in similar spirit, "Yes, and Borges, too, but just dabbling. To me," he went on, "*all* realism should be magical. All reality *is* magical" (McCaffrey, 142).

5 As I hope my study will show, particularly in the work of major American writers of Vietnam in their generation, I take the concept of literature as cultural revision outlined here, I should emphasize, to suggest something quite culturally specific and not just the restatement, for instance, of some rather traditional modernist conception of the artist as the creator of *kulchur*—neither a naive moral and philosophical didacticism nor some fascist mystagogy of art. What is suggested here is an art *at once* of the possible and of the newly plausible—a ground of genuinely new creation that in the same moment returns us to ourselves in enlarged dimensions of insight. In various forms, it is an idea that runs through the pronouncements of various major writers studied here in this text. Tim O'Brien, for instance, has described "the central theme of the novel" as "how we use our imaginations to deal with situations around us, not just to cope with them psychologically but, more importantly, to deal with them philosophically and morally" (Schroeder, 139).

Of fictional creation in general, Robert Stone has said to the same interviewer in a similar vein, "You make up things that didn't happen about people that never were in order to render in a way more truly events that did happen to people who really did exist. Fiction performs the same function for history or for life that dreaming performs for the mind" (Schroeder, 155). More recently, he has also written, arguing what he sees as an inherent morality function lodged in the act of creating "stories," "If we did not idealize ourselves, if we only accepted the reality of ourselves as we are most of the time, we would never be capable of the extensions of ourselves that are required of us" ("The Reason for Stories," 74). Likewise, of the role of the political novel in his work as a critical fiction, after comments on the contextualizing authority of imagination virtually identical to those above, he has said, "Its element is what I believe to be the transitory nature of moral perception. I think it's extremely difficult for people to identify and act upon the right. The world is full of illusion. We carry nemesis inside us—almost, it seems, by design. But we are not excused" ("We Are Not Excused," 36–37).

Of Vietnam "war stories" in particular, William Broyles, anticipating many of the thematic elaborations of O'Brien's *The Things They Carried*, posits ideas similar to O'Brien's and Stone's about the heuristic relation of facts to creative falsehoods as ones with the merit of being so new that they are also quite old. "I have never once heard a grunt tell a war story that wasn't a lie," he writes, "just as some of the stories that I tell about the war are lies. Not that even the lies aren't true, on a certain level. They have a moral, even a mythic, truth, rather than a literal one. They reach out and remind the tellers and listeners of their place in the world. They are the primitive stories told around the fire in smoky teepees after the pipe has been passed. They are all, at bottom, the same" ("Why Men Love War," 61).

6 As might be expected, the brilliantly original strategies of narration and struc-

ture in *Going After Cacciato* thus described have generated considerable academic discussion. Besides the analyses of Myers and Couser noted here and my own earlier one in *American Literature and the Experience of Vietnam*, see also, for instance, Nancy Anisfield, "Words and Fragments"; Tobey C. Herzog, "*Going After Cacciato*"; Michael W. Raymond, "Imagined Responses to Vietnam"; Eric James Schroeder, "The Past and the Possible"; Gordon O. Taylor, "Cacciato's Grassy Hill"; and Dennis Vannatta, "Theme and Structure in Tim O'Brien's *Going After Cacciato*." Also, as might be expected, each must thus concomitantly explore in its way the challenging issues, literary *and* moral and philosophical, posed by O'Brien's elevating of fictive imagination to a position coequal and correlative with the traditionally privileged status in experience-based fiction of the "real."

The general points explored in the academic literature, one should add, were at least suggested, as Thomas W. Myers notes in his truly excellent discussion already cited (*Walking Point*, 171–85), by a number of astute reviewers at the time of the novel's publication. See, for instance, Pearl K. Bell, "Writing About Vietnam," and, as already cited in my own text, Richard Freedman, "A Separate Peace." But perhaps O'Brien himself put the matter of the reality/imagination dialectic structuring the novel into simplest relief when he told an interviewer, "I think you could argue that *Cacciato* is the most realistic thing I've written. The life of the imagination is *real*—it's as fucking real as anything else, especially if you happen to be a follower of Fichte, who says that *nothing* is real but what is inside of our own heads" (McCaffrey, 142).

7 O'Brien himself, again, asked specifically about the repeated imagings of Cacciato's insistent fishing in bomb craters, would seem to suggest that this is finally the response the novel is intended to elicit. "That's the feeling I'm trying to evoke. That's exactly it. It's the sense that 'maybe there is something there that nobody else knows about.' A sense that 'well, it's not very likely, and yet maybe. . . .' It's the sense of 'maybe' that I really like about his character. And it is this sense that runs throughout the book. 'Maybe so'" (Schroeder, "Two Interviews," 150–51).

8 Both of these texts, along with several more, had previously been published independently over the past few years in *Esquire*, and others in the collection had likewise appeared in further serial publications and anthologies. In virtually every case, however, their literary thrust was to continue to extend "facts" and "fictions" into new dimensions of creative reciprocity, and the publication of the current work now also clearly attempts, within a composite critique of fictional structure, to address these issues within a larger pattern of intertextual relation.

9 Again, as if to enforce the point of the composite text at hand, these two excerpts were intially published as one story with two headings. See "Speaking of Courage," 135–54.

10 See Cornelius A. Cronin, "From the DMZ to No Man's Land," and Peter McInerney, "Straight and Secret History in Vietnam War Literature." Issues of experiential or historical versus literary narration are also discussed insightfully in Thomas Myers's discussion of the text in *Walking Point*.

11 In the *New Republic*, Randall Kennedy also noted the text's persistent identifications of its philosophical father, albeit in his opinion, along with the literary invocations of Conrad, in considerably oppressive measure, as Friedrich Nietzsche. The novel remained in his view, however, an important exploration of our culture's wish to indulge its most violent and imperialistic impulses (46–48).

12 As will be noted in subsequent discussions of the fiction of Robert Olen Butler, Winston Groom, and Larry Heinemann, one of the major achievements, from both an experiential and a mythic standpoint, of what might now be called "second stage" or "second generation" Vietnam novels has been their attempt to undertake in realistic and psychologically complex and serious ways a full-scale consideration of this perhaps most widely known and widely mythologized of specific forms of the emotional legacy of the war for many veterans. Curiously, one might also note in this regard, it therefore remains one of the chief ironies of the absorption of Vietnam texts into the process of cultural mythmaking at large, that a version of the problem and the metaphor was the subject, and one treated in many ways with prophetic perception and insight, of one of the very first novels to launch Vietnam fiction, David Morrell's *First Blood*. It, of course, was the genesis of *Rambo*.

For a recent discussion of psychological issues in Heinemann's *Close Quarters* and *Paco's Story*, Caputo's *Indian Country*, Bobbie Ann Mason's *In Country*, and John Nichols's *American Blood*, see also Thomas Myers's, "Dispatches from Ghost Country."

13 As will be seen in subsequent discussions, given Webb's own public visibility first as a military and later as a political figure, it is not simply speculation to suggest that, as an index of his explicit polemical revisionism, in each of his novels we are clearly given a Webb-like figure or figures with whose perspective we are basically invited to identify. In this text, for instance, although both Gilliland here and Goodrich in his concluding excoriation of self-righteous antiwar activists will articulate something like Webb's public positions, the central Webb stand-in is clearly the doomed warrior Hodges. In *A Sense of Honor*, that role will be shared by the tactical officer, the marine captain Lenahan, the much-wounded and much-decorated "soldier's soldier" restive under academy petty protocols, and the gung-ho fourth-classman, even down to a surprise loss in the annual boxing championships, Wild Bill Fogarty. (For a turn in the latter case on the considerable reciprocity of art and life, see, for instance, the account of Webb's own similar boxing experience at the Naval Academy with another future marine, Ollie North, in Robert Timberg, "The Private War of Ollie and Jim.") Finally, in *A Country Such as This*, a figure analogous to

all of the foregoing will be Judd Smith, decorated marine, "fighting preacher" from the hills of his beloved Appalachia, and ultimately member of Congress standing bravely against the minions of rampant liberalism.

14 In a letter to the author.


## AMERICAN DRAMATIST

1 A 1988 study, William W. Demastes's *Beyond Naturalism: A New Realism in American Theatre*, addresses in its main chapters the three writers named in just such a "major" configuration. It then goes on to discuss works by more recently emergent playwrights such as Charles Fuller, Beth Henley, and Marsha Norman.

2 For a study of the Vietnam plays in a basically tripartite relation, see my own earlier *American Literature and the Experience of Vietnam*; Barbara Hurrel, "American Self-Image in David Rabe's Vietnam Trilogy"; and Sidney Homan, "American Playwrights in the 1970s: Rabe and Shepard." For an illuminating dissection of the critical myth itself in the context of an overview of Rabe's career at large (and including, as noted subsequently, Rabe's own suggestion that he personally saw *The Orphan*, a third earlier play produced directly following *Pavlo Hummel* and *Sticks and Bones*, as completing a "Vietnam" trilogy), see Phillip C. Kollin, *David Rabe: A Stage History and a Primary and Secondary Bibliography*.

3 Although critical discussions of Rabe deal with him almost exclusively as a playwright, it should be noted that his career has also led him, as with the more widely known work of fellow Vietnam writer Michael Herr, into important writing for film. For discussions of Rabe's screenplays for the original film *I'm Dancing as Fast as I Can* (1982) and for Robert Altman's production of *Streamers* (1983), for instance, see Kollin, 77–83. More recently, Rabe has also received significant praise for the Vietnam combat film *Casualties of War* (1989). For a perceptive analysis of Rabe's dramatic screenplay, its relation to documentary sources, and the investigative journalism in which the film had its origins, see Pauline Kael, "A Wounded Apparition."

4 The best known of the three Vietnam works, it is also, however, clearly of initial composition in the period of *Pavlo Hummel* and *Sticks and Bones*, and in fact, as demonstrated by Kollin, its period of actual creation spans the time of composition of the other two plays (65).

5 In less happy intimation, as cited by Kollin (53), one can also find evidence to suggest origination of the "alternative trilogy" idea in a contemporary review of *The Orphan* by Clive Barnes.

6 This particular strategy of juxtaposition also repeats itself in virtually invariable form in the epigraphs to published versions of a number of Rabe's plays:

a parable translated from an Asiatic language is paired with an apothegm from one of the great all-time losers of America, Sonny Liston.

7 Indeed, in testament to the conviction we are repeatedly driven to in Rabe of the unending reciprocity of art and life, one can only marvel at the casting of the initial production of such a play with a virtual who's who of "hot" young aspiring stars renowned for their laid-back, "cool" style of performance: William Hurt, Harvey Keitel, Christopher Walken, Judith Ivey, Sigourney Weaver.

8 Albeit, as Rabe would have it in an afterword, by quite eccentric coincidence.

## POETS AFTER OUR WAR

1 As recently noted by Lorrie Smith, others that "remain largely ignored" (14) include McAvoy Layne's *How Audie Murphy Died in Vietnam* (1973), Bryan Alec Floyd's *The Long War Dead: An Epiphany* (1976), Gerald McCarthy's *War Story* (1977), and Perry Oldham's *Vinh Long* (1976). For representative surveys of the work of additional figures, see selections from Jan Barry, D. F. Brown, Horace Coleman, and Basil Paquet included in Ehrhart's *Unaccustomed Mercy* and from R. S. Carlson in *Genre*. For a detailed account of early veterans' publishing enterprises in poetry and fiction, see also Caroline Slocock, "Winning Hearts and Minds: The First Casualty Press."

2 As will be noted in an ensuing discussion of Michael Herr, a turn toward mixed-media expression has been one of the strongest impulses of Vietnam writers in their generation. In Herr's case it will involve important work on the films *Apocalypse Now* and *Full Metal Jacket* and on the text for *The Big Room*, a collection of paintings, by the artist Guy Peellaert, on the role of Las Vegas in American history and myth. Herr's cohort, the legendary Tim Page, has supplied the narration to a collection of his own photographs of the war entitled appropriately, in the several senses that might be construed, *Tim Page's Nam*. More recently, he has also produced a second volume of postwar photographs and accompanying text entitled *Ten Years After: Vietnam Today*. The memoirist-novelist Ron Kovic has written an essay introduction to a compelling collection of combat photographs by Dick Durrance entitled *Where War Lives*. The novelist Robert Stone has written the narrative for *Images of War*, a major study of the war as a medium of photographic documentary, in an important series produced by the Boston Publishing Company.

3 Balaban teaches at Penn State University. Ehrhart has taught at the Germantown Friends School, a distinguished Quaker institution. Huddle currently teaches at the University of Vermont, Komunyakaa at Indiana University, McDonald at Texas Tech University, and Weigl, after an extended period at Old Dominion University, also at Penn State.

4 It should be noted additionally here that Ehrhart's career as a Vietnam author

in his generation will always be of singular significance also in ways for which conventional criticism will never provide an adequate account. Specifically, one must note his championing of a "Vietnam" literature itself when there was virtually no one, so it seemed, in the United States who possibly cared to read it or hear about it. Likewise, one must acknowledge his ongoing support of fellow Vietnam writers whose work often benefited by the war's eventual reemergence as an object of popular fascination; of other poets who went on, for instance, to win the Lamont and Yale Prizes; and other novelists, memoirists, and cultural journalists who went on to win the Pulitzer Prize and the National Book Award. In sum, amidst the remarkable achievements of writing after our war, Ehrhart continues to deserve recognition, perhaps more than any other, as the Vietnam author in his generation who in fact made the idea of such a thing possible in the first place.

5 For provocative insights into the achievement of "voice" in Ehrhart's work in a discussion which couples it with that of Balaban and Weigl, along with a number of major writers of fiction from the generation of the war, see the chapter entitled "Vietnam: The American Ronin" in Michael Stephens's *The Dramaturgy of Style*.

6 All of Huddle's war sonnets discussed here, along with others, have been subsequently collected under the subtitle "Tour of Duty" in his second book of poetry, entitled *Stopping by Home*; and, in something of a recapitulation of the structure of *Paper Boy*, they are now combined with "domestic" sections of gathered individual poems of youth and elegiac memory entitled "Album," "Stopping by Home," and "Things I Know, Things I Don't."

7 The genius of such a figure in Vietnam writing, the same Shakespearean imaging of Vietnam in a history born of the deepest imaginings of American and Western cultural myth, can also be seen, as will be presently noted, in Frances Fitzgerald's similar invocations of *The Tempest* in *Fire in the Lake*. A chapter devoted, as I will observe, to the increasing resemblance of the American enterprise to previous colonialisms she calls "Prospero, Caliban, Ariel." Another, on the increasingly autocratic and brutal attempts of American proconsuls to bend the Vietnamese to their will she entitles, simply, "Prospero." To an ensuing one, entitled "Guerrillas," on the responses of supposed GVN minions "to this rage directed against them and to the destruction of their country by the Americans," she attaches a brilliantly selected epigraph from Shakespeare's play in which the last speaker is, of course, Caliban himself. "You taught me language," he says, "and my profit on't/Is, I know how to curse. The red plague rid you/For learning me your language!" (379).

8 One must also note here the titular honoring of the collection of stories by McDonald's Texan contemporary, Allen Wier. Like the poems in the section of the text introduced here, the latter comprise a similarly complex and moving meditation on history and family rooted deeply in the values of traditional life in the Southwest.

9 This sense of poetic growth and acknowledgment of poetic provenance, one should mention moreover, has been signaled not only in an impressive personal poetic canon but also in Weigl's work in editions of poetry and in collections of critical writing about poetry devoted to contemporaries including one old soldier in the quest for poetic sense making, James Dickey, and a younger one, Dave Smith. See his edited volumes, *The Imagination as Glory: The Poetry of James Dickey* and *The Giver of Morning: The Poetry of Dave Smith*.

## THE LITERATURE OF WITNESS

1 Although I wrote this discussion of *Winners and Losers* prior to reading Susan Jeffords's *The Remasculinization of America*, I would wish to note my concurrence with that writer's view of my earlier evaluation of *Winners and Losers* in *American Literature and the Experience of Vietnam* as subscribing to an interpretive poetics that, particularly in Emerson's case, severely limited my understanding of her revisionary project.

2 For a recent parallel study of the American conduct of the war written as specific analysis of the various discourses of techno-military "war management," see James William Gibson, *The Perfect War*. As Bruce Franklin argues in a review essay on that text, Gibson shows that the "managers of technowar" could of necessity, like Fitzgerald's sundry mission functionaries, only see "the foreign 'Other' merely as an inferior, primitive, underdeveloped version of their own war machine" (426). A quite original discussion on a related point, the unique problems of "technical" language attached to writing experience-based fiction about the war, is also Owen Gilman's "Vietnam Fiction and the Paradoxical Problem of Nomenclature" in *Search and Clear*. For personally helping to clarify my own understanding of Fitzgerald's particular critique of language here, and of the structure of analysis informing the work as a whole, I am also indebted to a student of mine in a recent seminar, Dan Peightel.

3 Contemporary criticism is virtually unanimous on an assignment of the work's genius to this extraordinary conflation of the "worlds" of Vietnam and Vietnam-era America in a single, endlessly self-elaborating continuum of violence and dread. Thomas Myers writes, for instance, "Stone achieves his horrible vision of cultural shift by tracing how a historical narrative such as the Vietnam war inflicts not only its substance but its tone and style on its authors and readers. The return home of Converse and Hicks is not the beginning of recovery from a terrible historical moment but a new encounter with its domestic variant, which is presented as a larger version of the affliction" (*Walking Point*, 199). See also Maureen Karaguezian, "Irony in Robert Stone's *Dog Soldiers*," and Frank W. Shelton, "Robert Stone's *Dog Soldiers*: Vietnam Comes Home to America."

4 To put the idea in the structural context of other well-known Vietnam narra-

tives in particular, this is to say that *Dispatches* as text of Vietnam witness may be said to embrace at once the perspectives of classic experience-based texts of the war—*A Rumor of War*, for instance, or *If I Die in a Combat Zone*, or *Born on the Fourth of July*—with combat participants become conscious mythic interpreters, as well as those of classic texts of imagination—William Eastlake's *The Bamboo Bed*, for instance, or Norman Mailer's *Why Are We in Vietnam?*—which in their mythic resourcefulness create an "experience" of Vietnam as true as any that ever existed in fact. Indeed, like the "literary" texts of creative dialectic it most closely resembles in this respect, Larry Heinemann's *Paco's Story*, for instance, or Tim O'Brien's *Going After Cacciato* and *The Things They Carried*, it simply makes explicit what is often in these other works implicit, the ideas of "witness" and "responsibility," for both writer and reader alike, as *always* matters ultimately of the shared "experience" of national culture.

5 Major critical discussions of *Dispatches* have from the outset centered rightly on the concept of "authorship" itself as constituted subject in the text. For discussions of the work as the account of Herr's attempt to position himself between the claims of "fact" and "fiction" see John Hellman's "The New Journalism and Vietnam" (revised and included in *Fables of Fact*) and his subsequent analysis in *American Myth and the Legacy of Vietnam*. In my own earlier book, I also noted Herr's primary identification as "subject" in the text of his own role as "public artificer." Enlarging on this concept, and in a way akin to the Heisenbergian analogy I pose below, Thomas Myers in his more recent and comprehensive analysis calls Herr "the historian as self-reflexive agent within his data." And he too begins by acknowledging Herr's connection with the complex strategies of the New Journalism. "Herr attempts," he writes, imaging Hellman's idea of the creative odyssey, "to discover within the materials of individual consciousness a lexicon and syntax with enough originality and power to do battle with those of the master narrative" (*Walking Point*, 148). He also, however, significantly locates the enterprise in a deeply American belief, especially characteristic, he notes, of the great American romantics, in the "organic power of the image and the word. . . . Herr reads his book of nature," Myers writes, "only to rewrite it as an individual spirit of history, as both complicating and completing artificer" (*Walking Point*, 149).

6 Text has been transcribed from the film.

7 In talking here about writing as intertextualizing activity in its relation to film and later to painting, I will obviously be required to address the latter as aesthetic texts. What I do want to disclaim from the outset is any specific critical expertise in these media beyond the discussion thus defined.

8 A similar confrontation, it should be added, and in just these symbolic terms, creates a major scene of surrealistic crisis in the novel. And, as a kind of telling true-life index of the work of literature and cultural revision, it is probably worth noting as well that virtually all the publicity materials for *Full Metal Jacket* featured exactly such a helmet with exactly such inscriptions—and some

machine-gun rounds in full metal jacket tucked into the helmet band for good measure — as master advertising logo.

9 Herr's multigeneric *Walter Winchell* (1990) is similarly provocative. It was published too recently for extended discussion here. As the author's preface reveals, however, the work continues to explore many of the creative concerns with issues of textuality and authority that have distinguished his career from the outset. "Even though *Walter Winchell* is based on the life of a real man and often uses his actual words," Herr writes, "it's a fiction, and it's in prose. So it must be a prose fiction. You could call it a screenplay that's typed like a novel, that reads like a novel but plays like a movie. Maybe it's a completely new form, or a wrinkle on an old form, or a mongrel. Maybe it's just a novel with a camera in it. Personally, my most ambitious claims for it are as an entertainment in the tradition of the Hollywood biopic, with the undertones of history spreading beneath the jokes in various bitter shades of dark" (v).

## CODA

1 As Thomas Myers has revealed, the works stand importantly together, in fact, as two of our most significant recent meditations on the problems of historical sense-making in postwar Vietnam narrative. Although my critical focus is more heavily oriented than his toward theoretical issues of language and meaning, my discussion throughout reveals its debts to his own quite original pairing of the texts in the chapter from *Walking Point* entitled "Shades of Retrieval."

2 Donald Ringnalda rightly connects this image, I believe, with the related one, from David Rabe's *Sticks and Bones*, of the "Vietnam War home movie" David tries to show his family in which he quite literally sees the remembered horror of the war while they, as well as the theater audience, see a screen "filled with flickering shades of green" on which there appears, in Harriet's own account, simply "nothing" (Rabe, 160; Ringnalda, "Chlorophyll Overdose," 125). For a discussion of *Meditations in Green* as a major text in the literature of homecoming, see also William J. Searle, "Walking Wounded: Vietnam Novels of Return," in Searle's *Search and Clear*.

# BIBLIOGRAPHY

Anisfield, Nancy. "Words and Fragments: Narrative Style in Vietnam War Novels." In *Search and Clear*, edited by William J. Searle, 56–61. Bowling Green, Ohio: Bowling Green State University Popular Press, 1988.

Asahina, Robert. "The Basic Training of American Playwrights: Theater and the Vietnam War." *Theater* 9, no. 2 (1978): 30–37.

Baker, Houston A. *Long Black Song: Essays in Black American Literature and Culture*. Charlottesville: University of Virginia Press, 1972.

Baker, Mark. *Nam: The Vietnam War in the Words of the Soldiers Who Fought There*. New York: Morrow, 1981.

Balaban, John. *After Our War*. Pittsburgh: University of Pittsburgh Press, 1974.

——. *Blue Mountain*. Greensboro, N.C.: Unicorn Press, 1982.

——, trans. and ed. *Ca Dao Vietnam: A Bilingual Anthology of Vietnamese Folk Poetry*. Greensboro, N.C.: Unicorn Press, 1980.

——. *Coming Down Again*. New York: Harcourt Brace Jovanovich, 1985.

——. *The Hawk's Tale*. San Diego: Harcourt Brace Jovanovich, 1988.

——. "Words for My Daughter." *Harper's Magazine*, January 1989, 42.

Balaban, John, with Geoffrey Clifford. *Vietnam: The Land We Never Knew*. San Francisco: Chronicle Books, 1989.

Barnes, Clive. "Rabe's *The Orphan* Arrives." *New York Times*, 19 April 1973, L+, 51.

Bates, Milton J. "Tim O'Brien's Myth of Courage." *Modern Fiction Studies* 33 (1987): 263–79.

Beidler, Philip D. *American Literature and the Experience of Vietnam*. Athens: University of Georgia Press, 1982.

Bell, Madison Smartt. *Soldier's Joy*. New York: Ticknor and Fields, 1989.

Bell, Pearl K. "Writing About Vietnam." *Commentary*, October 1978, 74–77.

Bellow, Saul. *Herzog*. New York: Viking Press, 1964.

Berry, D. C. *saigon cemetery*. Athens: University of Georgia Press, 1972.

Bloom, Harold. *Agon*. New York: Oxford University Press, 1982.

——. *Kabbalah and Criticism*. New York: Seabury Press, 1975.

Bonetti, Kay. "An Interview with Robert Stone." *Missouri Review* 6, no. 1 (1982): 89–115.

Brinkmeyer, Robert H. "Finding One's History: Bobbie Ann Mason and Contemporary Southern Literature." *Southern Literary Journal* 19, no. 2 (1987): 22–33.

Broyles, William, Jr. "Why Men Love War." *Esquire* 102 (November 1984): 55–58, 61–62, 65.

——. *Brothers in Arms*. New York: Knopf, 1986.

Bryan, C. D. B. "Barely Suppressed Screams: Getting a Bead on Vietnam Literature." *Harper's Magazine* 268 (June 1984): 67–72.

——. *Friendly Fire*. New York: G. P. Putnam's Sons, 1976.

Bunting, Josiah. *The Lionheads*. New York: George Braziller, 1972.

Butler, Robert Olen. *The Alleys of Eden*. New York: Horizon Press, 1981.

——. *Countrymen of Bones*. New York: Horizon Press, 1983.

——. *The Deuce*. New York: Simon and Schuster, 1989.

——. *On Distant Ground*. New York: Knopf, 1985.

——. *Sun Dogs*. New York: Horizon Press, 1982.

——. *Wabash*. New York: Knopf, 1987.

Campbell, Joseph. *The Power of Myth*. New York: Doubleday, 1988.

Caputo, Philip. *Del Corso's Gallery*. New York: Holt, Rinehart and Winston, 1983.

——. *Horn of Africa*. New York: Holt, Rinehart and Winston, 1980.

——. *Indian Country*. New York: Bantam, 1987.

——. *A Rumor of War*. New York: Holt, Rinehart and Winston, 1977.

Carlson, R. S. Excerpts from *Was That Someplace You Were? Selected Poems 1968–1987*. *Genre* 21, no. 4 (Winter 1988): 553–77.

Casey, Michael. *Obscenities*. New Haven: Yale University Press, 1972.

Chaillet, Jean-Paul, and Elizabeth Vincent. *Francis Ford Coppola*. New York: St. Martin's Press, 1985.

Christie, N. Bradley. "David Rabe's Theater of War and Remembering." In *Search and Clear*, edited by William J. Searle, 105–15. Bowling Green, Ohio: Bowling Green State University Popular Press, 1988.

Cobley, Evelyn. "Narrating the Facts of War: New Journalism in Herr's *Dispatches* and Documentary Realism in First World War Novels." *Journal of Narrative Technique* 16, no. 2 (1986): 97–116.

Cohen, Hennig, ed. *Selected Poems of Herman Melville*. Carbondale: Southern Illinois University Press, 1968.

Conroy, Pat. *The Lords of Discipline*. Boston: Houghton Mifflin, 1980.

Cooper, Pamela. "David Rabe's *Sticks and Bones:* The Adventures of Ozzie and Harriet." *Modern Drama* 29 (1986): 613–25.

Couser, G. Thomas. "*Going After Cacciato:* The Romance and the Real War." *Journal of Narrative Technique* 13, no. 1 (1983): 1–10.

Cowley, Malcolm. *Exile's Return*. Rev. ed. New York: Viking Press, 1951.

Cronin, Cornelius A. "From the DMZ to No Man's Land: Philip Caputo's *A Rumor of War* and Its Antecedents." In *Search and Clear*, edited by William J. Searle, 74–86. Bowling Green, Ohio: Bowling Green State University Popular Press, 1988.

——. "Historical Background to Larry Heinemann's *Close Quarters*." *Critique: Studies in Modern Fiction* 24 (1983): 119–30.

Currey, Richard. *Fatal Light*. New York: E. P. Dutton/Seymour Lawrence, 1988.

Del Vecchio, John. *For the Sake of All Living Things.* New York: Bantam Books, 1990.

———. *The 13th Valley.* New York: Bantam Books, 1982.

Demastes, William W. *Beyond Naturalism: A New Realism in American Theatre.* New York: Greenwood Press, 1988.

Dickey, James. Introduction to *Selected Poems of Edwin Arlington Robinson,* edited by Morton Dauwen Zabel. New York: Macmillan Company, 1965.

Didion, Joan. *The White Album.* New York: Pocket Books, 1979.

Duncan, David Douglas. *War Without Heroes.* New York: Harper and Row, 1970.

Durden, Charles. *No Bugles, No Drums.* New York: Viking Press, 1976.

Durrance, Dick. *Where War Lives.* With introductory essay by Ron Kovic. New York: Farrar, Straus and Giroux, 1988.

Eastlake, William. *The Bamboo Bed.* New York: Simon and Schuster, 1969.

Egendorf, Arthur. *Healing from the War.* Boston: Houghton Mifflin, 1985.

Ehrhart, W. D. *Going Back: An Ex-Marine Returns to Vietnam.* Jefferson, N.C.: McFarland, 1987.

———. *Passing Time.* New York: Avon Books, 1986.

———. *To Those Who Have Gone Home Tired.* New York: Thunder's Mouth Press, 1984.

———. *Vietnam-Perkasie: A Memoir.* Jefferson, N.C.: McFarland, 1983.

———, ed. *Carrying the Darkness: American Indochina—The Poetry of the Vietnam War.* New York: Avon Books, 1985.

———, ed. *Unaccustomed Mercy: Soldier-Poets of the Vietnam War.* Lubbock: Texas Tech University Press, 1989.

Ehrhart, W. D., and Jan Berry, eds. *Demilitarized Zones: Veterans After Vietnam.* Perkasie, Pa.: East River Anthology, 1976.

Emerson, Gloria. *Some American Men.* New York: Simon and Schuster, 1985.

———. *Winners and Losers.* New York: Harcourt Brace Jovanovich, 1976.

Emerson, Ralph Waldo. *Nature.* In *Selections from Ralph Waldo Emerson,* edited by Stephen E. Whicher. Cambridge, Mass.: Riverside Press, 1957.

Esslin, Martin. *The Peopled Wound: The Work of Harold Pinter.* Garden City, N.Y.: Doubleday, 1970.

Faulkner, William. *Absalom! Absalom!* New York: Modern Library, 1951.

———. *The Sound and the Fury.* New York: Vintage Books, 1956.

Ferrandino, Joseph. *Firefight.* New York: Soho Press, 1987.

Fitzgerald, Frances. *America Revised.* Boston: Atlantic Monthly Press, 1979.

———. *Cities on a Hill.* New York: Simon and Schuster, 1986.

———. *Fire in the Lake: The Vietnamese and the Americans in Vietnam.* New York: Random House, 1972.

Floyd, Bryan Alec. *The Long War Dead: An Epiphany.* New York: Avon, 1976.

Franklin, H. Bruce. "How American Management Won the War in Vietnam." *American Quarterly* 40 (1988): 422–27.

Freedman, Richard. "A Separate Peace." *New York Times Book Review*, 12 February 1978, 1, 21.

Fuller, Jack. *Fragments*. New York: Morrow, 1984.

Fussell, Paul. *The Great War and Modern Memory*. New York: Oxford University Press, 1975.

Garson, Barbara. *Macbird*. Berkeley, Calif.: Grassy Knoll Press, 1966.

Gibson, James William. *The Perfect War: Technowar in Vietnam*. New York: Atlantic Monthly Press, 1986.

Gilman, Owen. "Vietnam Fiction and the Paradoxical Problem of Nomenclature." In *Search and Clear*, edited by William J. Searle, 62–73. Bowling Green, Ohio: Bowling Green State University Popular Press, 1988.

——, and Lorrie Smith, eds. *America Rediscovered*. New York: Garland Publishing, 1990.

Glasser, Ronald J. *Another War, Another Peace*. New York: Summit Books, 1985.

——. *365 Days*. New York: George Braziller, 1971.

Gotera, Vincente F. "Bringing Vietnam Home: Bruce Weigl's *The Monkey Wars*." In *Search and Clear*, edited by William J. Searle, 160–69. Bowling Green, Ohio: Bowling Green State University Popular Press, 1988.

Graff, Gerald. *Professing Literature*. Chicago: University of Chicago Press, 1987.

Groom, Winston. *As Summers Die*. New York: Summit Books, 1980.

——. *Better Times Than These*. New York: Summit Books, 1978.

——. *Forrest Gump*. Garden City, N.Y.: Doubleday, 1986.

——. *Gone the Sun*. New York: Doubleday, 1988.

——. *Only*. New York: G. P. Putnam's Sons, 1984.

Groom, Winston, with Duncan Spencer. *Conversations with the Enemy*. New York: G. P. Putnam's Sons, 1983.

Halberstam, David. *The Best and the Brightest*. New York: Bantam Books, 1977.

——. *The Breaks of the Game*. New York: Knopf, 1981.

——. *One Very Hot Day*. Boston: Houghton Mifflin, 1977.

——. *The Reckoning*. New York: Morrow, 1986.

Hannah, Barry. *Airships*. New York: Knopf, 1978.

——. *Ray*. New York: Knopf, 1980.

——. *The Tennis Handsome*. New York: Charles Scribner's Sons, 1987.

Hasford, Gustav. *The Phantom Blooper*. New York: Bantam Books, 1990.

——. *The Short-Timers*. New York: Harper and Row, 1979.

Heinemann, Larry. *Close Quarters*. New York: Farrar, Straus and Giroux, 1974.

——. *Paco's Story*. New York: Farrar, Straus and Giroux, 1986.

Hellman, John. *American Myth and the Legacy of Vietnam*. New York: Columbia University Press, 1986.

——. *Fables of Fact*. Urbana: University of Illinois Press, 1981.

——. "The New Journalism and Vietnam: Memory as Structure in Michael Herr's *Dispatches*." *South Atlantic Quarterly* 79, no. 2 (1980): 141–51.

Hemingway, Ernest. *The Complete Short Stories of Ernest Hemingway.* New York: Charles Scribner's Sons, 1987.

———. *The Sun Also Rises.* New York: Charles Scribner's Sons, 1954.

Herlihy, James Leo. *Midnight Cowboy.* New York: Simon and Schuster, 1965.

Herr, Michael. *Dispatches.* New York: Knopf, 1977.

———. *Walter Winchell.* New York: Knopf, 1990.

Herr, Michael, with Francis Ford Coppola and John Milius. Narration for *Apocalypse Now.* Zoetrope Studios, 1979.

Herr, Michael, with Stanley Kubrick and Gustav Hasford. *Full Metal Jacket.* New York: Knopf, 1987.

Herr, Michael, with Guy Peellaert. *The Big Room.* New York: Summit Books, 1986.

Herzog, Tobey C. "*Going After Cacciato:* The Soldier-Author-Character Seeking Control." *Critique: Studies in Modern Fiction* 24 (1983): 88–96.

Homan, Sidney. "American Playwrights in the 1970s: Rabe and Shepard." *Critical Quarterly* 24, no. 1 (1982): 73–82.

Huddle, David. "Cousin," "Vermont," and "Words." In *Carrying the Darkness: American Indochina—The Poetry of the Vietnam War*, edited by W. D. Ehrhart. New York: Avon Books, 1985.

———. *A Dream with No Stump Roots in It.* Columbia: University of Missouri Press, 1975.

———. *The High Spirits.* Boston: David R. Godine, 1988.

———. *Only the Little Bone.* Boston: David R. Godine, 1986.

———. *Paper Boy.* Pittsburgh: University of Pittsburgh Press, 1979.

———. *Stopping by Home.* Salt Lake City: Peregrine Smith Books, 1988.

Hurrel, Barbara. "American Self-Image in David Rabe's Vietnam Trilogy." *Journal of American Culture* 4 (1981): 95–107.

Jameson, Fredric. "Postmodernism, or the Cultural Logic of Late Capitalism." *New Left Review* 146 (1984): 53–92.

Jeffords, Susan. *The Remasculinization of America: Gender and the Vietnam War.* Bloomington: Indiana University Press, 1989.

Jones, James. *Some Came Running.* New York: Charles Scribner's Sons, 1957.

Just, Ward. *The American Blues.* New York: Viking Press, 1984.

———. *The Congressman Who Loved Flaubert and Other Washington Stories.* Boston: Little, Brown, 1973.

———. *Honor, Power, Riches, Fame and the Love of Women.* New York: Dutton, 1979.

———. *Jack Gance.* Boston: Houghton Mifflin, 1989.

———. *Military Men.* New York: Knopf, 1970.

———. *Nicholson at Large.* Boston: Atlantic Monthly Press, 1975.

———. *Stringer.* Boston: Little, Brown, 1974.

———. *To What End.* Boston: Houghton Mifflin, 1968.

Kael, Pauline. "A Wounded Apparition." *New Yorker,* 21 August 1989, 76–79.

Karaguezian, Maureen. "Irony in Robert Stone's *Dog Soldiers.*" *Critique: Studies in Modern Fiction* 24 (1983): 65–73.

Karnow, Stanley. *Vietnam: A History.* New York: Viking Press, 1983.

Kennedy, Randall. Review of *Horn of Africa. New Republic* 183 (25 October 1980): 46–48.

Klinkowitz, Jerome. "Writing Under Fire: Postmodern Fiction and the Vietnam War." In *Postmodern Fiction: A Bio-Bibliographical Guide,* edited by Larry McCaffrey, 79–92. New York: Greenwood Press, 1986.

Kollin, Philip C. *David Rabe: A Stage History and A Primary and Secondary Bibliography.* New York: Garland Publishing, 1988.

Komunyakaa, Yusef. "Somewhere Near Phu Bai," "Starlight Scope Myopia," "Tiger Lady," "The Dead at Quang Tri," "After the Fall of Saigon." In *Carrying the Darkness: American-Indochina—The Poetry of the Vietnam War,* edited by W. D. Ehrhart. New York: Avon Books, 1985.

——. *Copacetic.* Middletown, Conn.: Wesleyan University Press, 1984.

——. *Dien Cai Dau.* Middletown, Conn.: Wesleyan University Press, 1988.

——. *I Apologize for the Eyes in My Head.* Middletown, Conn.: Wesleyan University Press, 1986.

Kovic, Ron. *Around the World in Eight Days.* San Francisco: City Lights Books, 1984.

——. *Born on the Fourth of July.* New York: McGraw-Hill, 1976.

Laing, R. D. *The Politics of Experience.* New York: Ballantine Books, 1967.

Lawson, Jacqueline E. " 'She's a pretty woman . . . for a gook': The Misogyny of the Vietnam War." *Journal of American Culture* 12, no. 3 (Fall 1989): 55–65.

Layne, McAvoy. *How Audie Murphy Died in Vietnam.* Garden City, N.Y.: Anchor Books, 1973.

Lomperis, Timothy J. *Reading the Wind: The Literature of the Vietnam War.* Durham: Duke University Press, 1987.

Lowell, Robert. *Lord Weary's Castle* and *The Mills of the Kavanaughs.* New York: World Publishing Company, 1961.

Lowenfels, Walter, ed. *Where Is Vietnam?* Garden City, N.Y.: Doubleday/Anchor Books, 1967.

McCaffrey, Larry. "Interview with Tim O'Brien." *Chicago Review* 33, no. 2 (1982): 129–49.

McCarthy, Gerald. *War Story.* Trumansburg, N.Y.: The Crossing Press, 1977.

McDonald, Walter. *After the Noise of Saigon.* Amherst: University of Massachusetts Press, 1988.

——. *Burning the Fence.* Lubbock: Texas Tech Press, 1981.

——. *Caliban in Blue.* Lubbock: Texas Tech Press, 1976.

——. *The Flying Dutchman.* Columbus: Ohio State University Press, 1987.

——. *Night Landings.* New York: Harper and Row, 1989.

McInerny, Peter. "Straight and Secret History in Vietnam War Literature." *Contemporary Literature* 22, no. 2 (1981): 187–204.

McShane, Frank. *Into Eternity: The Life of James Jones*. Boston: Houghton Mifflin, 1985.

Mahoney, Tim. *Holloran's World War*. New York: Delacorte Press, 1985.

———. *We're Not Here*. New York: Dell Publishing, 1988.

Mailer, Norman. *An American Dream*. New York: Dial Press, 1965.

———. *Why Are We in Vietnam?* New York: G. P. Putnam's Sons, 1967.

Marcuse, Herbert. *One-Dimensional Man*. Boston: Beacon Books, 1964.

Marshall, Kathryn. *In the Combat Zone: An Oral History of American Women in Vietnam*. New York: Harper and Row, 1984.

Mason, Bobbie Ann. *In Country*. New York: Harper and Row, 1985.

———. *Shiloh and Other Stories*. New York: Harper and Row, 1982.

Melville, Herman. *Billy Budd, Sailor*. Edited by Harrison Hayford and Merton J. Sealts, Jr. Chicago: University of Chicago Press, 1962.

———. "Hawthorne and His Mosses." In *Melville: Pierre, Israel Potter, The Piazza Tales, The Confidence-Man, Uncollected Prose, Billy Budd, Sailor*. New York: The Library of America, 1984.

Meriwether, James B., and Michael Millgate, eds. *Lion in the Garden: Interviews with William Faulkner*. Lincoln: University of Nebraska Press, 1968.

Merritt, William E. *Where the Rivers Ran Backward*. Athens: University of Georgia Press, 1989.

Miller, Arthur. *All My Sons*. New York: Dramatists Play Service, 1947.

———. *Death of a Salesman*. New York: Viking Press, 1981.

Morrell, David. *First Blood*. Philadelphia: M. Evans/Lippincott, 1972.

Morris, Willie. *James Jones: A Friendship*. Garden City, N.Y.: Doubleday, 1978.

Myers, Thomas. "Dispatches from Ghost Country: The Vietnam Veteran in Recent American Fiction." *Genre* 21, no. 4 (Winter 1988): 409–28.

———. *Walking Point: American Narratives of Vietnam*. New York: Oxford University Press, 1988.

Nelson, Marie. "Two Consciences: A Reading of Tim O'Brien's Vietnam Trilogy." In *Third Force Psychology and the Study of Literature*, edited by Bernard J. Paris, 262–79. Rutherford, N.J.: Fairleigh Dickinson University Press, 1986.

Nichols, John. *American Blood*. New York: Ballantine Books, 1988.

Nietzsche, Friedrich. *Untimely Meditations*. Translated by R. J. Hollingdale. Cambridge: Cambridge University Press, 1983.

Norman, Michael. *These Good Men*. New York: Crown Publishers, 1990.

O'Brien, Tim. *Going After Cacciato*. New York: Delacorte Press/Seymour Lawrence, 1978.

———. *If I Die in a Combat Zone*. New York: Delacorte Press, 1973. Parenthetical references are to the Dell (1979) edition, which contains significant revisions.

———. *Northern Lights*. New York: Delacorte Press/Seymour Lawrence, 1975.

———. *The Nuclear Age*. New York: Knopf, 1985.

———. "Speaking of Courage." *Granta* 29 (Winter 1989): 135–54.

———. *The Things They Carried.* New York: Houghton Mifflin/Seymour Lawrence, 1990.

Oldham, Perry. *Vinh Long.* Meadows of Dan, Va.: Northwoods Press, 1976.

Page, Tim. *Ten Years After: Vietnam Today.* Hong Kong: Thames and Hudson, 1987.

———. *Tim Page's Nam.* New York: Knopf, 1983.

Palm, Edward F. "James Webb's *Fields of Fire:* The Melting-Pot Platoon Revisited." *Critique: Studies in Modern Fiction* 24 (1983): 105–18.

Pelfrey, William. *The Big V.* New York: Liveright, 1972.

Pettit, Michael. *American Light.* Athens: University of Georgia Press, 1984.

Phillips, Jayne Anne. *Machine Dreams.* New York: Dutton/Seymour Lawrence, 1984.

Pratt, John Clark. *The Laotian Fragments.* New York: Viking Press, 1974.

———. *Vietnam Voices.* New York: Penguin Books, 1984.

Proffitt, Nicholas. *The Embassy House.* New York: Bantam Books, 1986.

———. *Gardens of Stone.* New York: Carroll and Graf, 1983.

———. "Pete Bravado's War and Peace." *New York Times Book Review*, 21 May 1989, 7.

Pynchon, Thomas. *Gravity's Rainbow.* New York: Viking Press, 1973.

Rabe, David. *The Basic Training of Pavlo Hummel* and *Sticks and Bones.* New York: Penguin Books, 1978.

———. *Goose and Tomtom.* New York: Grove Press, 1986.

———. *Hurlyburly.* New York: Grove Press, 1985.

———. *In the Boom Boom Room.* New York: Grove Press, 1986.

———. *The Orphan.* New York: Samuel French, 1975.

———. *Streamers.* New York: Knopf, 1977.

Ransom, John L. *Andersonville Diary.* Philadelphia: Douglass Brothers, 1883.

Raymond, Michael W. "Imagined Responses to Vietnam: Tim O'Brien's *Going After Cacciato.*" *Critique: Studies in Modern Fiction* 24 (1983): 97–104.

Ringnalda, Donald. "Chlorophyll Overdose: Stephen Wright's *Meditations in Green.*" *Western Humanities Review* 40, no. 2 (1986): 125–40.

———. "Fighting and Writing: America's Vietnam War Literature." *Journal of American Studies* 22, no. 1 (1988): 25–42.

Robinson, James A. "Soldier's Home: Images of Alienation in *Sticks and Bones.*" In *Search and Clear*, edited by William J. Searle, 136–46. Bowling Green, Ohio: Bowling Green State University Popular Press, 1988.

Rottmann, Larry, with Jan Barry and Basil T. Paquet, eds. *Winning Hearts and Minds: War Poems by Vietnam Veterans.* New York: McGraw-Hill, 1972.

Sack, John. *M.* New York: New American Library, 1966.

Sales, Roger. "Fathers & Fathers & Sons." *New York Review of Books*, 13 November 1975, 31–32.

Salisbury, Harrison E., ed. *Vietnam Reconsidered*. New York: Harper and Row, 1984.

Santoli, Al. *Everything We Had*. New York: Random House, 1981.

Schaeffer, Susan Fromberg. *Buffalo Afternoon*. New York: Knopf, 1989.

Schroeder, Eric James. "The Past and the Possible: Tim O'Brien's Dialectic of Memory and Imagination." In *Search and Clear*, edited by William J. Searle, 116–34. Bowling Green, Ohio: Bowling Green State University Popular Press, 1988.

———. "Two Interviews: Talks with Tim O'Brien and Robert Stone." *Modern Fiction Studies* 30, no. 1 (1984): 135–64.

Searle, William J. "Walking Wounded: Vietnam Novels of Return." In *Search and Clear*, edited by William J. Searle, 147–59. Bowling Green, Ohio: Bowling Green State University Popular Press, 1988.

———, ed. *Search and Clear: Critical Responses to Selected Literature and Films of the Vietnam War*. Bowling Green, Ohio: Bowling Green State University Popular Press, 1988.

Shakespeare, William. *Hamlet*. Edited by H. Jenkins. London: Methuen, 1982.

———. *Macbeth*. Edited by Kenneth Muir. London: Methuen, 1979.

———. *The Tempest*. Edited by Frank Kermode. London: Methuen, 1971.

Sheehan, Neil. *A Bright Shining Lie: John Paul Vann and America in Vietnam*. New York: Random House, 1988.

Shelton, Frank W. "Robert Stone's *Dog Soldiers*: Vietnam Comes Home to America." *Critique: Studies in Modern Fiction* 24 (1983): 74–81.

Slocock, Caroline. "Winning Hearts and Minds: The First Casualty Press." *Journal of American Studies* 16, no. 1 (1982): 107–17.

Smith, Lorrie. "A Sense-Making Perspective in Recent Poetry by Vietnam Veterans." *American Poetry Review* 51, no. 6 (November/December 1986): 13–18.

Spencer, Scott. "Times Square by Way of Saigon." *New York Times Book Review*, 3 September 1989, 10.

Stephens, Michael. *The Dramaturgy of Style: Voice in Short Fiction*. Carbondale and Edwardsville: Southern Illinois University Press, 1986.

Stone, Robert. *Children of Light*. New York: Knopf, 1986.

———. *Dog Soldiers*. Boston: Houghton Mifflin, 1973.

———. *A Flag for Sunrise*. New York: Knopf, 1981.

———. *A Hall of Mirrors*. Boston: Houghton Mifflin, 1967.

———. "Helping," *New Yorker*, 8 June 1987, 28–38, 41–45, 47.

———. "The Reason for Stories: Toward a Moral Fiction." *Harper's*, June 1988, 71–76.

———. "We Are Not Excused." In *Paths of Resistance: The Art and Craft of the Political Novel*. Edited by William Zinsser. Boston: Houghton Mifflin, 1989.

Stone, Robert, with Julene Fischer and the Picture Staff of Boston Publishing Company. *Images of War*. Boston: Boston Publishing Company, 1986.

Strouse, Jean. "Heebiejeebieville Express." *New York Times Book Review*, 16 March 1986, 1, 24–25.

Styron, William. *Sophie's Choice*. New York: Random House, 1979.

Tal, Kalí. "The Mind at War: Images of Women in Vietnam Novels by Combat Veterans." *Contemporary Literature* 31, no. 1 (Spring 1990): 76–96.

Tate, Donald. *Bravo Burning*. New York: Charles Scribner's Sons, 1986.

Taylor, Gordon O. "American Personal Narrative of the War in Vietnam." *American Literature* 52 (1980): 294–308.

——. "Cacciato's Grassy Hill." *Genre* 21, no. 4 (Winter 1988): 393–407.

Terry, Wallace. *Bloods: An Oral History of the Vietnam War by Black Veterans*. New York: Random House, 1984.

Thompson, Hunter S., with Ralph Steadman. *Fear and Loathing in Las Vegas*. New York: Popular Library, 1971.

Timberg, Robert. "The Private War of Ollie and Jim." *Esquire*, March 1988, 144–48, 150, 152, 154–55.

Truscott, Lucian K., IV. *Dress Gray*. Garden City, N.Y.: Doubleday and Company, 1979.

Vannatta, Dennis. "Theme and Structure in Tim O'Brien's *Going After Cacciato*." *Modern Fiction Studies* 28, no. 2 (1982): 242–46.

Vonnegut, Kurt, Jr. *Mother Night*. New York: Harper and Row, 1966.

——. "*Something Happened*." *New York Times Book Review*, 6 October 1974, 1–2.

Webb, James. *A Country Such as This*. Garden City, N.Y.: Doubleday, 1983.

——. *Fields of Fire*. Englewood Cliffs, N.J.: Prentice-Hall, 1978.

——. *A Sense of Honor*. Englewood Cliffs, N.J.: Prentice-Hall, 1981.

Weigl, Bruce. *Executioner*. Tucson, Ariz.: Ironwood Press, 1976.

——. *The Monkey Wars*. Athens: University of Georgia Press, 1985.

——. *A Romance*. Pittsburgh: University of Pittsburgh Press, 1979.

——. *A Sackful of Old Quarrels*. Cleveland: Cleveland State University Poetry Center, 1977.

——. *Song of Napalm*. New York: Atlantic Monthly Press, 1988.

——, ed. *The Giver of Morning: The Poetry of Dave Smith*. Birmingham, Ala.: Thunder City Press, 1982.

Weigl, Bruce, and T. R. Hummer, eds. *The Imagination as Glory: The Poetry of James Dickey*. Urbana: University of Illinois Press, 1984.

West, Nathaniel. *Day of the Locust*. New York: Random House, 1939.

Wheeler, John. *Touched with Fire: The Future of the Vietnam Generation*. New York: F. Watts, 1984.

Wier, Allen. *Things About to Disappear*. Baton Rouge: Louisiana State University Press, 1978.

Winn, David. *Gangland*. New York: Knopf, 1982.

Winthrop, John. *A Model of Christian Charity*. Edited by Samuel Eliot Morison. Old South Leaflets, no. 207. Boston: Old South Association.

Wittman, Sandra M. *Writing About Vietnam: A Bibliography of the Literature of the Vietnam Conflict.* Boston: G. K. Hall, 1989.

Wood, Michael. "A Novel of Lost Americans." *New York Times Book Review,* 18 October 1981, 1, 34.

Wright, Stephen. *M31: A Family Romance.* New York: Harmony Books, 1988.

———. *Meditations in Green.* New York: Charles Scribner's Sons, 1983.

Zins, Daniel L. "Imagining the Real: The Fiction of Tim O'Brien." *The Hollins Critic* 23, no. 3 (1986): 1–12.

# INDEX

*Adventures of Ozzie and Harriet, The,* 111–17

Altman, Robert: *Streamers* (film), 308 (n. 3)

Anisfield, Nancy, 306 (n. 6)

Asahina, Robert, 106

Asia Society, xii, 73, 74

Baker, Houston, 171

Baker, Mark: *Nam,* 2

Balaban, John, 4, 7, 55, 146, 147–57, 158, 170, 185, 192, 200, 309 (n. 3), 310 (n. 5); *After Our War,* 1, 147, 148–51; *Coming Down Again,* 147; *The Hawk's Tale,* 147; *Vietnam: The Land We Never Knew,* 147; *Words for My Daughter,* 147; *Ca Dao Vietnam,* 147, 150–51; *Blue Mountain,* 147, 151–55; *Remembering Heaven's Face,* 148

Banks, Russell, 200

Barnes, Clive, 308 (n. 5)

Barry, Jan, 146, 309 (n. 1)

Bates, Milton J., 12, 17, 19

Beale, Betty, xi

Beckett, Samuel: *Waiting for Godot,* 135

Beidler, Philip D., xi–xii, 107, 128, 151, 245, 272, 279, 301 (n. 2), 306 (n. 6), 308 (n. 2), 311 (n. 1), 312 (n. 5)

Bell, Madison Smartt: *Soldier's Joy,* 303–4 (n. 2)

Bell, Pearl K., 306 (n. 6)

Bellow, Saul: *Herzog,* 24

Berry, D. C.: *saigon cemetery,* 146

Berryman, John, 264

Black Americans: experience of Vietnam, 171

*Black Elk Speaks,* 98

Bloom, Harold, 302 (n. 2)

Bonetti, Kay, 259

Borges, Jorge Luis, 224, 304 (n. 4)

Brinkmeyer, Robert H., 303 (n. 2)

*Brothers in Arms,* 8

Brown, D. F., 309 (n. 1)

Browning, Robert: "Caliban Upon Setebos," 183–84

Broyles, William, 305 (n. 5)

Bryan, C. D. B., 65; *Friendly Fire,* 2

Bunting, Josiah, 303 (n. 1); *The Lion-heads,* 9

Butler, Robert Olen, 4, 7, 10, 52–63, 147, 307 (n. 12); *Countrymen of Bones,* 7, 10, 52, 56–57, 58–59; *Wabash,* 7, 10, 52, 56–57, 58–59; *The Deuce,* 7, 52, 55, 59–63; *The Alleys of Eden,* 7, 52–55, 58, 88; *On Distant Ground,* 7, 52–56, 58, 88; *Sun Dogs,* 52–55, 58, 88

Campbell, Joseph, 151

Caputo, Philip, 4, 6, 10, 20, 36–52, 58, 126; *A Rumor of War,* 2, 4, 6, 37, 39–42, 49, 81, 301 (n. 2), 312 (n. 4); *Horn of Africa,* 6, 10, 38, 42–45; *Indian Country,* 6, 18, 38, 48–52, 88, 307 (n. 12); *Del Corso's Gallery,* 6, 38, 42, 43, 45–48

Carlson, R. S., 309 (n. 1)

Casey, Michael: *Obscenities,* 146

Chaillet, Jean-Paul, 274

Chandler, Raymond, 275–76

Chopin, Kate: *The Awakening,* 258–64

Christie, N. Bradley, 104

Clifford, Geoffrey: *Vietnam: The Land We Never Knew,* 148

Cobley, Evelyn, 302 (n. 2)

Coleman, Horace, 309 (n. 1)

Coleridge, Samuel Taylor: "The Rime of the Ancient Mariner," 255

Conrad, Joseph, 39, 255, 307 (n. 11); *Heart of Darkness*, 42–45, 274–77, 280

Cooper, James Fenimore, 39, 42, 44–45

Cooper, Pamela, 111–12

Coppola, Francis Ford: *Apocalypse Now* (film), 264, 273–78

Couser, G. Thomas, 21, 306 (n. 6)

Cowley, Malcolm, 4

Crane, Stephen, 12, 39, 40, 42; "The Open Boat," 255

Cronin, Cornelius A., 39, 90, 307 (n. 10)

Crosby, Bing, 22

Cultural revision: literature as, xii–xiii, 2–3, 4, 5, 10, 20–21, 24, 29, 36, 38–39, 42, 43, 45, 52, 57, 59, 63–64, 67–69, 71, 74, 90, 97, 99–100, 103, 111–12, 116–17, 127, 133–34, 146, 147, 148, 150, 151, 153, 158, 161, 163–64, 171, 182, 183, 186–88, 191, 192, 193, 197, 200, 203, 204–5, 207–8, 209–10, 211–12, 214, 219, 221, 227, 237, 238, 249–50, 254, 262, 264, 266, 307 (n. 13), 311 (n. 1), 312 (n. 8)

Currey, Richard: *Fatal Light*, 10

Dante, 255

Del Vecchio, John: *The 13th Valley*, 10, 79, 303 (n. 1); *For the Sake of All Living Things*, 303 (n. 1)

Demastes, William W., 308 (n. 1)

Derrida, Jacques: *Glas*, 282

Dickey, James, 311 (n. 9)

Dickinson, Emily, 202, 255

Didion, Joan, 137, 140, 193, 259

Duncan, David Douglas, 47

Durden, Charles, 80; *No Bugles, No Drums*, 10

Durrance, Dick: *Where War Lives*, 309 (n. 2)

Eastlake, William: *The Bamboo Bed*, 208, 312 (n. 4)

Egendorf, Arthur: *Healing from the War*, 8

Ehrhart, W. D., 4, 146, 157–62, 170, 186, 205, 301 (n. 2), 309 (n. 3), 309–10 (n. 4), 310 (n. 5); "A Relative Thing," 145; *Carrying the Darkness*, 146; *Unaccustomed Mercy*, 146, 309 (n. 1); *Vietnam-Perkasie: A Memoir*, 157; *Going Back: An Ex-Marine Returns to Vietnam*, 157–58; *To Those Who Have Gone Home Tired*, 157–62; *Passing Time*, 158

Eliot, T. S., 148, 248, 255, 277

Ellison, Ralph: *Invisible Man*, 240

Emerson, Gloria, 5, 7, 208, 227, 237, 304 (n. 3); *Winners and Losers*, 2, 7, 208–14, 221, 301 (n. 1), 311 (n. 1); *Some American Men*, 7, 208, 214–21

Emerson, Ralph Waldo, 302 (n. 2); *Nature*, 288

Esslin, Martin, 122

Faulkner, William, xi; *The Sound and the Fury*, 84; *Absalom! Absalom!*, 164

Feminist criticism, 208, 227, 302 (n. 2), 311 (n. 1)

Ferrandino, Joseph: *Firefight*, 10

Fitzgerald, Frances, 5, 7, 55, 208, 221–37, 304 (n. 3); *Fire in the Lake*, 2, 7, 208, 217, 221–27, 301 (n. 1), 310 (n. 7), 311 (n. 2); *America Revised*, 7, 208, 227–33; *Cities on a Hill*, 7, 208, 233–37

Fitzgerald, F. Scott: *The Great Gatsby*, 286

Floyd, Brian Alec: *The Long War Dead*, 309 (n. 1)

Flynn, Sean, 279

Foster, Stephen, 132

Franklin, Bruce, 311 (n. 2)

Frazer, J. G., 277

Freedman, Richard, 20, 306 (n. 6)

Fromm, Erich, 12

Fussell, Paul, xii–xiii, 12

Fuller, Charles, 308 (n. 1)

Fuller, Jack: *Fragments*, 10

Garson, Barbara: *Macbird*, 118
Garwood, Robert, 79
Gibson, James William, 311 (n. 2)
Gilman, Jr., Owen W., 302 (n. 2), 311 (n. 2)
Ginsberg, Allen: "Wichita Vortex Sutra," 146
Gitelson, David, 155
Glasser, Ronald J.: *Another War, Another Peace*, 10; *365 Days*, 11
*Gomer Pyle, U.S.M.C.*, 106, 280
Gotera, Vincente, 191
Gothic fiction, 238
Graff, Gerald, 3
*Green Berets, The*, 275
Greene, Graham, 42–43, 255
Groom, Winston, 4, 10, 58, 79–90, 307 (n. 12); *As Summers Die*, 10, 79, 82–84, 87; *Forrest Gump*, 11, 79, 84–86, 87; *Conversations with the Enemy*, 79; *Only*, 79; *Gone the Sun*, 79, 81, 86–90; *Better Times Than These*, 79–82, 87, 88

Halberstam, David: *One Very Hot Day*, 9; *The Best and the Brightest*, 303 (n. 1); *The Breaks of the Game*, 303 (n. 1); *The Reckoning*, 303 (n. 1)
Hannah, Barry: *Airships*, 303 (n. 2); *Ray*, 303 (n. 2); *The Tennis Handsome*, 303 (n. 2)
Hard-boiled writing, 82–83, 134–35, 137, 275
Hasford, Gustav, 80; *The Short-Timers*, 10, 208, 278–79, 280–81, 303 (n. 1), 312 (n. 8); *The Phantom Blooper*, 303 (n. 1)
Hawthorne, Nathaniel, 56
Heinemann, Larry, 4, 10, 58, 80, 90–103, 307 (n. 12); *Paco's Story*, 1, 9, 11, 90, 97–103, 301 (nn. 1, 2), 307 (n. 12), 312 (n. 4); *Close Quarters*, 1, 10, 81, 90–98, 307 (n. 12)
Heller, Joseph, 239
Hellman, John, 6, 275, 301 (n. 2), 312 (n. 5)

Hemingway, Ernest, 18–19, 38–39, 40, 42, 45–46, 48, 54, 158, 171, 248; *The Sun Also Rises*, 19; "Soldier's Home," 113; *The Old Man and the Sea*, 255
Henley, Beth, 308 (n. 1)
Herlihy, James Leo: *Midnight Cowboy*, 52, 59
Herr, Michael, 5, 6, 7–8, 42, 237, 246, 255, 264–87, 304 (n. 3), 308 (n. 3), 309 (n. 2); *Dispatches*, 2, 8, 46, 54, 201–4, 208, 216, 249, 264–73, 274, 275, 276–78, 279–80, 297, 301 (nn. 1, 2), 311–12 (n. 4), 312 (n. 5); *Full Metal Jacket* (screenplay), 8, 264, 273, 278–81, 303 (n. 1), 309 (n. 2); *Apocalypse Now* (screenplay), 8, 264, 273–78, 309 (n. 2); *The Big Room*, 8, 264, 281–87, 309 (n. 2); *Walter Winchell*, 8, 264, 313 (n. 9)
Herzog, Tobey C., 306 (n. 6)
Historical fiction, 10–11, 52, 56–57, 74, 76
Homan, Sidney, 308 (n. 2)
Hope, Bob, 22
Hopper, Dennis, 274
Huddle, David, 4, 146, 162–71, 183, 309 (n. 3), 310 (n. 6); *A Dream with No Stump Roots in It*, 162; *The High Spirits*, 162; *Only the Little Bone*, 162; *Paper Boy*, 164–70, 310 (n. 6); *Stopping By Home*, 310 (n. 6)
Hurrel, Barbara, 308 (n. 2)
Hurt, William, 309 (n. 7)
*Honeymooners, The*, 125

*Images of War*, 309 (n. 2)
Ivey, Judith, 309 (n. 7)

Jameson, Fredric, 266
Jeffords, Susan, 302 (n. 2), 311 (n. 1)
John, Elton, 148
Joyce, James: *Ulysses*, 59, 62
Jones, James, 80, 83; *Some Came Running*, 83
Jung, C. J., 277

Just, Ward, 5, 303 (n. 1), 304 (n. 3); *The Congressman Who Loved Flaubert*, 10; *Jack Gance*, 10; *Nicholson at Large*, 10; *The American Blues*, 10, 288, 289–97, 299, 300, 313 (n. 1); *Honor, Power, Riches, Fame and the Love of Women*, 10–11; *Military Men*, 303 (n. 1); *Stringer*, 303 (n. 1); *To What End*, 303 (n. 1)

Kael, Pauline, 308 (n. 3)
Kafka, Franz, 255
Karaguezian, Maureen, 311 (n. 3)
Karnow, Stanley: *Vietnam: A History*, 157
Keitel, Harvey, 309 (n. 7)
Kennedy, Randall, 307 (n. 11)
Kerouac, Jack: *On the Road*, 244
Kesey, Ken, 246, 248
Klinkowitz, Jerome, 302 (n. 2)
Kollin, Philip C., 117, 118, 121, 133, 134, 308 (nn. 2–5)
Komunyakaa, Yusef, 4, 7, 146, 171–82, 183, 192, 301 (n. 2), 309 (n. 3); *I Apologize for the Eyes in My Head*, 171, 174–75; *Dien Cai Dau*, 171, 177–82; *Copacetic*, 171–74
Kovic, Ron, 39, 126, 309 (n. 2); *Born on the Fourth of July*, 2, 37, 81, 108, 300, 312 (n. 4); *Around the World in Eight Days*, 11
Kubrick, Stanley: *Full Metal Jacket* (film), 8, 264, 273, 278–81, 303 (n. 1), 312–13 (n. 8)
Kyd, Thomas, 148

Labinski, Leland, vii
Laing, R. D., 57–58
Lamour, Dorothy, 22
Lawson, Jacqueline, 302 (n. 2)
Layne, McAvoy: *How Audie Murphy Died in Vietnam* 309 (n. 1)
Lewis, Sinclair: *Elmer Gantry*, 236
Liston, Sonny, 309 (n. 6)
Literature of exhaustion, 2
Lomperis, Timothy J., xii, 301 (n. 2)

Lowell, Robert, 148; "Skunk Hour," 18; "Christmas Eve under Hooker's Statue," 192; "Children of Light," 240, 257
Lowry, Malcolm, 255

McCarthy, Gerald: *War Story*, 309 (n. 1)
McCaffrey, Larry, 302 (n. 2), 304 (n. 4), 306 (n. 6)
McDonald, Walter, 4, 146, 182–91, 309 (n. 3); *After the Noise of Saigon*, 183; *Burning the Fence*, 183; *Caliban in Blue*, 183; *The Flying Dutchman*, 183; *Night Landings*, 183, 188–91
McInerney, Peter, 5, 39, 307 (n. 10)
McPherson, Aimee Semple, 236
McShane, Frank, 80
Magical realism, 6, 11, 20, 296, 304 (n. 4)
Mahoney, Tim: *Halloran's World War*, 10; *We're Not Here*, 10
Mailer, Norman, 40, 243; *Why Are We in Vietnam?*, 54, 208, 240, 296, 312 (n. 4); *An American Dream*, 286
Mamet, David, 4, 104, 301 (n. 2), 308 (n. 1)
Manson, Charles, 118, 120
Marcuse, Herbert, 231
Marlowe, Christopher, 54
Marquez, Gabriel Garcia, 304 (n. 4)
Marshall, Kathryn: *In the Combat Zone*, 2
Mason, Bobbie Ann, 52, 126; *Shiloh and Other Stories*, 303 (n. 2); *In Country*, 303 (n. 2), 307 (n. 12)
Mather, Cotton, 276
Melville, Herman, 4, 20, 29; "Benito Cereno," 132; *Billy Budd*, 132–33, 192; "A March into Virginia," 133, 192
Merritt, William E.: *Where the Rivers Ran Backward*, 11
Morrell, David: *First Blood*, 307 (n. 12)
Morris, Willie, 80
Morrison, Jim, 276

Miller, Arthur: *All My Sons*, 112; *Death of a Salesman*, 112, 113
Milton, John, 148
Murphy, Audie, 106
Myers, Thomas, xiii, 10, 17, 21, 38, 49, 54, 90, 238, 246, 266, 267, 271, 272, 294, 297, 301 (n. 2), 302 (n. 2), 306 (n. 6), 307 (nn. 10, 12), 311 (n. 3), 312 (n. 5), 313 (n. 1)

Nashe, Thomas, 148
Nelson, Marie, 12, 17
Neorealism, 6, 56, 122, 282
Neotraditionalism, 38–39, 64, 80, 238–39
New journalism, 5–6, 221, 264, 312 (n. 5)
Nichols, John, 307 (n. 12)
Nietzsche, Friedrich, 248, 307 (n. 11); "On the uses and disadvantages of history for life," xi
Norman, Marsha, 308 (n. 1)
Norman, Michael: *These Good Men*, 8
North, Oliver L., 307 (n. 13)

O'Brien, Tim, 4, 6, 8, 10, 11–37, 38, 39, 58, 80, 304 (n. 4), 305 (n. 5), 306 (nn. 6, 7); *The Things They Carried*, vii, 6, 11, 15, 28–37, 93, 300, 305 (n. 5), 312 (n. 4); *Going After Cacciato*, xii, 1, 6, 9, 11, 16, 20–24, 28, 33, 93, 221, 296, 301 (nn. 1, 2), 304 (n. 4), 305–6 (nn. 6, 7), 312 (n. 4); *If I Die in a Combat Zone*, 2, 6, 11, 12–17, 19, 20, 33, 37–38, 312 (n. 4); *Northern Lights*, 6, 11, 17–20; *The Nuclear Age*, 6, 11, 18, 24–28
O'Connor, Flannery, 86
Oldham, Perry: *Vinh Long*, 309 (n. 1)
Owen, Wilfred, 158

Page, Tim, 155, 274, 276, 279; *Ten Years After*, 309 (n. 2); *Tim Page's Nam*, 309 (n. 2)
Palm, Edward F., 64
Papp, Joseph, 105

Paquet, Basil T., 146, 309 (n. 1)
Patton, George S., Jr., 210
Patton, George S., III, 210
Peelaert, Guy, 8, 281, 286, 309 (n. 2)
Peightel, Dan, 311 (n. 2)
Pelfrey, William: *The Big V*, 10
Pettit, Michael: *American Light*, 207
Phillips, Jayne Anne: *Machine Dreams*, 303–4 (n. 2)
Pinter, Harold, 122; *The Dumb Waiter*, 134
Political novel, 238–39, 254, 305 (n. 5)
Postmodernism, 4, 6, 7, 11, 16, 20, 36, 44, 56, 74, 136–37, 148, 207, 239, 244, 254–55, 256, 258, 264, 266–67, 276, 301–2 (n. 2)
Poststructuralism, 3, 32, 36, 136, 147, 208, 222, 237, 264–65, 272, 302 (n. 2)
Posttraumatic stress disorder, 49, 307 (n. 12)
Pound, Ezra, 148
Pratt, John Clark, 301 (n. 2), 303 (n. 1); *Vietnam Voices*, 8, 303 (n. 1); *The Laotian Fragments*, 9–10
Proffitt, Nicholas, 304 (n. 2); *The Embassy House*, 304 (n. 2); *Gardens of Stone*, 304 (n. 2)
Pynchon, Thomas: *Gravity's Rainbow*, 25

Rabe, David, 4, 7, 104–44, 192, 301 (n. 2), 308 (nn. 1–3), 308–9 (n. 6), 309 (nn. 7, 8); *Sticks and Bones*, 7, 104, 105, 110–17, 121, 122, 126, 301 (n. 1), 308 (nn. 2, 4), 313 (n. 2); *Streamers*, 7, 104, 105, 117, 122, 126–34, 137–44, 301 (n. 1), 308 (nn. 2, 4); *The Basic Training of Pavlo Hummel*, 7, 104, 105–110, 111, 117, 121, 122, 123, 126, 280, 308 (nn. 2, 4); *Hurly-burly*, 7, 105, 137; *In the Boom Boom Room*, 7, 122–26, 127, 141; *The Orphan*, 105, 117–22, 127, 134, 308 (nn. 2, 5); *Goose and Tomtom*, 105, 134–37; *Casualties of War* (screenplay), 308 (n. 3); *I'm Dancing*

Rabe, David (*continued*)
  *as Fast as I Can* (screenplay), 308
  (n. 3); *Streamers* (screenplay), 308
  (n. 3)
*Rambo*, 307 (n. 12)
Ransom, John L., 37
Raymond, Michael W., 306 (n. 6)
Reinhardt, Django, 240
Ringnalda, Donald, 298, 302 (n. 2), 313
  (n. 2)
Robinson, E. A., 239
Robinson, James A., 116, 128
Roethke, Theodore, 148
Rottmann, Larry, 146
Runyon, Damon, 134, 135; *Guys and
  Dolls*, 123–24

Sack, John, 80
Sales, Roger, 19
Salinger, J. D.: *The Catcher in the Rye*,
  59
Santoli, Al: *Everything We Had*, 2
Sassoon, Siegfried, 4, 158
Schaeffer, Susan Fromberg: *Buffalo
  Afternoon*, 303–4 (n. 2)
Schroeder, Eric James, 304 (n. 3), 305
  (n. 5), 306 (nn. 6, 7)
Searle, William J., 302 (n. 2), 313 (n. 2)
Shakespeare, William: *Hamlet*, 97–98;
  *Macbeth*, 137, 144, 155; *The Tempest*,
  183, 226, 310 (n. 7); *As You Like It*,
  258, 259, 261, 262; *King Lear*, 258,
  261, 262
Sheehan, Neil: *A Bright Shining Lie*, 8,
  301 (n. 1)
Shelton, Frank W., 311 (n. 3)
Shepard, Sam, 4, 104, 301 (n. 2), 308
  (n. 1)
Slocock, Caroline, 309 (n. 1)
Smith, Dave, 311 (n. 9)
Smith, Lorrie, 158, 159, 191, 195, 301
  (n. 2), 309 (n. 1)
Southern fiction, 82, 84, 303 (n. 2)
Spencer, Duncan, 79
Spencer, Scott, 59
*Star is Born, A*, 261
Steadman, Ralph, 281

Stephens, Michael, 301–2 (n. 2), 310
  (n. 5)
Stone, Dana, 279
Stone, Robert, 5, 7, 39, 42, 126, 140,
  201, 237–64, 301 (n. 1), 304 (n. 3),
  305 (n. 5), 309 (n. 2); *Dog Soldiers*, 1,
  7, 9, 237, 238, 245–49, 255–56, 301
  (nn. 1, 2), 311 (n. 3); *A Flag for Sunrise*, 7, 10, 43, 53, 206, 238, 249–56;
  *Children of Light*, 7, 138, 238, 240,
  256–64; *A Hall of Mirrors*, 238, 240–
  45, 255–56; "Helping," 239
Strouse, Jean, 252, 257
Styron, William: *Sophie's Choice*, 255

Tal, Kali, 302 (n. 2)
Tate, Donald: *Bravo Burning*, 10
Tate, Sharon, 120
Taylor, Gordon, O., 266, 306 (n. 6)
Terry, Wallace: *Bloods*, 2
Thomas, Dylan, 299
Thompson, Hunter S., 256, 281
Traven, B., 248, 249, 253, 260
Twain, Mark: *Huckleberry Finn*, 59

Vann, John Paul, 8
Vannatta, Dennis, 306 (n. 6)
"Vietnam: A Television History"
  (PBS), 157
Vonnegut, Jr., Kurt, xii, 239

Walken, Christopher, 309 (n. 7)
Weaver, Sigourney, 309 (n. 7)
Webb, James, 4, 10, 63–79, 303 (n. 1),
  307–8 (n. 13); *Fields of Fire*, 10, 63,
  64–69, 79, 81, 307 (n. 13); *A Country
  Such as This*, 10, 63, 69, 72–79, 307–8
  (n. 13); *A Sense of Honor*, 63, 69–72,
  307 (n. 13)
Weigl, Bruce, 4, 146, 153, 158, 178,
  191–205, 217–18, 301 (n. 2), 309
  (n. 3), 310 (n. 5), 311 (n. 9); *Song of
  Napalm*, 1–2, 191–92, 196, 200–205;
  *Executioner*, 191; *A Sackful of Old
  Quarrels*, 191; *A Romance*, 191, 192–
  97, 200; *The Monkey Wars*, 191,
  197–200

West, Nathanael, 243; *Day of the Locust*, 257

Wheeler, John: *Touched with Fire*, 1

Whitman, Walt, 149, 255

Wier, Allen, 310 (n. 8)

Winn, David: *Gangland*, 11

*Winning Hearts and Minds*, 146

Winthrop, John, 233, 236

Wittman, Sandra M., 302 (n. 2)

Wood, Michael, 238, 249–50

Wright, James, 193

Wright, Stephen, 5, 80, 126, 304 (n. 3); *Meditations in Green*, 1, 10, 11, 93, 296–300, 301 (nn. 1, 2), 303 (n. 1), 313 (nn. 1, 2); *M31: A Family Romance*, 11

Yevtushenko, Yevgeni, 173

Zins, Daniel L., 17